THE RISE AND FALL OF THE
HASHIMITE KINGDOM OF ARABIA

For my Parents

לאבי מורי, לאמי מורתי

JOSHUA TEITELBAUM

The Rise and Fall of the Hashimite Kingdom of Arabia

NEW YORK UNIVERSITY PRESS
WASHINGTON SQUARE, NEW YORK

First published in the U.S.A. in 2001 by
NEW YORK UNIVERSITY PRESS
Washington Square
New York, NY 10003

Typeset in Bembo by Bookcraft Ltd, Stroud, Gloucestershire
Printed in Malaysia

Library of Congress Cataloging-in-Publication Data
Teitelbaum, Joshua
The rise and fall of the Hashimite Kingdom of the Hijaz / Joshua Teitelbaum
p. cm.
Includes bibliographical references
ISBN 0-8147-8270-1 (cloth : alk. paper)
ISBN 0-8147-8271-X (pbk. : alk. paper)
1. Hijaz (Saudi Arabia)–History.
2. Arab countries–History–Arab Revolt, 1916–1918.
I. Title.
DS247.9.H45 T45 2001
953.8-dc21   00-051978

A sharif you may be, but you're hardly a king;
Though you kill barren camels, their fat you don't fling;
Though you carry long spears, you don't enter the ring;
Though you'd battle, a fox's howl makes you take wing;
Though you're quick on the trigger, no bullets ping.

The above is a poem by a bedouin opponent of Sharif Husayn. It is quoted, with permission, from Clinton Bailey, *Bedouin Poetry from Sinai and the Negev: Mirror of a Culture* (Oxford: Clarendon Press, 1991), p. 356.

ACKNOWLEDGMENTS

One who undertakes an enterprise such as this incurs many debts (intellectual and otherwise) along the way, and it is a pleasure to acknowledge them. My first thanks go to the Moshe Dayan Center for Middle East and African Studies at Tel Aviv University, which is an unequalled concentration of scholars on the Middle East. My friends and colleagues have been generous with their guidance and advice. The Dayan Center has been my professional home for many years; one can ask for no better.

Martin Kramer, Director of the Dayan Center, kept me going when my spirit flagged. I owe him a great deal for his patient, intellectual guidance while he steered me toward my goal and warned me away from tempting but dangerous avenues.

Itamar Rabinovich, former head of the Center and now President of Tel Aviv University, was instrumental in bringing me to the Center and has been a source of counsel throughout my academic career. Asher Susser, former head of the Center, was of great help during this project. He was always interested, and never lacked for an encouraging word.

Joseph Kostiner has been a mentor and friend for many years. Yosi was always cheerfully available to share with me his unique approach to the study of tribes and state formation, as well as his encyclopedic knowledge of the Arabian Peninsula. I am in his debt.

Ami Ayalon, Gad Gilbar, Ofra Bengio, Meir Litvak, Bruce Maddy-Weitzman, Yigal Sheffy, and Aryeh Shmuelevitz gave unstintingly of their time and expertise.

I would also like thank the following scholars at other institutions: Michael Barnett, Michael Bates, Ross Brann, David Dewitt, Werner Ende, Adam Garfinkle, Joel Migdal, David Owen, Barry Rubin, Jeffery Rudd, Adi Schnytzer, and Eliezer Tauber. William Ochsenwald, dean of scholars of the Hijaz, deserves special mention for his sharing of his knowledge on Arabian affairs. They have all given kindly of their considered opinion, but I absolve them of responsibility for the contents of this work; it remains mine alone.

Much of the research for this book was carried out during a two-year fellowship at the Jackson School of International Studies, University of Washington. Charlotte Albright, Jere Bacharach, Dorothy Becker, Martin Jaffee, Hillel Kieval, and Joel Migdal assisted greatly during my stay there.

My aunt and uncle in Seattle, Frances and Fred Rogers, made us feel welcome in the Great Pacific Northwest, and were a source of practical and financial assistance.

Without the generosity of Samuel and Althea Stroum, our stay in Seattle would not have been possible. I have benefited from the support of the Stroums at several stages in my academic life, and to them I offer my profound thanks.

I am indebted for additional financial support to the Moshe Dayan Center through its Moshe Dayan and Uriel and Lora Dann Scholarships (I regret that Uri, of blessed memory, did not live to read this work — his counsel has been sorely missed); the Avi Foundation; London B'nai B'rith; the Anglo-Jewish Association; and the Harry and Jenny Lewis Studentship.

During my work in the archives, I was greatly aided by the staffs of the Sudan Archives, Durham University (Lesley Forbes, Jane Hogan); the Public Record Office; the India Office; the archives of the French Ministries of Foreign Affairs and Defense; the Middle East Center, St Antony's College, Oxford; the Archives Centre, Churchill College, Cambridge; and the Liddell Hart Centre for Military Archives, King's College.

Marion Gliksberg, Marwan Hanania, Anat Lapidot, Edna Liftman, Amira Margalith, Marie Miran, Shira Ohayon, Dorit Paret, Soly Shahvar, Judy Shulevitz, and my uncle Morton Wagenfeld assisted in countless ways.

Aaron Roland has been generous of spirit and of pocket. I consider his enduring friendship a blessing in my life.

My thanks go to my very special editor and friend, Penny Beebe, for her devoted and expert work on the manuscript.

I am grateful to my parents-in-law, Hal (of blessed memory) and Marilyn Simkowitz, who cared about my work and helped whenever needed. I deeply wish Hal were still with us to see the completion of this project.

To Jacqueline, my inspiration, I owe more than anyone can imagine. She has been a profound source of advice and constant support, although at times she may have wondered if she was married to me or widowed by the Arab Revolt. I would not have been able to finish this without her. My three wonderful daughters, Dena, Rivital, and Ayalah, have grown up during the gestation of this work, and now they finally see what Abba was doing all the time.

I take special pleasure in thanking my parents and teachers, Rabbi David and Robin Teitelbaum, whose unwavering confidence in me made it all possible. Along with my dear brother Adam, they have been a source of tremendous support throughout this effort. I dedicate this book to them.

Tel Aviv JOSHUA TEITELBAUM
February 2001

CONTENTS

MAPS

TABLES

NOTATION, TRANSLITERATION
AND SOURCES

In order to facilitate reference to documentation, in the notes I have maintained capitalization, spelling of names and the writing of dates as they appear – often quite idiosyncratically – in the original sources.

During 1919, Husayn's newspaper, *al-Qiblah*, began printing the common era date as well as the *hijrah* date. Only the common era date is cited when available; otherwise, the *hijrah* date is given followed by the converted common era date. The conversion was carried out by the program 'CAL–1.3: A Calendar of Islamic and Christian Dates,' written by Jerzy Lacina of Poznan, Poland.

A simplified transliteration of Arabic is used, on the premise that those who know Arabic do not need full transliteration, and those who don't know the language would not find full transliteration useful. Long vowels are not distinguished from short ones, and *hamza* is used only in the middle of a word. Proper nouns with common English spellings are spelled in that manner: thus Medina, not al-Madinah; Mecca, not Makka; but Hashimite, not Hashemite.

This work uses the available Arabic, English, and French sources. It would have been useful to have explored Husayn's own archives, but these were not available. According to Professor 'Adnan al-Bakhit, who has overseen the publishing of Hashimite official papers in Jordan, Husayn's archives are not in Jordan. Chances are they were either destroyed in the Wahhabi takeover of Mecca, or they are in Saudi Arabia. The British representative in the Hijaz at the time, Reader Bullard, wrote to London: 'Bin Saud has got hold of all of Hussein's archives. He appears to be well acquainted with the correspondence between the Agency and Mecca, as was much amused by it.'[1]

---

[1] FO 682/22, Bullard to Mallet, 23 May 1925.

ABBREVIATIONS

AAS	*Asian and African Studies*
AB	Arab Bureau
AB	*Arab Bulletin*
AH	Arabie–Hedjaz
CP	Clayton Papers
EI^1	*Encyclopedia Islamica* (1st edition)
EI^2	*Encyclopedia Islamica* (2nd edition)
GA	*Gazetteer of Arabia*
GLLD	George Lloyd, Lord Lloyd of Dolobran, Papers
FO	Foreign Office
HA	*Handbook of Arabia*
HH	*Hejaz before World War One: A Handbook*
IJMES	*International Journal of Middle East Studies*
IO	India Office
MAE	Ministère des Affaires Etrangères
MES	*Middle Eastern Studies*
RMM	*Revue du Monde Musulman*
SHAT	Ministère de la Défense, Service Historique de l'Armée de Terre, Château de Vincennes, Paris
T	Treasury
WO	War Office
WP	Wingate Papers

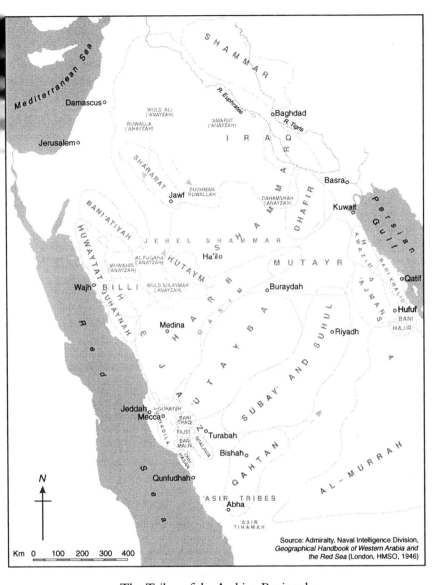

The Tribes of the Arabian Peninsula

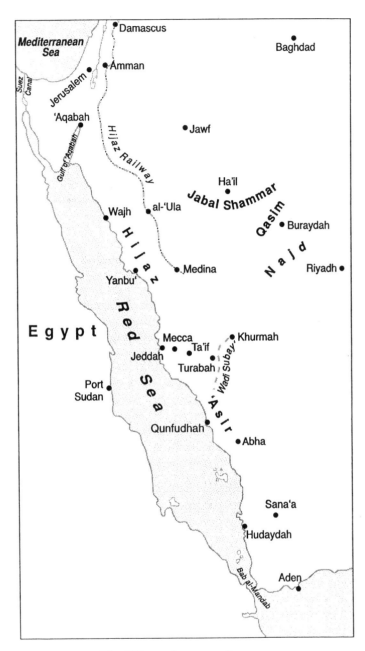

The Hijaz and surrounding areas

xviii

1

INTRODUCTION

'Before 1920 states in Arabia were little more than the assertions by oases of claims to tax their users, by religious dignitaries of claims to recognition, and military alliances among tribes.'[1]

The Hijaz in the early twentieth century

The IIijaz is *al-Ard al-Muqaddasah*, the holy land for Muslims. Stretching along the Arabian Peninsula's Red Sea coast from Yemen to 'Aqabah, it is made holy by its role in Islam as the birthplace of the faith. The Qur'an, the direct word of God, was revealed to the Prophet Muhammad while he was on retreat in a cave on Mount Hira, on the outskirts of Mecca. It was to Medina that Muhammad made his *hijra*, or migration from the unbelievers of Mecca in 622, and it is there that he is buried. Together the cities of Mecca and Medina are known as the *Haramayn*, after their two holy shrines (the *harams*): Mecca's Ka'aba and the Prophet's Mosque in Medina. Mecca's traditional sobriquet is *Makka al-Mukarramah* (Revered Mecca), and Medina's is *al-Madinah al-Munawwarah* (Brilliant Medina).

This land plays a role in two of Islam's 'five pillars': *salat* (prayer) and *hajj* (pilgrimage). Five times a day, Muslims are urged to turn in the direction of Mecca and pray. This direction is known as the *qiblah*. Muslims are also obligated, if financially able and in good health, to make the *hajj* to Mecca at least once in a lifetime. While in the Hijaz, they often visit the Prophet's Mosque in Medina, although it is a separate ritual and not part of the *hajj* proper.[2]

---

[1] M.E. Yapp, *The Near East since the First World War* (Harlow: Longman, 1991), p. 189.

[2] The pilgrimage to Medina is known as a *ziyarah*, or holy visitation. Among Shi'i Muslims, with their special veneration of the Prophet and his family, the *ziyarah* to Mecca takes on importance nearly equal to that of *hajj*. (See Werner Ende's admirable and exhaustive 'The *Nakhawila*, A Shiite Community in Medina, Past and Present,'

1

The pilgrimage and the Hijaz's centrality to Islam accounted for much of the region's social and economic life, as well as its politics. In what David Long has aptly termed the '*hajj* service industry,'[3] countless Hijazis were involved in transportation, housing, and overseeing the ritual observances of the *hujjaj*, or pilgrims. With the *hujjaj* usually numbering in the hundreds of thousands in the early twentieth century, it is not surprising that the pilgrimage and everything associated with managing Islam's holiest sites touched the lives of almost every Hijazi.

Yet the Hijaz was a harsh land: mostly rocky desert inhabited by nomadic and semi-nomadic tribesmen who made their living from alternately facilitating or robbing pilgrimage traffic. Government in the Hijaz was shared between the Ottoman Vali and the Amir of Mecca, who was a *sharif* (pl. *ashraf*), meaning a descendant of the Prophet. Since the Ottomans drew legitimacy from their control of the *Haramayn*, and since the Sharif could often be dismissed at Istanbul's whim (depending on the balance of power), both parties sought a successful *hajj*, which meant security on the roads. If pilgrims proceeded unhindered, they would report back home and encourage more Muslims to make the pilgrimage the following year. The Ottoman Sultan-Caliph received credit for living up to his designated role as Servant of the *Haramayn*, while the Sharif earned money and prestige as the practical head of the entire *hajj* service industry.

The Hijaz's place in Islam accounted for its relatively cosmopolitan nature when compared with much of Arabia. For centuries, Muslims from south-east Asia, the Indian sub-continent, North, West and sub-Saharan Africa, as well as the Middle East, had made their home in Islam's holy land. They had become an integral part of the society, and had made the Hijaz a center of a cosmopolitan scholarly community as well.[4] Jeddah's importance as a center of Red Sea trade contributed to its international flavor.

It was Jeddah's very cosmopolitan character that brought with it the interest of European powers. Britain, France, and Holland

---

Die Welt des Islams 37 [1997], pp. 263–348.)

[3] David Long, *The Hajj Today: A Survey of the Contemporary Muslim Pilgrimage* (Albany: SUNY Press, 1979).

[4] John Voll, 'Hadith Scholars and Tariqahs: An Ulama Group in the 18th Century Haramayn and Their Impact on the Islamic World,' *Journal of Asian and African Studies* 15 (1980), pp. 264–73.

all had substantial holdings in Muslim countries, and were keen to follow developments in the Hijaz for effect on their imperial holdings.

In October 1916, with British help, the Amir of Mecca, Husayn ibn 'Ali al-Hashimi (in English, Hashimite), began the rebellion later widely known as the Arab Revolt. Students of Middle Eastern history most often encounter Husayn as one of the two protagonists in the Husayn–McMahon correspondence, a series of letters which were instrumental in shaping the diplomatic history of the creation of several Middle Eastern territorial states after the First World War. Yet most have only a tangential familiarity with the state established by Husayn in the Hijaz, which lasted almost ten years, finally giving way to Saudi conquest in 1925.

In the early twentieth century the Ottoman Empire came to an end and broke up into smaller territorial states. The Hashimite Kingdom of the Hijaz was the first independent state to emerge from the Ottoman Empire in Asia, and thus represents an important example of the process of state formation in the post-First World War period in the Middle East in general, and in the Arabian Peninsula in particular. Husayn's short-lived polity, however, represents a case of failed state formation. History is generally written by the winners, and scholars have tended to study the winners.[5] Indeed, Husayn's failure remains in stark contradistinction to the oft-studied state-forming success of another Arabian leader, Ibn Saud of Najd. A comparison with the history of Saudi Arabia is thus often made a touchstone throughout this work.

Scholars have studied the history of the *Haramayn* in this period, the land to which millions of Muslims turn five times a day in prayer, largely in terms of Husayn's political role before the war, or as a theater of the Saudi conquest afterwards.[6] This study

---

[5] Although recently two other Arabian state-forming 'losers' have been studied: see Madawi Talal Al-Rasheed, *Politics in an Arabian Oasis: The Rashidi Tribal Dynasty* (London: I.B. Tauris, 1991); and Anne K. Bang, *The Idrisi State in 'Asir: Politics, Religion and Personal Prestige as Statebuilding Factors in Early Twentieth Century Arabia* (Bergen, Norway: Centre for Middle Eastern and Islamic Studies, 1996).

[6] Examples of those treating, for instance, the Husayn–McMahon correspondence are legion: Elie Kedourie, *In the Anglo-Arab Labyrinth: The Husayn–McMahon Correspondence and its Interpretations, 1914–1939* (Cambridge University Press, 1976); A.L. Tibawi, *Anglo-Arab Relations and the Question of Palestine, 1914–1921* (London: Luzac, 1978);

draws on previously unused or underutilized documentation from, *inter alia*, the British Public Record Office, the French archives, private papers and Husayn's newspaper, *al-Qiblah*, in hope of presenting a sharp and full picture of the social, political, and economic developments in the Hashimite Kingdom of the Hijaz.

Circumstances had dealt Husayn a fairly good opening hand when he began the Revolt. He enjoyed a certain degree of legitimacy as Amir of Mecca and as leader of the *ashraf* in the holy city. He was supported by the Arab nationalist societies in Syria. And, of course, he was the recipient of British guns, gold, and officers. Given this auspicious beginning, why – of all the states which emerged from the Ottoman Empire after the First World War – did Husayn's fail? This is the central question of this work, and the answer is to be found in an examination of the state created by Husayn, and particularly by focussing on the issues of revenue extraction, mechanisms of coercion, and coalition building.

Of tribes and chieftaincies: state formation in Arabian tribal societies[7]

The Hijaz was predominantly a tribal society. The literature is abundant on what constitutes a tribe or a tribal group,[8] yet for our purposes Kostiner's definition will suffice:

[A] tribe is ... a political unit that was identified or appeared in historiographical accounts as such. It consisted of a group of people who shared a common territorial base, true or mythological kinship ties, and a corporate existence. The members' political allegiance was to the tribe,

---

George Antonius, *The Arab Awakening: The Story of the Arab National Movement* (London: Hamish Hamilton, 1939). Understandably, books on Saudi Arabia, for example Gary Troeller's admirable *The Birth of Saudi Arabia, Britain and the Rise of the House of Saud* (London: Cass, 1976), treat the Hijaz only tangentially. The only book covering the period and subject under review is Randall Baker's hagiographic *King Husain and the Kingdom of the Hejaz* (New York: Oleander Press, 1979).

[7] This section has benefitted substantially from the introduction to Joseph Kostiner's masterly work, *The Making of Saudi Arabia, 1916–1936: From Chieftaincy to Monarchical State* (New York: Oxford University Press, 1993), pp. 3–11; only direct quotations are specifically cited.

[8] But see in particular Dale Eickelman, *The Middle East: An Anthropological Approach*, 2nd edn. (Englewood Cliffs, NJ: Prentice-Hall, 1989), pp. 73–94; 126–50; Fred Donner, *The Early Islamic Conquests* (Princeton University Press, 1981), pp. 11–49; Christine Helms, *The Cohesion of Saudi Arabia: Evolution of Political Identity* (London: Croom Helm, 1981).

and in return they received physical and economic protection and social status.[9]

Tribal groups were divided into sub-units, such as clans and families; if the sub-units were particularly large, they were often referred to as a tribe (*qabilah*, or *'ashirah*), although they were actually part of a larger whole. The cohesion of the members of a tribe (*'asabiyyah*, meaning *esprit de corps*) was strongest amongst nomadic tribes, and also remained an important source of identity in small oases and villages.

Often a very large tribe or several tribes would be part of a larger political framework, termed here a chieftaincy. Kostiner, drawing on the work of Kister, Serjeant and Donner, writes that the chieftaincy was the predominant form of political organization in Arabia until the twentieth century:

[C]hieftaincies consisted of loose tribal alliances based on power sharing, mutual responsibilities and duty-sharing relationships among nomadic tribal groups, sedentarized inhabitants centered in villages and towns, and a ruler who governed these alliances. The ruler was a member of a leading family of a major tribe who had both the authority and the obligation to maintain internal order in the chieftaincy, to protect his people (*himaya*), and to wage war against enemies. Sometimes he had religious authority as well. The nomads received the benefit of urban facilities such as markets ... and institutionalized religious rites. In return, they acknowledged the leader's authority, pledged their allegiance to him, and sometimes even paid tribute (or protection money, *khuwwa*) to the ruler. The sedentarized population had to fight for the state, pay tribute to the ruler and sometimes to the regional nomadic tribe, and provide facilities for the nomads, in return for trade benefits and protection.[10]

Borders between chieftaincies were not sharply defined, but were rather a function of the *dirah*s, the grazing zones of the tribes. The administration of the chieftaincy was quite simple, if non-existent, with practically no bureaucracy. It followed that '[t]he authority structures of a chieftaincy's various sectors were not controlled by the ruler but retained autonomy in the conduct of their internal affairs.'[11] Loyalties in chieftaincies were personal

---

[9] Kostiner, *The Making*, p. 3.

[10] *Ibid.*, pp. 3–4. See also Ernest Gellner, *Muslim Society* (Cambridge University Press, 1981), pp. 1–99.

[11] Kostiner, *The Making*, p. 4.

and provisional, and thus inherently unstable; tribes came and left the polity. Social cohesion and cooperation between the various tribes and between tribes and the ruler was not based on an over-riding loyalty, national or otherwise. To assure loyalty, the head of the chieftaincy had to provide the tribes with strategies or tools of survival other than those which the tribe might possess independently. These included protection, raiding to gain booty, and access to markets. At times, loyalty of tribes to the chief was augmented by a religious factor, as was often case with Islamically mobilized chieftaincies.[12]

The amirate of Mecca, which existed from about 968 to 1925, was just such a chieftaincy, although it differed from other Arabian chieftaincies in two main ways: the centrality of the Muslim pilgrimage (*hajj*) to the economy (as opposed to simple trade) and its political status as a 'state within a state,' a crucial part of the Ottoman Empire. A further significant difference was the existence of major cities such as Mecca and Jeddah – the latter was also a major port. Both Mecca as a pilgrimage center, and Jeddah, its entrepôt, were cosmopolitan places; their residents hailed from parts of the Islamic world as different from each other as Java, the Middle East, India and Central Asia.

As Kostiner has shown, although chieftaincies had a low degree of 'stateness,' they can develop attributes of stateness, such as a central government, an acknowledged territoriality, and a basic social cohesion whereby most segments of society recognize the right of the state to rule.[13] The Saudi chieftaincy in the twentieth

---

12 See also Ronald Cohen, 'Introduction' in Ronald Cohen and Elman Service (eds), *Origins of the State* (Philadelphia: Institute for the Study of Human Issues, 1978), pp. 1–17; Philip Khoury and Joseph Kostiner, 'Introduction: Tribes and the Complexities of State Formation in the Middle East' in Philip Khoury and Joseph Kostiner, *Tribes and State Formation in the Middle East* (Berkeley: University of California Press, 1990), pp. 1–24; Gellner, *Muslim Society*. Both Gellner and Kostiner are beholden in much of their analysis to Ibn Khaldun, *The Muqaddimah*, trans. Franz Rosenthal (Princeton University Press, 1967), vol. 2.

13 It is convenient to conceive of various states having a place on a continuum of 'stateness.' This continuum conceptually plots state attributes such as well-defined borders, central institutions and government, and legitimacy. See Gabriel Ben-Dor, *State and Conflict in the Middle East: Emergence of the Post-Colonial State in the Middle East* (New York: Praeger, 1983), who elaborates on J.P. Nettl's seminal 'The State as a Conceptual Variable' *World Politics* 20 (1988), pp. 559–92.

century gained these attributes as it developed into a monarchical state.

The Saudi state developed out of what Lapidus, looking at Islamic history, has termed the 'conquest movement.' Lapidus has shown that the early Islamic *ummah* and state (and later Islamic states) developed as a result of conquest; in fact, he states that the primordial tribal alliances known as Qays and Yaman actually arose in the post-Arab conquest garrison cities, as the Arabian conquerors became more conscious that they possessed an Arab identity. This conquest movement turned into an established state (higher on the continuum of stateness, or what Lapidus calls 'the routinization of conquest movements') when its leaders, the Umayyads and later the 'Abbasids, realized the necessity of developing a fiscal administration and relying on client military forces.[14]

Kostiner applies this idea of 'the routinization of conquest movements' to Saudi state formation and discusses the political environment, which was influenced by 'the unprecedented involvement of the Great Powers, particularly Britain, in the arena during World War I.'[15] The Great Powers gave political support to, and funded, Ibn Saud, the Idrisi of 'Asir, and Husayn ibn 'Ali as well. (Ibn Rashid of Ha'il received a subsidy from the Ottomans.) Husayn's ambitions went well beyond the Hijaz and even the Arabian Peninsula, and his massive subsidy from the British, who encouraged him to lead the Arab Revolt, alarmed Ibn Saud and other tribal leaders, as the local balance of power shifted. Kostiner quotes the High Commissioner of Egypt, Sir Reginald Wingate, who wrote in December 1917: 'the aggrandizement of the Shereef and extension of his influence ... alarmed Bin Saud and other chiefs who ... sought guarantees and material [aid] against him.' The First World War also wrought enormous changes in trade routes, as a result of the British blockade of coasts and tribal markets, as well as to the enmity between tribes supporting different rival chieftains, who in turn supported either the Ottomans or the British.[16]

---

14 Ira Lapidus, 'Tribes and State Formation in Islamic History,' in Khoury and Kostiner, pp. 25–47.

15 Kostiner, *The Making*, p. 6; Joseph Kostiner, 'Transforming Dualities: Tribe and State Formation in Saudi Arabia' in Khoury and Kostiner, pp. 226–51.

16 Kostiner, *The Making*, pp. 9–10.

After the war, Ibn Saud sought the means for more efficient expansion and more successful internal consolidation, and he resolved to demarcate the territory of the state more distinctly than the extant overlapping borders based on *dirah*s. Ibn Saud began thus to move towards a more tightly organized, quasi-modern state, 'replacing the provisional arrangements of the chieftaincy' with a stronger and more centralized government.[17] Many of the tribes in his chieftaincy were infused with the Wahhabi religious ideology; and the *Ikhwan*, tribal groups which became Ibn Saud's vanguard in this effort, developed a religious zeal and an *'asabiyyah* based on the Wahhabi *da'wah*. Ibn Saud's state had therefore developed a social cohesion and legitimacy that other chieftaincies lacked. Moreover, Wahhabi propagandizing was continuous throughout the area, reaching all social levels, as preachers spread the word far and wide, thereby strengthening Ibn Saud's leadership as the Imam of the Wahhabiyyah. It was this move towards a more modern type of state, which we may conceive of as an 'ascent' on the stateness continuum, that distinguished the development of the Saudi state from its main rival and the focus of our study, the Hashimite state of Husayn ibn 'Ali.

The overall question we must ask, therefore, is why did this not happen with Husayn, who had a better opening hand than Ibn Saud? Moreover, what kind of state was created by the Arab Revolt, and why did it not achieve the continuing dynamic of an expanding chieftaincy attained by Ibn Saud? Finally, what efforts, if any, were made to increase levels of stateness in the Hijaz, and did these increase or diminish the strength of the state?[18] In the following pages these questions are examined in detail, and a new understanding of the rise and fall of the Hashimite Kingdom of the Hijaz is offered.

[17] *Ibid.*, p. 11.

[18] My understanding of strong and weak states, and of the level of social control as a measure of state strength, is informed by Joel Migdal, *Strong Societies and Weak States: State–Society Relations and State Capabilities in the Third World* (Princeton University Press, 1988).

A note on the Hashimites and the Meccan Sharifate

The Sharifate, that is the position of ruler of Mecca by a *sharif* (pl. *ashraf*), endured from about 968 to 1925. All *ashraf* claim descent from Hashim ibn 'Abd Manaf, the eponymous founder of the Banu Hashim clan of the tribe of Quraysh, the tribe which held Mecca during the lifetime of the Prophet of Islam, Muhammad ibn 'Abdallah (d. 632). Hashim was the great-grandfather of the Prophet. The Prophet's daughter, Fatima, married his first cousin, 'Ali ibn Abi Talib (d. 661). Their two sons, Husayn (d. 680) and Hasan (d. 669), founded the two main branches of sharifian descent, known as the Husaynids and the Hasanids. In about the year 968, Ja'far ibn Muhammad ibn Husayn al-Amir, a descendant of the ninth generation after Hasan, asserted control of Mecca. From that time until the Saudi capture of Mecca in 1924, the Sharifate was held by the Hasanid *ashraf*. Medina, on the other hand, was often controlled by the other branch of *ashraf*, the Husaynids.[19]

Although the term Hashimite could technically be applied to all descendants of Hashim via the Prophet, including the Kings of Morocco, the 'Abbasid Caliphs, and the Fatimid Caliphs, the only family claiming the eponym Hashimite today is the ruling family of Jordan, the descendants of Sharif Husayn ibn 'Ali of Mecca, the subject of our study. Indeed, when the rulers of Jordan discuss the Hashimites *per se*, they begin from Sharif Husayn.[20] This family traces its ancestry from Hashim ibn 'Abd Manaf, through Hasan, Sharif Qitada (r. c.1200–1220) through Sharif Muhammad Najm al-Din Abu Numayy I (r. 1251–1301) and Sharif Muhammad Abu Numayy II ibn Barakat (r. 1524–1584). From Abu Numayy II, the Hashimites divided into three clans, the Dhawu Barakat, the Dhawu Zayd, and the Dhawu 'Abdallah ('Abadillah). From the seventeenth century until the end of Hashimite rule in the Hijaz, the struggle for the Sharifate was between these three branches.

[19] Given their descent, it is not surprising that at least until the second half of the fourteenth century, the *ashraf* of Mecca were followers of the party of 'Ali, Shi'is of the Zaydi sect. See: Richard Mortel, 'Zaydi Shi'ism and the Hasanid Sharifs of Mecca,' *IJMES* 19 (1987), pp. 455–72; Ende, 'The Nakhawila.' As will be seen, Medina was often independent of Meccan rule.

[20] See *al-Album al-Hashimi* (Amman: Shams Publishing, 1994).

A sub-clan of the Dhawu 'Abdallah was the Dhawu 'Awn, which is the sub-clan of the last Hashimite rulers of Mecca, and which struggled with the Dhawu Zayd until Husayn ibn 'Ali assumed the mantle of the Sharifate and secured it for the Dhawu 'Awn in 1908. Sharif Husayn ibn 'Ali was the last of the Dhawu 'Awn to rule Mecca.

2

THE SOCIAL AND POLITICAL LEGACY OF OTTOMAN RULE IN THE HIJAZ, 1840–1916[1]

The Sharifian state: the 'state within the state' on the eve of the Arab Revolt

From its founding in c. 968 until its demise in late 1925, the amirate of Mecca, which controlled most of the Hijaz, was governed locally by descendants of the Prophet Muhammad through his grandson Hasan (and are therefore sometimes known as the Bani Hasan), the offspring of the marriage of Muhammad's daughter Fatimah to 'Ali. The ruler of Mecca was called both the amir and the Sharif of Mecca. In later Western usage, he was often called the 'Grand Sharif.' We will refer to him as the Sharif, with an uppercase 'S,' to distinguish him from other *ashraf*.

The story of the relations between the Sharifian state from the end of the Egyptian occupation and the restoration of Ottoman

---

[1] The period from 1840 to 1908 has been well researched. The best studies for this period are: Saleh Muhammad al-Amr, *The Hejaz under Ottoman Rule, 1869–1914: Ottoman Vali, the Sharif of Mecca, and the Growth of British Influence* (Riyadh University Press, 1978); William Ochsenwald, *Religion, Society and the State in Arabia: the Hijaz under Ottoman Control, 1840–1908* (Columbus: Ohio State University Press, 1984); Butrus Abu-Manneh's 'Sultan Abdulhamid II and the Sharifs of Mecca (1880–1900),' *AAS* 9 (1973), pp. 1–21, is also very valuable. Less analytical but also valuable studies are Gerald de Gaury, *Rulers of Mecca* (New York: Roy Publishers, 1954; reprint, New York: AMS Press, 1982) and Fa'iq Bakr al-Sawwaf, *al-'Alaqat bayn al-Dawlah al-'Uthmaniyyah wa-Iqlim al-Hijaz, 1693–1443AH (1876–1916)* (n.p.: Matabi' Sijill al-'Arab, 1978). For a survey of Ottoman–Hijazi relations in the eighteenth century, see Abdulrahman Alorabi, 'The Ottoman Policy in the Hijaz in the Eighteenth Century: A Study of Political and Administrative Developments, 1143–1202 AH/1735–1788 AD', unpublished PhD dissertation, University of Utah, 1988.

11

rule in 1840,[2] was a roller-coaster ride of competition within the state apparatus, in which the Ottoman Vali and the Sharif vied for the upper hand, and for the opportunity to set the rules of the game in the relationship between state and society.

The structure of the Ottoman state in the Hijaz was unlike that in other Ottoman vilayets, or provinces; it was, rather, more like a 'state within a state,' where the Ottoman Vali and the Sharif each had their own administration, armed forces, courts, prisons, and representatives in the major towns. This state of affairs caused perpetual tension between the two authorities.[3]

Finances and economy in the Hijaz. The Hijaz had little in the way of natural resources; it was a poor place and was not located on any major trade routes. Except for some Red Sea trade at Jeddah, the Sharif and many other Hijazis survived on the remittances they received from the Ottomans, as well as on seasonal pilgrim-age-related income. This economic predicament made the Hijaz almost wholly dependent on the goodwill of the Ottoman Empire.

Ochsenwald has written that the vilayet of Hijaz was perhaps 'the Arab province most valuable to the Ottoman Sultan.'[4] Possession of the *Haramayn* was a *sine qua non* for any sultan-caliph, and to be seen as the defender and benefactor of Islam's two holiest cities was fundamental to the legitimacy and prestige of the ruler. Ruling the Hijaz was an emotionally potent political and religious asset for the Ottomans, but their possession of the region came at a double price: they shared its governance with the Sharif, and, unlike more conventional states and other vilayets, the Hijaz received massive amounts of imperial funds. Indeed, the Otto-man state in the Hijaz was more akin to the modern distributive states of the Persian Gulf, in that the sultan distributed more to the Hijaz than he received from it.[5] The 'Hijaz was too poor, too distant, and too accustomed to near-autonomy to submit to taxation.

---

[2] In 1803 the Al Sa'ud of Najd had occupied Mecca; they were removed by Muhammad 'Ali of Egypt – acting at the request of the Ottomans – in 1813, and direct Ottoman rule was re-established in 1840.

[3] Al-Amr, p. 12.

[4] William Ochsenwald, 'Ottoman Subsidies to the Hijaz, 1877–1886,' *IJMES* 6 (1975), p. 300.

[5] For a general analysis of the Ottoman revenue system in the nineteenth century, see Stanford J. Shaw, 'The Nineteenth-Century Ottoman Tax Reforms and Revenue System,' *IJMES* 6 (1975), pp. 421–59.

Hijazis ... did not pay taxes except in the disguised form of higher prices for goods taxed on entry to the Hijaz by sea.' The Ottomans actually operated at a deficit there, netting a small income only from customs at Jeddah.[6]

The residents of the Hijaz – the Sharif and his family among them – were dependent on Ottoman subsidies. Indeed, throughout the history of the Hijaz under Ottoman rule, various social groups established a right to receive gifts from the Ottoman central treasury, in what amounted to a large-scale patronage system. These funds contributed greatly to the coffers of the élite and stimulated an alliance between the upper levels of society and the Ottoman state. Other sources of income were numerous, for instance, taxes on camel hire and income from *awqaf* and other property, and donations from the pious abroad, particularly India.[7]

It is difficult to arrive at precise figures for imperial subsidies to the Sharif and his family, since contemporary documents give conflicting information, and in some Ottoman records the sums are often amalgamated with other subsidies to the Hijaz; nevertheless, the nature and breadth of the Ottoman contribution to the Sharifian state are evident, and they were substantial. It meant that the Sharif and all other Hijazi residents were quite dependent on Ottoman largesse.[8]

---

[6] William Ochsenwald, 'The Financial Basis of Ottoman Rule in the Hijaz, 1840–1877' in William Haddad and William Ochsenwald (eds), *Nationalism in a Non-National State: The Dissolution of the Ottoman Empire* (Columbus: Ohio State University Press, 1977), p. 133.

[7] FO 195/1514, Jago (Jeddah) to Granville, no. 3, 5 March 1885.

[8] The study of currency in the Ottoman Empire is made difficult due to changes and debasements over the years. To ease comparisons and thus save the reader trouble, I have followed the example of Frederick Anscombe in *The Ottoman Gulf: The Creation of Kuwait, Saudi Arabia, and Qatar* (New York: Columbia University Press, 1997), pp. xiii–xiv, and converted all non-British currencies to Ottoman lira (TL). Small sums are given in piasters of which there were 100 in a Turkish lira; larger sums are in Turkish lira, rounded to the nearest whole lira. Anscombe pegs the TL at roughly equivalent to 0.9 British pounds sterling for most of the period under discussion, as does Roger Owen, *The Middle East in the World Economy, 1800–1914* (London: Methuen, 1987), p. xiii. For discussions of money and finance in the Ottoman Empire, in particular, see Charles Issawi, *The Economic History of the Middle East, 1800–1914* (University of Chicago Press, 1966), pp. 517–24; Şevket Pamuk, 'Appendix: Money in the Ottoman Empire,' in Halik Inalcik with Donald Quataert, *An Economic and Social History of the Ottoman Empire, 1300–1914* (Cambridge University Press, 1994), pp. 946–85.

The best-known way in which the Ottomans subsidized the Hijaz was the *surre*, the yearly Ottoman donation to institutions and residents of the Hijaz, which was sent with the pilgrimage caravan from Damascus (sometimes referred to as the Syrian *mahmal*). In the mid-1880s, for example, the Ottomans budgeted over TL80,000 for the *surre*, although over half of that went for transportation costs (see Table 2.1). The budget for Mecca in 1884–1885 included about TL15,440 for payments to *ashraf* and *sadat*, and around TL12,000 for the purchase of wheat to be distributed (see Table 2.2). For the same fiscal year, the budget for the Hijaz vilayet included TL50,000 for the sultan's donation for the *mahmal*, sacred uses, and to tribes for security. Payment to *ulama*, *ashraf* and *sadat* totalled TL17,767; grains distributed in the Hijaz were budgeted for TL25,559 (see Table 2.3).

Ashraf and *sayyids*, as well as religious functionaries and just plain residents of the *Haramayn* had two other sources of income: the *Ikramiye* and the *Ôehadetname*. Sir Richard Burton, the British adventurer and traveler, writing of the 1850s, stated that the *Ikramiye* was money obtainable by almost any Medinan who traveled to Istanbul. The size of his gift was determined by his social class; *sayyids* received the greatest amount.[9] But there appears to have been some reform in this matter in the 1880s with the introduction of the *Şehadetname*, which was funded by a tax on the March salaries of Ottoman civil servants. A certificate – *Şehadet* – was issued to residents of the *Haramayn* with their name, age, eye color and height. In the fiscal year 1880–1881, the Ottomans budgeted TL70,348 for the *Şehadetname*, but the following year it was reduced to TL49,886 (see Table 2.4). A yearly lottery was held and the winners received funds from this source. In the 1880s, the number of residents receiving funds from this source was in the low hundreds.[10]

An indication of the magnitude of these sums can be derived from data we have on wages of laborers in the Hijaz. A *mu'adhdhin*

---

9   Richard Burton, *Personal Narrative of a Pilgrimage to al-Madinah and Meccah* (London: Tylston and Edwards, 1893), rpt. Dover, 1964, II, p. 7–8. Burton's view was that the terms *sayyid* and *sharif* in the Northern Hijaz 'applied indifferently to the posterity of Hasan and Hosayn.' He may also have amalgamated the *Ikramiye* together with the *Şehadetname*.

10 Ochsenwald, 'Ottoman Subsidies,' pp. 305–6; R. Tresse, *Le Pélerinage syrien aux villes saintes de l'Islam* (Paris: Chaumette, 1937), pp. 120–2. Ochsenwald, 'Ottoman Studies,' terms this certificate a *tezkere*.

Table 2.1. *SURRE* EXPENDITURES, MID-1880s

	In Turkish lira, rounded to the nearest lira
Transportation: provisions, payments to bedouins, salaries and expenses of *surre* staff	53,773
Donations to mosque officials, charitable institutions, *tekkes*	26,626
Total	80,399

Adapted from Ochsenwald, 'Ottoman Subsidies,' pp. 302–3.

Table 2.2. EXPENDITURES IN THE MECCA BUDGET OF
FISCAL YEAR 1300 (1884–5)

Payments to *ashraf* and *sadat*	15,441
Wheat purchased in Egypt	12,026
Salaries for Ka'ba officials	8,346
Miscellaneous and numerous other items	53,718
Total	89,529

Adapted from Ochsenwald, 'Ottoman Subsidies,' p. 302.

Table 2.3. EXPENDITURES IN THE HIJAZ VILAYET BUDGET OF
FISCAL YEAR 1300 (1884–5)

Army, navy, police	144,471
Sultan's donation for *mahmal*, other sacred uses, payments to tribes	50,000
Payments to *ashraf*, *sadat*, *'ulama*	17,767
Wheat, barley, lentils and beans distributed at Mecca, Medina, and Jeddah	25,559
Civil government salaries	17,300
Total	255,097

Adapted from Ochsenwald, 'Ottoman Subsidies,' p. 302.

Table 2.4. THE ŞEHADETNAME

Fiscal year 1296 (1880–1)	70,348
Fiscal year 1297 (1881–2)	49,886

Adapted from Ochsenwald, 'Ottoman Subsidies,' p. 305.

of the *Haram* at Medina received a salary of about two piasters a day in 1853, and a carpenter eight; in Ta'if in 1880 a skilled gardener was paid nearly four. Although meat was not common fare, a chicken cost about five piasters, while a kilogram of mutton cost more than four and a half; the estimated daily cost of food to sustain life was two to three piasters.[11] From this we can deduce that the amount distributed by the Ottomans in each year was substantial.

Another source of income for the Hijaz was Egypt. The money and payment in kind came with the Egyptian *mahmal* each year.[12] In 1880 grain valued at TL42,334 was sent from Egypt; in 1914 this was valued at TL31,858. Money was also earmarked for the inhabitants of the Hijaz: in 1890 and 1914 this amounted to TL4,251 and TL1,008, respectively. The *ashraf* of Mecca and Medina were budgeted to receive TL1,711 in 1888, but by 1914 this had dropped to TL1,008.[13]

Data are not widely available for the Sharif's subsidy from the Ottomans. In the 1810s the Sharif's subsidy was around TL9,600.[14] For the fiscal year 1871–2 the subsidy was valued at TL10,800. These monies were combined with a massive payment in kind of 228 tons of barley and other goods, mostly grains, which was valued in fiscal year 1854–5 at TL1,425.[15]

The greatest revenue accruing to the Sharifian coffers from anything resembling taxation came from taxing the use of camels, whether to carry *hujjaj* or merchant cargo. With respect to the former, the Iranian notable of Qajar Iran, Mirza Mohammad Hosayn Farahani, who made the pilgrimage in 1885, stated that there was a tax on the use of camels carrying pilgrims from Egypt to Medina, and that it went to the vali and the Sharif in order to pay tribesmen for permission to traverse their grazing areas.[16]

---

11 Ochsenwald, *Religion, State*, pp. 22–3.
12 The *mahmal* was the procession to Mecca from Egypt, which carried the *kiswa*, the embroidered covering for the Ka'ba.
13 Al-Amr, p. 23; Ibrahim Rif'at Pasha, *Mir'at al–Haramayn* (Cairo: Matba'at Dar al-Kutub al-Misriyyah, 1925), vol. 2, p. 360–1, which is a table detailing the gifts of the Egyptian authorities to the residents of the Hijaz for most of the years from 1880 to 1924.
14 Ochsenwald, 'The Financial Basis of Ottoman Rule,' p. 149.
15 *Ibid.*, pp. 146, 149.
16 Hafez Farmayan and Elton L. Daniel (eds), *A Shi'ite Pilgrimage to Mecca, 1885–1886: The Safarnameh of Mirza Mohammad Hosayn Farahani* (Austin: University of Texas Press, 1990), p. 193.

Muhammad Abu Liwa, who was chief dragoman to the travel agents Thomas Cook and Son, made the pilgrimage the next year. He recorded that the Sharif set the price for camel hire, which at the time was TL4.6 for the Mecca to Medina route and TL6.9 for a round trip. Someone who wanted to travel from Mecca to Medina and then to Yanbu' paid TL5.8. Abu Liwa recounts that most of this money went to the camel owner, and the rest was split between the Vali, the Sharif, the *mutawwif* (pilgrim guide and travel agent), and the *mukharrij* (the camel broker who collected the camels); TL0.23 was held as bond (*rahniyyah*) or insurance for the safe arrival of the pilgrim. (At other times, a parent or friend of the broker was imprisoned by the Sharif in lieu of this monetary guarantee.) Abu Liwa concluded his report with the age-old pilgrim's lament: 'A pilgrim in the Hedjaz lands is just as grass and a nice piece of meat […] every one likes to take a piece of it.'[17]

Many sources refer to the collusion between the Sharif and the Vali for the exacting of the camel tax. During the construction of the Hijaz railway, the British Consul at Jeddah, J.H. Monahan, had the impression that the Vali was interested in trying to delay construction, as he was 'mindful of his private interest in … camel transport.'[18] In some years the Sharif and the Vali reportedly colluded to raise the tax to about 50 per cent of the total charge. A portion of the Vali's share was pocketed by the Vali himself, while

---

[17] FO 685/2, Translation from the Arabic Journal of Mohammed Abou-Elewa's Pilgrimage, Cairo to Meccah, Medinah, and Back, 1886, undated. Yanbu' was the sea port closest to Medina, and was often used as a point of departure for those leaving the Hijaz after the *ziyarah*, as the pilgrimage to Medina is termed. An official at the British consulate in Jeddah, in a Memorandum on Camel Hire in the Hedjaz (FO 685/2, 11 April 1887, unsigned), substantially agrees with Abu Liwa's observations. See also Ali Ibrahim Kholaif, 'The Hijaz Vilayet 1869–1908: The Sharifate, the Hajj, and the Bedouins of the Hijaz,' unpublished PhD dissertation, University of Wisconsin-Madison, 1986, pp. 58–63; Rif'at Pasha, pp. 125–6; al-Amr, 2, p. 38.

[18] FO 195/2286, Monahan to Chargé d'Affaires, Constantinople, no. 17, 8 March 1908. For more information on the camel tax, see the following: FO 195/2126, Devey, Memorandum Respecting His Highness the Grand Sherif, undated (probably October 1902); FO 195/2148, Devey, Report on the Economic State of the Hejaz Vilayet during the Months January to April 1903, 13 May 1903; FO 195/2148, Devey, Report on the Hejaz Vilayet May to August Inclusive 1903, undated (probably early September 1903); Devey to O'Conor, Report on the Administrative and Economic State of the Hejaz for the Months March to June 1905, 19 July 1905.

another went to the budget of the vilayet.[19] The Sharif's total income from the tax on camel hire and various other exactions was estimated in the 1880s to be £150,000 sterling.[20] From camel sales in Mecca during the *hajj*, the Sharif also received half of one pound sterling for each camel, amounting to a total of £15,000 a year.[21]

While the historian Abu-Manneh probably exaggerated when he wrote that the Sharif 'was the ultimate administrator of the endowments of the [Meccan] *haram*,'[22] there is little doubt that he did have much income from the *waqf* (pl. *awqaf*) in the *Haramayn*.[23] Most available residences in Mecca were *waqf*, set aside to house pilgrims.[24] That the Sharif exerted some control over houses which were *waqf* may be deduced from Hurgronje's observation that during the absence of the Sharif, the Vali manipulated the title to many *awqaf* and acquired possession by means of a legal fiction.[25] In 1891–2 some *ashraf* petitioned the Porte for the dismissal of Sharif 'Awn al-Rafiq, charging, among other things, that he had embezzled *awqaf* funds.[26]

The sources also give us an indication of other forms of Sharifian income, a main one being the kickback by various functionaries for appointments approved by the Sharif. The most prominent of these was that of *mutawwif*, or pilgrim guide. A *mutawwif* had to receive a license (*taqrir*) from the Sharif. While theoretically the license was for life, it could be revoked by the Sharif for 'misconduct.' Thus, if a particular *mutawwif* fell into disfavor, his license might be withdrawn, or, if all the *mutawwifin* seemed to be doing rather well, an ordinance might be issued demanding the renewal of all licenses, for a fee.[27] Kholaif cites

19 Al-Amr, pp. 37–8; FO 195/2126, Devey, no. 84, Budget Estimate for the Jeddah District, 31 October 1902.
20 Kholaif, pp. 58–9.
21 *Ibid.*, pp. 60–1.
22 Butrus Abu-Manneh, 'Sultan Abdulhamid II and the Sharifs of Mecca (1880–1900)', *AAS* 9 (1973), pp. 3–4. Abu-Manneh brings no evidence for this assertion.
23 Ochsenwald, *Religion, Society*, p. 177.
24 *Ibid.*, p. 24.
25 C. Snouck Hurgronje, *Mekka. Die Stadt und ihre Herren* (The Hague: Nijhoff, 1888), pp. 164–165.
26 Ochsenwald, *Religion, Society*, p. 194.
27 C. Snouck Hurgronje, *Mekka in the Latter Part of the Nineteenth Century* (Leiden: Brill, 1931, rpt. 1970), pp. 78–9.

reports from the 1880s which estimate that the Sharif received £21,668 from various *mutawwifin* for the privilege of attending to pilgrims from specific geographical regions. British representative Devey stated that at least 800–900 *mutawwifin* paid 'baksheesh' of between £5 and £100 for the privilege of handling pilgrims from various classes. In 1901, he reported, it was said that one *mutawwif* paid £2,000 for the right to supervise pilgrims. 'The Sharif alone,' Devey concluded, 'appoints [and] is responsible for these nominations.'[28]

Yet the Sharif received an income from appointments other than those of *mutawwifin*; according to Hurgronje, what applied to the guild of *mutawwifin* applied to all the guilds in Mecca. For example, one who wanted to join the guild of the *zamazimah*, that is, those charged with the distribution of the holy waters of the well of Zamzam in the Meccan *Haram*, could 'secure for himself the Government[']s protection in [his] practise only by a license (*taqrir*) from the Grand Sherif [,and the] license [was] not granted for nothing.'[29] Camel brokers were also approved by the Sharif.[30]

Mechanisms of coercion: armed forces and the administration of justice. According to Ochsenwald, the Sharifian state 'generally relied on religious prestige and political and financial maneuvering to achieve its goals.'[31] Since most of the Sharif's income came from Ottoman subsidies, approving appointments, and various *awqaf*, he had little need for a large army to extract revenue. Income from the camel-hire tax and from appointments was collected easily by virtue of tradition, coercion rarely being used by the Sharif's small force.

In 1885 it was reported that the Sharif 'Awn al-Rafiq had a small personal guard, known as 'Baverdis', which he clothed, paid, and armed with Martini Henry rifles.[32] Another force was the Bisha,

---

[28] Kholaif, p. 61; FO 195/2126, Devey (Jeddah), undated (probably 11 October 1902), Memorandum Respecting His Highness the Grand Sharif.

[29] Snouck Hurgronje, *Mekka*, pp. 22, 28, 78.

[30] FO 685/2, Memorandum on Camel Hire in the Hedjaz, unsigned, 11[?] November 1987. In this memorandum, it is noted that only the 'Head Camel-Broker ... receives a Firman from the grand Sheriff and the Gov. Genl. at Mecca.' Farmayan, p. 194, states that 'a camel broker ... is designated by the Sharif for each [national] group of pilgrims.'

[31] Ochsenwald, *Religion, Society*, pp. 158–9.

[32] FO 195/1514, Abdur Razzack (Jeddah) to White, no. 23, 21 August 1885.

which was composed mostly of black men from Wadi Bisha, near Abha in 'Asir. In 1898 the Bisha had numbered about 300 men, but by the outbreak of the First World War it had grown to 500. Controlled by the Sharif, the Bisha spent most of its time guarding caravan routes.[33]

Ottoman troops were sometimes used for securing the roads from the depredations of nomadic and semi-nomadic tribal groups. In fiscal year 1884–5, for instance, the Ottomans budgeted TL144,714 out of a total Hijaz Vilayet budget of TL255,339 (see Table 3). This task was shared occasionally by the Sharif, who would enlist tribal levies to fight the offending tribal group, and, more importantly, make periodic payments to the tribal chiefs in exchange for keeping the peace.[34]

The Sharif/Vali dual authority in the Hijaz led to a complex allocation of the administration of justice.[35] Officially, cases involving nomads and *ashraf* were to be heard by the Sharif, while other cases were to be heard by the Qadi of Mecca, who was the religious and judicial representative of the empire. Yet justice was often dispensed personally by the Sharif, the Vali, or bedouin chiefs without regard for these divisions.

Sources of justice included arbitration, tribal customary law (*'urf*), Ottoman commercial law and Qur'anic law. The Ottoman courts applied the *shari'ah*, as did the Sharif on occasion. These courts were headed by Ottoman appointees, the highest of which was the Hanafi Qadi of Mecca, who appointed deputies in Rabigh, Ta'if, Lith and Qunfudah; the Qadi of Medina did the same in Yanbu', Wajh, Khaybar and Diba. Special Ottoman courts administered the laws of the new commercial codes of the nineteenth century. Consular courts tried individuals who could prove foreign nationality.

In dealing with tribal forces, the Sharif often resorted to his own form of ready justice. In 1905, for instance, the Sharif 'Awn al-Rafiq imprisoned two tribesmen from Wadi Fatimah. In response, his relatives kidnapped two foreigners in Mecca who enjoyed European protection. The next morning one of the pris-

---

33 Al-Amr, pp. 98, 105–6; FO 195/2126, Devey (Jeddah) to O'Conor [?], no. 82, 14 October 1902; FO 195/2286, Monahan (Jeddah) to Lowther, no. 65, 5 December 1908; Ochsenwald, *Religion, Society*, p. 158.

34 Ochsenwald, *Religion, Society*, pp. 207–8.

35 The judicial system in the Hijaz is discussed in *ibid.*, pp. 84–90.

oners was ordered to be executed: he was taken out in public and 'poignarded' by two Bisha soldiers.[36]

The Sharif's prisons were criticized by observers from the West:

The cruelty of confining a son of the desert in dark damp stifling cells of the Sherif's prisons, sometimes too loaded with chains, has [as a] ... not infrequent result, death within a few score weeks. One is tempted to say that where possible a return to the 'lex talionis' of the Koran viz 'Kisas' and 'Haddu' would be far preferable: for the grade of civilization in this district can be very little higher than that of Abyssinia, a degree or two above pure African savagery.[37]

Only a few months later, however, the British consul praised the new Sharif's ('Ali ibn 'Abdallah) administration of justice, noting that 'bedouin affairs have received careful and prompt attention, and the measures of simple justice or custom-law practised at Mecca have obtained Arab public approval.'[38]

On the eve of the 1916 Arab Revolt then, the Sharifate was financially dependent on the Ottomans and linked to the empire militarily and with respect to administration of justice. After the Revolt, Husayn ibn 'Ali would not only have to make up a tremendous financial shortfall, but maintain order on his own as well.

The structure of Hijazi society on the eve of the Arab Revolt[39] The two major structural components of Hijazi society on the eve of the Arab Revolt were the bedouin and the population of the major towns, Mecca, Medina and Jeddah. Bedouin – settled, nomads, and semi-nomads – were the single largest component of the Hijazi population. Townspeople were a distinct minority at the end of the nineteenth century; Medina, Jeddah and Mecca had a

---

[36] FO 195/2198, Devey (Jeddah) to O'Conor, 19 July 1905, Report on the Administrative and Economic State of the Hejaz, for the months March to June 1905.

[37] FO 195/2198, Devey (Jeddah) to O'Conor, 19 July 1905. For similar Muslim opinions of the Sharif's prison, see below.

[38] FO 406/24, Devey (Jeddah) to O'Conor, no. 107, 13 October 1905, Report on the Economic and Administrative Condition of the Hejaz Vilayet for the Quarter ended 30 September 1905.

[39] The best study of Hijazi society in this period is Ochsenwald, *Religion, Society*, pp. 3–127. I have developed Ochsenwald's work in directions that are appropriate for our discussion.

combined population of about 150,000, but the tribal population was estimated to be close to 400,000, including the tribes of 'Asir.[40]

Throughout most of the nineteenth century, chronic insecurity was the order of the day along the most important pilgrimage route, the Jeddah–Mecca road, as well as along the less important Mecca–Medina road. Since neither the Ottomans nor the Sharif had enough troops to prevent the raiding of pilgrimage caravans, safety depended on the goodwill of the bedouin, who sometimes even threatened Jeddah itself.[41] As a ruler with roots in the Hijaz, the Sharif knew the bedouin best, and it was his responsibility to make sure that they would not cause trouble. When the Sharif wanted to make difficulties for the Vali, he would incite the bedouin to prey on the pilgrimage traffic. Hurgronje wrote that 'it was not seldom that the rapacious bedouin rejoiced secretly in the support of the Shereef.'[42] It was this political and social constellation which determined relations between the Sharif, the Vali, and the tribes.

Bedouin rapaciousness was the result not of some inherently aggressive character, but of a more complex social and economic reality. Most of them lived at subsistence level, under a real threat of famine. Many lived in misery and poverty, whereas in the large towns the standard of living was far higher. The bedouin often resented the Sharif for not paying them fairly for their cooperation. They saw this neglect as a breach of trust and thus exacted their payment by harassing the *hujjaj* passing through tribal territory; pilgrims were often robbed or kidnapped and held for ransom, to be paid by the Sharif.[43]

The Sharif wielded some moral authority over those tribal groups who agreed to accept him as a mediator, as was sometimes the case with the Juhaynah and the Harb. When disputes arose between or within such tribes, they appealed to the Sharif and his decision was supposed to be final.[44]

---

[40] Ochsenwald, *Religion, Society*, pp. 17, 31.

[41] See, for instance, FO 195/2286: Husain to Lowther, no. 44, 9 September 1908; Husain to Lowther, no. 45, 10 September 1908; Monahan to Lowther, no. 53, 5 November 1908.

[42] Quoted in Kholaif, pp. 56–7.

[43] Kholaif, pp. 137–46, citing various British despatches from Jeddah.

[44] Al-Amr, p. 115. Regarding the Juhaynah and the Harb, see M. Oppenheim, *Die Beduinen*, 2 (Leipzig: Harrassowitz, 1943) pp. 360, 371.

Ira Lapidus has added greatly to our general understanding of
the social structure of the Muslim city and town; his analysis can
be applied to cities and towns in the Hijaz. The social basis of the
Muslim city was personal relationships, informally organized in
what he terms *'asabiyyat*, or 'factional units functioning as autonomous collectives.' Institutions were embodied in the person of
individuals, whose authority derived not from the office they held
but rather from the force of their own personality. The notion of a
notable who led such an institution was summed up in the word
shaykh, which

defines a diffuse realm of authority, radiating from the person of the
notable. In a society which functioned on the basis of personal authority
and personal influence without legally defined offices or corporate
organizations, in the context of loosely ordered institutions which
depended heavily on clientage, notables were the key to the operation of
society as a whole.[45]

Lapidus has also demonstrated the image of the city in Islamdom
to be distinct from that of the countryside. As a place where 'serious Islamic learning' and collective worship took place, it was
viewed by Muslims as a 'superior place for religious life.'[46] The
townspeople therefore usually felt the 'nomads to be dangerous
robbers who were irreligious, uncouth, and barbaric'; for their
part, the bedouin saw the townspeople as 'defiled by their inter-
marriages with foreigners, unhealthy, effete, and cowardly.'[47] Yet
despite this mutual disdain, there was a great degree of interde-
pendency. The bedouin needed the town for its markets, where
they could sell their animals and animal byproducts, as well as
purchase provisions, such as cookware and rice. The townsmen
often needed what the bedouin brought to them. Thus the biggest
weapon of the Sharif against the bedouin was cutting them off
from the markets of the towns.

The Hijaz differed from many other regions in the Middle East
because of the centrality of the pilgrimage to its social structure. In
other areas a landowning class developed, but the harsh terrain of

---

[45] Ira Lapidus, 'Muslim Cities as Plural Societies: The Politics of Intermediary Bodies,'
Proceedings of the International Conference on Urbanism in Islam, Tokyo, 1989, vol. 1, pp.
134–63.

[46] Ira Lapidus, 'Traditional Muslim Cities: Structure and Change,' in L. Carl Brown
(ed.), *From Madina to Metropolis* (Princeton University Press, 1973), pp. 51–69.

[47] Ochsenwald, *Religion, Society*, p. 30.

the Hijaz did not support agricultural development, preventing such a class from emerging. Instead, livelihood was gained from the pilgrimage and all activities associated with it (for example, shipping, housing, providing food, and *hajj* rite services). The commercial élite made their living from trade, and most had a hand in the pilgrimage as well.

In areas of the Middle East where no strong local ruler existed, a 'politics of notables' developed whereby the local élites, acting as intermediaries between the non-Arab officials and the populace, gained political influence; such was the case in Syria. But in areas with strong local rulers, such as Istanbul or Muhammad 'Ali's Egypt, no such politics developed; instead, court or bureaucratic politics prevailed. In the Hijaz, the situation was more akin to the latter case:[48] the Sharif was a local strong man at the head of a chieftaincy, and therefore no 'politics of notables' developed; the élite did not act as intermediaries, and thus did not develop any significant political power. Power was instead heavily centralized in the hands of the Sharif, although it depended on his ability to maneuver *vis-à-vis* the Ottoman government, which could usually remove him if it wished.

[As a result of] the extreme ethnic diversity of the commercial elite [in the Hijaz] they did not coalesce with the chief religious families … to wrest local political power from the amirs of Mecca. Since the Ottoman government … played a major role in providing food to the Hijaz … and the Ottomans supported the amirate, a possible alliance between the central government and the merchants was … averted. Individual merchants were co-opted into the ruling groups as advisers to the vali and the amir …. Wealthy individuals in the commercial élite could and did secure special treatment … from the government, but they did not seek political power.[49]

Taking the work of Albert Hourani and Philip Khoury together, it is possible to distinguish three types of notables in the late Ottoman Empire: the religious élite, comprising the *'ulama* and the

---

[48] See Albert Hourani, 'Ottoman Reform and the Politics of Notables' in William Polk and Richard Chambers, *Beginnings of Modernization in the Middle East: The Nineteenth Century* (University of Chicago Press, 1968), pp. 41–68. Hourani's essay actually lumps the Hijaz with Syria as the place where the 'politics of notables' were found 'in their purest form' (p. 52), but I believe him to be mistaken.

[49] Ochsenwald, *Religion, Society*, pp. 92–3.

ashraf; a secular élite composed of merchants, *mashayikh* of quarters, bedouin chieftains and tax farmers; and the *aghawat*, the chiefs of local Ottoman military garrisons.[50]

In the Hijaz on the eve of Husayn's rule, there does not appear to be any evidence that the last category was present,[51] so we are concerned only with the religious and secular élites. To make the categorization of these élites more applicable to the Hijaz, they are divided here into the urban lay élite: merchants, heads of quarters, heads of guilds, and *hajj* service industry leaders (for example *mutawwifin*); the religious élite: the *'ulama* and the *ashraf*; and the tribal élite.

The urban lay élite: merchants. Commerce in the Hijaz was centered in Jeddah and was often dominated by three main houses: 'Ali Rida, Nasif, and Banajah. Since they did not seek political power, the merchant families simply went about their business making money. If the Sharif was particularly oppressive, they kept their heads down until better times.

Jeddah was widely considered the best port on the Red Sea.[52] With little in the way of natural resources and agriculture in the Hijaz, it was through Jeddah that most of the area's food arrived. The trade from India was of particular importance, many of the goods being re-exported by the merchants to Egypt.

Jeddah was also by far the main entrepôt for the *hujjaj*. Muhammad al-Sha'afi's statistical studies have shown a correlation between the number of pilgrims and the volume of foreign trade at Jeddah, a correlation also reported anecdotally by British observers. The pilgrims affected both import and export trade as well. The more pilgrims there were at Muna to make a sacrifice at the end of the *hajj*, the more hides there were to export. Mer-

---

[50] Hourani, pp. 48–9; Philip Khoury, 'Continuity and Change in Syrian Political Life: The Nineteenth and Twentieth Centuries,' *American Historical Review*, vol. 96 (December 1991), pp. 1334–95; Philip Khoury, *Urban Notables and Arab Nationalism: The Politics of Damascus 1860–1920* (Cambridge University Press, 1983), pp. 10–13. There were persons designated *aghawat* in the Hijaz, but there this term referred to the attendants of the Medinan *haram*; see Shaun Marmon, *Eunuchs and Sacred Boundaries in Islamic Society* (New York: Oxford University Press, 1995).

[51] A military tour in the Hijaz was considered hardship duty, and it may have been that the Ottoman commanders simply preferred to keep their stay there short, thus not leaving enough time for their formation into 'notables.'

[52] Much of the information on the commerce of Jeddah is taken from Muhammad S. al-Sha'afi, *The Foreign Trade of Juddah* (n.p.: privately published, 1985).

chants involved in the shipping business stood to gain or lose by the number of pilgrims each year. As Consul Devey summed it up: 'The pilgrimage is the mainstay of trade; a good pilgrim season implies increased shipping, low freights, money brought into the country and brisk business.'[53]

Jeddah was a particularly cosmopolitan Islamic city, and its most influential merchant families originated outside the Hijaz. The richest merchant family in Jeddah was the house of 'Ali Rida, who were Sunni Persians.[54] The 'Ali Ridas had a long history in Jeddah, beginning with the arrival of Zaynal in the 1840s. Zaynal eventually brought over his much younger brother 'Abdallah, and together they founded the merchant house; 'Abdallah was the head of the family on the eve of the Revolt and throughout the rest of the period of this study. Both married wives from the Nasif family.

The business developed primarily in the 1880s when 'Abdallah was sent to Bombay and Calcutta to establish purchasing offices, a move enabling the family to buy Indian products at cheaper prices than other merchants could. Of particular importance was the concession which it gained to act as agent for the Mogul Shipping Line, which at the time held a monopoly on the pilgrim traffic between India and the Hijaz. The business apparently held most of the Indian trade in its hands, after wresting it from the foreign trading houses of Jeddah. The family was also heavily involved in the pearling industry.[55]

Qasim ibn Zaynal 'Ali Rida was chosen for the Ottoman Parliament in late 1908 as the representative from Jeddah;[56] Muham-

---

53 Devey (Jeddah), Report for the Years 1900–1904 on the Trade of the Hejaz, Diplomatic and Consular Reports, no. 3483, July 6, 1905.

54 Background on the 'Ali Rida family is taken from Michael Field, *The Merchants: The Big Business Families of Saudi Arabia and the Gulf States* (Woodstock, NY: Overlook Press, 1984), pp. 15–19, 21–6; FO 882/20, Jeddah Personalities by Capt. Young, December 1919 (henceforth, Young, Jeddah Personalities); Muhammad 'Ali Maghribi, *A'lam al-Hijaz fi al-Qarn al-Rabi' 'Ashar lil-Hijrah*, vol. 1 (Jeddah: Tihamah, 1981), pp. 37–40, 139–42, 279–90 (henceforth, Maghribi).

55 Muhammad 'Ali ibn Zaynal 'Ali Rida was known as '*malik al-lu'lu' fi al-'alam*' ('the pearl king of the world' – Maghribi, p. 283).

56 The election had difficulty getting under way, as no one registered to vote, fearing conscription. In the event, the Ottomans ordered the three *mashayikh* of Jeddah's quarters to choose 200 from each district. These chose a body of twenty-five, who finally voted. Qasim received the largest number of votes: eight; two or three were from his relatives and the others from business associates. Little interest was taken in

mad 'Ali ibn Zaynal, the family's philanthropist, founded a chain of schools – the Falah schools – first in Jeddah and in Mecca, and later in Bahrain, Bombay and Dubai.[57] He was once also an Ottoman MP. 'Abdallah was *qa'im maqam* of Jeddah in the late Ottoman period, under Husayn, and into the Saudi period.

The Banajah family was of humble Hadrami origin but had become a great merchant house. By 1858 Yusuf ibn Ahmad Banajah was a major Hijazi merchant, although hard times may well have preceded his success. In the 1850s Yusuf lent money to the Ottoman treasury. On the eve of Sharif Husayn ibn 'Ali's rule, the patriarch of the family was 'Abd al-Rahman ibn Muhammad, who together with his brother 'Abdallah Pasha and son Muhammad Salim, dominated the import and export trade in spices, rice, flour and sugar with India and Egypt. 'Abd al-Rahman was banker to the Vali Ratib Pasha and, following the 1908 Young Turk Revolution was arrested by those investigating Ratib's finances. 'Abdallah owned most of the property in Jeddah's northern quarter, as well as over 400 *feddans* in Egypt.[58]

The Nasif family – connected to the 'Ali Ridas by two marriages – was of modest Egyptian origin, and its patriarch was 'Umar Nasif. The Nasifs prospered as merchants, no doubt partly because they were the agents (*wakil*) for the Dhawu 'Awn Sharifs in Jeddah, looking after their properties and business interests. 'Umar built the largest and most well-appointed house in Jeddah, the famous Qasr Nasif, and the Sharifs stayed there when in town. It was a kind of social salon where Jeddah's merchants gathered, and foreign consuls visited.

---

the election (FO 195/2286: Monahan [Jeddah] to Lowther [Constantinople], no. 53, 5 November 1908; Monahan to Lowther, no. 57, 10 November 1908). For information on the activities of Qasim and other Hijazi deputies in the Ottoman parliament, see Sabine Prator, *Der arabische Faktor in der jung-turkischen Politik. Eine Studie zum osmanischen Parlament der II. Konstitution (1908–1918)* (Berlin: Klaus Schwarz Verlag, 1993).

57 According to Maghribi (p. 283), he founded these schools first in the Hijaz as a way of combating Young Turk efforts at Turkification (*tatrik*).

58 FO 371/16878/E 3745, Personalities in Saudi Arabia, enclosed in Ryan (Jeddah) to Simon (London), no. 187, 19 June 1933 (henceforth, Ryan, Personalities); Young, Jeddah Personalities; Ochsenwald, *Religion, Society*, pp. 109–10, 216; FO 195/2286, Mohammed Hussain, Acting British Consul (Jeddah), to Lowther (Constantinople), no. 39, 25 August 1908; Ochsenwald, 'Nationalism,' p. 136.

On the eve of Husayn's rule, the most prominent Nasif was 'Umar's grandson, Muhammad Husayn. British documents noted that Muhammad was a 'Wahhabi by conviction, even before the Sa'udi invasion,' and a French note illuminates this remark. Muhammad Husayn Nasif was reportedly influenced by the reformer Muhammad 'Abduh while in Egypt and upon his return attacked the local Sufis and threw stones at them. He was described as an intimate friend of Rashid Rida and was *al-Manar's* correspondent in the Hijaz. It is clear that this influential man held strong *salafi* tendencies that made him sympathetic to Wahhabism. Muhammad established a famous library in his house, consisting mostly of *salafi* texts.[59]

The urban lay élite: shaykhs of quarters and guilds. Like other Middle Eastern cities, Mecca, Jeddah and Medina were divided into quarters (*harat*), each headed by its own *shaykh*. The *shaykh*s of the professions and the quarters were usually nominated by the important men of each profession or quarter, and the nomination was approved by the Sharif of Mecca and the head of the municipality (*ra'is al-baladiyyah*) in Jeddah. These *shaykh*s often served the Sharif by mobilizing their constituents to attend meetings and issue declarations in his favor.[60]

Mecca had about thirteen quarters, each with its own flag. According to Ihsanullah, the Indian agent for the British in Mecca in 1920, the *Shaykh al-Hara* stood at the head of a council that decided matters of the quarter and reported to the Sharif.[61] Hurgronje wrote of 'feuds lasting years' whereby a man from one quarter could not venture into another. Disputes often ended with a death, which necessitated the payment of blood money, a sum decided by the *shaykh*s of the quarters involved.[62]

---

[59] MAE, Arabie–Hedjaz 24, Capitaine ['Ibrahim'] Depui (Paris) to Minister [of Foreign Affairs], personality profiles of Jeddah residents, 28 September 1924 (henceforth, Depui, Personalities); MAE, Djeddah (consulat), Carton no. 24, card catalog of Hijazi personalities, undated (henceforth, French personality cards); SHAT, 7 N 2139, M. Benazzouz (Jeddah), Note sur Mohammed Nacif, 23 June 1917; Young, Jeddah Personalities; Ryan, Personalities; Maghribi, pp. 209–15; obituary in *al-'Arab*, 6 (September 1971), part 1, pp. 63–5.

[60] FO 882/23, Ihsanullah (Mecca) to British Agent, 19 May 1920.

[61] *Ibid.*

[62] Snouck Hurgronje, *Mekka*, p. 9. Those who carried out such fighting were known as *ayyal al-harah*, the quarter's brave fighting toughs. They were sometimes imprisoned for such activity, but the punishment was light: they were not chained, and were allowed

Jeddah had four quarters: Harat al-Sham, containing government offices and foreign missions and companies; Harat
al-Mazlum; Harat al-Yaman, in which were situated the agencies
of the various *mutawwifin*; and Harat al-Bahr, which held fisher-
men, seamen, and ships' suppliers. Residents of each neighborhood felt a common *'asabiyyah* (*esprit de corps*), and prevented those
perceived as undesirable from entering.[63]

Guilds in the Hijaz could be divided into two types: those associated with the *'hajj* service industry' and those not. Of the latter,
there were silk merchants, boatmen, jewelers, sellers of prayer
beads, butchers, camel brokers, masons, and porters. At times in
Mecca, Medina, and Jeddah there was even a chief merchant, recommended by the Vali and appointed by the Grand Vezir. The
mashayikh of the guilds were sent a mantle (*jubbah*) of honor by
the Sharif as a sign of their official nomination.[64]

Given the character of the Hijaz, the most socially significant
guilds were those associated with the *hajj* service industry, and the
most prominent of these was the *mutawwifin*. The *mutawwif* was
both religious guide and travel agent; he not only helped pilgrims
to carry out the *hajj* in the manner prescribed by Islam, but handled their accommodation and transportation as well. A *mutawwif*
specialized in pilgrims from a particular region, so that a *mutawwif*
who handled pilgrims from Egypt was known as *shaykh* of the
Egyptians. All the *shaykhs* dealing with a particular region were
grouped in a guild, headed by a *Shaykh al-Mashayikh*. The man
who represented the most general interests of all the *mutawwifin*
was known as *Shaykh al-Mutawwifin*. This leader was appointed by
the Sharif, probably from amongst a select group of obvious candidates. In Medina there were guides called *muzawwirin* (from the
ziyarah, or holy visitation to Medina), who guided the pilgrims
around the sacred sites. It is not clear if they were organized into a
guild.[65]

---

visitors who came throughout the day to drink tea (FO 882/23, Ihsanullah [Mecca] to
British Agent, 19 May 1920). Urban gangs were a region-wide phenomenon in the
Middle East at least from the Middle Ages: see, for example, Ira Lapidus, *Muslim Cities in
the Later Middle Ages*, p. 105; Juan Cole and Moojan Momen, 'Mafia Mob and Shi'ism in
Iraq: The Rebellion of Ottoman Karbala, 1824–1843,' *Past and Present* 112 (August 1986),
pp. 116–18 and the sources cited therein for a typology of these gangs.

63 Maghribi, pp. 58–9.
64 Ochsenwald, *Religion, Society*, pp. 113–14; Hurgronje, *Mekka*, pp. 29–30.
65 Snouck Hurgronje, *Mekka*, pp. 25–9; Long, pp. 31–2.

The *mutawwif*s were represented in Jeddah by *wukala* (agents, sing. *wakil*). The guild of the *wukala* was headed by a *Shaykh al-Wukala* and, like that of the *mutawwifin*, was subdivided according to the region of origin of the *hujjaj*.[66]

The third important *hajj* service industry guild was that of the *zamazimah* (sing. *zamzami*), which monopolized the distribution of the water from the famous well of Zamzam in the Meccan *Haram*. This trade necessitated a *taqrir*, or license from the Sharif.[67]

The religious élite. The highest religious official in the Hijaz was the Hanafi *qadi* of Mecca (the Hanafi *madhhab* was the official Ottoman school of jurisprudence). The next most powerful officials were the directors (*shaykh*) of the Meccan and Medinan *Harams*. The *'ulama* of each town were headed by a *shaykh*, the *Shaykh al-'Ulama*, who was Shafi'i, the *madhhab* of most Hijazis. On the eve of Husayn's rule, the position was held by Shaykh Ahmad Zawawi. The *mufti* of the Hanafi *madhhab* was 'Abd al-Rahman Sarraj, who was succeeded by his son 'Abdallah, and both may also have been the *qadi* of Mecca. The *qadis*, the *mufti*s of the *madhahib* and other religious appointments were made by the Sharif and the central government in Istanbul.[68] There does not seem to have been an official position of *Qadi al-Quda*, although the Hanafi *qadi* may have been regarded as such.

These men in the uppermost echelons of the religious establishment were financially supported by the Ottomans and they did not therefore usually challenge the government, although they were not beyond supporting one Sharifian branch against another. In turn, the Ottomans enjoyed the legitimacy conferred on them by these men.[69]

If there was any social group that approximated the concept of hereditary nobility, it was the descendants of the Prophet. Those who traced their ancestry to Muhammad's grandson Hasan were

66 Long, p. 31; Snouck Hurgronje, *Mekka*, pp. 24–5.
67 Snouck Hurgronje, *Mekka*, p. 22.
68 Ochsenwald, *Religion, Society*, pp. 50–3, 176; Snouk [sic] Hurgronje, 'Some of My Experiences with the Muftis of Mecca (1885)', *Asian Affairs* 8, part 1 (February 1977), pp. 25–37; Hurgronje, *Mekka*, pp. 182–4; Young, Mecca Personalities; SHAT, 7 N 2139, Cheikh Ahmed Zouaoui Mufti Chafeite et Vice-Président du Sénat Arabe, note by M. Benazzouz (Mecca), 7 January 1917; 'Abd al-Rahman Sarraj's son, 'Abdallah, was elected to the Ottoman Parliament in 1908 (Kayali, pp. 208–9.)
69 Ochsenwald, *Religion, Society*, pp. 55–6.

called *ashraf*, and those who descended from another grandson, Husayn, took the title *sayyid* (pl. *sadat*). For much of the nineteenth century, these were headed by a *Naqib al-Ashraf* and a *Naqib al-Sadat*. Sometimes, however, these posts were combined in one person, and often the Sharif of Mecca himself headed the *ashraf*.[70]

In parts of the empire other than the Hijaz, the *naqib* was a post 'which conferred the most social prestige, though not necessarily the most political influence,'[71] and, like other notables, he performed an intermediary function between the state and the local populace.[72] There is no indication whatsoever that in the Hijaz the *naqib* held any political power; in fact, with the top *sharif* being the most powerful figure in the country, there is no reason to believe that the position of the *Naqib al-Ashraf* was anything more than symbolic. As the Hijaz was in essence a Sharifian state run by *sharif*s, the real contest for power was between competing branches of the *ashraf*; in our case, between the Dhawu 'Awn and the Dhawu Zayd, whose competition for the position of Sharif of Mecca formed the principal political ambit of the Meccan élite.

The Shayba family was prestigious because of its hereditary ownership of the keys to the Ka'bah. It had held this position from *Jahiliyyah* times, and note was taken of their role by Nasir-i Khusraw when he visited the city in 1050 and by Ibn Jubayr when he did the same in 1183–4.[73] Burton called them 'the true *sangre azul* of Al-Hijaz.'[74] Their primary income was from selling pieces of the *kiswah*, the Ka'bah's black, gold-embroidered covering, and from entrance fees when the edifice was opened to the public; often a rich Muslim would have the Ka'bah opened for him specially, for which the Shayba would be handsomely rewarded.[75] Hasan Shayba was elected as representative of Mecca to the Ottoman Parliament in 1908 along with Sharif Husayn's son 'Abdallah; on the eve of Husayn's rule, Muhammad Salih Shayba was the head of the family.[76]

---

[70] *Ibid.*, p. 53.

[71] Khoury, *Urban Notables*, p. 14.

[72] Ochsenwald, *Religion, Society*, p. 53.

[73] F.E. Peters, *Mecca: A Literary History of the Muslim Holy Land* (Princeton University Press, 1995), pp. 140–141, 280–282.

[74] Burton, vol. 2, p. 468.

[75] Snouck Hurgronje, *Mekka*, p. 21.

[76] FO 195/2350, Monahan (Jeddah) to Lowther (Constantinople), 23 March 1910; FO 195/2376, Abdurrahman (Jeddah) to Lowther, no. 44, 4 November 1911; Ochsenwald,

The tribal élite. Relations with the tribal élite were both monetary and social. The Ottomans kept detailed records of payments in cash and grain to tribes,[77] and the Sharif probably also made some payments. The Sharif sometimes made tribal alliances via marriage, as in the case of Sharif Muhammad ibn 'Abd al-Mu'in, who married a daughter of a chief of an 'Asiri tribe. He was most intimately involved in the affairs of the tribes closest to Mecca, notably the Harb. At times, the Sharif would attempt to oust a tribal chief, as happened with the Ahamidah section of the Harb in 1853.[78] In some cases, the Sharif appointed, probably with tribal consent, an 'amir' of a sub-tribe. Sharif Ahmad ibn Mansur, known in 1905 as 'Amir al-Harb,' resided at Mecca, and was held responsible for the affairs of the Masruh Harb. The man who held this position had influence with the Masruh, and as a result enjoyed the favor of the Sharif.[79] The existence of several other individuals with similar titles who resided in towns suggests that the title 'amir' of a tribe was more often an indication of that man's closeness to the Sharif rather than any consensus that he was a leader of a tribal group.

In regions not immediately surrounding the major cities, but along certain pilgrimage routes, the tribal élite often had direct relations with the Ottomans, sometimes circumventing the Sharif. Thus the Ottomans were able to determine who would be 'amir' of the Juhaynah in 1914, when they replaced 'Ali ibn 'Abdallah with Muhammad 'Ali al-Badawi at Yanbu'.[80]

In general, unlike the urban élite, tribal leaders played an intermediary role between their minions on the one hand, and the Sharif and the Ottomans on the other. Ochsenwald records that during the pilgrimage often about ten Harb members were kept in Mecca as hostages until the safe return of caravans through Harb territory.[81] But the tribes were divided into many sections and sub-sections and the authority of leaders was often weak; loosely

---

Religion, Society, p. 54; Young, Mecca Personalities; *AB* no. 66, 21 October 1917.

[77] Ochsenwald, *Religion, Society*, pp. 32–3.

[78] *Ibid.*, p. 35.

[79] FO 195/2198, Vice-Consul Mohammed Husain to Devey, in Devey to O'Conor, 9 January 1905; Young, Jeddah Personalities. Sharif Husayn ibn 'Ali designated his son 'Abdallah as 'amir al-'Utaybah.'

[80] *Arabian Personalities*, pp. 12, 15.

[81] Ochsenwald, *Religion, Society*, p. 33.

defined grazing zones, raiding, and a general mutual animosity kept
tribal groups at odds with each other. The Sharif and the Ottomans
exploited this situation to play the game of divide and rule. It was
not until the Arab Revolt, catalyzed by a massive influx of British
gold and guns, that a real tribal confederation was formed.

The notables' lack of involvement in politics in the Hijaz is particularly striking when a comparative look is taken at their central
intermediary role in Damascus. If, for example, we look at the
activities of the post-1840 advisory council set up by the Ottomans as part of the series of reforms known as the *tanzimat*, we see
that it was an instrument with which notables increased their
influence; they could often refuse approval to the Vali in certain
areas, and they directly controlled *awqaf*, relief for the poor, and
the election of village and guild *mashayikh*. It was the highest
appeals court in the *vilayet*, settling commercial disputes and
shari'ah court cases. Rather than the *tanzimat* being the result of
top-down reform from Istanbul, the Damascus council was one
tool for making the interests of the notables quite clear, so that the
final product was transformed by a process of bargaining instead
of being an imposition from Istanbul.[82]

But in the Hijaz, where the notables did not perform an intermediary role, there is no evidence that advisory councils, which
had been established in some towns, were at all effective, either as
a way of increasing Ottoman centralization or as an instrument
with which the local élite could control politics and the economy.[83] The notables of the Hijaz usually stayed out of these matters; the religious and tribal élite collected their subsidies, and the
commercial élite kept on trying to make money in good times and
in bad. Competition for political control was therefore primarily
centered on the Vali and the Sharif, with the élites on the sidelines.
Sometimes the Vali led the decision making, but at other times the
Sharif had the upper hand.

A note on Medina on the eve of the Arab Revolt

Medina was, in the words of Hasan Kayali, 'a gray zone between
Damascus in the north and Mecca in the south, the two regions to

[82] Elizabeth Thompson, 'Ottoman Political Reform in the Provinces: The Damascus
Advisory Council in 1844–45,' *IJMES* 25 (1993), pp. 457–75.
[83] Ochsenwald, *Religion, Society*, p. 184, n. 15; al-Amr, p. 73.

which it was linked politically and economically.'[84] Throughout the nineteenth century, the capability of the Sharifian state to rule in Medina fluctuated and was often quite limited. Indeed, throughout much of its history Medina was under the control of the Shi'i Husaynid *ashraf*, sometimes known as *sadat*, while Mecca was under the Hasanids.[85] Although the Ottoman *muhafiz* was supposed to be under the authority of the Vali, he often acted independently of both the Vali and the Sharif. He sometimes also held the title of *Shaykh al-Haram al-Nabawi*. Osman Pasha, who held the post from 1891 until the year of Husayn's accession, 1908, was authorized to communicate directly with Istanbul.

Sharifian control over Medina lessened with the extension of the Hijaz railway to Medina in 1908 and with the Young Turks' strategy of using it as a means of projecting Ottoman power deep into the Arabian Peninsula. In 1910 the Young Turks changed the status of the city from a *sancak* of the Hijaz Vilayet to an independent *sancak* answerable directly to the Interior Ministry in Istanbul. When Husayn protested, he was reminded that he was tasked only with bedouin and pilgrimage affairs, and that he would continue to be responsible for these issues under the new arrangement.

With this step, Medina became more integrated than ever before into the ambit of Ottoman policies. The Committtee of Union and Progress had more support there and was more active than in Mecca, and the Ottomans took a greater interest in centralizing reforms in Medina. Sharif Husayn's interests in Medina were looked after by the Shi'i Sharif Shahhat bin 'Ali, who, under Husayn's instruction, tried to thwart Ottoman designs in the town.[86] Shahhat was to give Husayn much trouble after the

---

84 Hasan Kayali, 'Arabs and Young Turks: Turkish–Arab Relations in the Second Constitutional Period of the Ottoman Empire,' unpublished PhD dissertation, Harvard University, 1988, pp. 218–19. Kayali's dissertation has since been reworked and published as *Arabs and Young Turks: Ottomanism, Arabism, and Islamism in the Ottoman Empire* (Berkeley: University of California Press, 1997).

85 See Ende, 'The *Nakhawila*'; see also Richard Mortel's pioneering work: 'The Origins and Early History of the Husaynid Amirate of Madina to the End of the Ayyubid Period,' *Studia Islamica* 74 (1991), pp. 63–78; 'The Husaynid Amirate of Madina during the Mamluk Period,' *Studia Islamica* 80 (1994), pp. 97–123. Also of use is 'Arif Ahmad 'Abd al-Ghani, *Ta'rikh Umara al-Madinah al-Munawwarah* (Damascus: Dar Kinan lil-Tiba'ah wal-Tawzi' wal-Nashr, 1996).

86 Al-Amr, pp. 75–6; Ochsenwald, *Religion, Society*, pp. 106, 210, 212; Kayali, pp. 211–22, 238–39; Mary Wilson, 'The Hashemites, the Arab Revolt, and Arab Nationalism' in

Revolt, and actually prevent the Sharif from taking full control after the fall of Medina in 1919.

Thus on the eve of the Revolt, Sharifian control of Medina was tenuous, to say the least, although the Revolt had the sympathy of the tribes who opposed the railway. During and after the Revolt, the Sharif of Mecca would fail to assert control over this second of the *haramayn*.

The social and political legacy of Ottoman rule was, essentially, an urban and tribal population accustomed to being on the receiving end of Ottoman financial largesse. The residents of the Hijaz thus enjoyed a special place and status within the empire, and were not – understandably – about to forfeit it easily. But centuries of Ottoman dependency on the Sharif to control the tribes also gave him the upper hand against Istanbul when the Revolt broke out. It would be a kind of guerrilla warfare to which the tribes were accustomed, but to which the Ottomans were not.

The élites were not party to politics, and although they may have limited and thus diluted Sharifian power (after all, the Sharif did have to behave according to certain socially determined norms and conventions), the evidence shows no real indication of this. Instead, the arena of political contest was between the Sharif and the Vali and between the two main houses of *ashraf*, the Dhawu 'Awn and the Dhawu Zayd.

When the Revolt broke out, the Sharif's challenge would be to a great extent financial: how was he to replace the Ottoman payments which had been so fundamental to the socioeconomic system in the Hijaz? Until the Revolt, Sharifian rule constituted a limited state within the state, but now the Sharif would be faced

---

Rashid Khalidi, Lisa Anderson, Muhammad Muslih, and Reeva Simon (eds), *The Origins of Arab Nationalism* (New York: Columbia University Press, 1991), pp. 204–21; on Shahhat and his brother Nasir, see Ende, pp. 281–5.

with all state tasks, including control of Medina. The remainder of this work is the story of his failure.

3

SHARIF HUSAYN AND HIS AMBITIONS

THE BACKGROUND TO THE ARAB REVOLT

The milieu: intrigue in Mecca and Istanbul

Sharif Husayn ibn 'Ali was born in Istanbul in 1853 or 1854.[1] His grandmother was Circassian and his mother Yemeni, although very little is known of his early life. He first visited Mecca in 1856 at the age of three, when his grandfather, Muhammad ibn 'Awn, began his second term as Sharif. He remained there until 1858, when Muhammad died, and returned with his family to Istanbul. After the death of his father, 'Ali, the family went back to Mecca to live with his uncle, 'Abdallah, who had succeeded Muhammad as Sharif of Mecca. Husayn remained at Mecca, where life at the Sharif's included competition for the Sharifian succession between the rival Dhawu Zayd and his own Dhawu 'Awn branches of the Meccan *ashraf*, until the assassination of Sharif Husayn ibn Muhammad ibn 'Awn in 1877. Sultan Abdulhamid brought back the aging Sharif 'Abd al-Mutalib ibn Ghalib of the Zaydi branch, and Husayn, then in his twenties, returned to Istanbul. It is not known whether this was a forced or a voluntary return.

In Istanbul, Husayn, along with others of the Dhawu 'Awn and former Sharif 'Awn al-Rafiq ibn Muhammad ibn 'Awn, began plans to restore the Dhawu 'Awn to the Sharifate, and may have

---

1 Randall Baker, *King Husain and the Kingdom of Hejaz* (Cambridge: Oleander, 1979), pp. 6–11; *Arabian Personalities of the Early Twentieth Century* (Cambridge: Oleander, 1986), rpt. of internal Arab Bureau publication, Cairo, 1917, pp. 54–5. There seems to be some discrepancy about Husayn's date of birth. Ochsenwald, *Religion, Society*, p. 217, states that he was born in 1853–4 (probably based on the *hijri* date of 1270); Baker, p. 6, writes 1853.

37

even visited foreign embassies. This activity aroused Abdulhamid's ire, since the Sultan feared that Britain sought to transfer the caliphate to the *ashraf* of Mecca, an idea which had been under discussion by members of the Ottoman constitutional movement and in the British press.[2] Husayn was therefore soon returned to the Hijaz. While in Mecca, he seems to have intrigued against his uncle Sharif 'Awn al-Rafiq, who had replaced the deposed 'Abd al-Muttalib in 1882. 'Reports ... reached Abdul-Hamid, depicting young Husain as a wilful and recalcitrant person whose views, on the rare occasions when he consented to express them, revealed a "dangerous" capacity for original and independent thinking.'[3] He was therefore recalled to Istanbul in February 1893. His cousin, Sharif 'Ali ibn 'Abdallah ibn Muhammad ibn 'Awn, succeeded 'Awn al-Rafiq upon the latter's death in 1905. He continued to intrigue against 'Ali and on his own behalf, until his appointment in 1908.[4]

It was traditional for the Sultan to keep possible heirs to the Sharifate in Istanbul, where he could keep his eye on them and hold them in reserve in case the incumbent Sharif needed to be replaced. The *ashraf* were well treated and paid, and some even served on the Council of State. In 1886 five sons or grandsons of Sharif Muhammad ibn 'Awn, including Husayn ibn 'Ali, served in this capacity.[5] He married into the Turkish élite when he wed Adile Hanim, the granddaughter of Mustafa Reşid Paşa (1800–1856), a reformer and Grand Vezir to Mahmud II and Abdulmecid.[6]

Both Istanbul and Mecca were centers of political intrigue. In Istanbul, this focussed on the court of Abdulhamid at Yildiz Palace, where power and decision making had become radically centralized. The Sultan kept an estimated retinue of at least 12,000 and a security detail of about 15,000 stationed in the vicinity of Yildiz. He 'padded the payrolls to an unheard-of extent with

[2] See the excellent article by S. Tufan Buzpinar, 'Opposition to the Ottoman Caliphate in the Early Years of Abdulhamid II: 1877–1882,' *Die Welt des Islams* 36 (1996), pp. 59–89.

[3] Antonius, p. 72; Baker, p. 7.

[4] Al-Amr, p. 134.

[5] Ochsenwald, *Religion, Society*, p. 7.

[6] Mary Wilson, *King Abdullah, Britain, and the Making of Jordan* (Cambridge University Press), p. 14.

secret agents, sons, sons-in-law, or protégés of men of influence, and actual or potential members of the opposition, whom he sought by such means to buy off and neutralize.' So centralized was decision making that valis, ambassadors and military commanders communicated 'as much with the palace secretariat as with the ministries to which they were nominally attached.' To obtain a position of power anywhere in the empire, and certainly in the Hijaz, would require of the aspirant both patience and craftiness.

Abdulhamid was 'strange, complex, and psychologically unsettled.' The Sultan-Caliph was distinctly paranoid, '[r]eportedly afraid to handle any documents which had not been specially "disinfected," to drink any coffee or smoke any cigarettes not specially prepared before his eyes by servants who did nothing else, or to eat any food but that prepared in a special kitchen that served him alone.' His spy network was legendary, employing such types as Fehim Paşa, 'a baby-faced psychopath,' whom he put in charge of Yildiz security. Fehim led a force of criminals who rounded up real or imagined opponents and tortured them in his house.[7]

To increase his influence among Arabs and bring adherents to his caliphate and pan-Islamic vision, the Sultan-Caliph surrounded himself with Arabs. One was his second secretary, the Syrian 'Izzat Pasha al-'Abid, who was widely hated. Others were Shaykh Abu al-Huda al-Sayyadi of Aleppo, Muhammad Zafir of Tripolitania, and Ahmad As'ad of the Hijaz. Sharif 'Awn al-Rafiq's son had married Ahmad As'ad's daughter in 1896.[8]

Although intrigue in Istanbul and Mecca was usual, the sources are unusually silent on Husayn's personal involvement. There is, however, little doubt that Husayn worked to undermine the rival Dhawu Zayd family, led by Sharif 'Abd al-Muttalib, and this fact, taken with a comment attributed to 'Ali Haydar, also of the Dhawu Zayd, suggests that Husayn was crafty indeed. The Otto-

[7] Carter Findley, *Bureaucratic Reform in the Ottoman Empire: The Sublime Porte, 1789–1922* (Princeton University Press, 1980), pp. 227–239; all quotations are from Findley. See also George Antonius, *The Arab Awakening: The Story of the Arab National Movement* (London: Hamish Hamilton, 1939), pp. 61–78.

[8] Ochsenwald, *Religion, Society*, pp. 209–10; Butrus Abu-Manneh, 'Sultan Abdulhamid II and Shaikh Abulhuda Al-Sayyadi,' *MES* 15 (1979), pp. 131–53; Jacob Landau, *The Politics of Pan-Islam: Ideology and Organization* (Oxford: Clarendon Press, 1990); Kramer, *Islam Assembled*, p. 6. 'Izzat Pasha was later to suggest a Sharifian Caliphate in secret talks with the British (see below).

man reformer, Midhat Pasha, had been exiled by Abdulhamid to Ta'if, a temperate mountain resort for Mecca's wealthy, in 1882. The Vali was given instructions to do away with him, and he was strangled in prison in 1883. 'Ali Haydar – Husayn's rival for the Sharifate – accused Husayn of complicity in the assassination, claiming that he had forged letters from 'Abd al-Muttalib to the British, asking them for help. The Sultan, perhaps illogically, perhaps not, assumed that 'Abd al-Muttalib and Midhat had been in league against him, and this doomed 'Abd al-Muttalib who was removed from the Sharifate.[9]

When he became Sharif in 1908, Husayn ibn 'Ali was well equipped with an understanding of politics in Mecca and Istanbul. His political education included centralization and paranoia. His understanding of governance, acquired at the feet of Abdulhamid, would have a profound influence on him when he came to be the Sharif of Mecca and its Amir.

The Young Turk Revolution and Husayn's appointment as the Sharif of Mecca and its Amir

Sultan Abdulhamid had been in power since 1876. In July 1908, he was forced to reinstate the constitution in a revolt which was to be known as the Young Turk Revolution.

Husayn's appointment as Sharif on 1 November 1908[10] was due both to his 'schooling' in Meccan and Istanbul politics and to the political circumstances of the Young Turk Revolution. The Young Turk drama which had been playing out in Istanbul had its corollary in the *Haramayn*. The Vali was recalled following a mutiny by the Seventh Army Corps. Sharif 'Ali ibn 'Abdallah ibn Muhammad ibn 'Awn, who had been appointed Amir in 1905,

---

[9] George Stitt, *A Prince of Arabia: The Emir Shereef Ali Haider* (London: Geo. Allen and Unwin, 1948), pp. 75–7. For a description of Midhat's detention in Ta'if, see Ali Haydar Midhat Bey, *The Life of Midhat Pasha* (London: John Murray, 1903); on Midhat's activities in Syria, see Shimon Shamir, 'Midhat Pasha and the Anti-Ottoman Agitation in Syria,' *MES* 10 (1974), pp. 115–41.

[10] Confusion exists as to the actual date of Husayn's appointment. Ochsenwald, who examined Ottoman archives, gives the official date of appointment as 1 November (Ochsenwald, *Religion, State*, p. 217). Hasan Kayali, who also examined the Ottoman archives, notes that the official date of the appointment was 24 November, but that there is earlier documentation, from at least 12 November, in which Husayn is titled 'Amir of Mecca' (Kayali, diss., p. 204).

remained in Ta'if, too scared to come to Mecca. The Local Committee of Union and Progress (CUP) sympathizers – the Young Turks' political organization – in that mountain resort humiliated him by forcing him to stand next to some common folk and state that he was no different from them. He was then sworn on the Qur'an to uphold the constitution. 'Ali's reign, however, lasted only about three years, and he was replaced following disturbances which broke out as a result of rumors that the CUP was going to limit the Sharif's authority.[11] 'Ali was replaced by 'Abd al-Ilah ibn Muhammad ibn 'Awn, but the latter died before leaving Istanbul. Husayn was appointed to replace 'Abd al-Ilah and made his way to the Hijaz.

There are signs of British involvement in Husayn's appointment to the Sharifate. While in Istanbul, he was in contact with HMG's ambassador, Lowther, to whom he had secretly sent 'a very friendly message expressing his feelings of gratitude to England for her sympathy towards the Ottoman constitutional movement.' Lowther described him as 'an upright man' who had written to 'influential Arab chiefs in the Hejaz,' urging them to think kindly of Britain.[12] Also, given British sympathy for reform, the Sultan may have acted to conciliate London. Historical memory in British circles includes indications that the appointment was obtained with British help. An intelligence summary written for the Egyptian Expeditionary Force (EEF) noted: 'Kiamil Pasha, the Grand Vizier, consulted a representative of our Embassy and the result was the nomination of Husein.'[13]

Husayn's appointment by Abdulhamid was a calculated risk. The latter was suspicious of Husayn's ambition, but he knew that 'Ali Haydar was the CUP's candidate, while Husayn, the Sultan

11 Wilson, *King Abdullah*, pp. 14–15; FO 195/2286, Hussain to Lowther, no. 39, 25 August 1908.

12 FO 371/561, Lowther (Constantinople) to FO, no. 802, 24 November 1908.

13 WP, 148/9/68–69, King Husein of Hejaz and His Sons, attachment to Political Intelligence Summary, no. 6, 25 May 1918. This document casts doubt on Elie Kedourie's statement that there 'seems to be no basis for the frequent assertion that Husayn was appointed on the recommendation of the British' (*Arabic Political Memoirs and other Studies* (London: Cass, 1974), p. 160, n. 58); Wilson, *King Abdullah*, p. 15. The British Naval Intelligence Division, writing in *A Handbook of Arabia* (London: HMSO, 1920), p. 110, also notes: 'Hussein was appointed as a man of pacific character, likely both to serve the Porte's purposes and also to keep on good terms with ourselves.'

believed, favored neither the CUP nor the constitution.[14] By
appointing a conservative, Abdulhamid most probably hoped to
avoid trouble in the Hijaz, which was so crucial to his status and
legitimacy. 'Abdallah reports that his father received a memorandum from the Grand Vezir, assuring him that the Amirate of
Mecca was connected directly to the caliphate and that the constitution had not changed this relationship. 'Abdallah also recalls his
father's saying that after appointing him Sharif, Abdulhamid
spoke to Husayn about his fear of the Unionists. Husayn promised the Sultan-Caliph asylum in the Hijaz should he need it.
Husayn thus assumed leadership of the Hijaz with a feeling that
his position was secure, and was determined to preserve all the
entitlements and traditions of a position that in his view was equal
to that of the Grand Vezir and the Khedive of Egypt, second only
to the position of the Crown Prince himself, and certainly not to
the Vali of the Hijaz.[15]

The British and Husayn's ambitions: Caliphate and territorial borders

Husayn had planned for a long time to reach the Sharifate, and it
was now his. In March 1924, after Turkey's Mustafa Kemal
('Ataturk') abolished the caliphate, Husayn declared himself
Caliph. While it is impossible to determine when the notion first
occurred to him, the issue of an Arabian and/or Sharifian Caliphate had been floating about since at least the fifteenth century.
Husayn may, therefore, have harbored such a notion throughout
his adult life.[16]

[14] Al-Amr, pp. 134–5; Wilson, *King Abdullah*, pp. 15–16; Baker, 15–16; Ochsenwald, *Religion, State*, p. 217; C. Ernest Dawn, *From Ottomanism to Arabism: Essays on the Origins of Arab Nationalism* (Urbana: University of Illinois Press, 1973), pp. 4–6. This did not stop Rashid Rida, an opponent of Abdulhamid, from referring to Husayn as 'the constitutional amir' (*al-amir al-dusturi*). Rida most probably did not understand that Husayn was appointed by Abdulhamid to thwart the Young Turks in the Hijaz, and referred to him as the constitutional amir because he was appointed after the constitution had been restored. Many in the Hijaz believed the same thing (see *al-Manar*, 19 May 1909).

[15] Sulayman Musa, *Al-Harakah al-'Arabiyyah: Sirat al-Marhalah al-Ula lil-Nahdah al-'Arabiyyah al-Hadithah* (Beirut: Al-Nahar, 1982), pp. 48–9; 'Abdallah ibn al-Husayn, *Mudhakkirati* (Jerusalem, 1945), pp. 27–8.

[16] For a more detailed analysis of Husayn's perception of a post-Ottoman Islamic polity, see Joshua Teitelbaum, 'Sharif Husayn ibn Ali and the Hashemite Vision of the

The notion of a Sharifian Caliphate in Mecca was not entirely of European derivation, as suggested or implied by several researchers. C. Snouck Hurgronje, probably the first scholar to assert decisively that the idea had solely European roots, wrote in 1917 that '[t]he idea of a caliphate of the Shereefs of Mecca [was] ventilated, more than once, by this or that European writer on Islam, but, in the Moslem world, it [was not] broached, and no one of the Shereefs from the House of Katada – rulers in Mecca ... ever since the year 1200 AD – ever thought of such a thing.'[17] Recent research has demonstrated, however, that the idea was older and more deeply rooted than scholars have thought. Richard Mortel has shown that at least three Muslim historians from the fifteenth century mentioned the idea quite positively. For example, a fifteenth-century historian of Mecca, Taqi al-Din Muhammad ibn Ahmad al-Fasi, amidst a discussion of the Zaydi Shi'i sympathies of the *ashraf* of Mecca, wrote of Sharif Abu Numayy, who ruled Mecca from 1254 to 1301 that, '[w]ere it not for his madhhab, he would have been [a] suitable [choice] for the caliphate; he was a Zaydi, as were his relatives.'[18]

The trail of this idea can be picked up again in the middle of the nineteenth century. In 1858, Muslims in northern Syria who were disappointed with Ottoman reforms imagined how the establishment of a 'new Arabian state under the sovereignty of the Shereefs of Mecca' might be,[19] and in 1860 British government circles considered the idea 'of using the Grand Sheriff as a kind of Caliph' to oppose the French in Egypt.[20]

While there was little evidence of wide, grassroots support for a Sharifian Caliphate in the Middle East, the defeat of the Ottomans

---

Post-Ottoman Order: From Chieftaincy to Suzerainty,' *MES* 34 (1998), pp. 103–22.

17 C. Snouck Hurgronje, *The Revolt in Arabia* (New York: Putnam, 1917), pp. 34–5.

18 Mortel, pp. 461–2. The other two historians were Taqi al-Din Ahmad ibn 'Ali al-Maqrizi (d. 1442), and Jamal al-Din Abu al-Mahasin Yusuf ibn Taghribirdi (d. 1470). Al-Fasi's singling out of Abu Numayy was most probably due to his reigning during the time of the destruction of the 'Abbasid Caliphate by the Mongols in 1258; Hurgronje, *Mekka*, pp. 183–4, also notes that the Sharifs of Mecca were at one time Zaydi Shi'is.

19 FO 78/1389, J.H. Skene (Aleppo) to Earl of Malmesbury, no. 33, 7 August 1858, enclosing copy Skene to Charles Alison, no. 20, 31 July 1858; this document is quoted in Musa, *Al-Harakah al-'Arabiyyah*, p. 57, where sovereignty is translated as *mulkiyyah*.

20 FO 78/1514, December 12, 1860, cited in G.P. Gooch and Harold Temperley (eds), *British Documents on the Origins of the War, 1898–1914*, vol. X, Part II: *The Last Years of Peace* (London: HMSO, 1938), p. 824. The editors note that there 'is no real evidence of Arab support for the idea.'

in their war with Russia in the winter of 1877–8 raised questions in Britain and the Arab world as to the suitability – on practical as well as on religious grounds – of the Ottomans to hold the caliphate.

The candidacy of the Sharif of Mecca, from the tribe of Quraysh, was put forward by John Louis Sabunji, G.C.M. Birdwood, James Zohrab, and even by Jamal al-Din 'al-Afghani' al-Asadabadi, although by the latter a bit less enthusiastically. Most active on behalf of the idea – Muslim or European – was Wilfred Scawen Blunt, who was in contact with all the above.[21] Blunt espoused a spiritual caliphate, not unlike the papacy.[22] The renowned Turcologist, J. Redhouse, took the side of the Ottomans.[23]

In about 1880 in Bukhara, evidence shows, Muslims sought to establish a Muslim federation with the Sharif of Mecca as the Caliph,[24] and towards the end of the century, the idea was bandied about rather widely. British Muslim Marmaduke Pickthall noted that in Syria from 1894 to 1896 he heard 'Muslim Arabs talking more than once' about the Sharif of Mecca's becoming 'the spiritual head of the reconstituted realm of El Islam, [and] the Khedive of Egypt the temporal head.'[25]

Discussion of an Arabian–Sharifian Caliphate spread in the Arab world with the 1902–3 serialization of 'Abd al-Rahman al-Kawakibi's (c. 1849–1902) book *Umm al-Qura* in Rashid Rida's *al-Manar*. This work purports to be the minutes of a secret Muslim society that worked in Mecca to create a Sharifian Caliph-

21 Kramer, *Islam Assembled*, pp. 10–22. Sabunji was a former Syrian Catholic priest turned journalist from Diyarbekir who settled for several years in England; Birdwood was an Indian civil servant; Blunt was a 'poet, politician and pamphleteer' (Sylvia G. Haim, 'Blunt and al-Kawakibi,' *Oriente Moderno* 35 (1955), pp. 132–43, quotation on p. 137) who travelled in the Middle East and wrote *The Future of Islam* (London, 1882), in which he put forward the case for the Sharifian Caliphate; Zohrab was British consul, Jeddah, from October 1878 to July 1881.
22 Kedourie, *England and the Middle East*, pp. 52–4.
23 See also Buzpinar, 'Opposition to the Ottoman Caliphate.' Buzpinar notes that in 1876, two leaders of the Ottoman constitutional movement, Midhat Pasha and Namik Kemal, discussed the idea of transferring the Caliphate – after its separation from the Sultanate – to the Sharif of Mecca. He stresses, however that 'the circumstances surrounding this plan remain extremely obscure' (p. 63).
24 Haim, 'Blunt and al-Kawakibi,' p. 136, n. 2.
25 Quoted in Sylvia G. Haim, *Arab Nationalism: An Anthology* (Berkeley: University of California Press, 1962), p. 28.

ate which would have temporal power only in the Hijaz.[26] James Zohrab, British representative in Jeddah, wrote home extensively, beginning in 1879, of the rumored existence of a 'secret society' in Mecca whose objective was 'to restore the Khalifate to the Arabs of the Hedjaz.'[27] Zohrab was in the Hijaz during the tenure of Sharif Husayn ibn Muhammad ibn 'Awn (and into the second term of Sharif 'Abd al-Muttalib).

Negib Azoury, a Syrian Christian and founder of the *Ligue de la Patrie Arabe* in 1904, published a manifesto in which he called for the Hijaz to be independent and ruled by a Caliph who would be a religious figure for all Muslims.[28]

In the early twentieth century, we have evidence that the notion of a Sharifian Caliphate was also about in Syria. The US Vice- and deputy Consul-General in Beirut noted in December 1912: 'As long as the Sultan was also the Khalifa the religious bond that held the Kurds and Arabs to the Empire was strong; but with Abdul Hamid's deposition this bond was snapped; the only Khalifa recognized is the Sherif of Mecca.'[29]

It is clear then, that the idea was afoot in the nineteenth century, and as al-Afghani makes clear, the *ashraf* of Mecca were well aware of it. Blunt wrote in 1885 that '[a]mongst other things, [al-Afghani] [said] that it was he himself who had suggested to the Sherif [Husayn ibn Muhammad ibn 'Awn] ... [that he] claim the Caliphate, but El Huseyn ... said it was impossible without armed support, and the Arabs could never unite except in the

---

26 It has been shown that Kawakabi borrowed his ideas on the Caliphate from Blunt (Haim, 'Blunt and al-Kawakibi'); Elie Kedourie, *Arabic Political Memoirs*, pp. 107–14.

27 FO 195/1251, Zohrab (Jeddah) to Marquis of Salisbury, no. 34, 6 August 1879 (quoted); FO 78/3314, Zohrab (Jeddah), 8 February 1881, quoted in Kramer, p. 15. Other Zohrab dispatches are in FO 78/3131, FO 78/2988, FO 78/3314, and are quoted extensively in Kramer, pp. 14–15. One can only speculate on the reasons for Zohrab's flights of fancy. Perhaps the consul, who was constantly complaining about the lack of funds for his post, was interested in increasing his importance to London: 'The Consulate at Jeddah does not appear to have attracted the attention on the part of Her Majesty's Government which the importance of the position merits,' he wrote (FO 685/1, Consul James Zohrab's letter book, Report on the Establishment required to carry on the duties of Her Majesty's Consulate at Jeddah [September 1879]).

28 Eliezer Tauber, 'Three Approaches, One Idea: Religion and State in the Thought of 'Abd al-Rahman al-Kawakibi, Najib 'Azuri and Rashid Rida,' *British Journal of Middle Eastern Studies* 21 (1994), pp. 190–8.

29 Quoted in Wilson, *Lawrence*, p. 946.

name of religion.'[30]

All this suggests that Sharif Husayn ibn 'Ali assumed office at a time when the idea of a Sharifian Caliphate was in wide circulation. But, perhaps even more importantly, the *ashraf* of Mecca had a collective memory of primacy stemming from their origins in the Prophet's house, the Banu Hashim (hence the term Hashimite, to be used later by Husayn), and the Prophet's tribe, Quraysh.[31] There was no reason, therefore, that an ambitious man such as Husayn would not have considered the possibilities, should the opportunity present itself.

Kitchener's tantalizing intimation. In 1914 the opportunity was presented by none other than Field Marshal Earl Kitchener of Khartoum, who had been appointed Minister of War in August. Kitchener was a figure of mythic proportions in Britain and in most of the world, the avenger, in the Battle of Omdurman (1898), of the death of General Charles Gordon at the hands of the Mahdi of the Sudan fifteen years earlier.[32] As war clouds gathered over Europe, his assumption of the post in the War Office was seen by Britons as the key to safe passage through the storm. It was no accident that those charged with raising an army turned to his stern, mustachioed visage to call Britons to arms in the famous 'Your Country Needs You' recruitment poster. ('And the men came because Kitchener asked them,' wrote George Arthur, Kitchener's biographer.[33])

Kitchener lived at a time when the threat of a mysterious religious uprising in 'the East' had captured the British public's imagination. John Buchan, the famous novelist and author of *The Thirty-Nine Steps* (later made into a film by Alfred Hitchcock),

[30] Quoted in Kramer, *Islam Assembled*, p. 20.
[31] On these feelings of primacy, see Yisrael Gershoni, 'Ha-Leom Ha'Aravi, Beyt Hashim ve-Suriya Ha-Gedola Bi-Khtavav shel 'Abdallah, Part One,' *Ha-Mizrah He-Hadash* 25 (1975), pp. 1–26.
[32] In a humiliating defeat for the empire, Gordon was killed by the Mahdist forces in late January 1885. Kitchener recaptured Khartoum at the Battle of Omdurman on 1 September 1898, thereby restoring British honor.
[33] George Arthur, *Life of Lord Kitchener* (New York: Macmillan, 1920), vol. 3, p. 14. Kitchener died in 1916 when his ship struck a mine and sank in the North Sea. Arthur saw fit to end his hagiographic tribute thus: 'And if, in any sense or degree *laborare est orare* [to work is to pray], may it not be thought of him that no life could present itself as a more proper prelude to the further life of full freedom and fair beauty ....' (vol. 3, p. 372).

who was wartime Director of Information, popularized this idea in his 1916 espionage thriller, *Greenmantle*. Sir Walter, a Foreign Office official, calls secret agent Richard Hannay to his office:

'There is a dry wind blowing through the East, and the parched grasses wait the spark. And the wind is blowing towards the Indian border. Whence comes that wind, think you?'

Sir Walter had lowered his voice and was speaking very slow and distinct. I could hear the rain dripping from the eaves of the window, and far off the hoot of taxis in Whitehall.

'Have you an explanation, Hannay?' he asked again.

'It looks as if Islam had a bigger hand in the thing than we thought,' I said. 'I fancy religion is the only thing to knit up such a scattered empire.'

'You are right,' he said. 'You must be right. [...] There is a Jehad preparing. [...] Supposing there is some Ark of the Covenant which will madden the remotest Moslem peasant with dreams of Paradise? What then, my friend?'[34]

Having first-hand experience of a violent religious movement in the Sudan, Kitchener sought to avoid such a situation in the future, or, failing that, to harness it for Britain. Lord Kitchener, it has been noted, 'had cherished for a long time the idea of an Arab Caliphate.'[35] And it was Kitchener, it seems, who gave Sharif Husayn ibn 'Ali the idea that the time for a Sharifian Caliphate had come.

The Hashimites' first overtures to the British came in 1914, in meetings in Cairo between 'Abdallah, Kitchener, and Ronald Storrs, Kitchener's oriental secretary in Cairo in February and April. In these meetings, the Sharif was said to be interested primarily in maintaining the amirate of the Hijaz in his and his family's name. But when hostilities were declared between Britain and the Ottoman Empire on 31 October 1914, Kitchener sought to take advantage and fired off a message to 'Abdallah in which he raised the issue of the Caliphate for the first time. Kitchener's draft, embellished with 'profuse magniloquence' by Storrs, was despatched the next day. Kitchener asked for the help of the Arab nation and added a fateful phrase:

[34] John Buchan, *Greenmantle* (London: Nelson, 1916), pp. 16–17.
[35] Jukka Nevakivi, *Britain, France and the Arab Middle East, 1914–1920* (London: Athlone Press, 1969).

It may be that an Arab of true race will assume the Caliphate at Mecca or Medina, and so good may come by the help of God out of all the evil that is now occurring.[36]

Coming from a man of Kitchener's stature, representing powerful Britain, these were heady words. It would be hard to imagine a comment more likely to confirm Husayn's sense of his natural importance and rightful role in the Muslim world, and to whet his appetite for the Caliphate. With respect to that office, Storrs had faithfully translated Kitchener's words. However, the translation greatly exceeded Kitchener's draft with respect to the Arabs, essentially presuming and presenting as a *fait accompli* that the Sharif already headed a widespread Arab movement.[37]

But Husayn was cautious, answering Kitchener's message with restraint. He was reluctant to revolt, he said, for the time was not right. In the first place, as part of their effort against the Ottomans, the British had impeded Egyptian grain shipments to the Hijaz, and he implied that this would have to be rectified. In the second place, Husayn said, the issue of the Caliphate was a complicated one. He cautiously commented that the Ottomans' 'rule projects … deeds … contrary to religion. The Caliphate means this, that the rule of the book of God should be enforced, and this they do not do.'[38] As Kedourie points out, Husayn was hesitating over something that had been talked about for years, yet no opportunity had presented itself. Indeed, about a year later, an associate of

---

[36] Kedourie, *England and the Middle East*, pp. 48–54; Kedourie, *Anglo-Arab Labyrinth*, pp. 16–19 (the Kitchener quote is on p. 19).

   Kedourie and Dawn have debated Husayn's Caliphate aspirations in the pages of *IJMES* (9 [1978], pp. 120–30; 10 [1979], pp. 420–6). The exchange demonstrates how two scholars examining the same documents can reach similar conclusions but exaggerate their differences. Kedourie argues that Husayn became more interested in the Caliphate after the Kitchener message. Dawn says that the Caliphate 'was of interest to Husayn primarily as an instrument in his efforts with the British to gain kingship for himself and as much territory as possible for himself and the Arabs' (p. 423). Dawn denies not that Husayn was interested in the Caliphate, but that it was an ultimate goal. The present author would note only that Husayn's being interested in the Caliphate at all demonstrates just how grand were his ambitions.

[37] Kedourie, *Anglo-Arab Labyrinth*, pp. 19–20. The text of Storrs' translation, taken from the papers of Husayn's son, Amir Zayd, is in Sulayman Musa, *Al-Thawrah al-ʿArabiyyah al-Kubra: Watha'iq wa-Asanid* (Amman: Da'irah al-Thaqafah wal-Funun, 1966), pp. 15–16.

[38] L/P&S/18/B22, 'Shorthand Note taken by Messenger [Ali Asghar] of a discourse by the Sherif of Mecca,' undated [but from early December 1914]. This paper is also in WP, 134/8/114–116, where it is dated 9 December 1914.

'Abdallah from Mecca told a British official in Sudan that the Sharif was carefully canvassing opinion on the issue.[39]

In his belief that the caliphate could be maneuvered into his hands, Husayn was sustained by the determined energy of 'Abdallah, whose influence Kedourie sees behind the famous letter of 14 July 1915, which initiated the so-called Husayn–McMahon correspondence. The letter demanded – apparently for the first time – that 'Great Britain ... agree to the proclamation of an Arab Caliphate for Islam.'[40] Repeating exactly the terms of the 'Damascus Protocol' presented to Faysal by representatives of the secret Arab nationalist societies in May 1915 in Damascus,[41] he demanded Arab independence in an area including most of the modern-day Arabian Peninsula, parts of southern Turkey, Iraq, Syria, Israel, the West Bank and the Gaza Strip, Jordan, and Lebanon. The Sharif was well aware of the Hijaz's precarious economic dependence on the pilgrimage, which would worsen after the Hijaz was cut off from the Ottoman center, and he knew that the *haramayn* would therefore require a connection to the greater Arab hinterland. In his letter to Husayn of 30 August 1915 High Commissioner McMahon twice reiterated Kitchener's loaded intimation of the previous year, and there was no reason for Husayn not to hope and believe that he was the object of suggestion. The letter went even further, noting that Britain would welcome the caliphate's reversion to a 'true Arab born of the blessed stock of the Prophet,' a reference to Quraysh and perhaps the Banu Hashim.[42]

Most probably, what both Kitchener and McMahon had in mind was a spiritual caliphate *à la* Blunt ('a papacy of Islam'), a notion then popular in Europe.[43] The idea of a separate spiritual caliphate had also been making the rounds in the Arab world for decades, and the notion was held by such luminaries as Muham-

[39] FO 371/2428/112369, memorandum on the Sherif of Mecca, Symes (Erkowit), 15 July 1915 (India Office Print, B. 211). The document is also discussed in Kedourie, *Anglo-Arab Labyrinth*, p. 65.
[40] Kedourie, *Anglo-Arab Labyrinth*, p. 4; Husayn's letter of 14 July 1915 is in Antonius, p. 414.
[41] The Damascus Protocol is in Antonius, pp. 157–8.
[42] McMahon to Husayn, letter of 30 August 1915, in Antonius, pp. 415–16.
[43] Kedourie, *England and the Middle East*, pp. 52–4; Thomas Arnold, *The Caliphate* (London: Routledge & Kegan Paul, 1965), pp. 146–7, 170–1, 189–200.

mad 'Abduh, 'Abd al-Rahman al-Kawakibi, and Rashid Rida.[44] But even if Husayn had been aware of the idea of a separate spiritual and temporal caliphate, he did not subscribe to this notion. There is no reason to believe that Husayn had in mind any type of caliphate other than the traditional Sunni type, involving temporal as well as a form of spiritual authority or right to lead the *ummah* stemming from his being descended from Quraysh and the Prophet.[45]

For Husayn, whose sense of his rightful place in history was driven in part by the need to be well remembered, creating a worthy Muslim Arab replacement for the Ottoman Empire was essential; rebellion alone would merely single him out as a leader who helped to destroy a legitimate Muslim government in exchange for a truncated Hijazi state. Rather, he saw himself as a Caliph who would protect the Muslim world from the anti-religious trends that now controlled the Ottoman Empire, and restore the caliphate to its rightful occupant, a descendant of the Prophet's house.

Hashimite contacts with Arab nationalists

There can be no doubt that the contacts of Husayn and his sons with underground Arab nationalist societies fed Husayn's caliphal and territorial ambitions. Many Arabs worked on his behalf.

As early as 1911, he received from some Arab members of the Ottoman Parliament a letter of support for his activities against the Ottoman Vali (on these activities, see later on in this chapter). These deputies gave him their blessing for the religious leadership (*ri'asah diniyyah*) of the Arab regions.[46] In that same year, 'Ali Rida al-Rikabi, the Ottoman Muhafiz of Medina, wrote to Istanbul complaining of Husayn's anti-Ottoman activities, and noted that he was assisted by 'the revolutionary Society of the Arab Revival'

---

44 Buzpinar, 'Opposition'; Tauber, 'Three Approaches.'
45 Indeed, Husayn's newspaper *al-Qiblah* was later to take issue with the notion of a separation between the spiritual and temporal function of the Caliph; Islam, wrote *al-Qiblah*, does not recognize a spiritual Caliphate akin to the Papacy (*al-Qiblah*, 21 Shawwal 1335 [9 August 1917]).
46 The letter's authenticity is disputed in Anis Sayigh, *Al-Hashimiyyun wa-al-Thawrah al-'Arabiyyah al-Kubra* (Beirut: Dar al-Tali'ah, 1966), pp. 22–4, but Dawn, pp. 11, believes the letter to be authentic. The text of the letter is in Musa, *al-Harakah al-'Arabiyyah*, p. 57. Notice that *ri'asah diniyyah* might signify a separation between temporal and religious leadership.

which aimed to set up Husayn as Caliph.[47] While 'Abdallah was in Cairo in 1914, Rashid Rida made him a member of his Society of the Arab Association, informing him of the society's plan for a pact of Arabian Peninsula rulers with Husayn as president of the pact's council. In late 1915 Rida proposed making Husayn Caliph, and he gave a copy of the proposal to the British.[48]

Once the First World War began, the Arab nationalist societies of al-Fatat and al-'Ahd were active in recruiting the Hashimites to lead them. Husayn was approached several times in 1915 in Mecca, as was Faysal during his visits to Damascus. Husayn's ambitions were thus augmented, as was the possibility of implementing them. At a family conference in Ta'if in June 1915, it was decided in principle to initiate a revolt and to begin negotiations with Britain.[49]

One of Husayn's lobbyists was the same 'Izzat Pasha mentioned earlier as one of Abdulhamid's court Arabs. After being removed from office following the Young Turk revolution, he had settled in Paris, living on the fortune he had made under the *ancien régime*. McMahon met with him in December 1914, and in early January 1915 'Izzat stopped by the Foreign Office for a chat. 'Izzat argued on behalf of an Arab caliphate as a rallying point for the Arabs against the Ottomans. His candidate was Husayn, and he proposed that one of Husayn's sons be brought incognito to Egypt to meet with the High Commissioner. The file on this visit contains a minute by Foreign Secretary Grey directing that the India Office and Kitchener be asked if they would approve a reply that Britain would 'gladly [?] give their support if desired to an Arab Caliphate of the true race.'[50] Interestingly, the language was that of Kitchener's telegram of 31 October 1914.

---

47 Eliezer Tauber, *The Emergence of the Arab Movements* (London: Frank Cass, 1993), pp. 49–50. Tauber (p. 43) writes that this society was the 'first true Arab society of the twentieth century.'

48 Tauber, *Emergence*, p. 115; FO 882/15, Rashid Rida, General Organic Law of the Arab Empire, attached to a note by Storrs to Clayton, Cairo, 5 December 1915, cited in Tauber, *Emergence*, pp. 116–17.

49 Eliezer Tauber, *The Arab Movements in World War I* (London: Frank Cass, 1993), pp. 57–82.

50 FO 371/2979/1286, Minutes and memorandum by 'Izzet Pasha, 4 [?] January 1915. Kitchener approved, the India Office did not, and 'Izzat Pasha received a negative reply; see Kedourie, *Anglo-Arab Labyrinth*, pp. 28–9; H.V.F. Winstone, *The Illicit Adventure* (London: Cape, 1982), pp. 174–5. For more on 'Izzat Pasha, see Martin Kramer, 'Azoury: a Further Episode,' *MES* 18 (1982), pp. 351–8.

We should not close without discussing claims to the caliphate by the Hashimites themselves, before the Revolt. (After the Revolt began, such claims became progressively more explicit.) Statements on the Caliphate by Husayn and 'Abdallah cited by Kedourie, yet attacked by Dawn as inconclusive, can now be given further weight. In late December 1915 Husayn wrote Sudanese leader Grand Qadi 'Ali al-Mirghani discussing the possibility of the former assuming the caliphate:

I had not claimed before to be the qualified chief of the Emirs (the Caliph) but I explained to them more than once that I was ready to extend my hand to any man who would come forward and take the rein of authority. I was, however, chosen in every quarter and even forced to take up the question of their future prospects.[51]

In February 1916, when a messenger delivered a letter from Husayn to McMahon, he also stated that 'Abdallah had requested £3,000 sterling 'for [him] and [his] scheme'; when questioned, the messenger explained that 'Abdallah's scheme was to choose a 'powerful Islamic Committee from the Arab countries to offer his father the Khalifate. The latter is aware but feigns ignorance of these measures.' Storrs sent the money, a response that must have greatly increased Husayn's hope of the caliphate.[52]

In October 1916, a few months after the Revolt broke out. 'Abdallah asked Storrs during a meeting in Jeddah if he would address his father by the title *amir al-mu'minin*, a title most properly attached to the Caliph. (Storrs knew this, and demurred.)[53]

---

51 F0 371/2767/30674, McMahon to Grey, no. 26, 7 February 1916, enclosing Hussein to Sayyid Ali El Morghani, 28 December 1915, cited in Kedourie, *Anglo-Arab Labyrinth*, pp. 122–3. Mirghani had a month earlier written Husayn, presumably with Wingate's authority, urging the Sharif to 'rise and take over the reins of the holy Arabian Koreishite Khaliphate, which you represent, being a direct descendant of our Holy Prophet' (Kedourie, *Anglo-Arab Labyrinth*, pp. 42–3).

52 FO 371/2767/45855, McMahon to FO, no. 42, 29 February 1916, enclosing note on the verbal messages from 'Abdallah, and FO 141/461/1198/48, Memorandum of R. Storrs, 11 March 1916, both cited and discussed in Kedourie, *Anglo-Arab Labyrinth*, p. 123.

53 FO 882/5, Storrs' diary of visit to Jeddah, 17 October 1916; Kedourie, *Anglo-Arab Labyrinth*, pp. 144–5. Dawn's contention (*IJMES* 10 [1979] p. 424) that the title claimed by Husayn, *amir al-mu'minin*, 'had long since lost its connection with the caliph and had become a rarely used title of honor' conflicts with that of Gibb: 'until the end of the Caliphate as an institution, *amir al-mu'minin* was employed exclusively as the protocollary title of a caliph, and among the Sunnis its adoption by a ruler implied a claim to the office of caliph' (H.A.R. Gibb, 'Amir al-Mu'minin,' *EI²*).

Husayn's Caliphate and territorial ambitions were influenced, therefore, by three factors. First, there was the general idea – current in Muslim circles from at least the fifteenth century – that the Sharif of Mecca was the legitimate claimant to the caliphate. Second, communications from both the British and Arab nationalists after he assumed the Sharifate in 1908 augmented his caliphate ambitions and brought them into the realm of what he thought might actually be attainable. Third, the British and the Arab nationalists also influenced Husayn to believe that he had support for his ambition to achieve Hashimite territorial sovereignty over much of the Arab world. In may be assumed, therefore, that these elements combined to create in Husayn's mind a powerful mix of personal aspirations and the perceived ability to implement them.

Husayn in the Hijaz, 1908–1916: tribes, tribal borders and local ambitions in the Arabian arena

Husayn faced several difficulties when he assumed the Sharifate in 1908, arriving in the Hijaz on 3 December. To create a chieftaincy, he needed to assert autonomy from the Vali and consolidate his influence among the Hijazi tribal and urban élite. But in so doing, it was essential that he not be so audacious as to cause his own removal.

The Sharif who preceded Husayn, 'Ali ibn 'Abdallah, had established a *modus vivendi* with the tribes, acting more honestly and efficiently. The Ottomans had also established order by constructing guardhouses and extending telegraph lines from Damascus to Medina and Mecca. But the extension of the Hijaz railroad to Medina in the fall of 1908, and the possibility that it would soon reach Mecca (it never did), caused a general tribal uprising in the Hijaz.[54] Security was so poor that Monahan, the British consul, requested that a British warship be ready during the pilgrimage season.[55]

In general, while Ottoman control was potentially much easier to maintain – troop transportation being vastly improved – the

---

[54] Ochsenwald, *Religion, Society*, pp. 214–15. For a detailed discussion of bedouin opposition to the Hijaz railway, see Hans-Jürgen Philipp, 'Der Beduinische Widerstand gegen die Hedschasbahn,' *Die Welt des Islams* 25 (1985), pp. 31–83.

[55] FO 195/2286, Monahan (Jeddah) to Lowther, no. 53, 5 November 1908.

bedouin felt their livelihood threatened, as the railway largely alle-
viated the need for the hiring of camels. If money could not be
earned that way, it would have to be got by raiding and plunder. In
response, the Ottomans sent troops and increased payment.[56]

At the beginning of Husayn's rule it was not entirely clear who
was in charge in the Hijaz. The deposed Sharif, 'Ali ibn 'Abdallah,
a representative of the old Ottoman regime, found refuge in Ta'if,
where he had the support of many bedouin. The local branch of
the CUP was composed of officers, military physicians, and several notables who were forced to join and swear fealty to the constitution. It also seemed to exercise some control, as did the
Ottoman civil administration. Initially, the CUP seemed to have
much local support, and *'huriyyah'* (freedom) was the talk of the
day. But, fearing conscription, the residents of Jeddah refused to
register to vote for the new parliament, as a result of which the
government told the shaykhs of the neighborhoods to select those
who would vote.[57]

Creating a chieftaincy: asserting power over the tribes. The most pressing problem upon Husayn's assumption of office and around
the time of his arrival in the Hijaz was the need to assert control
over the tribes, which had become quite violent, mostly around
Medina.[58] 1908 had in fact been a year of tremendous tribal
problems before his arrival in early December: the Egyptian
mahmal was been attacked by the Banu 'Awf between Medina
and Yanbu' on 24 February, claiming arrears on money due to
them, although the head of the *mahmal* did pay them handsomely himself. Several dozen *shaykhs* of tribes around Jeddah
and Medina were under house arrest in Mecca, as was Husayn
ibn Mubarak, the *shaykh* of the port of Rabigh on the coast
between Jeddah and Yanbu'.[59] Monahan reported that Rabigh

---

56 Ochsenwald, *Religion, Society*, pp. 215–16.
57 FO 195/2286, Hussain (Jeddah) to Lowther, no. 39, 25 August 1908; FO 195/2286,
Monahan (Jeddah) to Lowther, no. 53, 5 November 1908; Ochsenwald, *Religion,
Society*, p. 217.
58 By late 1907, some of the bedouin had become so audacious that they ran away with
the cricket stump in the middle of a match played by the Mohomedan Cricket Club of
Jeddah! (FO 685/3, Honorary Secretary to the Mohomedan Cricket Club, Jeddah, to
British Consul, Jeddah, 29 September 1907).
59 FO 195/2286, Monahan (Jeddah) to O'Conor, no. 6, 14 March 1908; FO 195/2286,
Monahan (Jeddah) to Chargé d'Affaires (Constantinople), no. 17, 8 May 1908. The

was under siege by bedouin trying to prevent the landing of material for the railway. Travelers were instructed not to venture even two miles outside the walls of Jeddah.[60] In early May the mail from Istanbul was plundered between Jeddah and Mecca.[61] The imprisoned tribal leaders were released on 28 May; nonetheless, bedouin continued to skirmish with troops just outside Medina.[62] The Ottomans, by way of a ruse, succeeded in pre-empting an attack on their troops by unidentified Masruh – who blamed the Banu 'Ali Harb for inciting them – two miles from Medina; three prisoners taken by the Ottomans were beheaded, and their heads displayed for two days on the gates of Medina.[63] In early September, the Jid'an (who had also been responsible for acts of piracy in Jeddah harbor) attacked a caravan only 500 meters from the Jeddah city walls. The city notables requested that the Ottomans give them rifles for self-defense.[64] In October and November there were further skirmishes around Medina with the Banu 'Ali and the Banu 'Awf. The inhabitants, now armed by the Ottomans, joined troops in carrying out reconnaissance and engaged the tribesmen in skirmishes around the town.[65]

Following his arrival in the Hijaz Husayn promised to restore order quickly.[66] One of his first acts in this respect came during the pilgrimage, which fell on 1 January 1909, when he

Banu 'Awf were a sub-tribe of the Masruh section of the Harb tribe. Information on tribes and tribal personalities is gleaned from three main sources: *Gazetteer of Arabia (GA)*; *Hijaz before World War One: A Handbook (HH)*; and the *Handbook of Arabia (HA)*, under the relevant entries. All these texts caution that the internal organization of the larger tribes is not always entirely known.

60 FO 195/2286, Monahan (Jeddah), to O'Conor, 19 March 1908.
61 FO 195/2286, Monahan (Jeddah) to Chargé d'Affaires (Constantinople), no. 17, 8 May 1908.
62 FO 195/2286, Monahan (Jeddah) to Chargé d'Affaires, 29 May 1908.
63 FO 195/2286, Hussain (Jeddah) to Chargé d'Affaires, no. 33, 30 July 1908. The Bani 'Ali are a clan or sub-tribe of the Masruh section of the Harb.
64 FO 195/2286, Hussain to Lowther, no. 44, 9 September 1908; FO 424/217, Hussain to Lowther, no. 47, 22 September 1908. The Jid'an were a clan of the Zubayd sub-section of the Masruh section of the Harb.
65 FO 196/2286, Monahan to Lowther, no. 60, 18 November 1908; FO 424/117 Devey (Damascus) to Lowther, no. 63, 17 November 1908. An account of the near siege of Medina by the tribes in 1908 is given in A.J.B. Wavell, *A Modern Pilgrim in Mecca* (London: Constable, 1913), pp. 80–9.
66 FO 195/2286, Monahan to Lowther, no. 65, 5 December 1908.

insisted that the Syrian *mahmal* use a route of his choosing from Mecca to Medina. The *Amir al-Hajj*, 'Abd al-Rahman Pasha al-Yusuf, wanted to take the caravan by sea because he feared bedouin attack. This was an unheard-of route, and Husayn believed that al-Yusuf, a CUP sympathizer, wanted to show that the Sharif was incompetent. Husayn denied the Pasha's request and had the Syrian *mahmal* travel under the escort of his brother, Sharif Nasir, after having paid off the bedouin on the route.[67]

While there were still reports throughout 1909 of widespread looting and violence, including attacks on the Syrian *mahmal*, Husayn eventually brought matters under control.[68] Monahan reported in October 1909 that the Harb tribe had almost totally submitted 'to the government, or rather to the Grand Sharif representing the government.' He recorded that Shaykh 'Abd al-Muhsin ibn 'Asim, a Harb chieftain, had capitulated to two of Husayn's sons.[69] Bringing the tribes to heel to a greater extent than anyone before him, Husayn had begun to create his chieftaincy. His next step would be to expand it.

Relations with expanding chieftaincies in Najd and 'Asir.   Pacification of local tribes, primarily the Harb, opened for Husayn the possibility of embarking on his next important task – expansion – in the course of which he could use to his advantage the very Harb with whom he had come to terms.

Conveniently for Husayn, expanding his chieftaincy served his goals while fulfilling a duty to the Ottomans, since his rivals were also Istanbul's: the Idrisi of 'Asir, and 'Abd al-'Aziz ibn 'Abd al-Rahman Al Sa'ud (henceforth, Ibn Saud) of Najd. Like Husayn,

---

[67] That Husayn might have been trying to humiliate the Unionists is buttressed by the fact that the Egyptian *mahmal did* go by sea to al-Wajh, and then overland to Medina. Husayn was on good terms with the Khedive of Egypt. FO 195/2320, Monahan to Lowther, no. 24, 21 May 1909, Mohammad Husain's Haj Report for 1908/09, 19 May 1909; Dawn, p. 7; 'Abdallah, pp. 44–5; Khoury, *Urban Notables* p. 87.

[68] FO 195/2320, Monahan to Ambassador, 20 January 1909; FO 424/219, Devey (Damascus) to Lowther, no. 17, 23 March 1909; FO 424/219, Monahan to Lowther, no. 14, 27 March 1909; Richardson to Lowther, no. 45, 30 August 1909; Richardson to Lowther, 6 October 1909.

[69] FO 195/2320, Monahan to Lowther, 2 November 1909. On 'Abd al-Muhsin: 'Lives at Khalis [Khulays – near the coast between Jeddah and Rabigh – author]. Hereditary standard bearer of the Harb. About fifty-five. A noted warrior and reputed just' (*HH*, p. 58).

these two leaders were expanding their chieftaincies. His first target was the rising power of the Al Sa'ud of Najd.[70]

In 1902 Ibn Saud had captured Riyadh from Ibn Rashid of Ha'il, signalling the beginning of the third Saudi state. By the end of March 1904 Ibn Saud had captured Qasim (its main cities were 'Anayzah and Buraydah), an important trading region in northern Najd long coveted not only by the Saudis but also by Ibn Rashid, and the Sharif of Mecca.[71] The *dirah*s of two important tribes of Qasim, the Mutayr and the 'Utaybah, covered the eastern part of the Hijaz and Qasim; parts of these tribes had declared for Ibn Saud in 1902.[72]

Ottoman attempts to assert control in Qasim met with little success; Ibn Saud was appointed *qa'im makam* of southern Najd, but he continued to reduce Ottoman authority; by 1907, Lorimer reports, there were fewer than fifty Ottoman troops in Qasim.[73] If the Ottomans wanted to reassert some control there and rein in Ibn Saud, they would have to enlist the help of the Sharif of Mecca.

In 1905 Ibn Saud, still weak and reaching an accommodation with the Ottomans, had asked Husayn's predecessor to intervene on his behalf,[74] thus indicating – in Arabian tribal practice – a kind

---

70 The conflict with Ibn Saud is discussed first because it happened first, although the Idrisi was actually more of a threat to Husayn at this early stage.

71 R. Bayly Winder, *Saudi Arabia in the Nineteenth Century* (London: Macmillan, 1965), p. 150, caught the nature of Qasim when he wrote: 'The towns of Qasim, [in their] valiant efforts to remain independent of sharifs, Rashids or Sauds, were another important factor which helped undermine what Faisal [ibn Turki, of the second Saudi state] was building. The farmers and traders of this province knew that they could not rule Arabia, but on the other hand they did not want to be ruled either by Ha'il or Riyadh. Frequently they fought the stronger of these two on a kind of rough balance of power theory.'

72 For details on the Mutayr and the 'Utaybah, see *HA*, pp. 67–9, 83, 609; *GA*, pp. 342–9; John Lorimer, *Gazetteer of the Persian Gulf, Oman, and Central Arabia* (Calcutta: Government Printing House, 1908–1915), 2, pp. 178–84, 1284–91. As Winder notes, it was the 'Utaybah going over to Ibn Rashid in 1884 that signalled the real end of the second Saudi state (Winder, pp. 269–70).

73 Lorimer, 1, pp. 1140–44; 1154–56; 1178.

74 FO 195/2198, Memorandum by Muhammed Hussein (Jeddah), 3 January 1905, enclosed in Devey to O'Conor, 4 January 1905. Goldberg, writing of Ibn Saud's diplomacy with the British and the Ottomans, does not mention this channel of communication (Jacob Goldberg, *The Foreign Policy of Saudi Arabia: The Formative Years, 1902–1918* [Cambridge, MA: Harvard, 1986]). Such moves were not unprecedented in Hijazi–Najdi relations. In 1846–7, Muhammad ibn 'Awn, Sharif Husayn's

of subservience to the Sharif of Mecca. By 1908, when Husayn came to power, Ibn Saud had become much stronger. At the *hajj* of 1909 he addressed representatives of various tribes in Qasim, adjuring them to submit to him instead of to Ibn Saud. May witnessed an expedition led by 'Ali and 'Abdallah against the Mutayr and the 'Utaybah; although they stopped short of entering Qasim proper, the small force, which included about 140 bedouin (probably Harb), handily mauled the Mutayr in several engagements east of Medina; 'Abdallah sustained a slight wound in one of these engagements.[75]

Preferring distant rulers to proximate ones, the residents of Qasim had indicated to Husayn that they favored his rule over that of Ibn Saud. In 1910, Husayn decided to move against Ibn Saud in Qasim and to collect the funds owed from that region, which had been in arrears for many years. Although the campaign was nominally in the name of Istanbul, the Ottoman commander-in-chief refused to send troops to accompany Husayn. Thus operating more on his own behalf than on that of the Ottomans, Husayn left Ta'if for Qasim near the end of July.

In the ensuing skirmishes, the Hashimites had the good fortune to capture Sa'd, Ibn Saud's favorite brother; the Najdi leader had no choice but to sue for terms. He consented not to tax the 'Utaybah and the Mutayr, and to pay Mecca tribute. 'Abdallah later admitted that Ibn Saud and Qasim had never actually forwarded the tribute and that his father had been satisfied with Ibn Saud's admission of his rights.[76] But the whole episode greatly

---

grandfather, attempted an invasion of Qasim. He was accompanied by a rival Saudi ruler, Khalid ibn Sa'ud. According to Winder, this campaign was 'presumably' because Faysal ibn Turki had refused to pay a tribute to the Ottoman sultan through the Sharif. After much posturing on both sides, Faysal agreed. The evidence as to whether or not the amir of Najd continued to pay this amount is inconclusive (Winder, pp. 157ff., 179–82).

75 *AB* no. 77, 27 January 1918; Dawn, p. 7; *RMM* 10 (1909), p. 503.

76 It is interesting to note that the messenger between Husayn and Ibn Saud was none other than Khalid ibn Lu'ayy, the amir of Khurma. Another 'ibn Lu'ayy' had been a go-between in similar circumstances in the nineteenth century (Winder, p. 180), and this one would cause much trouble for Husayn in the future. Information on the Qasim expedition of 1910 and the events leading up to it may be found in FO 195/2320, Monahan to Lowther, no. 25, 30 May 1909; Monahan to Lowther, no. 26, 30 May 1909; FO 195/2350, Monahan to Lowther, no. 30, 11 June 1910; FO 195/2350, Abdur Rahman to Lowther, no. 41, 14 July 1910; FO 424/224, Abdur Rahman to Lowther, no. 44, 5 August 1910; FO 195/2350, Abdur Rahman to Lowther, 17

increased the regional prestige of Husayn ibn 'Ali and began a severe enmity between the two leaders, each of whom attempted to expand his nascent chieftaincy.

Ibn Saud began taxing the 'Utaybah again the next year. In response, Husayn moved to halt trade and communications between Najd and the Hijaz, encouraging the looting of any goods sent to or from Najd.[77] By 1915 relations had deteriorated so much that 'Abdallah made another incursion into Qasim and proceeded beyond, to Sudayr. Meanwhile, Ibn Saud subdued the 'Ujman tribe of distant al-Hasa, on the Persian Gulf coast. 'Abdallah defeated some sympathizers of Ibn Saud, and collected tribute from parts of the 'Utaybah.[78]

In late 1914, in the midst of this tension between the Hijaz and Najd, the British had begun to negotiate a treaty with Ibn Saud. Signed on 26 December 1915, the treaty involved the British recognition of Ibn Saud as the independent ruler of Najd, al-Hasa, Qatif, Jubayl and associated territories.[79] It is not known if Husayn was aware of the treaty, which had the effect of committing the British to Saudi claims to vaguely defined territories, some of which were claimed by Husayn, with whom the British had no agreement. It also represented a British incursion into a conflict between two growing and competing chieftaincies.

As serious as Ibn Saud's activities were, Sharif Husayn became preoccupied with the potentially more dangerous threat from 'Asir. The *dirah*s of that region's tribes crossed into contiguous territory, north, south, and east.[80] 'Asir was important to Husayn for two reasons: first, the tribes of Ghamid and Zahran straddled

---

September 1910; FO 195/2350, Abdur Rahman to Lowther, no. 54, 11 October 1910; FO 371/2128/13871, Mallet to Grey, no. 193, 18 March 1914; *AB* 76, 13 January 1918; *AB* no. 77, 27 January 1918; Troeller, pp. 38–9; Dawn, pp. 6–7; Goldberg, p. 137; Philby, *Arabian Jubilee* (New York: John Day, 1953), pp. 26–7; al-Amr, p. 140; Baker, pp. 25–6; Goldrup, pp. 110–34. Husayn's correspondence with the Ottomans concerning the expedition is covered in Kayali, *Arabs and Young Turks*, pp. 162–3.

77 FO 195/2350, Abdur Rahman to Lowther, no. 39, 11 October 1911.

78 WP 140/3/67–70, Director, Arab Bureau, to Residency (Cairo), 11 September 1916; FO 371/3044/35392, A.T. Wilson (Iraq Section, Arab Bureau), to Director, Arab Bureau, 12 January 1917; Goldberg, pp. 137–8.

79 For the text of the treaty, see J.C. Hurewitz, *The Middle East and North Africa in World Politics: A Documentary Record* (New Haven: Yale Univerxsity Press, 1972), p. 58.

80 'Asir was never a whole politically, except theoretically in that it formed a *sancak* of the vilayet of Yemen.

both the Hijaz and 'Asir, and, second, his influence over them was threatened by the Idrisi himself – Sufi master, sharif, and the region's new rising star, who was developing his own chieftaincy.

The Idrisi was a charismatic figure and a religious reformer who had sometimes been vetted as a candidate for the caliphate.[81] As he gained followers among the tribes, miraculous tales were told about him and his works. Reports began to flow into Jeddah in early 1909 about a 'Mehdi, otherwise called a Hadi, who is said to be invulnerable [to] bullets, having appeared in Assir.'[82] Although disclaiming any grand intentions, he soon earned the title of 'Pretender' in British correspondence, and moved to institute the *shari'ah* in his domain.[83]

Husayn's interest in 'Asir was also a function of tribal politics. As the Idrisi's movement began to grow in 1909 and 1910, he threatened the Sharif's hold over parts of the tribes of Ghamid and

---

81 Sayyid Muhammad ibn 'Ali ibn Muhammad ibn Ahmad ibn Idris, known as 'al-Idrisi,' was the leader of a Sufi *tariqah* which was connected by marriage to the Sanusiyyah order of North Africa. The latter had been founded by Muhammad ibn 'Ali al-Sanusi, who had met the mystic Ahmad ibn Idris (the founder of the Ahmadiyyah [Idrisiyyah] order), native of Fas, at Mecca, where he had been preaching since 1799. The Sanusiyyah were quite powerful in the major towns and among the tribes, and for this reason they were watched carefully by the Sharifs of Mecca. Ahmad ibn Idris himself eventually acquired land at Sabya in 'Asir, where he died in 1837, and where he was presumably buried. Sayyid Muhammad was born in Sabya in 1876, and was educated at al-Azhar and by the Sanusi. He returned to 'Asir about 1906 and began his activities (Ochsenwald, *Religion, Society*, pp. 46–7; *AH*, pp. 26–7; *EI²*). For detailed studies of the Idrisi and the amirate of 'Asir, see Anne Bang, *The Idrisi State in Asir, 1906–1934: Politics, Religion and Personal Prestige as Statebuilding Factors in Early Twentieth-Century Arabia* (Bergen, Norway: Centre for Middle Eastern and Islamic Studies, 1996); Johannes Reissner, 'Die Idrisiden in 'Asir. Ein historischer Überblick,' *Die Welt des Islams* 21 (1991), pp. 164–92.

82 FO 424/219, Monahan to Lowther, no. 14, 27 March 1909.

83 For reports on the appearance of the Idrisi and his qualities and purported goals, see the following: FO 195/2320, Richardson (Hudaydah) to Lowther, no. 12/E, 14 April 1909; FO 424/220/34999, translation of extract from the *Yeni Gazeta* of 6 September 1909, enclosed in Lowther to Grey, no. 734, 13 September 1909; FO 424/250/4235, Lowther to Grey, no. 55, Annual Report for 1909 on Turkey, 31 January 1909; FO 424/231/25598, Memorandum respecting affairs in Asyr, in Kitchener to Grey, no. 66, 9 June 1912; FO 424/232/32964, Memorandum respecting Rebellion in Asir, Cheetham (Ramleh) to Grey, no. 82, 28 July 1912. The Idrisi's institution of the *shari'ah* and his confrontations with the Ottomans regarding it are interesting when we remember that one of the declared reasons for the Sharif's revolt was the low to which the Young Turks had brought the *shari'ah*. Husayn himself moved to institute the *shari'ah* as soon as the Revolt began (see Chapter 4).

Zahran. Many of the Ghamid acted as porters in the Hijaz during the pilgrimage season. In the summer of 1910 both tribes proclaimed their allegiance to the Idrisi. As punishment, the Sharif ordered the expulsion of all members of the Ghamid and Zahran tribes from Mecca and Jeddah – a form of economic pressure on potential fifth columnists. The Idrisi also sent men to collect taxes from the Dhawi Hasan at Lith on the coast (between Jeddah and Qunfudhah); Lith had in the past paid a tax on cattle and sheep to the Sharif.[84]

Husayn's connection with 'Asir involved more than financial and political matters. His family, the Dhawu 'Awn, was closely related to two important personages in 'Asir: the paramount Shaykh of the Banu Shihr al-Sham, Sa'id ibn Fa'iz Walad Fa'iz ibn Qurum ('Abdallah was raised by his great-grandmother, who was of the Banu Shihr); and the 'A'idh family of Abha, which had risen against the Ottomans in 1905.[85]

The Idrisi's rebellion against the Ottomans began in early 1909. The main town of northern 'Asir, Abha, was eventually cut off. By March, Ottoman weakness had led to an agreement whereby the Idrisi would be responsible for collecting *zakat* in 'Asir and the Tihamah north of Hudaydah, and all other taxes would be abolished. Moreover, the Ottomans reportedly agreed to abolish the *qanun* and institute the sole use of *shari'ah* law.[86] The Idrisi was appointed *mutasarrif* of 'Asir, and although this step appeared to have ended the revolt, it was really only the end of the first battle. Husayn was alarmed, and wrote to the Ottomans expressing his concern.[87] The result was that the Idrisi became stronger and more entrenched, and he was propagating a dangerously messianic message.

In 1910 the Idrisi attempted to expand his reach, trying to collect taxes from tribes in areas between the Hijaz and 'Asir, such as at Lith. The Sharif, feeling personally threatened, began to prepare an expedition against the Ghamid and the Zahran.[88] In that

84 FO 195/2350, Monahan to Lowther, 18 June 1910; FO 195/2350, Abdur Rahman to Lowther, no. 41, 14 July 1910; *AH*, pp. 44–5.

85 *AH*, pp. 48, 101; 'Abdallah, p. 9; FO 406/22, Devey to O'Conor, no. 64, 10 June 1905.

86 FO 371/1006, Richardson (Hudaydah) to Lowther, no. 8/E, 4 April 1909. See also FO 424/224/26784, a report by the Idrisi, enclosed in Lowther to Grey, no. 501, 20 July 1910.

87 Kayali, *Arabs and Young Turks*, p. 163.

88 FO 195/2350, Abdur Rahman to Lowther, 14 July 1910.

same year, the Idrisi destroyed some Ottoman fortifications and telegraph installations and tightened his control of the area around Abha, again virtually cutting it off. There were reports that the Idrisi was cooperating with the equally rebellious Imam Yahya of Yemen. By January of 1911, the Idrisi had issued a call to the inhabitants of 'Asir to rise up in *jihad* against the infidel Ottomans. His standard was a red (green was also reported) flag emblazoned with the words '*la ilaha illa allah*' (there is not God but God).[89]

Istanbul requested the aid of Husayn and his sons in suppressing the Idrisi. Having gained the submission of the Hijazi Harb, the Sharif was happy to oblige, as such a campaign afforded him the opportunity to ingratiate himself with the Ottomans and to limit the threat to his domain from the Idrisi's expanding chieftaincy.

The Sharif left Mecca on 15 April 1911 with his sons 'Abdallah and Faysal. He had about 5,000 bedouin irregulars with him (mostly Harb), although over half appeared to have dropped away by the time he reach Qunfudhah on or about 29 April 1911. On about 3 May a column of bedouin and Turkish regulars led by 'Abdallah set out to relieve Abha, only to be defeated at Quz Aba al-'Ir, a six-hour ride inland from Qunfudhah. 'Abdallah was wounded in the leg during this encounter.

Towards the end of May 1911, another expedition, led by Faysal, attacked Quz and put the Idrisi's men to flight. On 16 or 17 July 1911 Abha was relieved by a combined Ottoman–Sharifian force. By August the Sharif and his sons were back in Ta'if, and were given a grand reception.[90] It was difficult to tell who had

89 FO 195/2350, Monahan to Chargé d'Affaires, 13 December 1910; FO 424/226/1652, Richardson to Marling, no. 37/E, 15 December 1910; FO 424/226/1659, Proclamation of Seyyid Idris of Yemen, enclosed in Marling to Grey, no. 30 11 January 1911; FO 195/2736, Monahan to Lowther, no. 24, 10 June 1911.

90 FO 195/2376, Richardson to Lowther, no. 12/E, 24 February 1911; FO 195/2376, Richardson to Lowther, no. 20/E, 27 March 1911; FO 195/2376, Monahan to Lowther, 15 March 1911; FO 195/2376, Monahan to Lowther, no. 16, 26 March 1911; FO 195/2376, Monahan to Lowther, no. 21, 2 May 1911; FO 195/2376, Monahan to Lowther, no. 22, 25 May 1911; FO 195/2376, Monahan to Lowther, no. 24, 10 June 1911; FO 195/2376, Monahan to Lowther, no. 26, 20 June 1911; FO 195/2350, Richardson to Lowther, no. 38/E, 22 July 1911; FO 195/2376, Abdur Rahman to Lowther, no. 32 A, 13 August 1911; FO 195/2376, Abdur Rahman to Lowther, 11 August 1911; FO 195/2376[2350?], Richardson (San'a) to Lowther, no. 41/E, 14 September 1911; FO 424/232/32932, Cheetham to Grey, no. 82, Memorandum respecting Rebellion in Asir, 28 July 1912.

done most of the fighting, the Sharif's men or the Ottoman regulars; according to Kayali, who has checked Ottoman sources, Husayn's achievements were quite modest.[91]

The political meaning of the Sharif's 'Asir expedition was apparent to British and French observers. Monahan wrote:

The Grand Sharif since his triumphant return to the Hejaz has become exceedingly independent [of the Ottomans], and is likely to give much trouble to the government. The Sharifian prison for Bedouins in Mecca, which, since the advent of freedom [a reference to the Young Turk revolution], has been in a doubtful position, is now a firmly established institution, and the Grand Sharif is asserting his power of life and death over the Bedouins. At the reception held on his arrival at Taif he violently and publicly abused some Sharifs of the Daui Zeid ... He has caused four carriages brought by speculators into Mecca for the conveyance of pilgrims to be burned, on the ostensible grounds that immorality was being practised in them.[92]

The French envoy reported that no one doubted that the Sharif had undertaken the expedition for his own benefit. The Ottomans had sent a special envoy to present Husayn with the *plaque de l'Imtiaz,* which the envoy saw as *'une pure comédie,'* given the self-serving nature of the 'Asir campaign and that the Idrisi was still in power.[93]

Several authors have emphasized the role of the 'Asir campaign in Husayn's relations with the Ottomans, but the tribal dimension of the conflict with the Idrisi has been undervalued. 'Abdallah noted the Ottoman cruelty to the tribes, as did Husayn and the Idrisi. Suleiman Paşa, Ottoman *mutasarrif* of 'Asir in 1908–12, stressed that his conflict with Husayn was not because of an argument over who was responsible to the Porte in 'Asir, but because Husayn wanted to demonstrate magnanimity and forgive the tribes of 'Asir in an official proclamation. Husayn attempted to appoint his relative, Hasan ibn 'A'idh, as deputy *mutasarrif,* and

91 Kayali, *Arabs and Young Turks,* p. 164.
92 FO 195/2376, Monahan to Lowther, no. 36, 18 September 1911. The member of the Dhawi Zayd who was abused was Sharif Nasir ibn Muhsin who had been in the Vali's welcoming party; see also FO 195/2376, Abdur Rahman to Lowther, no. 44, 4 November 1911).
93 MAE, Djeddah (consulat), carton no. 24, Consul to Ambassador (Constantinople), 2 September 1911.

appoint another associate to be the *qa'im maqam* of the Bani Shihir.[94]

The Idrisi continued to maintain his headquarters at Sabya and his wide influence over the tribes. The war between Italy and the Ottoman Empire (September 1911 to October 1912) afforded him another chance of pursuing his ambition of freeing himself from Istanbul. Italian ships operated against Ottoman coastal installations along the Red Sea and actively aided the Idrisi. Istanbul's forces in the port of Luhayyah (between Hudaydah and Jizan) were besieged by the Italians from the sea and the Idrisi by land. Sharif Faysal fought alongside Ottoman troops with about 1,500 bedouin and 400 bisha and 'uqayl. Faysal's campaign was essentially a failure, as the Idrisi was not substantially weakened.[95] As an agreement ending the conflict with Italy neared in October 1912, Husayn urged the Porte not to allow the Idrisi to benefit from his rebelliousness. Istanbul, however, pardoned the Idrisi.[96]

In March 1913, not too long after the signing of a peace treaty between Italy and the Empire, the Ottomans tried again to reach accommodation with the Idrisi. He rejected their advances because of their refusal to grant him greater autonomy, including his own flag and coinage, and perhaps because of covert Italian support, which continued even after the treaty had been signed.[97] As the world war approached, the British capitalized on Idrisi–Ottoman mutual antipathy. Contacts began in September 1914, and by February 1915 the India Office had approved a subsidy of about £5,000 in arms and cash.

On 30 April 1915 the Idrisi signed a treaty with the British in which he agreed to go to war against the Ottomans in exchange for arms and funds. The British claimed that they wished 'solely to see the various Arab rulers living peacefully and amicably

---

94 'Abdallah, pp. 66–67; 'Mudhakkirat Sulayman Pasha,' *Al-'Arab*, 6 (February 1972), pp. 409–17, cited in al-Amr, p. 153.

95 FO 424/230/10206, Kitchener to Grey, no. 10, 8 March 1912; FO 424/232/32964, Cheetham to Grey, no. 82, Memorandum respecting Rebellion in Asir, 28 July 1912; al-Amr, p. 157. See also John Baldry, 'The Turkish–Italian War in the Yemen, 1911–1912,' *Arabian Studies* 3 (1976), pp. 51–65.

96 Kayali, *Arabs and Young Turks*, p. 165.

97 On the negotiations for an arrangement with the Idrisi, see FO 424/238/20498, Richardson to Lowther, no. 10, 25 March 1913; FO 424/239/38869, Richardson to Marling, no. 23, 28 June 1913.

together, each in his own sphere';[98] such a wish, however, could never come true with three competing chieftaincies in the Arabian Peninsula. As in the case of Ibn Saud, the treaty only served to increase the competition between the chieftains. The treaty galled Husayn, who saw the Idrisi as a 'man whom no one recognizes to be anything, having made himself sheikh, and landed in some place which was not ruled by anyone.'[99]

Relations with the Vali and the urban élite. As noted above, from the outset Husayn saw himself as having a personal mandate from the Sultan-Caliph to act with autonomy such as that granted to the Khedive of Egypt. He was the representative of the *ancien régime*, not beholden to the CUP or the Vali of the Hijaz. His actions and high-handed tactics in relation to these two actors bear out this assessment.

The story of Husayn's arrival in the Hijaz is illustrative. Even before his coming Husayn telegraphed an order for the appointment of his representative at Medina, a town where Sharifian predominance over the Ottomans was never certain. The military officers of the CUP were, in his view young, unsophisticated upstarts. When a CUP delegation met him in Jeddah, it greeted him expectantly as the 'constitutional amir' who '[knew] the spirit of the age' and would abandon the old ways of Sharifs 'Awn al-Rafiq and 'Ali. He wasted no time in disabusing them of that notion: 'This is the land of Allah. Nothing will have validity here but the *shari'ah* of Allah, which comprises *al-amr bil-ma'ruf wal-nahi 'an al-munkar* (enjoining good and forbidding evil).' It was the Sultan who had proclaimed the constitution, and it was the Sultan who was *Khadim al-Haramayn al-Sharifayn*. He concluded, 'The constitution of the land of Allah is the *shari'ah* of Allah and the Sunnah of his Prophet.'[100]

---

98 Briton Cooper Busch, *Britain, India, and the Arabs, 1914–1921* (Berkeley: University of California Press, 1971), pp. 216–27; WP, 134/4/5–6, gist of telegram from Resident, Aden, to Viceroy of India, undated [about 20 March 1915], and Viceroy's reply; copy of treaty in FO 371/2786/66940, dated 30 April 1915; WP, 135/5/7–11, Clayton to Wingate, April 1915.

99 L/P&S/18/B446, The Seven Independent Arabian States, Memorandum by W.J. Childs in 1916, enclosed in FO to IO, 27 December 1935.

100 'Abdallah, pp. 34–35; On Husayn's arrival, see FO 195/2286, Monahan to Lowther, no. 65, 5 December 1908; al-Amr, pp. 136–7; Baker, pp. 20–1; Dawn, pp. 5–6.

Husayn arrived in the Hijaz at a time of discontent with the tactics of the local branch of the CUP. The CUP had been belligerent with the local élite. The notables of Jeddah refused to register to vote for the new parliament, fearing taxation and military service. In October 1908, having set up a municipality under its own direction in Jeddah, the CUP attempted to collect taxes there and in Mecca, among them a tax from street vendors. A riot ensued, forcing the CUP to give up the idea. A month later, the CUP tried to collect a tax for Mecca's cemetery, to cover general sanitation and costs for each funeral.[101] The resultant protests took on the character of a general demonstration against the CUP, with cries of 'down with the red Tarboushes.' Monahan assessed that the riot was partly in response to a rumor that the CUP intended to abolish the Sharifate. The CUP did succeed in instituting a lighting and cleaning tax in Mecca, where they hung hundreds of petroleum street lamps,[102] but on the whole the Ottoman state was not strong enough to enforce significant taxation.

Although members of the urban élite were not always on good terms with the Sharif, they knew that he counterbalanced the Vali and guaranteed their special status as residents of the *haramayn*; that is, they paid no taxes, received subsidies, and were exempt from conscription. By April 1909 Husayn seems to have done well in his efforts to undermine the authority of the CUP. Those who had been arrested during the demonstrations were never tried and soon released,[103] most probably through the intervention of the Sharif, who stood to benefit with the local populace for acts of munificence. From about March 1909, the CUP in Mecca and Jeddah seems to have been seriously handicapped in its functioning.[104] By July 1911, Monahan reported, the CUP had 'died a natural death' in Mecca and Jeddah. All 'Turks resident in Mecca and Jeddah had ceased to visit the [CUP] clubs, partly through indif-

---

101 FO 195/2286, Monahan to Lowther, no. 53, 5 November 1908; FO 195/2286, Monahan to Lowther, no. 60, 18 November 1908.

102 FO 424/217, Monahan to Lowther, no. 64, 2 December 1908; FO 424/224/23944, Monahan to Lowther, 7 June 1910; see also Elie Kedourie, *Arabic Political Memoirs and other Studies* (London: Cass, 1977), pp. 145–6.

103 FO 424/219/15577, Monahan to Lowther, no. 15, 5 April 1909; FO 424/221/37537, Richardson (Jeddah) to Lowther, no. 45, 30 August 1909.

104 FO 424/219/15577, Monahan to Lowther, no. 15, 5 April 1909.

ference and partly for fear of the Grand Shereef, who had also deterred the Arabs from becoming members.'[105]

Sharif Husayn also out-maneuvered the numerous Valis who were sent to the Hijaz during his tenure. By mid-1911, the British reported that the Valis had virtually abandoned 'to the Grand Sharif the functions of Government at Mecca.'[106] Of Vali Hazim Bey, who held office in 1911, Acting British Consul Abdur Rahman wrote, 'He was Vali of the Hejaz for over six months, and all this time he was in Ta'if. The sum total of his work here is next to nothing.'[107] At least ten Valis came and went during the Ottoman period of Husayn's reign.[108]

Husayn took steps to curry favor with the local élite. He announced upon his arrival that rather than keep his income from the tax on camel transport, which amounted to about £300 a month, he would use it to help fund an improvement in the Jeddah water supply.[109] The local élites often chafed under Ottoman measures; when, in August 1909, the Vali announced a plan to strengthen the Ottoman currency at the expense of the many other currencies extant in the Hijaz, it was opposed by both merchants and foreign firms.[110] The plans, following Husayn's announcement that he would improve the water supply, must have increased the aggravation of the élites with the Ottomans and strengthened Husayn's position with them. Husayn thus gained

105 FO 424/231/13624, Monahan to Lowther, 7 March 1912. The CUP fought back, but to little avail. Its short-lived newspaper, *al-Shams al-Haqiqah*, attacked Husayn for corruption and 'spending his large revenues on banquets which require four or five male cooks' (FO 424/219/13685, Monahan to Lowther, no. 12, 12 March 1909; Kedourie, *Arabic Political Memoirs*, p. 147).
106 FO 195/2376, Monahan to Lowther, no. 19, 18 April 1911.
107 FO 195/2376, Abdur Rahman to Lowther, no. 44, 4 November 1911.
108 Kayali brings in the Ottoman perspective, noting that the Hijaz's harsh climatic and geographical conditions led officials to consider such a posting hardship duty. Many of them therefore may have been eager to shorten their tenure regardless of Husayn's efforts (Kayali, *Arabs and Young Turks*, pp. 165–6).
109 FO 195/2286, Monahan to Lowther, no. 65, 5 December 1908; FO 195/2286, Monahan to Lowther, no. 60, 18 November 1908; FO 195/2320, Monahan to Lowther, no. 24, 21 May 1909, enclosing Mohammad Husain's Haj Report for 1908/09, 19 May 1909. His salary at this time was TL12,000, and his total income about £20,000. In 1910 it was reported that despite several efforts, nothing had been done in this respect and that the Sharif had taken back his offer (FO 424/224/23944, Monahan to Lowther, 7 June 1910).
110 FO 424/221/37537, Richardson (Jeddah) to Lowther, no. 45, 30 August 1909.

the important support of the urban élite by controlling the tribes and by loosening the power of the CUP. The tribes, the urban élite, and the CUP/Vali – all were played off one against the other to Husayn's advantage.

Medina was the area in which Ottoman control grew strongest after Husayn came to power, especially after the extension of the railway to Medina in 1908, and later in July 1910 when the city was separated from the Hijaz vilayet and made a *mutasarrifiyyah* under the direct control of the Ottoman central government. There was still a division of authority, with the Sharif's courts hearing all cases involving bedouin, but the Ottoman presence was very strong.[111]

Ottoman attempts to extend the Hijaz railway beyond Medina gained momentum in 1912, following the conclusion of the war with Italy. Husayn, of course, opposed the Medina–Mecca and Jeddah–Mecca extensions. He was believed by most observers to be encouraging bedouin attacks on the railway and other Ottoman installations. In late 1911 or early 1912, Husayn let it be known that he was planning an expedition against Ibn Saud, but it never took place, and its organization was a pretext to avoid convening a meeting of tribal shaykhs. The Ottomans pressed him to find out exactly how much money the tribes wanted to stop their raiding and allow the railway to be completed. But since he wanted the raiding to continue, he never convened such a meeting. The railway was attacked with varying frequency until 1916. Telegraph wires were cut and there was an assault on the railway itself and on Ottoman barracks just outside Jeddah and Medina.[112]

In early 1912, the Hashimites began to voice their discontent with the Ottomans in unprecedented ways. In what appears to be the only contemporary record of 'Abdallah's thinking on this sub-

---

111 Ochsenwald, *Hijaz Railroad*, pp. 128–9.
112 FO 195/2320, Monahan to Lowther, no. 24, 21 May 1909, Mohammed Husain's Haj Report for 1908/09, 19 May 1909; MAE (Nantes), Djeddah (Consulat), carton no. 24, anonymous memorandum; Shipley (Jeddah) to Lowther, no. 29, 18 June 1912; FO 424/238/24670, Lowther to Grey, no. 252, 29 May 1913; MAE, Djeddah (consulat), vice-consul to ambassador, carton no. 3, 8 March 1914; FO 371/2130/15057, Abdur Rahman to Mallet, 11 March 1914; MAE, Djeddah (consulat), vice-consul to ambassador, Constantinople, carton no. 3, 15 March 1914; FO 371/2130/12652, Kitchener to FO, 21 March 1914; FO 371/12919, Mallet to FO, 23 March 1914; FO 371/2130/18245, Enclosure in Mallet to FO, no. 258, 17 April 1914; FO 371/2480/1761, Blackwell (Home Office) to FO, 4 January 1915.

ject, 'Abdallah confided to the French consul prior to his departure for Cairo. He spoke of his disgust with the Turks, announcing that he was giving up his seat in the parliament because he *'ne voul[ait] plus avoir rien en commun avec ces gens là.'* He talked about *'la tyrannie des turcs, de la haine des arabes contre eux, de la nécessité de mettre fin à cette tyrannie avec une franchise et une violence fort surprenantes.'* The French consul surmised that 'Abdallah's trip was aimed at gaining the support of the Khedive against the Turks, and vouched for the accuracy of the following quotation from 'Abdallah: *'Qu'y aurait-il d'étonnant ... à ce que l'Arabie et l'Egypte ne forment un jour qu'un seul état? Pensez-vous que les turcs seront éternellement les maîtres ici?'*[113]

Matters between Husayn and the Vali had significantly worsened with the appointment of Vehib Bey in 1914. He was a Vali of a different character, and he was determined to put an end to Husayn's growing power. Vehib ordered the Sharif's guard to hand over their guns, which they did.[114] Lawrence reported that 'Abdallah had confided to him that during Vehib's tenure he had contemplated taking several pilgrims of European nationality hostage in order to have the Powers force the Ottomans to grant the Hijaz more autonomy.[115] It was this Vali who precipitated the visits of 'Abdallah to Cairo in February and April 1914 in search of British support. Vehib, in attempting to take over much of the Sharif's functions, dismissed some of Husayn's supporters from government positions. He also announced several improvements in public works and services.[116] British Vice-Consul Abdurrahman wrote:

113 MAE, Djeddah (consulat), consul to Minister of Foreign Affairs, 29 January 1912. This conversation sheds new light on 'Abdallah's frame of mind before his 1912 Cairo visit. Dawn (pp. 58–61), has sifted through the historical record and determined that the visit occurred under circumstances which remain unclear. He believes that 'Abdallah did meet Kitchener on this visit, as does Musa (*Al-Harakah al-'Arabiyyah*, pp. 66–7). Kayali (*Arabs and Young Turks*, p. 170), states that this may have been his first contact with the British.

114 FO 371/2130, Mallet to FO, no. 258, 17 April 1914, enclosing memorandum by Devey (Damascus), dated 2 April 1914.

115 Kedourie, *England and the Middle East*, p. 49.

116 These included the *mutasarrif* (of Jeddah, probably), the chief clerks of two courts, the director of the public debt, and the municipal doctor of Jeddah. The *qadi* of Jeddah was threatened with replacement (MAE, Djeddah [consulat], vice-consul to minister of foreign affairs, no. 11, 26 February 1914).

[Husayn] was, up to the arrival of the new Vali, the sole monarch of the
Hedjaz and his word was law in this country. The Grand Shereef is
naturally opposed to any reform and wants that everything should run in
ancient rut [sic]. All departments in Mecca and Jeddah were under the
authoritative guidance of the Shereef and the Turkish Government only
in name. Every Vali who came here during the [preceding] five years had
to be either slave of the Grand Shereef or be summarily dismissed. The
Turkish Government ... is in [a] different mood now ... The new Vali
... confiscated all authority from the grand Shereef and wishes to do
away with [the] dual government.[117]

Vehib often complained to Istanbul of the Sharif's efforts to limit
his authority. He urged that Husayn be replaced and that the
Sharif's two sons serving in the Ottoman parliament, 'Abdallah
and Faysal, never be allowed to leave the capital. He concluded
that Husayn would not hesitate to cooperate with the enemy
should it attack the Red Sea coast. This tension was well known:
the French vice-consul thought the threat so serious that he
expected the central government was going to replace Husayn
with 'Ali Haydar of the Dhawu Zayd *ashraf*.[118]

But the Sharif's influence over the bedouin was supreme at this
stage, and his incitement of them forced Vehib Bey to come to
terms. He agreed to send a telegram together with Husayn to
Istanbul putting forth Husayn's demands: (1) That the government should abandon the idea of further construction of the railway in the Hijaz; (2) That the Jeddah court of justice, known as
the *'adaliyyah*, should deal only with foreigners; and (3) The Hijaz
should remain free of conscription. Istanbul agreed to these
demands.[119] Meeting them must have certainly increased the
influence of the Sharif.

Prelude to revolt: food, guns and gold. 'Abdallah's earlier 'overtures
of 1914' to the British were at first rejected, even though there is
some evidence of encouragement. Certainly nothing substantive

117 FO 371/2130/15057, Abdurrahman to Mallet, no. 16, 11 March 1914;
118 Kayali, *Arabs and Young Turks*, p. 184; MAE (Nantes) Djeddah (consulat), vice-consul
to ambassador, Constantinople, no. 6, 9 February 1914.
119 FO 371/2130, Abdurrahman to Mallet, no. 17, 19 March 1914; MAE (Nantes),
Djeddah (consulat), vice-consul to ambassador, Constantinople, 15 March 1914; FO
371/12919, Mallet to FO, 23 March 1914. See also FO 371/2130/6672, Kitchener to
Grey, no. 22, 6 February 1914; FO 371/2130/12652, Kitchener to FO, 21 March 1914;
Kedourie, *Anglo-Arab Labyrinth*, pp. 4–10; Ochsenwald, 'Opposition,' pp. 304–5.

was given to the Hashimites.[120] But after the departure of Vehib, Husayn's principal worry was getting food to the Hijaz. In an early December 1914 meeting between Storrs' messenger and the Sharif on the roof of his palace, Husayn was essentially noncommittal. He chided the British because their offer had 'simply [come] late, and if she had granted our demand when we made it [a reference to 'Abdallah's Cairo meetings], things would have been better.' Husayn said that his people were already helping the British by not aiding the Turks, and 'perhaps causes might spring up which would break these relations [with the Ottomans] before [your messenger, 'Ali] arrives in your country.' Meanwhile, he concluded, 'we simply pray her [Britain] to facilitate the question of [the import of] grains ... Be it as it may we shall not turn against her or aid her enemy. She shall see.'[121]

Husayn could not but have felt his acute dilemma. How long could he equivocate? Kitchener's intimation of the caliphate must have been tempting, along with the prospect of being rid of Ottoman rule. In January 1915, so the story goes, one of Sharif 'Ali's men found a case among Vehib's possessions which included plans to assassinate or depose Husayn.[122] If true, the event would certainly have motivated Husayn to side with the British. On the other hand, in November 1914 the Sultan-Caliph had declared a *jihad*, and he was expected by Istanbul to lend his prestige to the effort. The decision to break or stay with Istanbul, the legitimate Islamic state and the source of so much money, must have taxed the diplomatic skills of a local ruler caught between two great powers.

Throughout the first half of 1915, Husayn continued to equivocate, promising to support the Ottomans. Meanwhile, in response to Husayn's efforts, the High Commissioner in Egypt approached the Foreign Office with a request to allow limited food shipments to Jeddah; it was approved in May 1915, with an

---

120 Kedourie, *Anglo-Arab Labyrinth*, pp. 4–10.
121 WP, 134/8/114–116, Shorthand notes taken by X of a discourse by Sherif of Mecca, which took place in privacy on the roof of his palace, initialed R[onald] S[torrs], 9 December 1914. Another report of this messenger is in Storrs, pp. 174–6. See also Kedourie, *Anglo-Arab Labyrinth*, pp. 15–17; and Musa, *Al-Harakah al-'Arabiyyah*, pp. 142–3.
122 S. Mousa, 'Sharif Husayn and Developments Leading to the Arab Revolt,' *New Arabian Studies* 1 (1993), pp. 36–53; Kayali, *Arabs and Young Turks*, pp. 189–90.

apparently salutary effect on the way the local populace perceived the British and a concomitant rise in Husayn's prestige. Following promises of support from Arab leaders in Syria, the Hashimites met in June in Ta'if and decided, in principle, to revolt.[123]

Husayn needed one more thing from the British before he could begin the rebellion: money. Once the uprising began, his sizeable income from the Ottoman treasury would be immediately terminated. Moreover, it was also uncertain whether the pilgrimage would continue and to what extent, so this source of income was threatened, too. And, finally, he needed the funds to pay the bedouin, who would have little reason otherwise to cooperate. In messages received in February 1916, Husayn asked for £50,000, arms, and foodstuffs.[124] The cash was promised to be given to Husayn later, once it was confirmed that the uprising had actually taken place (see Chapter 5).

The actual timing of the Revolt may have been influenced by a flare-up in the already turbulent relations between the Sharif and the Ottomans. In 1916 Faysal met in Damascus with Arab nationalists while his son 'Ali was in Medina rustling up tribal support and interfering with the Ottoman administration there. Moreover, the Ottomans were pressing for Hijazi troops (the ever-feared conscription), and a declaration of *jihad* from Mecca. Husayn pressed for greater autonomy in exchange, not only for the Hijaz, but – following support gained from Arab activists – for Syria and Iraq as well. The Ottomans replied that Faysal would never be seen again if the troops were not sent. They agreed to send Faysal to Medina to get armed men, and the Sharif turned

<hr/>

[123] WP, 134/6/11–12, FO to Residency (Cairo) no. 230, repeated by Clayton to Wingate, received Erkowit on 14 May 1915; see also WP, 134/6/36–37, Clayton to Cheetham, 20 May 1915; WP, 134/7/1–3, Abdel Kadir El Mackawee (Aden) to Wingate, 9 June 1915; WP, 136/1/146–147, Report of the 3rd visit of Messenger 'G' to the Sherif Hussein Ibn Ali in Mecca, 25 January 1916; FO 371/2778/187291, McMahon to FO, no. 427, 3 June 1916 and associated papers; FO 371/2770/12036, IO to FO, P 198, 18 January 1916, and associated papers; 'Abdallah's cover letter to Storrs, covering Husayn's first letter of the Husayn–McMahon correspondence, 14 July 1915, in Antonius, pp. 413; Tauber, *Arab Movements*, p. 65; Mousa, 'Sharif Husayn'; Kayali, *Arabs and Young Turks*, pp. 190–2.

[124] The Sharif asked for 20,000 sacks of rice, 15,000 of flour, 3,000 of barley, 150 of coffee, 150 of sugar, 5,000 rifles 'modern pattern' and 100 boxes of cartridges of a kind of which he enclosed samples (WP, Clayton to Wingate, no. 163, received 29 [24?] February 1916).

this to his advantage. He had already assembled levies at Medina under 'Ali, for the ostensible purpose of sending them to fight for the Ottomans. But the Ottomans had also amassed significant forces at Medina, and Husayn feared that they might be instructed to depose him. When Faysal arrived at Medina, he and 'Ali left, and on 9 June 1916 at B'ir al-Mashi, on the way to Mecca, Faysal wrote Jemal Pasha that unless Husayn's demands were met, relations would be severed. On that same day the Revolt began with an attack on the railway.[125]

---

[125] Tauber, *Arab Movements*, pp. 78–82; Djemal Pasha, *Memories of a Turkish Statesman – 1913–1919* (New York: Arno, 1973), pp. 214–37; Kayali, *Arabs and Young Turks*, pp. 190–2. Faysal apparently wanted to start a revolt among Arab officers in Syria, but was unsuccessful due to the efforts of Jemal Pasha (see WP, 136/2/88–91, Clayton to Wingate, no. 163, received 24 [29?] February 1916; WP, 136/6/29–30, Wingate to C.E. Wilson, 7 May 1916). There is some confusion about the actual day the Revolt was inaugurated.

4

EXPANDING THE CHIEFTAINCY

THE ARAB REVOLT, 1916–1917

Scholars have studied two Arabian chieftaincies – the Saudi state based in Riyadh, in Najd, and the Rashidi state, based in Ha'il, in Jabal Shammar.[1] During times of expansion, these states were successful in providing tribes with certain 'attraction factors' – resources and benefits which proved more attractive than those offered by opposing chieftaincies.

The political configuration of the Rashidi chieftaincy (1836–1921) was based on an agreement among Shammar chieftains (*shaykhs*), each one the head of his own *'ashirah* (tribal section), that a member of the Al Rashid should be their amir. This was primarily a blood connection, augmented by protection arrangements (*khuwwa*) and the coalescing of commercial interests. The *shaykhs* were expected to take part in Ibn Rashid's raids, and he in turn provided them with regular seasonal subsidies, as well as gifts of rice, coffee, dates, clothes, and, above all, weapons. This chieftaincy fielded an armed force that included tribal warriors, mercenaries and slaves, and it expanded beyond the immediate area of Ha'il to incorporate Jawf in the north and Qasim and Riyadh in Najd. In 1891 the Rashidis captured Riyadh and forced

---

[1] The best study of Saudi Arabia in terms of tribes and state formation is Joseph Kostiner, *The Making of Saudi Arabia, 1917–1939: From Chieftaincy to Monarchical State* (New York: Oxford University Press, 1993). The best study of the Rashidi state, from the same perspective, is Madawi Al Rasheed, *Politics in an Arabian Oasis: The Rashidi Tribal Dynasty* (London: I.B. Tauris, 1991), and her comparative article, 'Durable and Non-Durable Dynasties: The Rashidis and Sa'udis in Central Arabia', *British Journal of Middle Eastern Studies* 19 (1992), pp. 144–58. Recently, a short study of the Idrisi state of 'Asir has been completed: Anne Bang, *The Idris State in 'Asir, 1906–1934: Politics, Religion and Personal Prestige as Statebuilding Factors in Early Twentieth Century Arabia* (Bergen, Norway: Centre for Middle Eastern and Islamic Studies, 1996).

the Saudis into exile; during the First World War they supported the Ottomans, and the Rashidi state came to an end in 1921 when Ibn Saud captured Ha'il.

Ibn Saud's chieftaincy was similar to Ibn Rashid's in many ways, but it had distinct differences. First, it confederated several tribes, whereas Ibn Rashid's chieftaincy was based on the Shammar. Second, it harnessed the power of the Wahhabi *da'wah* (message, or creed) as its cohering ideology. Ibn Khaldun commented that the unifying power of religion strengthened dynastic rule, which was made possible by tribal solidarity (*'asabiyyah*).[2] A decisive external factor, British support, made Ibn Saud victorious over his Rashidi rival.

Sharif Husayn came to the Sharifate of Mecca in 1908, and, until he began the Revolt in 1916, he had made no bid for tribal solidarity, and his religious appeal was limited. His *modus operandi* – payments to the tribes that controlled the *hajj* traffic – was made possible by the subsidies he received from the Ottomans. When he revolted against Istanbul, these funds vanished; he now had to keep the tribes' support with funds that he did not have. His Revolt involved an expansion that had continuously to enlist more tribes, and more of each tribe. The territorial goal, no longer limited to the Hijaz, depended on a tribal confederacy, which itself depended on the attraction factors of money and arms from the British, and plunder from the Ottomans. There is no indication that a cohering ideology – such as Arab nationalism – generated political or social integration in the Hijaz, and Husayn's religious pronouncements seemed to have been designed for Muslims outside the Hijaz over whom he eventually hoped to rule. The state, rather, perpetuated the traditional tribal institution of raiding (*ghazw*); only this time, the institution was put in the service of a grand movement, with massive British support.[3] Financial backing and the provision of war *matériel* on this scale

---

2 Ibn Khaldun, *The Muqaddimah: An Introduction to History*. (London: Routledge & Kegan Paul, 1987), pp. 125–7.

3 'For a tribe's consent to join a Hashemite alliance, it was paid a large sum, rather than being fully integrated into the new alliance or being required to reform its basic values or structure' (Joseph Kostiner, 'The Hashemite "Tribal Confederacy" of the Arab Revolt, 1916–1917,' in Edward Ingram [ed.], *National and International Politics in the Middle East: Essays in Honor of Elie Kedourie* [London: Cass, 1988], pp. 126–43, [quote on p. 135]).

were unprecedented for any foreign power in the Arabian
Peninsula.

Forming alliances with tribal groups

The process of forming the necessary tribal alliances before and
during the Revolt was one of protracted bargaining. The tribal
chiefs were fairly autonomous, and their consent to join was
entirely conditional on the fulfilment of Sharifian promises for
money, plunder, and rifles. Istanbul also had these incentives to
offer, and the principal, if not the sole, obstacle to keeping the
tribes from going over to the Turks was that the Hashimites,
backed by the British, offered more of them. The long halts at
Rabigh and Yanbu', Wajh and 'Aqabah (see below) frustrated
many observers; Lawrence, however, saw them for what they
were: long bargaining sessions necessary for adding further rungs
on the ladder of alliances that would allow the Revolt to progress
northwards. Besides promising guns, money and booty, the
Sharifs, and particularly Faysal, were constantly involved in mediation between and among rival tribes. Faysal was engaged in such
activity practically all day and every day. He adjudicated not only
feuds between tribal groups, but within them and between individuals.[4] This mediation increased the prestige of the Sharifate
which already enjoyed some prestige because of its Hashimite
lineage.

These factors would allow the tribal armies to be kept in the
field much longer than they were accustomed to (and to go out of
their *dirah*s), for their warfare usually consisted of raiding and
returning to base. Tribal autonomy, however, was strong, and
given the right circumstances tribal groups might change sides. It
therefore bears stressing that these alliances were by nature temporary, and when the incentives dwindled, trouble was bound to
appear (as will be seen in Chapter 8). The Sharif's hold on the
tribes was therefore tenuous.[5]

[4] *AB*, no. 36, 26 December 1916; *AB*, no. 43, 28 February 1917; see also Ronald Colman,
    'Revolt in Arabia, 1916–1919: Conflict and Coalition in a Tribal System', unpublished
    PhD dissertation, Columbia University, 1976, p. 126.
[5] For an excellent analysis of these factors, see Colman, especially pp. 123–45; Kostiner,
    'Tribal Confederacy'.

The first incentive to the tribes to join the alliance was gold – British sovereigns. Husayn considered this subsidy his due, for having forfeited the Ottoman remittances, he now needed not only to replace them, but to better them. At the beginning of the Revolt, when the British hesitated to fully commit resources and funds, Sharif Shakir ibn Zayd, 'Abdallah's friend and companion who was often designated 'Amir of the 'Utaybah,' told Storrs: 'Do the English not see that if the Sherif is not able to redeem his money promises to the Arabs, he will be a liar proved and lose his honour before them? Then where will be success?'[6] C.E. Wilson, British 'Pilgrimage Officer' in Jeddah, wrote, 'The allegiance of the tribes is a very precarious plant whose roots need constant feeding with gold.'[7]

Another move that helped the Sharif's efforts was his distribution of rifles to the bedouin. In the first six months of the Revolt, about 54,000 rifles and 20 million rounds of ammunition were distributed; by June 1917, these figures had risen to approximately 71,000 rifles and over 40 million cartridges. Complaining about the massive number of rifles being distributed, the British did not understand that to the bedouin the rifles had become personal property, not 'ordnance' issued temporarily by the military to its soldiers. Lawrence wrote that Faysal curried favor with the tribes by, *inter alia*, paying the large sum of £1 for each captured Turkish rifle – and then returning it to the taker. (It was reported that Ibn

---

[6] FO 371/2773/122968, report by Storrs on his trip to the Hijaz in early June, enclosed in McMahon to Grey, no. 141, 15 June 1916. For more on Sharif Shakir, see *al-Album al-Hashimi*, p. 109.

[7] *AB*, no. 91, 4 June 1918. The issue of the subsidy is dealt with in detail in Chapter 5. There had been no British representation at Jeddah since the outbreak of the war. C. E. Wilson, who had been Governor of Port Sudan, was suggested for this position by McMahon who thought such a 'colourless' title would 'avoid giving colour to idea of our assumption of (?control) in Hedjaz' (FO 371/2773/133810, McMahon to FO, no. 565, 10 July 1916).

Wilson made a point of not assuming Arab garb, in contrast to Lawrence: 'I informed Sherif I could not dress like an Arab and he agreed that I need only put the usual scarf and "oqal" over my helmet. The Sherif himself does not care a rap what I wear and laughed when I told him that there was nothing about not wearing a helmet in the Koran. I took up this line about dress because I consider that to have complied with the request "in toto" would not be in keeping with the prestige of custom of British officers, and the sooner the Arabs know this the better' (FO 686/33, Wilson, note for files, undated, but probably from October 1916).

Saud had bought over 300,000 rounds and many rifles from the bedouin, only to use them later against Husayn.)[8]

Another important tool in mobilizing the tribes was control of their cultivated areas and markets. As long as the Ottomans controlled these, the tribes concerned tended to be pro-Istanbul. Dominating the markets, and having the prerogative to deny access to them, thus became one of Husayn's objectives.[9]

From Mecca to Wajh: June 1916–January 1917

On 5 June 1916, Husayn's sons 'Ali and Faysal, supported by some Harb, 'Utaybah and Juhaynah, raised the standard of the Revolt outside Medina. Faysal had gone there as part of a ruse, purportedly to organize volunteers for the sultan's *jihad*. The Revolt was initiated without much advance planning and was declared earlier than expected because of the arrival of Ottoman reinforcements. Despite doing some damage to the railway north of the town, the rebels were pushed back by the Ottomans. Faysal had counted on the people of al-'Awali, a 'garden suburb' a few miles east of the town occupied mostly by Banu 'Ali Harb, to control Medina's water supply and deny it to the Ottomans, but instead they went over to the Ottomans and were massacred. Continued Ottoman sorties pushed Faysal out of Medina's environs and west to the region of Yanbu', where he met the British officer Charles Wilson in late August 1916. This was to be his first meeting with a British official.[10] The failure to capture Medina demonstrated the precariousness of tribal support for the Revolt, as well as the durability of Ottoman influence in the Medina region – it would last until after the conflict.[11]

Meanwhile, in Mecca, Husayn had begun planning those aspects of the Revolt which would be centered there. He was also trying to form alliances with the nearby tribes and the townsfolk of Mecca. The latter, because of their financial dependence on the

---

[8] FO 882/5, report by Lawrence (also excerpted in *AB*, no. 31, 18 November 1916); Colman, pp. 80–5.

[9] Colman, pp. 93–5.

[10] *HH*, p. 51. *AB*, no. 14, 7 August 1916; *AB*, no. 28, 1 November 1916; *AB*, no. 31, 18 November 1916; *AB*, no. 52, 31 May 1916; FO 882/5, report by Lawrence, 27 October 1916; Eliezer Tauber, *The Arab Movements*, pp. 80–2.

[11] It should be remembered that the capacity of the Sharifian state in Medina was actually quite limited in any case.

Ottoman Empire, were reluctant, and in March 1916 Husayn tried to starve them into 'cooperation.' He asked the British to blockade the Hijazi coast and cut off its trade; the townsfolk could perhaps be convinced to cooperate in order not to lose their livelihood, and, in fact, their food supply.[12] The total blockade went into effect on 15 May 1916, and its announcement was communicated to 'the Arab Chiefs and the Sheikh of Jeddah' by the commander of the British man-of-war *Suva*.[13]

It was a master stroke – Husayn had calculated correctly. In mid-May 1916, meetings of notables, merchants, heads of guilds, *'ulama*, and the *shaykh*s of the quarters were held in Mecca, some of which were attended by 'Abdallah. Those present bemoaned the calamity of the blockade and talked about concluding peace with Britain. At some meetings, oaths of allegiance to the Sharif were sworn. The Ottoman acting governor and commandant of Mecca, Bimbashi Mehmed Zia Bey, wrote that 'an attitude of distrust of the [Ottoman] Government began to appear among the people, and words to the following effect were current: "Let us invite British protection," "Let us declare our independence," "Expel all the Turks from Hejaz".' On 17 May, the Ottomans deployed troops in Mecca in preparation for a revolt. Husayn protested, saying that the comments made at the meetings had been misinterpreted and that the troops would cause unnecessary alarm. By the night of 9 June, the Ottomans noticed suspicious

---

12 Antonius, p. 191. That the blockade was instituted at Husayn's request is attested to by McMahon, who telegraphed the FO on 4 June 1916: 'Our blockade of Hedjaz which it should be remembered was instituted at the urgent and repeated request of Shereef himself.' (FO 371/2778/187291, no. 487). The British had initiated a partial blockade as early as late 1914, which led Husayn to complain about the lack of grains in the Hijaz (WP 134/8/114–116, Shorthand notes taken by X of a discourse by Sherif of Mecca, which took place in privacy on the roof of his palace, 9 December 1914). In mid-1915, the British decided to allow restricted imports of food to Jeddah via Port Sudan and Suakin at the urging of McMahon, who believed that stoppage of supplies alienated the Arabs (WP 134/6/11–12, Clayton to Wingate, repeating FO to High Commissioner, received Erkowit 14 May 1915; WP 134/6/36–37, Clayton to Cheetham, 20 May 1915). This policy met with approval in the Hijaz (WP 136/1/146–147, Report of the third visit of Messenger 'G' to the Sherif Hussein Ibn Ali at Mecca, 25 January 1916). See also Colman, pp. 96–101, and Sheila Scoville, 'British Logistical Support to the Hashemites of Hejaz: Ta'if to Ma'an, 1916–1918,' unpublished PhD dissertation, University of California, Los Angeles, 1985. pp. 51–3.

13 Text in *AB*, no. 21, 15 September 1916; WP 136/6/29–30, Wingate to Wilson, 7 May 1916.

movements by armed men around Mecca, and the first shots were fired on 10 June, soon after morning prayer. Zia Bey telephoned Husayn: 'The Bedouin are revolting against the Government; find a way out.' Husayn replied sarcastically, 'of course we shall,' and hung up.[14] The Revolt had begun in Mecca the Revered.

The tribes around the Holy Cities, mostly Juhaynah, Harb, and 'Utaybah, had already been operating for years against the Ottomans in opposition to the Hijaz railway.[15] In addition to tribal forces, the Sharif had at his disposal several hundred 'regulars,' probably Bisha troops.[16] Most of the Ottoman troops in the area of Mecca were with the Vali in Ta'if, leaving only about 1,400 troops in the holy city itself. Husayn's forces captured Mecca within the space of two days, and two weeks later he took two forts in the hills outside the city.

On 16 June, after a fierce fight, Jeddah fell to the Sharif's forces, aided by the British seaplanes of the carrier *Ben-my-Chree*. Rabigh fell soon after (to a local revolt); Yanbu' was taken at the end of July. Ta'if resisted 'Abdallah and his 'Utaybah throughout the summer, strengthened by Ottoman troops which had left Mecca; but almost before the Hashimites knew what was happening, the Ottomans had amassed large numbers of troops in Medina and its environs. It was apparent that the Ottomans were setting their sights on Rabigh, which, if seized, would be a staging ground for a counterattack on Mecca. However, Rabigh was taken in June by Husayn bin Mubarak, the powerful *shaykh* of the Zubayd section of the Masruh Harb.

In 1915 Bin Mubarak had helped Husayn by facilitating the landing of British ships and delivering their supplies to the Sharif.[17] Early in 1916 he had raised 4,000 men and stolen a large sum of Ottoman money that was on its way from Mecca to

---

14 *AB*, no. 21, 15 September 1916.

15 FO 371/2773, McMahon to FO, 8 June 1916, cited in Colman, p. 60. According to McMahon, when the Revolt broke out these tribes were already enlisted. This is only partially true, as Husayn Mubarak's Harb were still in opposition (see below).

16 According to a French report, while 'Bisha' were men from Wadi Bisha that had a tradition of serving with the Sharif (see Chapter 1), it soon became the generic description of all 'non-tribal' recruits from the Hijaz, regardless of whether they came from Wadi Bisha or not (SHAT, 7 N 2139, Brémond, no. 14, 'Notes sur les tribus des ahl el Hedjaz,' 17 January 1917).

17 FO 882/15, L.F. Nalder, Inspector, Suakin District, to Governor, Red Sea Province, 22 December 1915.

Medina.[18] When he took Rabigh, it appeared that he had joined the Revolt.

But Bin Mubarak's affiliation with Husayn proved unreliable, for in July, after the Ottomans had reportedly offered him £50 a month, Bin Mubarak was made Pasha.[19] Towards the end of that month, he opposed an attempt by the British to land an Egyptian artillery battery and supplies at Rabigh, and by late summer, having received only nominal provisions, Faysal's men found themselves ill equipped. British officers saw an Ottoman flag flying over Rabigh, and spies reported that several Turks were in town. Kinahan Cornwallis of the Arab Bureau commented, 'Sheikh Hussein Mabeiriq is supreme in his own territory and has always been independent of the Sheriff.'[20]

Because of Bin Mubarak's influence over the Masruh Harb, his obvious willingness to cooperate with the Ottomans raised a serious question on the Hashimite side: whether or not British troops should be sent to hold Rabigh. The British wanted to send them, and Faysal agreed, but Husayn believed that having Christian troops fighting under his command would damage his prestige among Muslims.[21]

Meanwhile, Mubarak continued to play both sides of the game, demonstrating the difficulties an independent tribal leader could present. On 8 September, with the British and Faysal convinced of his treachery, he came to Husayn's youngest son Zayd and swore his loyalty to the Sharif, denying that he had kept any of the supplies or had had dealings with the Ottomans. Faysal, though, was not convinced of this change of heart.

The first stage of the Rabigh crisis abated when news reached the region of the fall of Ta'if on 22 September. This, combined with Faysal's minor success when the Ottomans tried to force the Darb Sultani, led to an increase in morale. When, at about the same time, 'Ali arrived with about 1,000 men, Mubarak fled to the hills; in a search of his home in Rabigh, diverted stockpiles of British supplies were found. A few months later the British were

---

[18] *HH*, pp. 65.

[19] FO 882/4, Ruhi (Jeddah) to Storrs, 2 August 1916.

[20] FO 371/2775/196445, Captain Kinahan Cornwallis to Director, Arab Bureau, report on mission to Jeddah, 8 July 1916.

[21] WP, 141/7/50–51, Wilson to Sharif, telephone message, 12 October 1916.

reporting that Mubarak 'had made his way to Medina and definitely joined the Turks.'

However, Rabigh remained a problem that worsened with every Arab defeat from October to December 1916: if the Ottomans were to take Rabigh, Mubarak would join them; if the Sharif appeared stronger, he would go over to the Sharif. But the Sharif could appear stronger only by having British troops there, and this he refused to do. Husayn was caught in a dilemma; his Revolt was based, according to his proclamation, on Islamic principles. His rival and Ottoman-sponsored pretender to the Sharifate, 'Ali Haydar, was already in Medina, proclaiming that the Sharif was in league with infidels. On the other hand, Husayn's situation was desperate, and, in an effort to win over Bin Mubarak, he reportedly sent him £2,000.

In December the Revolt was near collapse. The few victories of Husayn's forces had been offset by several major defeats, an imbalance that greatly affected tribal recruitment. Matters looked so bleak that Wingate wired the Foreign Office: 'Captain Lawrence reports that Emir Faisal's position has changed from that of a leader of the tribes to a tribal leader.'[22] There were problems with supplies and communications, and the survival of Husayn's Revolt hung on the British Navy's Red Sea patrol which prevented an Ottoman advance on Rabigh and Yanbu'.[23]

As the year 1916 drew to a close, Faysal began to consider that the only way out of the Rabigh trap and the whims of Shaykh Mubarak was an aggressive thrust up the coast to Wajh. It was that thrust which would effectively solve the conundrum of Rabigh and its Shaykh Mubarak.[24]

---

22 FO 371/2776/262389, Sirdar (Khartoum), to FO, no. 79, 13 December 1916.

23 Wilson, *Lawrence*, p. 340.

24 The saga of Husayn Bin Mubarak is covered in many sources. The most important are: H.V.F. Winstone, *The Diaries of Parker Pasha* (London: Quartet, 1983), pp. 120–3; 130, 132, 155, 175; Wilson, *Lawrence*, pp. 297–300, 1030; *SPW*, pp. 77, 94; FO 371/27775/196445, K. Cornwallis to Director, Arab Bureau, report on mission to Jeddah, 8 July 1916; FO 882/4, Ruhi to Storrs, 2 August 1916; WP, 140/1/108–109, Clayton to Wingate, 4 September 1916; FO 371/2778/176250, McMahon to FO, 5 September 1916; WO 158/627, Chief, Egyptforce to Dirmilint, 17 November 1916; FO 371/2776/251855, Wingate to FO, no. 77, 13 December 1916; see personality profile in *HH*, p. 65, and in *AP*, pp. 14–15; see also the following in *AB*: no. 18, 5 September 1916; no. 20, 14 September 1916; no. 23, 26 September 1916; no. 24, 5 October 1916; no. 25, 7 October 1916; no. 31, 18 November 1916; no. 36, 26 December 1916.

The Sharif's predicament with respect to a British landing at Rabigh illustrates some of the central problems he faced during the Revolt. The British troops were certainly deemed necessary by all involved, including Faysal. On at least two occasions, Husayn himself even agreed to their despatch, although he requested that they be Muslim troops; this became a moot point, as there was no way, the British said, that they could provide these. On the other hand, the Arab leaders were wary of British help; even the arrival of only a few British officers had caused initial difficulties. The main sticking point, as Husayn and his supporters explained it, was that the chief thrust of Ottoman propaganda and of the one whom they had appointed to take his place as Sharif, 'Ali Haydar, was that Husayn had sold himself to the British. Even a small force, which would soon be exaggerated along the grapevine, would play right into their hands.

This explained Husayn's hesitancy and vacillation. Fu'ad al-Khatib, a Syrian in Husayn's service, put forth some interesting arguments against the British troops that revealed the precarious status of the Revolt in its initial stages: the tribes whom the Sharif wished to win over would go over to the Ottomans if they thought that the Hijaz was being turned over to Christians; any Christian soldier captured would be paraded among all the tribes to show that the Sharif intended to put the Hijaz under foreign rule; he would lose support among Muslims in Iraq and Syria; and there would be opposition at Mecca by those already predisposed against the Sharif.

Husayn bridled at his dependence on the British. Often, he blamed the British for his dilemma; they had, he claimed, promised to cut the railway from Damascus to Medina. If they had done so, there would have been no emergency at Rabigh. There is no evidence that such a commitment had ever been made by the British, and Husayn could produce no documents attesting to it, although he claimed to have such a document from the High Commissioner in his possession.[25] These were the accusations of a man who was already beginning to see that his alliance with the British was unequal and that he had not developed alternative sources of power. He was totally dependent on them, and while

---

[25] FO 686/6, Report by George Lloyd, n.d., from December 1916; GLLD, 9/8, Lloyd to Wingate, Report on the Hejas [sic], 22 December 1916; FO 882/3, Statement on Hedjaz taken from Fuad Eff. El Khatib, 1917.

they needed his support, they also had other obligations, military and political.

On 10 or 11 December, with the Rabigh situation critical, Husayn agreed in writing to the sending of British troops, only to retract his agreement the next day. Wingate, who believed strongly that the troops were necessary, told Wilson to get a positive reply, but the Sharif still refused. He brought Wilson a statement of the Qadi of Mecca in support of his refusal. Wingate then asked the Foreign Office for an ultimatum, stating to the Sharif that if he refused this time, the offer would not be repeated. At about this time (mid-December), the threat receded as the Ottomans began to believe that they had overextended themselves in the direction of Rabigh and Yanbu'. On 5 January 1917, it was reported that the Sharif had again, in a formal application, asked for the troops to be sent. Wingate rushed to arrange to send them. The Sharif had, however, played a clever game and had made his application by telephone, allowing him to easily repudiate his agreement. Wilson argued, successfully, that the request should be made in writing, and that the Sharif be held responsible for assuring the troops' positive reception by the local Arabs. Both the Foreign Office and the War Office supported this view. The Foreign Office added that the Sharif would be obligated to issue a suitable proclamation to the Muslim world explaining the presence of Christian troops. The Sharif refused these conditions, but requested that the troops be held in reserve should the necessity arise. On 10 January, Wingate reported to the Foreign Office that the Sharif had made his refusal final, and that he had acknowledged that he could not count on such British assistance in the future. Wingate rightly assumed that the Sharif's *volte face* was a result of the improvement in the military situation.[26] (Indeed, less than two weeks later, Wajh was in the hands of Faysal's troops, thereby ending the threat to Yanbu' and Rabigh.)

[26] Wilson, *Lawrence*, pp. 342–6, 1047–8; FO 686/6, report by George Lloyd on meeting with Sharif, n.d., from December 1916; all of the following, in WO 158/627: Chief, London, to Chief, Egypforce, no. 26663, 16 December 1916; Chief, Egypforce, to Chief, London, no. AM 1475, 5 January 1917; High Commissioner, Egypt, to FO, no. 15, 6 January 1917; Wilson to Arbur, no. W. 142, 7 January 1917; Chief, London, to Chief, Egypforce, no. 27639, 8 January 1917; Wilson to Arbur, no. W. 146, 8 January 1917; FO to High Commissioner, no. 19, 8 January 1917; Arbur to Wilson and Sirdar, no. AB. 562, 9 January 1917; Wilson to Arbur, no. W. 161, 9 January 1917; Wingate to FO, 12 January 1917.

In Rabigh and Yanbu', Faysal mediated between the Harb and the Juhaynah. He also effected a reconciliation between the Masruh Harb who were with the Ottomans, and the Banu Salim Harb who were with the Sharif.[27] Nevertheless, the temporary nature of the various reconciliations was evident from the occasional mutual raiding that still went on.[28] 'Abdallah, who was near Medina, did not come to Rabigh because the tribes concentrated there were mostly 'Ali's Harb, with which 'Abdallah's 'Utaybah were not on good terms.[29] This showed the problem of fighting with a force comprising tribes from different *dirah*s; tribesmen could rarely be used in areas outside their *dirah*: if they were, they often wanted to return home and were harder to keep in the field.[30]

The period of the Rabigh crisis, from July 1916 to January 1917, while frustrating to many British officials, was also a time for Faysal to cement alliances that would be necessary for progression further north. Initially, the situation was bad and there were several desertions stemming from low morale and the feeling that the Ottomans would arrive any day. The fate of the people of al-'Awali (the tribal group who had revolted with Faysal at Medina and were punished by the Ottomans) and other earlier examples of Ottoman revenge were not conducive to supporting the losing side.[31] The Revolt was threatened by an Ottoman occupation of the homes and palm groves of the tribesmen who had joined Faysal. If this happened in any serious fashion, they would melt away to protect their families and economic base.[32] The Juhaynah, wrote Lawrence, might 'fall away ... since they depend entirely on Wadi Yenbo for their existence .... [I]ts lower course contains twenty-four oases of running water and palm-gardens, with a population of perhaps 20,000, mostly slaves, who cultivate the land. The entire tribe ... feeds on the produce of this valley,

27 *AB*, no. 28, 1 November 1916; Colman, pp. 125, 128.

28 Colman, p. 124.

29 FO 371/2776, Pearson, aboard HMS *Dufferin*, off Rabigh, to Arab Bureau, 7 October 1916, cited in Colman, p. 127.

30 Colman, pp. 141–142; *AB*, no. 36, 26 December 1916.

31 *AB*, no. 36, 26 December 1916; *AB*, no. 27, 26 October 1916; Colman, p. 118; Ende, 'The Nakhawila.'

32 Colman, p. 122.

whose occupation, as it is surrounded by rather easy down-country, seems a feasible operation for a considerable Turkish force.'[33]

To sum up, Faysal initially overcame the problems in mobilization with money and rifles, and subsequently had enough successes to be convincing. His personality apparently contributed as well: 'He is accessible to any man who stands outside his tent till he is noticed,' wrote Lawrence, 'and never cuts short a petitioner. He hears every case, and if he does not settle it himself, calls one of his staff to settle it for him. His patience is extreme, and his self-control rather wonderful.'[34] Unlike Ibn Saud, there is little indication that Sharif Husayn himself had a direct connection to the tribes or that he was a charismatic leader. And unlike in the case of Ibn Saud's Wahhabi *da'wah*, there was no ideological attraction for the tribes. But Faysal was charismatic, and he set himself up as an indispensable leader.

The next rung in the ladder north was to win over the Billi in the vicinity of Wajh and their chief, Sulayman ibn Rifadah (Ibn Rifadah). Faysal's move up the coast to Wajh would eliminate the problem of Ottoman attacks on Yanbu' and Rabigh. Such a deployment, an elongation of the Sharifian forces along a north–south axis, would be a serious threat to the railway. The move had been discussed since mid-November 1916, but the Billi were key to its success; to win them over, it was necessary to negotiate with Ibn Rifadah, who, like Husayn ibn Mubarak at Rabigh, led an autonomous tribal polity in the environs of Wajh which was also courted by the Ottomans. Ibn Rifadah was a typical waverer. He was initially seen as pro-Sharif, and there were discussions in early August about supplying him, but soon afterwards those active in the Revolt became suspicious.[35]

The British first approached him on 3 September, but unsuccessfully. Colonel Alfred Parker, who liaised for a time with the Arab forces, interviewed Ibn Rifadah on 16 September 1916 and reported the latter's claim that while personally he supported the

---

[33] *AB*, no. 31, 18 November 1916.

[34] *AB*, no. 36, 26 December 1916.

[35] WP, 139/1/60–61, RNO, Port Sudan, to Hakimam, Khartoum, 3 August 1916; *AB*, no. 14, 7 August 1916; 'Sherif has received letters from Suliman Rifada and states he is alright but meanwhile the latter is, somewhat naturally, taking as much gold as the Turks will give him' (FO 371/2775/182184, Wilson to McMahon, no. 4, 24 August 1916, enclosed in McMahon to Grey, no. 210, 5 September 1916).

Sharif, the Turks were paying many of his tribesmen and that his interests were with the Turks, who had taken him to Damascus where they had decorated and rewarded him. He asked that the British stop blockading his coast.[36] While in late September winning over Sulayman seemed rather hopeless, the Sharif had begun soon afterwards to forbid his markets to the Billi as a pressure tactic, and sent Ibn Rifadah a twenty-day ultimatum (expiring 15 November).[37]

Faysal's efforts to mobilize the tribes while at Yanbu' prior to the advance on Wajh were greatly facilitated by British gold. Even allowing for exaggeration, Lawrence seems to have captured the moment:

[T]he Sherif is generally regarded with great pride, and almost veneration, as an Arab Sultan of immense wealth, and Feisal as his War Lord. His cause has for the moment reconciled the inter-tribal feuds, and Feisal had Billi, Juheinah, and Harb, blood enemies, fighting and living side by side in his army. The Sherif is feeding not only his fighting men but their families, and this is the fattest time the tribes have ever known; nothing else would have maintained a nomad force for five months in the field.[38]

By late November, Faysal had won over a cousin of Sulayman, Hamid Ibn Rifadah, who succeeded in cutting Turkish lines of communication between Wajh and al-'Ula,[39] which was a significant precursor to the advance on Wajh. A British intelligence report from the field noted: '[I]f Wejh can be taken by Faisal … there appears to be reasonable grounds for hoping that the Northern Juheina, a considerable portion of the Billi, and Nuri Nawaf [sic] of Jawf with his tribesmen would all actively cooperate.'[40] While a force of 500–550 men, mostly Juhaynah, Harb and Bisha, made for Wajh on board the HMS *Hardinge*, other ships in the Red

---

36 *AB*, no. 23, 26 September 1916; *HH*, pp. 52, 72–3.

37 *AB*, no. 31, 18 November 1916, citing Lawrence report, 30 October 1916, Yanbu' (also in FO 882/5).

38 *AB*, no. 31, 18 November 1916 (also in FO 882/5).

39 *AB*, no. 34, 11 December 1916.

40 FO 686/6, Intelligence Report, 28 12 1916. 'Nuri Nawaf' referred either to Nuri al-Sha'lan, the paramount chief of the Ruwalah, based primarily at Jawf, or his son, Nawwaf. Faysal had been in contact with Nuri since 1915 or 1916 when he was considering a Revolt in Syria. The British also wanted to establish an airstrip at Jawf (WO 158/626, minute by Clayton on Nuri Sha'lan, 15 November 1916). He was sympathetic to Husayn, but was never totally committed because the Turks controlled his markets.

Sea patrol carried supplies up the coast, with the original intention of making a simultaneous attack with Faysal. This party made a landing at Wajh on 23 January, On 4 January, Faysal began his march north, and he turned it into a spectacle. Even allowing for Lawrence's hyperbole, the procession of over 10,000 must have been a sight to see:

> The march became rather splendid and barbaric. First rode Feisal in white, then Sharraf at his right in red head-cloth and henna-dyed tunic and cloak, myself on his left in white and scarlet, behind us three banners of faded crimson silk with gilt spikes, behind them the drummers playing a march, and behind them again the wild mass of twelve hundred bouncing camels of the bodyguard, packed as closely as they could move, the men in every variety of coloured clothes and the camels nearly as brilliant in their trappings. We filled the valley to its banks with our flashing stream.[41]

Lawrence noticed that even though there were tactical difficulties with the movement of such a mass of people, Faysal's 'reasons for taking with him so large a force were moral and not tactical.'[42] The goal of such a mass movement was to show the tribes the glory and unstoppable nature of the Sharifian advance. Indeed, it was an ancient form of psychological warfare. As he approached Wajh and tribal *shaykh*s began coming in, Faysal wrote letters to *shaykh*s of the Huwaytat, Billi and Bani 'Atiyah, informing them of his pending arrival. The message was most certainly understood.[43]

To be able to leave Yanbu' lightly defended – and moving to Wajh would do just that – Faysal conceived a plan to have 'Abdallah move to Wadi 'Ays, about 100 kilometers north of Medina astride the railway. Supplies could be fed in from Yanbu'. On 9 January 'Abdallah confirmed that he would be moving to Wadi 'Ays, and on or about 18 January news arrived that while on his way there 'Abdallah had captured Sherif Bey, who, according to Lawrence, was a former brigand from Smyrna who had taken up with the Young Turks. Among his personal effects were £20,000 in coin, costly presents, pistols and rifles. The news elated all present, delaying Faysal's advance. 'Abdallah arrived at Wadi 'Ays soon afterwards.

---

41 *SPW*, pp. 140–1.
42 FO 686/6, report by Lawrence, undated, probably late January–early February 1917.
43 *SPW*, p. 151.

By the time Faysal reached Wajh on 25 January, it was already in the hands of the 500 or so troops which the *Hardinge* had landed on 23 January. Admiral Wemyss had decided against waiting for the planned rendezvous with Faysal since he believed that he could no longer feed the men on board and keep proper sanitation. The original landing party helped themselves to looting, which they felt to be their just reward. Ibn Rifadah escaped.[44]

In strictly strategic terms, the combined move to Wadi 'Ays and to Wajh lengthened the Arab front along the railway, threatened Medina and eliminated the threat to Yanbu', Rabigh, and Mecca. In terms of tribal rivalries, alliances, and state building, there were two major results. First, with respect to the Juhaynah, Lawrence wrote that all the tribe's fighting men left the tribe's *dirah* and moved 200 miles north without the goal of attacking another tribe. This was new behavior, and it was in the service of the developing tribal chieftaincy. Second, the capture of Wajh began to bring in much of the Billi, as soon as the column crossed into their *dirah*, which began at Wadi Hamd. In the future, Faysal would also bring in the Huwaytat and the Bani 'Atiyah, an alliance that would enable the capture of 'Aqabah, and end the Hijazi stage of the Arab Revolt.[45]

From Wajh to 'Aqabah: January to July, 1917[46]

The Hashimites had envisioned Syria as part of a post-war Arab state headed by them, and they believed that it had been promised to them by the British. There had been plans for the Revolt to actually begin in Syria, and Faysal had been in contact with Arab nationalists and tribal leaders there. But once in Wajh, the next step became crucial. Now that Faysal had taken Wajh, Brémond, chief of the French mission in the Hijaz, lobbied for the landing of

---

44 An undated and unsigned memo on Ibn Rifadah found in the files of the British Agency in Jeddah notes that the shaykh was loyal to the Turks all along, and 'was blown up at Kalaat el-Akhdar by Sharifian troops on 12 December 1917' (FO 686/137).

45 This section on the advance on Wajh is based primarily on *SPW*, pp. 137–64; George MacMunn and Cyril Fall, *Military Operations: Egypt and Palestine, From the Outbreak of the War with Germany to June 1917* (London: HMSO, 1928), pp. 234–7; Wilson, *Lawrence*, pp. 348–58; Lawrence in *AB*, no. 41, 6 February 1917; *AB*, no. 42, 28 February 1917; FO 686/6, report by Lawrence, undated, probably late January–early February 1917.

46 This section draws on Wilson, *Lawrence*, pp. 359–417; primary sources are cited in specific notes.

allied troops at 'Aqabah in order to block a Hashimite advance on Syria, which the French coveted. The British wanted Faysal to concentrate on Medina, where an Ottoman garrison was still holding out, and continued to do so until January 1919. But Faysal was influenced by Lawrence, who, in February 1917 (according to his biographer Jeremy Wilson) told Faysal about the May 1916 Sykes–Picot Agreement to divide the former Ottoman Empire between the British, French and Russians. Lawrence impressed upon him the need to capture the Syrian interior in order to be in a strong bargaining position opposite France after the war. A thrust north along the right flank of General Allenby's Egyptian Expeditionary Force (EEF) would assure arms and supplies. Knowledge of Sykes–Picot must have added to Faysal's sense of urgency and made him more determined than ever to concentrate his efforts on the north.

The British interest in Medina derived primarily from their fear that Ottoman troops holding the city might go to Palestine and aid the Ottomans fighting the British there. Britain was also sensitive to French objections to an Arab thrust into Syria. Nonetheless, in April 1917 Faysal and Lawrence planned to take 'Aqabah. Lawrence was convinced that when the occupation of 'Aqabah was a *fait accompli*, the High Command would be grateful. He later wrote, 'So I decided to go my own way, with or without orders.'[47]

Faysal delayed, however, feeling that he needed to establish good relations with the tribes to the north. The British High Commissioner in Egypt and Husayn wrote to Faysal, telling him to head east and occupy a position on the railway such as al-'Ula (due east of Wajh), but Faysal argued that he was still too busy bringing in tribes and keeping them on his side. He assured his father that, before long, Mecca would 'soon hear of the capture of El Ula or Medain Salah.'[48] He apparently made no serious efforts in this direction – his mind was set on Syria.

The move to 'Aqabah was made possible by developments in tribal bargaining, which at times enhanced Faysal's position and at times held him back. As the *Arab Bulletin* reported in early February, the Billi 'came in as one man to be enrolled' immediately after the fall of Wajh. They were followed by sections of the Banu

[47] *SPW*, p. 226.
[48] FO 686/10, Joyce (Wajh) to Wilson, 2 April 1917, forwarding Faysal to Sharif.

'Atiyah and the Huwaytat under 'Awda Abu Tayh and Shadhli Alyan. Professions of allegiance had also arrived from the Ruwallah of Nuri Sha'lan, the leaders of Karak (the Majalis), and Fawwaz al-Fa'iz, the head of the major section of the Banu Sakhr.[49] But it was also reported that, for reasons which remain unclear, the Billi were not cooperating; they may have been difficult because Faysal had no funds, camels or rifles to give them, despite Faysal having wired Wilson and his father repeatedly for them. (Joyce, who was responsible for British logistics at Wajh and later 'Aqabah, supported many of these requests, stressing that it would be difficult to keep so many men in the field without them.) Moreover, the Juhaynah were growing uncomfortable being so far away from their *dirah*, and were 'gradually slipping away.'[50]

Faysal reported a constant stream of tribal leaders throughout March, April and May 1917, including sections of the Banu Sakhr, Shararat, Huwaytat and Ruwallah, the most important being the latter two. 'Awdah Abu Tayh himself arrived in early April, as did five *shaykhs* of Nuri Sha'lan's Ruwallah, including a favorite nephew.[51] 'Awdah was a legendary figure, and his enthusiasm for the Revolt fed on his extreme dislike of the Turks. According to the Czech explorer Alois Musil, who was friendly with 'Awdah, the Ottomans issued a warrant against him in 1908 for having shot two gendarmes who came to arrest him for not paying tribute. 'Awdah claimed that he had paid it; when they tried to arrest him, he shot them both.[52] Lawrence recalled 'Awdah's horror when,

49 *AB*, no. 41, 6 February 1917.
50 FO 882/6, Lawrence notebook entry, 14 February 1917, cited and quoted in Wilson, *Lawrence*, p. 367; FO 686/10, Faysal to Wilson, 27 March 1916; FO 686/10, Wilson to Husayn, 30 March 1917, relaying message from Faysal, 28 March 1917; FO 686/10, Joyce to Wilson, no. 472, 2 April 1917, relaying message from Faysal to Sharif; FO 686/6, Joyce to Wilson, received Jeddah 4 April 1917; FO 686/6, part 2, Joyce to Director, Arab Bureau, received Jeddah 20 [30?] April 1917. The absence of the Billi was noted even after the capture of 'Aqabah (see *AB*, no. 57, 24 July 1917; Bassett to Arbur, no. W. 175, 27 October 1917, relaying message from Faysal to Husayn, via Joyce, noting that Zayd wanted to replace Sulayman ibn Rifadah with his cousin, Hamid ibn Rifadah as head shaykh of the Billi).
51 *AB*, no. 45, 23 March 1917; FO 686/10, Wilson to Husayn, 30 March 1917; *AB*, no. 47, 11 April 1917; FO 686/10, Wilson to Husayn, 6 April 1917, relaying message from Faysal; FO 686/6, part 2, Joyce (Wejh) to Director, Arab Bureau, 9 April 1917; *AB*, no. 48, 21 April 1917.
52 Alois Musil, *The Northern Hegaz: A Topographical Itinerary* (New York: American Geographical Society, 1928), p. 8.

while visiting Faysal, he suddenly recalled that he was wearing false teeth provided by the Turks. He promptly left Faysal's tent and destroyed them. (After the capture of 'Aqabah Wingate sent him an Egyptian dentist to make him another set.[53]) In Lawrence's *Seven Pillars of Wisdom*, 'Awdah is cruel, bloodthirsty, audacious, and extremely anti-Turk. Lawrence wrote:

He loses no opportunity of adding to his enemies and relishes the new situation most because it is an ideal excuse to take on the Turkish government. 'To the Mutessarif of Kerak from abu Tayi … greeting. Take notice to quit Arab territory before the end of Ramadan. We want it for ourselves. Should you not go, I declare you outlawed and God will decide between us.'

Faysal's success at bringing in tribes was due in part to the material advantages he provided for them. (On 21 February the War Office approved for this purpose an additional 30,000 rifles and 15 million rounds.) The other basis of his success was the settling of disputes among tribal groups. As stressed before, the tribes were autonomous; all alliances were temporary and predicated on Faysal's personality, guns, ammunition, British sovereigns and the promise of plunder. The Huwaytat made up with the Banu Sakhr, and Faysal persuaded 'Awdah to make a peace offering to a rival Huwaytat clan led by Hamid al-'Ar'ar ibn Jazi, who was pro-Ottoman and had been decorated by the empire in late January or early February 1917.[54] In one of the best-known cases of the settling of feuds, in March 1917, Lawrence executed a man rather than let a blood feud develop.[55]

The advance on 'Aqabah from Wajh began 9 May: it included Sharifs Nasir and Shakir, 'Awdah, the Syrian Nasib al-Bakri, Lawrence and about forty-five tribesmen. The party carried £20,000 in gold sovereigns and large quantities of explosives. Nasir and 'Awdah spent much time recruiting around Ma'an and 'Aqabah, and the latter went to Nuri Sha'lan to explain what was happening. Lawrence, too, set out for Syria, and met Sha'lan. The party reunited at Ba'ir, north-east of Ma'an on 28 June. On 2 July, the

---

53 *AB*, no. 57, 24 July 1917; *SPW*, p. 222. Musil, p. 8, recounts stories of 'Awdah eating the heart of his kills.

54 *AB* no. 45, 23 March 1917; *AB*, no. 47, 11 April 1917; Colman, pp. 125–7; Musil, pp. 7, 13, 18.

55 *SPW*, p. 181; Wilson, *Lawrence*, pp. 382, 1061–2.

Ottoman garrison was defeated at Abu al-Lisan. This was followed by the move on 'Aqabah, which was captured after a charge by 'Awdah; the town surrendered on 6 July 1917. Faysal arrived from Wajh in August; the Revolt in the Hijaz was now over.

The capture of 'Aqabah wrought several changes in the nature of the Revolt, had long-term implications for relations between Faysal and Husayn, and shaped Husayn's concept of his state. The British High Command had discussed the possibility that once Faysal's troops headed north they would be under the control of Allenby's EEF, which was still, in the summer of 1917, blocked outside Gaza. Lawrence, Clayton and Allenby all supported a move north by Faysal to harass the Ottoman flank. Allenby, however, would need Husayn's agreement that Faysal be subordinate to Allenby. Lawrence met Husayn on 22 July to discuss the matter. Husayn agreed, because he wanted his troops to advance into Syria. He sent Faysal a letter, giving him a free hand dealing directly with Allenby, to 'facilitate the cooperation between my army and that of Great Britain.' The British may have thought that Faysal was now authorized to deal with them independently, but this was not the case. Moreover, the letter did not state that Faysal would be under Allenby's command. Clayton had an inkling that Husayn would begin to make things difficult for Faysal but wrote: '[Husayn] has given his approval for the above arrangements and every effort will be made to prevent him [from] interfering with Emir Feisal.'[56]

Tribal brinkmanship: confrontation at Qunfudhah

While Husayn was concentrating on the Revolt in the Hijaz, to the south in 'Asir were the problems of the Idrisi's rival chieftaincy and the ensuing competition for tribal support. In early 1916, the Sharif had been in touch with the Idrisi, in hopes that he would join Husayn in the Revolt. His efforts to coopt the 'Asiri chieftain yielded no actual agreement, for this man, whom the Sharif regarded as an upstart and 'a poor type of Azhar student, a man who will sell you a charm to hang round your neck for a few

---

[56] Baker, pp. 135–6; Wilson, *Lawrence*, pp. 418–35; WO 158/629, Clayton to General Staff Operations, 9 August 1917.

piastres,'[57] had his own plans.

In about mid-June 1916, the Idrisi began preparations for an attack on Qunfudhah, Abha and Muhayl. He announced these plans to the Political Resident in Aden, alluding to his contacts with Husayn. The Resident wished him success.[58] His references to the Sharif were mere window dressing, an appeal to British sentiments about Arab working with Arab.[59] The British appeared to be unaware that, beyond the goal of fighting the Ottomans, the Idrisi had the more specific goal of extending his domain northwards toward the Sharif's territory.

It will be remembered from Chapter 2 that the British had signed a secret treaty with the Idrisi in April 1915: he would fight the Ottomans and the British would supply him. On 18 July British ships began bombarding Ottoman-occupied Qunfudhah. One ship conveyed the Idrisi garrison, mostly tribesmen from Birk. The Idrisi flag was raised.

Husayn reacted strongly upon hearing that the Idrisi had been aided by his allies, the British. At the end of July, in an act of brinkmanship, he instructed his loyalist Nasir ibn Muhammad of Lith (Nasir had taken Lith for the Sharif in June) to head for Qunfudhah. The British naval officers held firm, and told Nasir that the port was under British protection; if Nasir attacked, the British would defend.

It does not seem that Husayn wished to carry the Arab Revolt southward; more probably, he wanted to prevent the Idrisi from

57 FO 686/37, Wilson to Director, Arab Bureau, 29 November 1917, enclosing note by Cornwallis.
58 WP, 140/3/99, Political Resident, Aden, to Idrisi, no. 552, 14 June 1916. British responsibility for the Idrisi was under the Aden Residency which answered to the Indian Government. Aden was not enthusiastic about his prospects, and was lackadaisical about providing the Idrisi with arms and ammunition. In the end, Aden provided only 3,000 guns and 200,000 rounds of ammunition out of the 6,000 rifles and 11 million rounds authorized (Busch, p. 229). Clayton, who seems to have understood from the beginning what made the Revolt run, wrote Wingate: 'I only hope that Aden will adequately support the Idrisi. It is extraordinary how lukewarm our Government are in the help they give their friends. They do not yet seem to have learnt from the Germans, and even the Turks, that money spent generously at the right moment saves subsequent expenditure of millions. It is time we gave up our purist ideas [and] traditions about bribery and realized that – in many cases – friendship comes to those who pay for it.' (WP, 136/2/42–45, Clayton to Wingate, 4 February 1916.)
59 FO 371/2773, Resident (Aden), to Foreign (Simla), 30 June 1916.

moving further north. In any case, Husayn's move seems to have caught the British off guard, and seems to have been one of the very first occasions when officials higher up realized that Husayn did not hold sway in Arabia in the way that some tended to attribute to him. Confusion also reigned because communications were carried out by wireless involving British ships anchored off Qunfudhah and Jeddah, the Naval Command in Port Sudan, Wingate in Khartoum, McMahon in Cairo and the Foreign Office in London.

Meanwhile C.E. Wilson, who was billeted aboard HMS *Dufferin* which was moored off Jeddah before taking up his post as Pilgrimage Officer, was asked to tell the Sharif that if he persisted in his move on Qunfudhah, it would delay the arrival of his arms, food and money and would moreover complicate relations with HMG.

The Idrisi's attack on Qunfudhah had begun before he enlisted the support of the nearby Hali tribes, and when the British warned Husayn to leave Qunfudhah alone, he produced a letter from thirteen shaykhs in the area, including those of Hali, who stated their refusal to be led by the Idrisi. Wilson urged McMahon to have HM's ships hold their fire and instead remove the Idrisi's garrison from the town. Apparently unaware of the treaty between the British and the Idrisi, Wilson telegraphed, 'I hope information is being sent me giving full particulars as to any existing treaties, agreements or promises made to Sherif, Idrisi or any other Arabian chiefs by HM Govt.'[60]

As the British attempted negotiations in the first days of August, the Sharif stood firm. He chided the British for having conveyed Idrisi troops to Qunfudhah if they were really his allies, said that the situation could not be arbitrated until the Hijaz was free of Ottoman troops, and demanded that the British either remove the Idrisi or stand aside as the necessary battle ensued. Indeed, Husayn told the British that they must choose between him and the Idrisi; he believed that much of 'Asir and its tribes belonged to the Hashimites, particularly after he had captured Qunfudhah for the Ottomans a few years earlier.

As the confrontation reached the brink, both sides became more committed to battle, spurred on by the concomitant threat

---

60 WP, 139/1/10–14, Wilson to RNO, Port Sudan, 2 August 1991.

to their prestige if one or the other backed down. The Sharif believed that any backing down would undermine his ability to enlist tribes and continue the war effort. He held firm, and would accept no compromise offered by the British, who were slowly beginning to realize that the two rulers had more against each other than in common as part of some grand, British-inspired notion of Arabs united against the Ottomans. McMahon was soon convinced that the Idrisi should withdraw from Qunfudhah, since Husayn was the main Arab protagonist in this war and said that control of the town could be decided after it.

When the Idrisi was ordered to withdraw within forty-eight hours, he protested against the humiliation of having been given such an ultimatum and begged to have twenty days so that representatives of the two sides could meet and his prestige would not be destroyed. On 21 August the meeting took place on board HMS *Northbrook* anchored off Birk. The Sharifian representative said everything up to Birk belonged to Husayn, the Idrisi's representative rejected the claim, and they agreed to postpone the discussion of boundaries. They settled on a withdrawal that would enable the Idrisi to save face, and the evacuation was completed by 25 August 1916.

The crisis at Qunfudhah has a tribal dimension whose particulars most British officials did not consider.[61] Scholarship, too, has also tended to focus on the diplomatic aspects of this episode, without taking fully into account its tribal underpinnings.[62] But the conflict was essentially that: a conflict between two leaders of tribal chieftaincies over influence among certain tribal groups along their borders. Both the Idrisi and Husayn were concerned lest their behavior in the confrontation undermine their influence among these tribes. Clearly, there was still much rancor left over from the battle of 1911, when several *shaykhs* – representing nearly all the tribes on the Qunfudhah–Muhayl road – deserted the Idrisi and joined the Sharif and the Ottomans. In response, the Idrisi took many of the *shaykhs*' sons hostage. Five years later, on the eve of the Sharif's uprising, these leaders had been intriguing with the Sharif to secure their return, and it was these *shaykhs* who signed

---

61 An exception was Lt. L.F. Nalder, a political officer from the Red Sea patrol assigned to the Idrisi.

62 See, for instance, Busch, pp. 236–43.

the document that Husayn submitted to the British in claiming Qunfudhah.[63]

One of the Idrisi's aides, Sayyid Mustafa al-Idrisi, speaking with the British in Cairo, put his master's goals into surprising perspective. He said, 'By the present incident of Kunfida, the Sherif lost the active help of the Idrisi against the Turks, our common enemy ... As far as I know the Idrisi will not object to the Sharif of Mecca having a suzerainty over the whole of Arabia as a Khalif of the Moslems, or even as Sultan of the Arabs, provided the Sherif will not interfere with him in his own region, and does not trespass on his limits. There is, therefore, no meaning in the Sherif maintaining his claim to Kunfida as he can be general master of all of Arabia. The Idrisi has greater influence in Arabia than the Sherif of Mecca seems to think.'[64] The comment was either a recognition of the Idrisi's own limitations, or a ruse.

The Sharif's hold on Qunfudhah was tenuous, as demonstrated less than two months later when the town was recaptured by the Ottomans, assisted by the Hali, which had previously supported the Sharif. The *Arab Bulletin* noted that the Ottomans soon withdrew somewhat inland out of fear of a British naval bombardment, but their move intimidated the 'Utaybah tribesmen holding the town for the Sharif. In early December 1916 the 'Utaybah deserted Qunfudhah and set the local market on fire, an illustration of the unstable, *ad hoc* nature of Husayn's chieftaincy. Muhammad Nasir, Husayn's loyalist, escaped by dhow to Lith.[65]

---

63 This analysis of the confrontation at Qunfudhah in 1916 is based primarily on documents in the Wingate Papers: see the telegraph traffic and other correspondence in 136/4/59–61; 139/1/7–101; 139/2/9–12, 31–33, 66–71, 93–97; 139/3/16–17, 23, 64–67, 96; 139/4/12–13; 139/6/74; 139/7/15. Of particular interest is a series of letters between the Idrisi and the officers of the Red Sea patrol, as well as a cogent analysis by Nalder, all in one packet with a covering letter by R. Wemyss, Vice Admiral, Naval Commander-in-Chief, East Indies and Egypt, to McMahon (WP, 140/3/80–101). Also consulted were FO 371/2774/14935, McMahon to FO, no. 643, 31 July 1916; FO 371/2774/151769, McMahon to FO, no. 655, 3 August 1916; FO 371/2774/153550, McMahon to FO, no. 668, 5 August 1916; FO 371/2774/154595, FO to McMahon, no. 675, 7 August 1916; FO 371/2774/151769, FO to McMahon, no. 664, 8 August 1916; FO 371/2774/158847, McMahon to FO, no. 688, 13 August 1916; FO 371/2774/170494, McMahon to FO, no. 731, 29 August 1916; *AB*, no. 11, 17 July 1916; *AB*, no. 13, 1 August 1916; *AB*, no. 14, 7 August 1916; *AB*, no. 15, 10 August 1916; *AB*, no. 16, 18 August 1916; *AB*, no. 17, 30 August 1916. See also Busch, pp. 236–43; for details on the tribes involved, see *AH*.

64 *AB*, no. 30, 15 November 1916.

65 *AB*: no. 26, 16 October 1916; no. 27, 26 October; no. 37, 4 January 1917.

The British signed a supplemental treaty with the Idrisi on 22 January 1917 – motivated mostly out of suspicion of Italian designs in the Red Sea – under which he would occupy Kamaran Island, a pilgrimage quarantine station.[66] In the constant circle of intrigue among the British, the Idrisi, the Imam of Yemen, Ibn Saud and the Sharif, the Sharif was now concerned lest the Idrisi form an alliance with the Imam. As 1917 wore on, the Sharif grew increasingly suspicious of British contacts and agreements with the Idrisi (as well as with Ibn Saud; see below). The British assured Husayn that nothing in their treaty with the Idrisi would hinder the Revolt, but the Sharif claimed that by not blockading 'Asir the British were in effect aiding the Ottomans. In May and June 1917 he urged the British to put pressure on the Idrisi and Ibn Saud to recognize him as leader of the Arab movement. Meanwhile Wingate, in Egypt, was unwilling to approach the Idrisi formally on the subject.[67]

In mid- and late summer 1917, both Imam Yahya of Yemen and the Idrisi asked the British for support, each claiming to have won over the important Hashid and Bakil tribal confederation. Yahya was ready to go over to the British if they would guarantee to remove the Idrisi from 'Asir and turn it over to him, an offer that was rejected outright. But operating on the premise that the Idrisi had made tribal gains, Wingate endorsed an infusion to the Idrisi of £25,000 and necessary foodstuffs. The Idrisi seemed ready to take action against the Ottomans in Yemen, and Wingate and the Resident in Aden were relieved to think that he would not be infringing on Husayn. The Resident noted that the Idrisi was being spoken of in many letters as 'our master and ruler.' The Foreign Office sanctioned additional funds to the Idrisi for doling out to various tribes, by which action the British believed that they had done all that was politically and diplomatically feasible to

---

66 Busch, pp. 238–41; FO 371/3042/39128, supplemental treaty with the Idrisi, enclosed in Major-General J.M. Stewart Political Resident, Aden to Secretary to the Government of India, Foreign Department, Delhi, 26 January 1917.

67 FO 371/3045/23976, Wingate to FO, no. 85, 30 January 1916; FO 371/3042/39128, IO to FO, 19 February 1916, enclosing Agreement with the Idrisi Saiyid regarding the Farasan Islands and other Matters, 22 January 1916; FO 686/34, Husayn to High Commissioner, 28 April 1917; FO 371/3054/11799, IO to FO, no. P. 2152, 12 June 1917; FO 371/3054, Secretary of State for India to Viceroy, Foreign Department, no. P 2502, 23 June 1917; FO 371/3054/137978, Wingate to FO, no. 730, 12 July 1917.

encourage the Idrisi to act.[68]

The clash at Qunfudhah showed continuity from the past. There may have been an *Arab* Revolt going on, but the network of social and political interaction was still very much dominated by tribal considerations and relations with rival leaders of tribal confederacies.

The Saudi challenge

Husayn's other continuing nemesis during the Revolt was Ibn Saud. Their rivalry for control of the tribes, particularly the 'Utaybah, was longstanding. Husayn's own greater aspirations, and the large sums of money given to him by the British for distribution among the tribes, aggravated the relationship with Ibn Saud, who had no equivalent source of funds. One might assume that Ibn Saud had in the back of his mind the intention of regaining his patrimony in the Hijaz – occupied during the first Saudi state (1744–1818) – when the proper time arrived. Husayn would have no place in this scheme, of course.

When the Revolt broke out, 'Abdallah's 1915 move against Ibn Saud in Qasim was still fresh (see Chapter 2). According to one report, Ibn Saud felt particularly bitter about the event, because it had occurred when he was suppressing the 'Ujman further east, and thus was ill prepared at Qasim.[69] Now, in 1917, the two were being pushed to cooperate with each other under British tutelage. India and other officials in the Gulf and Iraq tended to support Ibn Saud, while London and Cairo leaned toward Husayn.

The two protagonists began diplomatic contacts because the British wished it, but they despised each other. Husayn feared that his tribes would succumb to the Wahhabi *da'wah*, while Ibn Saud feared Hashimite encroachment on Najd. While sometimes showing a glimpse of understanding, the British often failed to

---

68 FO 371/3045/14243, Resident, Aden, to IO, no. 409 AP, 20 July 1917; FO 371/3056/165854, Wingate to FO, no. 890, 23 August 1917; FO 371/3056/180312, FO to Wingate, no. 877, 7 September 1916; FO 371/3056/176298, Resident, Aden, to FO, no. 449, 9 September 1917; FO 371/3056/183233, Resident, Aden, to FO, no. 456 AP, 20 September 1917; FO 371/3056/189747, Wingate to FO, no. 1025, 1 October 1917; FO 371/3060/214021, Resident, Aden, to FO, 13 October 1917; FO 371/3056/196702, FO to Wingate, no. 979, 15 October 1917; FO 371/3056/205118, Wingate to FO, no. 1121, 25 October 1917; *AB*, no. 68, 7 November 1917; *AB*, no. 71, 27 November 1917.

69 *AB*, no. 33, 4 December 1916.

fathom that the Arabian tribal system, and not the British war effort, determined the behavior of the two men.

Massive British funds given to the Hashimites had by now brought much of the 'Utaybah over to Husayn. 'Abdallah, who was put in charge of them, and his protégé, Shakir ibn Zayd, apparently considered themselves bedouin of the 'Utaybah tribe.[70] Ibn Saud regarded this state of affairs as a move against him.

In the summer of 1916, when the Revolt broke out, Ibn Saud was in a weak position tribally, his following having been depleted by Husayn and 'Abdallah. Remarkably, he even asked Husayn for a loan of £6,000; he was granted £2,000. There is evidence that in the years 1913–14, and at least until early 1915, when both stepped up their actions against the Ottomans, Ibn Saud and the Sharif were on fairly good terms. Captain Shakespear reported that they were in correspondence when he first visited Riyadh in spring 1915, and had been 'acting in concert' in January 1915 ('Abdallah did not make his move on Qasim until November of that year). This may explain Husayn's willingness to give him a loan. He gave the Sharif in return 'two dromedaries, two high bred horses and other things.' 'We inform your Grandeur,' he continued, 'that we are loyal and obedient and ready to serve. We and our people are ready to obey your demand, may God grant you victory.'[71] But when the British officially communicated the news of the Revolt's outbreak to Ibn Saud, noting that the Sharif had declared the independence of 'the Arabs' as a whole, Ibn Saud communicated to Sir Percy Cox his fear that the Sharif might claim parts of Najd. Ibn Saud felt that the Sharif had been carried away by ambition. He said that he and Husayn had long been at odds over interference in Najd, that Najd would refuse to be under anyone else but himself, and that anyhow, in Mecca the Sharif had never been independent, having only recently become so.[72]

70 FO 686/6, part two, Lawrence to Wilson, 16 April 1917, report on visit to 'Abdallah in Wadi 'Ays.
71 FO 371/3044/35392, report on relations with Ibn Saud, A.T. Wilson, Iraq section, Arab Bureau, to Director, Arab Bureau, Cairo, 12 January 1917). FO 371/2783/23312 report by Ruhi, 25 October 1916, enclosed in McMahon to FO, 3 November 1916 (also excerpted in *AB*, no. 29, 8 November 1916); Kostiner, dissertation, pp. 37–8.
72 FO 371/2776, Ibn Saud to Cox, 19 Ramadan 1334 [20 July 1916]; Colman, p. 284; Goldberg, p. 140; see also FO 686/14, Arbur (Basra), to Arbur (Cairo), 5 September 1916, citing a communication from Ibn Saud, 25 June 1916.

When Husayn wrote to Ibn Saud in early August 1916 request-ing assistance, he may already have conceived of himself as the leader of all the Arabs and Ibn Saud as a mere follower, and may well have interpreted Ibn Saud's earlier gifts as a sign of subservi-ence. On 13 August Ibn Saud sent a straightforward answer: any help that he would offer would depend on Husayn's noninter-ference in the tribes and territories of Najd. Reaffirming his posi-tion on the matter, Ibn Saud asked the British where HMG stood,[73] and it was at this stage, in late September and early October 1916, that they decided to tell Husayn about their 1915 treaty with Ibn Saud, in order that his reply to the ruler of Najd would be appropri-ate.[74] At the instruction of the Foreign Office, Wilson assured Husayn that HMG was encouraging Ibn Saud to support him. But Wilson also reminded the Sharif that he 'had agreed that treaties made by His Majesty's Government with other Arabic Chiefs should be respected' and told Husayn that there was nothing in the treaty that was incompatible with 'the engagements' made between him and the British.[75] Husayn now realized that his own allies had promised to recognize the territories of his principal rival.

The British had hoped to influence the tenor of Husayn's response to Ibn Saud's statement of 13 August, but the Sharif had already written him a stinging reply on 5 September 1916: 'Your observations ... can only emanate from a man bereft of his reason or [having] an absent mind.' The Sharif's letter, wrote Cox wryly, 'was[,] to say the least[,] unconciliatory.'[76]

Throughout the following months, Ibn Saud was solicitous of the British wish that he cooperate with Husayn, but he had little intention of helping his rival. On 30 October 1916, replying to 'Abdallah, who had also written to him requesting support, he said that he was ready to help, but that he could not attack the Otto-

---

73 FO 371/2044, Ibn Saud to Husain, 13 Shawwal 1334 [13 August 1916]; FO 371/2769/180391, Arab Bureau (Cox), Basra, to [Arab] Bureau, Cairo, no. 4523, 8 September 1916; Goldberg, p. 140.

74 FO 371/2769/187737, FO to McMahon, no. 776, 23 September 1916; FO 686/14, Arbur to Wilson, no. I.G. 1543, 30 September 1916.

75 FO 686/14, Wilson to Husayn, 3 October 1916; see also Goldberg, p. 148.

76 FO 371/3044/35392, A.T. Wilson, Iraq section, Arab Bureau, to Director, Arab Bureau, Cairo, 12 January 1917, cover letter and enclosing Ibn Saud to Husayn, 13 Shawwal 1334 [13 August 1916] and Husayn to Ibn Saud, 6 Dhu al-Qa'dah 1334 [5 September 1916].

mans because would leave his flank open to Ibn Rashid, the tribal ruler of Ha'il.[77]

Ibn Saud went out of his way to show his goodwill to the British, tolerating insults from Husayn that at any other time might have been settled by the sword. He even offered, in communications with Cox, to send one of his sons with a fighting force to help Husayn, but Ibn Saud required first that the Sharif send him a letter requesting this.[78] The situation was a paradigmatic example of the best of Saudi diplomacy. On the one hand, Ibn Saud knew the British would realize that his offer involved, as a guarantee of good faith, the tribal custom of sending a son to be hostage; on the other hand, Ibn Saud would have known that Husayn would not send such a letter. Ibn Saud's forbearance was surely tried when he learned that Husayn contrived to be proclaimed King of the Arabs by the notables of Mecca. Husayn wrote to him about this development, signing himself 'King of Arabian Countries.'[79] (See below.)

Ibn Saud's diplomacy was successful: the British granted him a small six-month subsidy of £5,000 a month; 3,000 rifles were also promised. His cooperation with HMG contrasted sharply with Husayn's self-aggrandizement. By the end of the year, the Foreign Office regarded Ibn Saud's approach as 'very satisfactory,' while the Sharif was disparaged for 'repelling' the ruler of Najd 'whom the British Government had attracted to his support.'[80] This was an early indication that Husayn was to have trouble keeping the British – his sole source of real support – on his side.

In early 1917, the British informed Husayn that his Najdi rival was now receiving a regular subsidy and had been given 3,000 rifles. Faysal reasoned that Husayn might not be so angry at the growing British–Saudi relationship if HMG could persuade Ibn Saud to recognize the Sharif at least as 'leader of the Arab movement.' Sykes endorsed this, but it was rejected by Cox, who

[77] FO 371/2782/322002, Ibn Saud to Sherif Abdulla, 15 Dhu al-Hijjah [30 October 1916], enclosed in Lt. Col. C.E. Wilson to Sir A.H. McMahon, no. 14, 5 November 1916. Excerpts also in *AB*, no. 32, 26 November 1916.

[78] FO 371/2769/E 22470, Cox to GI, 13 November 1916, and FO 371/2769/E 236884, Cox to GI, 21 November 1916, both cited in Goldberg, p. 144.

[79] FO 371/3044. Husain to Ibn Saud, 18 Muharram 1335 [15 November 1916], enclosed in Ibn Saud to Cox, n.d., enclosed in Cox to Arab Bureau, 1 February 1917, cited in Goldberg, p. 148. Husayn was proclaimed King of the Arab Lands in October 1916.

[80] Goldberg, p. 148.

argued that it would make Ibn Saud suspicious of Britain.[81]

Throughout the summer of 1917, Husayn rained down insult after insult on Ibn Saud. He called Ibn Saud 'as convicted a *kafir* (infidel) as the Turks,' and said that Ibn Saud should 'first come and kiss [his] feet.'[82] He accused the Najdi ruler of using the arms provided by Britain to stir up a movement against him (there is no reason to doubt this). Ibn Saud's continuing strategy was to ingratiate himself with HMG – he turned a deaf ear to the insults and sent 'Abdallah a friendly letter and a valuable brood mare.[83]

That the threat of Ibn Saud occupied the Hashimites nearly as much as the Revolt was exemplified by 'Abdallah's singular lack of participation in the war effort. The British had often complained about 'Abdallah's attitude. Lawrence visited him in Wadi 'Ays in March 1917. 'Abdallah, he wrote, spent his time playing practical jokes on one hapless Muhammad Hasan and did not seem interested in attacking Medina.[84] To the British such 'indolence' was incomprehensible, as they did not realize that 'Abdallah was guarding the Hashimite flank in what amounted to an unannounced second front, and extending his hold over the 'Utaybah, a position essential to preventing a Wahhabi expansion into the Hijaz.[85]

Inevitably, Husayn stood out in sharp contrast to Ibn Saud, angering the British by not putting his rivalries aside for the sake of larger British war goals. Less canny than Ibn Saud, perhaps, and certainly less effective as a strategist, Husayn seems not to have

---

81 FO 686/14, Pearson, Jeddah, to Husayn, 14 February 1917; FO 371/3054/117999, J.E. Shuckburough, India Office, to Under Secretary of State, Foreign Office, 12 June 1917 [650]; Goldberg, pp. 153–154. This request was repeated to Sykes during a meeting between Faysal, Husayn, Picot and Sykes in Jeddah on 20 May 1917, where Faysal said that his father agreed 'to cooperate with France in Syria … and England in Mesopotamia but we ask for help from England with Idrisi and Ibn Saud without in any way infringing on their independence. We beg that Great Britain will endeavour to induce them to recognize [the] King's position as leader of the Arab movement' (FO/371/3054/101269, Sykes (Aden), to FO, 24 May 1917). This meeting is discussed further below.

82 Goldberg, p. 155; Colman, p. 338–339.

83 Bassett to Arbur, no. W 1031, 1 June 1917; FO 686/14, Joyce, Wajh, to Clayton, GHQ, Cairo, 10 June 1916 [616]; FO 686/14, Fu'ad al-Khatib to Bassett, 30 May 1917.

84 FO 686/6, part 2, report of visit to Wadi 'Ays, 16 April 1917 (also excerpted in *AB* no. 51, 23 May 1917). Both 'Abdallah and his father had a penchant for practical jokes; see 'Abdallah, pp. 11–13.

85 Colman, p. 286.

understood the British as well as his rival did. Ibn Saud used the period of the war in the Peninsula to increase Wahhabi propaganda, strengthen his hold over tribes, squeeze a subsidy out of the British and simultaneously prove to them how reasonable he was. Any credit Husayn had with the British was seriously eroded, and his relations with Ibn Saud were in large part responsible.

Trying to reconcile the unreconcilable: Hashimite ambitions vs. British and French territorial imperatives

Husayn to the Islamic world: the initial proclamations of the Revolt. Husayn was acutely aware that in leading a revolt against the Ottoman Sultan-Caliph, he had rebelled against the centuries-old Islamic order. To affirm that he was not causing *fitnah* (divisiveness in the community of believers), he repeatedly claimed that he was doing his duty to rebel against a leader who violates the *shari'ah*. This justification appears in a series of proclamations and articles published in early issues of Husayn's newspaper, *al-Qiblah*.[86]

The first proclamation, published in Egypt on 25 Sha'ban 1334 [26 June 1916],[87] was primarily a diatribe against the CUP; it was guilty, Husayn insisted, of oppressing the Hijazi economy, murdering Arab nationalists, and violating the *shari'ah*. Husayn bemoaned the economic woes of the Hijaz caused by the entry of the Ottomans into the First World War, and by the ensuing British blockade (for which, it will be remembered, he was greatly responsible): 'The middle class,' he proclaimed, '[has been forced to] sell the doors of their houses, their chests of drawers and even the wood from the ceilings of their houses, after selling all their furniture and clothes in order to appease their hunger.' He decried the brutality of the ruling Ottoman triumvirate of Enver, Talaat, and Jemal, in the hanging of twenty-one Arab nationalists. And he attacked, at length, the CUP

---

86 The text of these proclamations can also be found in: *RMM* 46 (1921), pp. 1–22; *RMM* 47 (1921), pp. 1–27, *RMM* 50 (1922), pp. 74–100, where they appear in Arabic and French; the first proclamation appears in English in FO 371/2775/196445. They have been discussed in William L. Cleveland, 'The Role of Islam as a Political Ideology in the First World War,' in Edward Ingram (ed.), *National and International Politics in the First World War: Essays in Honor of Elie Kedourie* (London: Cass, 1986), pp. 84–101; and in Dawn, pp. 75–86.

87 It was not published in *al-Qiblah*, which appeared first on 15 Shawwal 1334 [14 August 1916].

for changing and violating the *shari'ah*. His proclamation mentioned an article in an Istanbul paper that was 'disrespectful' of the Prophet, and he attacked the CUP for rejecting the *shar'i* rules of inheritance which give a man a portion double that of a woman. Moreover, the CUP had ordered the troops fighting Husayn not only to break the fast of Ramadan, but also to shell the Ka'ba.[88]

The second proclamation, dated 21 Dhu al-Qa'dah 1335 [20 September 1916],[89] blamed the triumvirate for causing the downfall of the Empire by alienating Britain and France, and further crimes against the *shari'ah* were elucidated, particularly relating to the honor of women. Ottoman soldiers had taken the young girls (*mukhaddarat*) of the 'Awali bedouin, near Medina, to the military barracks, an act 'condemned by the Islamic *shari'ah* and the Arab [sense of] honor.' Cemal was accused of organizing a women's society in Syria, and forcing the society to hold a reception where the women sang to the men. They had therefore disobeyed the word of God by violating the honor of women, and the 'Islamic state' (*dawlat al-Islam*) had been sacrificed to the personal ambitions of the triumvirate. This proclamation embodied Husayn's idea of the lawful state: it had to be headed by a Caliph, embrace all the *ummah*, and rule according to the *shari'ah*. Ottoman rule, according to Husayn, clearly no longer fitted the bill.[90]

The third proclamation, dated 4 Safar 1335 [10 December 1916][91] was the first issued after Husayn assumed royal dignity, and is signed 'King of the Arab Countries.' In this proclamation he elaborated on the link between Arabism and Islam, declaring that national (*qawmiyyah*) and patriotic (*wataniyyah*) duty was the same as the religious duty of the Muslim, namely, to follow the *shari'ah* and to revolt against those who 'took the religion of God as an amusement and as a game.'[92] The fourth proclamation, dated 10 Jumada al-Ula 1335 [4 March 1917], was important for announc-

---

88 First proclamation, *RMM* 46 (1921), pp. 20–21.
89 There is some confusion over the date of this proclamation. The versions published in *AB* no. 25, 7 October 1916 and in *RMM* 47 (1921), pp. 12–13, are dated 11 Dhu al-Qa'dah 1334 [9 September 1916]. The text in Musa, *Watha'iq*, pp. 77–81, and in *al-Qiblah*, no. 11, 21 Dhu al-Qa'dah 1334 [20 September 1916] carries that date.
90 Dawn, pp. 81–82.
91 The text in *RMM* 47 (1921), pp. 5–11, carries the date Saffar 1335 [November 1916]; the text in Musa, *Watha'iq*, and in *al-Qiblah*, no. 31, 3 Saffar 1335 [10 December 1916] carries that date.
92 Dawn, p. 77.

ing the omission of the Sultan's name from the *khutbah*, a move which Husayn declared he had previously avoided out of reverence for tradition.[93]

Other statements at the beginning of the war, written by Husayn, *al-Qiblah*'s editor Muhibb al-Din al-Khatib, or Fu'ad al-Khatib, were published in early issues of *al-Qiblah*.[94] The premiere issue of the paper, in August 1916, for example, had pre-empted an Ottoman accusation of *fitnah* (internecine fighting): the Turks had abandoned religion, and this in itself was '*fitnah* in every sense of the term.'[95] The Young Turks' treatment of the Caliph was also attacked: they had imprisoned him and many '*ulama*, thus humiliating the Caliphate and shaming Islam before the world. Those who behaved in such a manner, wrote *al-Qiblah*, had 'exceeded the divine statutes of God, and he who transgresses the divine statutes is an oppressor.'[96] And finally, expressing the perceived integral link between Arabs and Islam, the paper attacked the Young Turks for proposing a translation of the Qur'an into Turkish, for a 'Qur'an not in Arabic is an imperfect Qur'an, and a copy of it remains *jahiliyyah*.' An article by Fu'ad

---

93 Text in Musa, *Watha'iq*, pp. 78–82, where it is dated 10 Jumada al-Ula 1335 [3 March 1917]; and in *al-Qiblah*, no. 58, 11 Jumada al-Ula 1335 [4 March 1917].

94 Muhibb al-Din al-Khatib (1886–1969) was born in Damascus and embodied 'all the ideological complexities of the Ottoman–Arab Muslim élite of his generation.' For him, 'Arab rights and Islamic order ... were inseparable parts of the political whole' (Cleveland, p. 87). Muhibb al-Din al-Khatib and Fu'ad al-Khatib both had connections to British intelligence (see *AB*, no. 37, 4 January 1916). The idea for publishing *al-Qiblah* originated with Syrians in Cairo, who proposed it to the British. It won the hearty endorsement of Fu'ad, who wrote Clayton that 'there is not the least doubt, that it will always remain loyal to the Allies and particularly to Great Britain.' The British funded it, supplied the equipment, and endeavored to furnish the paper with 'favourable and authentic war news.' Despatches from Cairo were thoroughly examined before they were sent on to Mecca. As Clayton wrote: 'The first number of the Kibla was naturally read over rather carefully in the Arab Bureau, as it was an experiment and required careful checking.' (FO 882/14: W.H. Deedes to General Staff Officer [Intelligence GSOI], 19 August 1916, enclosing note by Fu'ad al-Khatib, 19 July 1916; Clayton to Private Secretary, Khartoum, 25 July 1916; and WP 140/5/68–70, Clayton to Wingate, 21 September 1916. See also Bruce Westrate, *The Arab Bureau: British Policy in the Middle East, 1916–1920* [University Park, PA: Pennsylvania State University Press, 1992], pp. 110–11.)

95 *Al-Qiblah*, no. 1 15 Shawwal 1334 [14 August 1916], quoted in Cleveland, p. 89.

96 *Al-Qiblah*, no. 10, 17 Dhu al-Qa'dah 1334 [14 September 1916]; no. 1 15 Shawwal 1334 [14 August 1916], both cited in Cleveland, p. 91.

al-Khatib exhorted all Muslims to fight on behalf of the father-
land, and for the cause of Muslims everywhere.[97]

Thoroughly grounded in Islam, whose message the Arabs had
the most right to carry, the Revolt presented itself to the Islamic
world. But what was Husayn planning?

'King of the Arab nation'. On 29 October 1916, Colonel Wilson in
Jeddah received the following telegram:

According to wish of public and assembled Ulema the Great Master, His
Majesty Our Lord and Lord of all el-Hussein Ibn Ali has been
recognized as King of Arab nation and he will be recognized as religious
head until Moslems are of one opinion concerning Islamic Caliphate ...

The telegram was signed by 'Abdallah as Minister for Foreign
Affairs. The news was unnerving to British officials, who had seen
no indication that Husayn had intended to make such a move.
'This is rather a bomb,' minuted a Foreign Office official drily.[98]
British astonishment notwithstanding,[99] Husayn's move was
entirely consistent with his pretensions. Indeed, the issue had
been raised twice on earlier occasions, but the British had not
dealt with it seriously.

The first inkling of Husayn's intentions had come in July. The
British had broken the cipher used to encode telegrams passing
between Muhammad Sharif al-Faruqi, the Hashimite representative in Egypt, and Husayn, and were in the habit of monitoring
their communications. On 10 July 1916 Faruqi telegraphed
Husayn that he had had an interview with McMahon. The meeting was a complete fiction, however – Faruqi was in Cairo and
McMahon in Alexandria. The telegram read, 'I have discussed
with the High Commissioner regarding the title of King of the
Arabs and I saw him willing to admit this idea with the greatest

---

[97] *Al-Qiblah*, no. 3, 22 Shawwal 1334 [21 August 1916], cited in Cleveland, pp. 90–1.

[98] FO 371/2782/218006, McMahon to FO, no. 945, 31 October 1916, transmitting
Wilson's no. 436 of 29 October 1916, which includes 'Abdallah's announcement; FO
371/2782/217652, 'Abdallah (Mecca) to FO, 29 October 1916, minute by George
Clerk dated 31 October 1916. Husayn's title was rendered by the Hashimites into
English as 'King of the Arab Nation,' into French as *'Roi de la nation arabe,'* and into
Arabic as *'malik al-bilad al-'arabiyyah.'*

[99] 'The telegram of Emir Abdulla was a complete surprise to me,' wrote Wilson to
McMahon (FO 371/2782/23317, Wilson to McMahon, no. 12, 31 October 1916,
enclosed in McMahon to Grey, 9 November 1916).

facility.'[100] And a few weeks before Husayn's assumption of kingship, 'Abdallah had approached Storrs in Jeddah on this matter, asking if the British would address Husayn publicly as *amir al-mu'minin* (commander of the faithful). Storrs told 'Abdallah that this form of address was reserved for the Caliph, and said that HMG had already distanced itself on the issue of the Caliphate. 'Abdallah then requested the title of Majesty (*jalalah*) and King (*malik*); Storrs demurred. Storrs informed 'Abdallah that Husayn had better rule more of at least the Hijaz before assuming such a title.[101] Nevertheless, 'Abdallah's efforts had demonstrated Husayn's real aspirations, and presaged Husayn's assumption of royal dignity.

This assumption of kingship took place at his palace in Mecca, with assorted guests in attendance. The event was carefully orchestrated by 'Abdallah, on the pretext of celebrating the Muslim new year, 1335, which began on 28 October 1916. It was to seem like a guileless response to a demand made spontaneously by the notables and *'ulama*. A long address and a petition from the *'ulama* and notables recognizing Husayn as King of the Arabs was read by a religious official, and the reading was frequently corrected by 'Abdallah, who knew the text by heart (a sure indication of his authorship). The head of the French mission in the Hijaz, Colonel Brémond, reported that his French Muslim officers present at the occasion had difficulty understanding the address, as it was delivered 'in very classical Arabic with a Syrian accent, no word of which [they] understood.' 'Abdallah telegraphed Brémond announcing his father's new title, and added that Brémond's Muslim aide Lieutenant Colonel Cadi *'ainsi que tous les membres de votre respectable mission assistaient à la cérémonie.'*[102]

---

[100] FO 371/2782/242008, McMahon to Grey, no. 334, 21 November 1916, enclosing Wilson to McMahon, no. 15, 11 November 1916. See also reference to this in an intercepted and deciphered telegram, FO 686/9, Mohd. Sherif El Farouki, Agent in Egypt, to Sub Minister of Foreign Affairs, Mecca, 29 Muharram 1335 [24 November 1916].

[101] FO 371/2782/220973, Storrs' diary of visit to Hijaz, enclosed in McMahon to Grey, 25 October 1916; see also Kedourie, *Anglo-Arab*, pp. 144–5.

[102] FO 371/2782/242002, Wilson to McMahon, no. 14, 5 November 1916; FO 371/2782/220734, McMahon to FO, no. 960, 2 November 1916, transmitting telegrams from Brémond passed on by French Military Attaché (Doynel de San Quentin) in Cairo. When Cadi found out that it was now trumpeted throughout Mecca that he had just congratulated the Sharif on becoming King in the name of France, he immediately took to bed with a diplomatic 'fever.'

'Abdallah had managed to force the merchants, *shuyukh al-harat* and notables of Jeddah into a coalition with Husayn. Several notables who were close to 'Abdallah were instructed to spread rumors that Husayn had been recognized by England, France, Russia and Italy as well as all the neutral countries. They were also to keep a record of those who decorated their shops and houses in honor of the event. A committee of some major figures in town held a reception. And the merchants, *shuyukh al-harat* and notables were ordered to send a boilerplate congratulatory telegram, whose text had been authored by 'Abdallah. The head of the telegraph office was instructed not to send any telegrams which deviated from the formula. Over 2,500 telegrams of congratulations reached the Sharif from Jeddah, wrote *al-Qiblah*.[103] Even taking exaggeration into account, 'Abdallah, it appeared, had done his work well, to the discomfort of those whom he had coerced. It was the assessment of a British agent that 'the people in Jeddah are not pleased with the Sherif declaring himself King.' Those who had sent telegrams or who in other ways had expressed support for Husayn were now bound to him in writing. If Husayn failed, the Ottomans would not treat them kindly.

The text of articles in *al-Qiblah* and of the announcement of Husayn's new title stopped just short of proclaiming him Caliph. The Revolt was aimed, he declared, not at the reigning Caliph but at the CUP. Nevertheless, the language was so suggestive that his intentions were unmistakable.

The petition, read out as a proclamation by 'Abdallah, reflected the same theory of the primacy of the Arabs in Islam first articulated by al-Kawakabi, elaborated upon by Rashid Rida and later echoed by 'Abdallah in his memoirs, that 'God singled out the children of Isma'il' and that the Arabs were the most exalted of nations because they spread the message of *tawhid*. Quoting Muslim (the compiler of a canonical compilation of *hadith*s), the petition stressed that the Prophet had been chosen because he was an Arab, of Quraysh, of the Bani Hashim. The petition then

---

103 FO 371/2782/23317, Wilson to McMahon, no. 12, 31 October 1916, enclosed in McMahon to Grey, 9 November 1916. *Al-Qiblah*, 3 Muharram 1335 [29 October 1916]. On 1 November 1916, Wilson telegraphed that there had been official announcement stating that 'Our Allied Governments … had sent congratulations to Shereef expressing pleasure at his action' (FO 371/2782/219490, Wilson to McMahon, no. 452, 1 November 1916, relayed in McMahon to FO, no. 955, 1 November 1916).

turned to Husayn, praising his connection to the Prophet, and stating that the petitioners did not know a more pious and god-fearing amir. He was the 'Savior of Islam,' and he would lead the Arabs to freedom from those who had oppressed them. The petition then stated, 'We recognize His Majesty our lord and master al-Husayn ibn 'Ali as our King, we the Arabs, and he will act amongst us according to the book of God Almighty and the laws of His Prophet, prayer and peace upon him.' It concluded with an oath of allegiance (*mubaya'ah*) to him as their 'religious authority [*marja' dini*] ... pending the decision of the Islamic world in the matter of the Islamic Caliphate.'[104] Although the petition declared him King of the Arabs and not Caliph, the qualifications specified for the former included those for the latter.

An account of the event was printed in *al-Qiblah* alongside the text of the petition; it endeavored to show that the *'ulama* and the notables had spontaneously come to Husayn. All had gathered, it was reported, for the purpose of persuading Husayn to assume the mantle of 'King of the Arabs (*malik 'ala al-'Arab*) and [to be] their religious authority (*marja' dini*) until the Islamic world reached a unanimous opinion in the matter of the Islamic Caliphate.' Shaykh 'Abdallah Sarraj, head (*ra'is*) of the *'ulama* of Mecca and chief *qadi* (*qadi al-quda*), entered the Hashimite Palace to inform Husayn that the crowd demanded that he come to them. The groups submitted the petition to Husayn when he joined them. He exclaimed, 'I have never thought it necessary for you to do such a thing ... I swear to you by Almighty God that this had never occurred to me.' The audience then insisted that he accept their wishes, he complied, and a proclamation was read establishing his new title. Fu'ad al-Khatib then stepped forward to proclaim the loyalty of Syrians to the new King.[105]

Husayn also caused a *fatwa* to be issued and sent to India's Muslims. The text begins with an attack on the CUP who 'had evil intentions towards our religion.' One had only to go to Istanbul, continued the *fatwa*, to see 'Moslem women employed in the

---

104 *Al-Qiblah*, 3 Muharram 1335 [29 October 1916]. A translation of parts of the petition can be found in Kedourie, *Anglo-Arab*, pp. 145–6.

105 *Al-Qiblah*, 3 Muharram 1335 [29 October 1916]. Husayn also published a speech of Sami al-Bakri, of the Damascus Bakris, stating that 'the Syrians and the Iraqis are happy today with the swearing in of their king' (*al-Qiblah*, 10 Muharram 1335 [5 November 1916]).

Postal and Finance Administration in the same way as men are –
with perfect coquetry and unveiled, meeting men of various
nationalities and going about their business. To obey these people
would be to disobey God; so we chose to invoke their anger, and
not that of God.' An article had appeared in an Indian paper that
assessed the Ottomans as unqualified for Caliphate. The *fatwa*
mentioned this article, and continued:

Today we do not know of any Moslem ruler more righteous and fearing
God, than the son of His Prophet, who is now on the throne of the Arab
Country. We do not know anyone more zealous in religion, more
observant of the Laws of God in words and deeds, and more capable of
managing our affairs in what would please God, than he is. The Arabs
have proclaimed him King over them only because in doing so they
would be serving their religion and country. As to the question of the
Khalifat, in spite of all that is known of the deplorable condition in which
it is situated at the present moment, we have not interfered with it at all
and will remain as it is pending the final decision of the whole
Mohammedan world.

The *fatwa* was signed by all the leading *'ulama* of Mecca.[106] As Ruhi
wrote, the proclamation was 'a step towards the Caliphate.'[107]

A few months after the assumption of the kingship *al-Qiblah*
printed the speech of 'a representative of Medina' under a banner
bismillah headline. The 'representative' addressed the Sharif as
'His Highness [*jalalah*] our Master [*mawlana*] *Amir al-Mu'minin*
and the Caliph of the Messenger of the Lord of the Worlds our
Lord and Lord of all, Sharif al-Husayn bin 'Ali.'[108] Numerous articles asserted the illegitimacy of the Ottoman Caliphate and the
qualifications of Quraysh and the Prophet's house.[109]

---

106 FO 371/2783/255868, McMahon to Grey, 2 December 1916, enclosing the *fatwa*
which is enclosed in Wilson to Director, Arab Bureau, 14 November 1916.

107 FO 371/2782/23317, Note by Hussein Effendi Ruhi, 30 October 1916, enclosed
Wilson to McMahon, no. 12, 31 October 1916, enclosed in McMahon to Grey, 9
November 1916.

108 *Al-Qiblah*, no. 56, 4 Jamadi al-Ula 1335 [25 February 1917]. Husayn's response,
printed in the same issue, was typically self-deprecating, stating only that the people of
the country had decided to abide by the decision of the rest of the Muslim world on the
Caliphate issue.

109 See for example, the following in *al-Qiblah*: a two-part article by F[u'ad al-Khatib?], 27
Jamadi al-Thani [19 April 1917] and 2 Rajab 1335 [23 April 1917], denying the
Ottoman claim to the Caliphate; an article published on 25 Jamadi al-Ula 1335 [18
March 1917] quoting an article from the Cairene paper *al-Kawkab* which calls into

Confusion and dismay: the British respond to Husayn's new title. In early Islamic history the title *malik* had been a term of abuse and 'came to connote the temporal, mundane facet of government – the antithesis of *khalifa* and *imam*[,] which signified piety and righteousness.' By Husayn's time numerous Muslim rulers had been influenced by Western cultures in adopting the title of king.[110] Husayn used the word in this European sense, perhaps to establish equality with his British and French counterparts. Other titles, such as amir or sultan, which might have recommended themselves, were deemed inappropriate to Husayn's position. Ibn Saud and the Idrisi were amirs, and the sultan in Istanbul was still, at least on paper, recognized by Husayn. As 'Abdallah told Wilson: 'The people here have declared him to be the King of the Arabs in order to show that they are not under any other power.'[111]

Husayn, too, explained the title of King of the Arabs to Wilson, saying: 'The people of the country want ... to explain to the whole world their intentions and plans in order to avoid suspicion as to other Amirs and Sheikhs of Arabs.'[112] 'Other Amirs and Sheikhs of Arabs' referred to the Idrisi and Ibn Saud, and Husayn wanted to present the British (and the French) with an accomplished fact. By having himself declared king not only of the Hijaz but of the Arabs as a whole, he put the British on notice that he was advancing himself as the sovereign in the territories mentioned, but not mutually agreed upon, in the Husayn–McMahon correspondence.

Speaking with Wilson on the telephone 'Abdallah insisted that neither Ibn Saud nor the Idrisi should worry the British. The former, 'Abdallah said, was 'a Sheikh of Arabs and would not interfere with his work or his land. Let every one rule his part, it does not make any difference.' Concerning the Idrisi, 'Abdallah remarked, 'He is a man who is not recognized by anyone to be anything. He

question the right of the Ottomans to the title of *Khadim al-Haramayn al-Sharifayn* when one *haram* was under the control of 'our King al-Husayn bin 'Ali al-Qurayshi;' an article published on 17 Jamadi al-Thani 1335 [9 April 1917] comparing Husayn's efforts for progress on behalf of the Arabs as unprecedented since the time of the *rashidun*.

110 Ami Ayalon, 'Malik,' *EI²*; see also Ami Ayalon, 'Malik in Middle Eastern Titulature,' *Die Welt des Islams* 23–24 (1984), pp. 306–19.

111 FO 371/2782/242002, Telephone message by Emir Abdulla, 1 November 1916, enclosed in Wilson to McMahon, no. 14, 5 November 1916.

112 FO 371/2782/24002, Telephone [statement] by the Sherif of Mecca himself, 2 November 1916, enclosed in Wilson to McMahon, no. 14, 5 November 1916.

has made himself sheikh and landed in some places which were not ruled by anyone.' The preceding remarks with respect to Ibn Saud hint at a view that was developing in Hashimite circles, that of Husayn as the acknowledged suzerain of the Arabs. 'Abdallah elaborated on this. He stated that the British had already promised the Hashimites that the 'Kingdom of the Sherif will be up to Iraq.' Since Ibn Saud's territory was between the Hijaz and Iraq, and 'Abdallah had said that Ibn Saud's boundaries would be accepted, he must have had the idea of a suzerainty in mind (for a detailed discussion of the suzerainty idea, see Chapter 7).[113]

Husayn's domestic social concerns were also behind the declaration of kingship. According to Fu'ad al-Khatib, Husayn had engineered the *bay'ah* (swearing of fealty) at the Ka'ba, believing that the act would bind to him those merchants and other notables still hesitating or still clinging to the old and comfortable order. Husayn's hunch proved correct, said al-Khatib, because everyone, in fact, now feared what the Ottomans would do to them if Husayn's cause failed. Now they would fight for the Sharif in their own defense. Khatib also stressed that by forming such a grand thing as a kingdom of all the Arabs, Husayn would not only show the world their independence from the Ottomans, but also could employ 'a great number of influential people,' thereby gaining their loyalty. He noted in particular Shaykh Shayba (the hereditary holder of the keys to the Ka'ba) in this regard.[114]

It is quite possible that Husayn believed the British were ready to recognize him as King of the Arabs, despite Storrs' warning to 'Abdallah.[115] Particularly in the light of Faruqi's telegram which falsely reported that McMahon had approved of the title king,[116]

---

[113] FO 371/2782/24002, Telephone message by Emir Abdulla, 1 November 1916, enclosed Wilson to McMahon, no. 14, 5 November 1916.

[114] FO 882/3, Statement on Hedjaz taken from Fuad Eff. El Khatib by Wilson, 1917. For a copy of 'Ali Haydar's proclamation, see FO 371/2776/231939, McMahon to Grey, no. 221, 12 September 1916.

[115] FO 371/2782/242008, McMahon to Grey, no. 334, 21 November 1916, enclosing Wilson to McMahon, no. 15, 11 November 1916.

[116] Husayn mentioned this in a telegram to Faruqi: 'your notice … of [Britain's] strong desire for the title "Sultan of the Arabs" …' In the same telegram he stresses that 'they had approved and considered fit for us the title of "Arab Caliph" and "Sultan of the Arabs" with all the authority which these titles involve.' (FO 686/9, Fuad El Khotib, Sub-Minister of Foreign Affairs, Mecca, to Sherif el Faroki, our Agent in Egypt, 22 November 1916).

the Sharif may well have assumed that the British, who had never officially recognized him as King of the Arabs, would not oppose his being such. In the telephone conversation between 'Abdallah and Wilson on 1 November 1916, 'Abdallah said that HMG had previously addressed the Sharif as king, but at that time he had been satisfied with the title of amir; the assumption of the title should therefore not have come as a surprise to the British.[117] In a letter to Wilson three days later, Husayn went even further, stating that 'His Majesty's Government has addressed me as the Caliph which is a higher dignity than Kingship'; therefore assuming the title of king, a lesser title, needed no official notification, the king reasoned.[118] This kind of disingenuousness would become the king's trademark, and this time it initiated a frantic British search through their archives. In this case, the only relevant document the British could find was Kitchener's letter to 'Abdallah of 31 October 1914 which he had concluded with the observation that an Arab might become caliph at Mecca or Medina.[119] But the British had never addressed him as caliph, or king. When confronted with this 'Abdallah finally admitted that the British had never addressed the Sharif by either title.[120]

The exchanges on this issue brought about the first stanza in what would become Husayn's continuing refrain: 'Please tell His Excellency [the High Commissioner] that if any misunderstandings may arise between me and His Majesty's Government, I will resign from this business.'[121] His assumption of royal dignity put the British (and indeed the French) in the awkward position of having to decide whether or not to recognize him as 'King of the Arabs.' While still undecided, the British addressed him with the

117 FO 371/2782/242002, Transcript of a telephone conversation between Wilson and 'Abdallah, 1 November 1916, enclosed in Wilson to McMahon, no. 14, 5 November 1916.
118 FO 371/2782/24002, Husayn to Wilson, 4 November 1916, copy enclosed in Wilson to McMahon, no. 14, 5 November 1916. See also FO 371/2782/242008, transcript of telephone conversation between Wilson and Husayn, 6 November 1916, enclosed in Wilson to McMahon, no. 15, 11 November 1916, enclosed in McMahon to Grey, no. 334, 21 November 1916. The same argument was advanced by Husayn in a conversation in Jeddah in December 1916 (*AB* no. 36, 26 December 1916).
119 FO 371/2782/228344, McMahon to FO, no. 1004, 13 November 1916.
120 FO 371/2782/226649, Sirdar to FO, no. 12, 10 November 1916.
121 FO 371/2782/24002, Telephone, by the Sherif of Mecca himself, 2 November 1916, enclosed in Wilson to McMahon, no. 14, 5 November 1916.

'sufficiently noncommittal' *sahib al-siyada* (approximately, 'his lordship'). Wingate and the India Office deprecated the FO suggestion of *malik al-haramayn* (king of the two holy shrines) as having too much religious significance, and both supported 'King of the Arabs in the Hedjaz' instead.[122] It was McMahon who eventually came up with a title all could agree on: 'King of the Hijaz'; the French Middle East envoy Georges Picot agreed, and Wingate was consequently authorized to recognize him as *Malik al-Hijaz*, with the honorific *siyada*.[123]

Neither the British nor the French immediately publicized their recognition of Husayn. But on 17 December 1916 'Abdallah sent a telegram to Faruqi in Cairo whose content was a figment of his imagination: 'three days ago the British Government began addressing my Master and Lord with the address and title of ... Galalat [Majesty] of Arabians.' Faruqi then handed the Cairo paper *al-Muqattam* an announcement that Britain, France and Russia had recognized Husayn as 'King over the Arabs.' The announcement was initially suppressed by the Arab Bureau's censors, but now that Husayn's move was known, Wingate proposed that the recognition of Husayn by Britain and France – as King of the Hijaz only – be published in the Cairo press.[124] Official French recognition of Husayn as King of the Hijaz was granted on 26 December 1916.[125] This limited recognition offended Husayn, who henceforth reminded the British of it regularly.

The extent of Hashimite ambitions becomes clear to the British.

'For Heaven's sake let us be straight with the old man; I am convinced it will pay in the end.' (C.E. Wilson, Jeddah, March 1917)

At the time Husayn declared himself king in October 1916, the Arab Revolt had accomplished little, and in fact was in great

---

[122] FO 371/2782/244179, Wingate to FO, no. 53, 3 December 1916. [79]; FO 371/2782/249498, Secretary of State [for India] to Viceroy, P 5097, 7 December 1916, and Viceroy, Foreign Department to IO, 8 December 1916.

[123] FO 371/2782/251737, Memorandum by Sir R. Graham, 11 December 1916.

[124] FO 686/9, Arbur to Sirdar, no. AB 429, 17 December 1916, transmitting intercepted and deciphered telegram from Minister of Foreign Affairs (Mecca), to Faroki (Cairo); FO 686/9, Arbur to Sirdar, no. AB 440, undated, but probably on 19.12.16; FO 371/2782/258154, Wingate to FO, no. 92, 20 December 1916.

[125] Dan Eldar, 'French Policy towards Husayn, Sharif of Mecca,' *MES* 26 (1990), pp. 329–49.

difficulty. The British and French had not had to concern themselves all that much with Hashimite aspirations, but assuming the kingship put them on notice that Husayn was after something grand, and it was only after the capture of Wajh in January 1917 that the allies began to consider their Hashimite option more seriously.

It appears that it was Lawrence who first revealed the Sykes–Picot Agreement to the Hashimites in February 1917, in a conversation with Faysal.[126] This had led Faysal to concentrate on moving north, towards Damascus, not east, towards Medina. Captain Joyce wrote from Wajh on 23 March 1917 saying that he could not understand why Faysal did not move on the Hijaz railway: 'It appears to me he is too inclined to concentrate his ideas on the North and Syria whereas so far as my information goes Medina should be the first objective of all the Sherif's Forces and I have endeavored to explain this clearly to him.' About a week later, his suspicions grew more serious:

I am still of the opinion that Sherif FAISAL's whole attention is directed towards the North and he cares little about the fate of MEDINA which he insists is a foregone conclusion and should be the work of ABDULLA and ALI ... I feel sure it would be advantageous if the limits of the HEDJAZ operations could be defined as soon as possible ... I have endeavoured to confine FAISAL to local ambitions and Military operations, but from somewhere he has developped [sic] very wide ideas and I would like to feel certain they are in accordance with the General plan.

Throughout April, Joyce was becoming increasingly impatient with Faysal, and seems to have been quite surprised when Faysal 'announced to Col. Newcombe and myself that the Hedjaz could never be an independent country owing to its more or less barren soil, and that only by having Syria could it possibly be maintained. I feel confident that it is essential that the limits of the Arab movement be defined as soon as possible.'[127]

At about the same time that Lawrence let on to Faysal about the French plans for Syria, the Hashimites began to object strongly to all kinds of French plans for the Hijaz itself. Husayn, knowing full well that the French aspired to control Syria, but believing or

126 Wilson, *Lawrence*, pp. 361–362.
127 FO 686/6, Joyce (Wajh), to Wilson, 24 March 1917; FO 686/6, Joyce (Wajh), to Wilson, received Jeddah 4 April 1917; FO 686/6, part 2, Joyce (Wajh), to Director, Arab Bureau, 15 April 1917.

hoping that the British would control the French, was careful not to let the French get control of anything in the Hijaz. This did not deter Brémond, who was very diligent in promoting French commercial interests in the *Haramayn*. While one must not discount that Husayn may have wanted to play off the two allies against each other, it appears that the initiative for several projects came from Brémond himself, although the French portrayed the initiatives as coming from Husayn.

French attempts to influence policy in the Hijaz began in earnest in February 1917, when the French approached the British concerning the sending of North African physicians to the Hijaz. They stated that Husayn had requested it, although this is doubtful. The request made the rounds in London, and was rejected since it would require a British countermove to maintain London's primacy, which in turn would only make Husayn appear dependent on Christian powers.[128] Brémond's next project involved construction of major railway lines throughout the Hijaz and the building of ports at Yanbu' and Rabigh.[129] This was followed by proposals for a wireless installation; minting currency for the Hijaz (Brémond suggested to Husayn that it be on the metric system, in other words, compatible with the French franc rather than the English pound); and a proposal for a North African pilgrim hostel to compete with one already in use for Egyptian pilgrims. But probably the most ambitious of the French schemes was to reopen the Jeddah branch of the French-controlled Imperial Ottoman Bank and have it act as Husayn's banker.[130] All these

---

128 FO 371/3049/28859, Jules Cambon (French Ambassador to London) to Arthur Balfour, 5 February 1917; FO 371/3049/36361: Hirtzel, IO, to Under Secretary of State, FO, no. P. 681, 14 February 1917; Balfour to Cambon, no. W. 36361/17, 23 February 1917.

129 SHAT, 7 N 2139, Note sur les Chemins de Fer et Ports du Hedjaz, Brémond, no. 46, 8 March 1917, copy directed to Le Ministre de la Guerre, Paris.

130 On the wireless project, see: FO 371/3050/56860, Cambon to Balfour, 15 March 1917; and FO 371/3050/W.64012/17, Balfour to Cambon, 30 March 1917. On the French sponsored *takiyyah*, see: SHAT, 7 N 2139, Benazzouz, Hôtellerie de la Mecque, Note de Monsieur Benazzouz, 3 March 1917; SHAT, 7 N. 2139, Brémond to le Ministre de la Guerre, no. 63, 28 March 1917; and FO 371/3058/28165, Cambon to Balfour, 3 February 1917. On the currency issue, see: SHAT, 7 N 2139, Brémond to Ministre de la Guerre, no. 60, 25 March 1916. On the Bank issue, see, for example: FO 371/3045/49721, George Lloyd to Balfour, 5 March 1917. Robin Bidwell, in his 'The Brémond Mission in the Hijaz, 1916–1917: A Study in Inter-Allied Cooperation,' in R.L. Bidwell and G.R. Smith (eds), *Arabian and Islamic Studies: Articles Presented to R.B.*

efforts angered Wingate in particular, and Husayn was noncommittal on all of them, much to London's satisfaction.[131] These activities led to demands for the mission to be recalled; Brémond left Arabia in December 1918, although the mission lingered on in an attenuated form until August 1920. For the Hashimites, these French efforts were dangerous signals of Paris' ambitions. Husayn, for his part, could rely on the British to keep the French off his back, at least in the Hijaz.[132]

From February 1917 onwards, the Hashimites and their officials left no doubt in conversations with British officials that they expected to rule Syria and Iraq. Although this had not been agreed to by the British, Husayn insisted that it was so, although he could not produce any documentation to back it up.[133] British officials began advocating that Husayn be made aware of the Sykes–Picot Agreement. C.E. Wilson, who was in almost daily contact with Husayn and seemed ill at ease when explaining the contradictions in British commitments, wrote Clayton that London had to be honest with the Sharif. 'I feel very strongly that the settlement of Syria etc., should not be arranged behind his back, so to speak … For Heaven's sake let us be straight with the old man; I am convinced it will pay in the end.'[134]

The French and English thus reached, at about the same time, the conclusion that the terms of the Sykes–Picot Agreement had to be made known to Husayn. And so, the Sykes–Picot mission

---

Serjeant (London: Longman, 1983), pp. 182–95, states categorically that he had 'not found any trace' of French suggestions to build a railway or to provide coinage 'in the records of the [Brémond] Mission.' On the contrary, there is ample evidence in the records of these suggestions, but they may have indeed been difficult to locate due to the scrambled nature of these papers. See also E. Brémond, *Le Hedjaz dans la Guerre Mondiale* (Paris: Payot, 1931).

131 See, for example, FO 371/3051/66635, Wingate to FO, no. 344, 29 March 1917; and FO 371/3051/70709, Wingate to FO, no. 368, 4 April 1917.

132 Probably the most important result of French intrigue in the Hijaz was that it pushed Wingate in April 1917 to insist that Whitehall establish once and for all with the French that the Hijaz was outside their area of influence. After many months of negotiations, this issue was settled in a *Projet d'Arrangement*, finalized in October 1917, recognizing the predominance of British interests in the Hijaz, albeit not granting them any monopoly on commercial ventures. See the voluminous correspondence on this issue in FO 371/3054 and FO 371/3056.

133 Kedourie, *Anglo-Arab*, pp. 152–8.

134 FO 882/12, Wilson to Clayton, 21 March 1917, quoted in Wilson, *Lawrence*, pp. 361–2.

was born.[135] After meeting with three prudently chosen Syrian Muslim 'delegates' in Cairo,[136] Sykes made his way to the Hijaz, where he was instructed to 'reassure' Husayn concerning French aims in 'the interior of Syria,' and to establish that his rule could not be forced on the Arabs there or in Baghdad, where Britain would 'retain the position of military and political predominance which our strategical and commercial interests require.'

Sykes met Faysal at Wajh on 2 May 1917. One can only imagine how Faysal must have felt at this meeting, since he already knew from Lawrence that the British would not support him against France in Syria. Sykes telegraphed that he had 'explained to him principle of Anglo–French agreement regarding Arab confederation,' and, he added blithely, '[a]fter much argument he accepted principle and seemed satisfied.'[137] But Sykes' self-satisfied assertion that he had convinced Faysal was belied by Faysal himself, who confided to Wilson (at this time they were on a British ship carrying Sykes from Wajh to Yanbu') his suspicions of the French. He asked Wilson to tell them 'they were not wanted and if I did not, he would.'[138]

Sykes' interview with Husayn on 5 May 1917 revealed some of Husayn's personal concerns about the path he had chosen. As will be remembered, he was quite conscious of his rebellion against the established Islamic authority. Not to achieve something at least approaching what he had rebelled against seemed to him inconceivable, and would have left him open to charges of *fitnah*. He therefore told Sykes 'that unless Arab Independence is assured he feared that posterity would charge him with assisting in the overthrow of [the] last Islamic power without setting up another in its place.' At this interview, Sykes seemed satisfied with what he

---

[135] The main secondary source for this section is Kedourie, *Anglo-Arab*, pp. 159–84; unattributed quotations are from there. Where appropriate, specific references to primary sources are made.

[136] During this meeting, Sykes wrote, the goal was 'to manoeuvre the delegates, without showing them a map or letting them know that there was an actual geographical or detailed agreement, into asking for what we are ready to give them' (FO 882/16, Sir T.B.M. Sykes to Sir G.M.W. Macdonough [DMI, War Office], no. 19, 30 April 1917, quoted in Wilson, *Lawrence*, p. 403).

[137] FO 371/3054/93335, Wingate to FO, no. 496, 7 May 1917, relaying Sykes' telegram from Jeddah, 6 May 1917.

[138] CP, 470/6/19819, Wilson to Clayton, 5 May [?] 1917; see also Wilson, *Lawrence*, pp. 390–2.

had achieved with Husayn, and he asked Wingate to tell Picot that both Faysal and Husayn 'now stand at the same point as was reached at our last joint meeting with the three Syrian delegates in Cairo.'[139] But Sykes told little of what transpired between the two at this meeting.

After Sykes met with Faysal – this time also with Picot – at Wajh again on 17 May, a meeting, he reported, which yielded little progress,[140] Sykes returned to Jeddah and met Husayn once again on 19 May 1917. Present at this meeting were Faysal, Husayn, Sykes, Picot, Fu'ad al-Khatib and Louis Massignon who acted as interpreter. According to Fu'ad, Sykes insisted that Picot's arrival be accompanied by much ceremony and honors. Sykes was sensitive to French concerns but not to Hashimite ones, as all this pomp and circumstance let all of Jeddah know that the French were coming, and people were aware that they had designs on Syria. Husayn was thus immediately put in an awkward position. Fu'ad reported that after the meeting 'people of the highest classes came asking what happened[:] "Did you give Syria to France [and] betray your country?" We said only that France had sent a visitor to see the King.'[141]

Kedourie has made his way through the labyrinthine documentation surrounding the meetings with Husayn, and demonstrated beyond a doubt that Husayn was informed of the Sykes–Picot Agreement during his talks with the agreement's namesakes.[142] But this did not mean that he had in any way given

139 FO 371/3054/93335, Wingate to FO, no. 496, 7 May 1917, relaying Sykes' telegram to Wingate, Jeddah, 6 May 1917. A short note on the 2 May meeting with Faysal and the 5 May meeting with Husayn in the *AB* (no. 50, 13 May 1917), mentions that Sykes had reported that both leaders had 'been brought to understand that they have to deal with an indivisible Entente; that under whatever overlord, an enlightened progressive régime must be established in Syria; and that certain districts of the latter, which present peculiar difficulties, must remain under special tutelage in any event.'
140 Even though at the previous meeting Sykes had proclaimed Faysal 'satisfied,' Faysal could not have been and therefore it was unrealistic to expect any other result, particularly with Picot around.
141 Sykes' telegram on the meeting is in FO 371/3054/101269, Sykes to FO, 24 May 1917; Fu'ad's report is in GLLD 9/9, Note by Sheikh Fu'ad el Khatib taken down by Lt. Col. Newcombe, undated, attached to Wilson to Clayton, 21–25 May 1917.
142 Kedourie, *Anglo-Arab*, pp. 165–167. Kedourie's position on this issue is further buttressed by Jeremy Wilson (*Lawrence*, p. 1068), who notes that on Lawrence's copy of the *AB*, no. 50, 13 May 1917, which carries a report on Sykes' first discussions with Husayn and Faysal, Lawrence wrote: 'S–P treaty explained in general terms.'

his acquiescence to their terms; he basically relied on the British to protect what he believed were his interests, yet to please Sykes, who was more concerned with the French than with the Hashimites, Husayn bowed to Sykes' pressure and made a declaration, to the meaning of which he would not have agreed had he known what it really meant. At the 19 May meeting, Sykes had 'urged upon [Husayn] the essential importance of European advisers [in Syria and Iraq] having executive authority'; Husayn, Sykes reported, 'naturally disliked the idea, and Fuadd [sic] said that would be the end of Arab independence.' On 20 May 1917 Husayn had Fu'ad state '[t]hat His Majesty the King of Hedjaz learned with satisfaction that the French Government approved Arab national aspirations [and] that as he had confidence in Great Britain he would be content if [the] French Government pursued [the] same policy towards Arab aspirations on Moslem Syrian littoral as British did in Bag[h]dad.'[143]

This change had been accomplished by intense pressure from Sykes, who was more concerned with getting Husayn to satisfy Picot than with making sure the King understood to what he was agreeing. That this was the case is quite clear from detailed testimony by Fu'ad, Newcombe, and Wilson.[144] Husayn wanted to please Sykes, and believed that Sykes would protect his interests *vis-à-vis* the French. Moreover, he knew that McMahon's letter of 24 October 1915 favoring Britain in Iraq was limited to issues of foreign policy and economic interests.[145] If Sykes wanted him to make some kind of statement to Picot, Husayn figured, then he would favor him with it. His statement was only verbal, and when asked he refused to give Picot a written version of it.[146] He probably believed that the McMahon letter, a written 'commitment,' as opposed to a verbal one, was his 'ace in the hole.'[147]

---

143 FO 371/3054/101269, Sykes (Aden) to FO, 24 May 1917.

144 GLLD 9/9, Wilson to Clayton, 21–25 May 1917, enclosing Note by Lt.-Col. Newcombe DSO, 20 May 1917 (misdated 20 March 1917), and Note by Sheikh Fu'ad el Khatib taken down by Lt. Col. Newcombe, undated.

145 'The Sherif has gone trumps on a letter he has from Sir Henry MacMahon ...' (GLLD 9/9, Wilson to Clayton, 21–25 May 1917).

146 GLLD 9/9, Wilson to Clayton, 21–25 May 1917.

147 'Faisal and Fuad expressed their fear that we and the Sherif may have different ideas as to the meaning of the McMahon letter to which the Sherif always refers and would have liked the Sherif to have produced the letter at the meeting, but whenever either say anything the Sherif simply says "I have the word of Great Britain in writing, and that is

Soon after his meetings with Sykes and Picot, Fu'ad went to Cairo, where he gave an interview to a British official.[148] The official, writing to Sykes, quoted Fu'ad as saying that 'King Hussein never understood either from you or from Monsieur Picot, that France would have control over the Syrian Littoral, but that it would be granted the preference for financial and economic concessions.' Husayn said as much to Lawrence on 28 July 1917:

[Husayn] is extremely pleased to have trapped M. Picot into the admission that France will be satisfied in Syria with the position of Great Britain in Iraq. That, he says, means a temporary occupation of the country for strategical and political reasons (with probably an annual grant to the Sherif in compensation and recognition) and concession in the way of public works. 'I was ready without being asked to guard their interests in the existing railways, and assist their schools; but the Hedjaz and Syria are like the palm and fingers of one hand, and I could not have consented to the amputation of any finger or part of a finger without leaving myself a cripple.' In conclusion the Sherif remarked on the shortness and informality of conversations, the absence of written documents, and the fact that the only change in the situation caused by

---

sufficient"' (GLLD 9/9, Wilson to Clayton, 21–25 May 1917). It is probable that the Sharif did not produce the letter because it was not as convincing as he would have liked it to be.

That Sykes was not playing it straight with Husayn tremendously disturbed the British officials on the scene. Their statements are sincere and made out of their sense of fair play. Newcombe wrote: '[A]n interview of a few hours debarring all investigation of the subject entails throwing great responsibility on our Govt., to see the Sherif or Arab cause through to the end; otherwise we are hoodwinking the Sherif and his people and playing a very false game in which officers attached to the Sherif's army are invariably committed and which I know causes anxiety in several officers' minds, in case we let them down' (GLLD 9/9, Note by Lt. Col. Newcombe DSO, 20 May 1917 [misdated 20 March 1917], enclosed in Wilson to Clayton, 21–25 May 1917). Wilson was very upset about the whole episode: 'Is the Sherif living in a fool's paradise? If so he will have a very rude awakening and once his trust in Great Britain has gone we will not get it back again.' Wilson then – perhaps influenced by the histrionics of his charge – offered to resign: 'If we are not going to see the Sherif through and we let him down badly after all his trust in us the very "enviable" post of Pilgrimage Officer at Jeddah will be vacant because I certainly could not remain' (GLLD 9/9, Wilson to Clayton, 21–25 May 1917). This policy made Lawrence positively suicidal, inspiring his ride to Syria. In his diary he wrote: 'Can't stand another day here. Will ride north and chuck it.' In a note he meant to leave behind he scribbled: 'Clayton. I've decided to go off alone to Damascus, hoping to get killed on the way; for all sakes try and clear this show up before it goes further. We are calling on them to fight for us on a lie, and I can't stand it' (Wilson, *Lawrence*, p. 410).

[148] FO 882/16, George Lloyd [?], Ismailia, to Sir Mark Sykes, 27 July 1917. The signature is undecipherable, but it is apparent from the content and style that the official was fairly high up in the Cairo intelligence establishment.

the meeting was the French renunciation of the ideas of annexation, permanent occupation or suzerainty of any part of Syria – 'but this we did not embody in a formal treaty, as the war is not finished. I merely read out my acceptance of the formula *"as the British in IRAQ"* proposed to me by M. Picot, since Sir Mark Sykes assured me that it would a satisfactory conclusion to the discussion'. [149]

These meetings also gave occasion to learn more about Husayn and the caliphate. Fu'ad told Picot: [W]e, the Arabs, must have [the Caliphate] ourselves ... If the Mohammedan world is not contented and if Syria is not under an Arab Kingdom, but an Arab King exist[s] only in the Hedjaz, how can the Khalifa be acknowledged by all Mohammedans as being Arab?'[150]

Soon after the Sykes–Picot mission left Jeddah, Sykes submitted for comments a draft joint memorandum that set out what should be the Franco–British policy in the Middle East. In regard to Husayn and his ambitions, the text was clear: the British continued to think of him and his successors in terms of being a titular suzerain over the Arab countries. The emphasis was on 'titular,' as Clayton made apparent to a US official in Cairo. In answer to a direct question, Clayton replied: '[W]hile the King of the Hedjas [sic] would probably entertain ambitions to extend his authority, the British had no intention of permitting the Kingdom of the Hedjaz to embrace but little, if any, more than what has been known as the Turkish province of the Hedjaz.'[151]

The die was cast, and the conflict between Hashimite aspirations and British considerations in Europe would dog the relationship between the two until the demise of the Kingdom of the Hijaz. Husayn's cantankerous behavior – probably born out of bitterness at the loss of what he thought should have been his glorious destiny – would be his undoing when the fire of the Wahhabi *da'wah* began to lap at the Ka'ba. He would have to modify his goals, and

---

[149] FO 371/3054/174974, Wingate to Balfour, no. 179, 16 August 1917, enclosing a report by Lawrence of an interview with Husayn on 29 July 1917, dated 30 July 1917. Emphasis in original.

[150] GLLD 9/9, Note by Sheikh Fu'ad el Khatib taken down by Lt.-Col. Newcombe, enclosed in Wilson to Clayton, 21–25 May 1917.

[151] Rashid, pp. 31–3, US Vice-Consul in Charge, Cairo, Paul [signature illegible], to US Secretary of State, date unclear, but from November 1917, received in Washington 20 December 1917.

this he did later, when he began to develop his own ideas on suzerainty.

The Hashimite tribal confederacy which expanded during the Arab Revolt differed from other Arabian chieftaincies in several respects. While alliances were made with tribes, they lacked the necessary *'asabiyyah* provided by kinship in the Shammar-based Rashidi chieftaincy or the ideological cohesion present in the Wahhabi creed of the Saudi chieftaincy. Perhaps most importantly, Husayn's leadership was neither charismatic nor based on a personal connection with tribal leaders, as was Ibn Saud's. His son Faysal was charismatic and did make such connections, but no sooner had he moved north of 'Aqabah than these relations loosened greatly, and the Hijaz was left with the uninspiring Husayn, who neither formed personal connections with tribal leaders, nor did he or his movement represent their aspirations. Lacking these qualities, Husayn chose to rely primarily on an outside power to support his chieftaincy. He expected and received massive funding and arms, but his expectations that the British would run political interference for him with the French and his Arabian rivals was foolhardy. This was unfortunate, for chieftaincies were inherently unstable; when he lost favor with the British, his chieftaincy had nothing to fall back on.

It also worth stressing that the tactics of the Revolt were often determined by having to come to terms with strong tribal autonomy – tribal leaders were reluctant to give this up and join the Revolt. At Rabigh and Wajh, movement was halted while tribal alliances were formed. Yet even these alliances were fickle, as demonstrated by the cases of Ibn Mubarak at Rabigh and Ibn Rifadah at Wajh.

From the beginning of the Revolt until the capture of 'Aqabah, the period discussed in this chapter, the main efforts at state formation were directed towards the creation of a tribal confederacy which expanded northwards. This period also saw the beginnings of developments in economic integration, increased methods of control, the formation of a central government, and other aspects of state development. These were not however the focus of Husayn's attentions in the Revolt's first year; but after the capture of 'Aqabah in the summer of 1917, Faysal's force came under the control of General Allenby's Egyptian Expeditionary Force (EEF), and the Hijaz itself was no longer a theater of operations.

Ibn Saud became an even greater problem, and when the British made clear that they would no longer support Husayn's territorial ambitions, Husayn was forced into dealing with the mechanics of state formation in the Hijaz itself. This effort is therefore studied in the next two chapters.

5

THE STATE'S MECHANISMS OF COERCION

THE ADMINISTRATION OF JUSTICE AND THE ARMED FORCES

One of the ways in which states become strong *vis-à-vis* their societies is by developing methods of coercion to force society to obey the will of the state, as defined by the ruler or rulers. Husayn, appointed Sharif in 1908, had an idea of what was needed to build his state. By clothing his authoritarianism in the fabric of the *shari'ah*, he represented the administration of justice by the state as the will of God. He also developed his armed forces as another means of coercion, used first against the Ottomans during the Revolt and then against Ibn Saud.

The administration of justice

'The [common people] … when the times seem out of joint, appeal, in concert with the 'Ulama, to the Sacred Law, and, in every political revolution, are thrilled by the expectation that at last the Mahdi is coming who will give back to that Law its own.'[1]

Historically, the Ottomans had a difficult time applying the various *tanzimat* reforms in the Hijaz.[2] It would therefore stand to reason that similar difficulties were encountered in the area of legal reform. Indeed, it seems that *nizamiyye* courts did not exist in the Hijaz – there were only *shar'i* and commercial courts,[3] the latter made necessary by the large number of foreign subjects with

---

[1] Snouck Hurgronje, *Mekka*, pp. 182–3; 189–90.
[2] See al-Amr, pp. 60–89.
[3] On the commercial courts, see Ochsenwald, *Religion, State*, pp. 84–90.

126

consular backing and the importance of Jeddah as an international port.

Before 1916 the *shari'ah* courts seemed to have functioned under the Ottomans' typical leniency in the application of the *hudud* (sing. *hadd*) punishments, the Qur'anic penalties prescribed for certain crimes, such as the amputation of a hand or foot for theft.[4] Snouck Hurgronje, writing of the late nineteenth century, hints that the *hudud* were used, but that the religious law, 'by its marvelously mild application ... secures a way out for all offenders.'[5] Ochsenwald, who covers the period 1840–1908, confirms the lax use of the *hudud*. He notes that '[p]unishment for such crimes as burglary and forgery consisted of flogging and short prison sentences.'[6] Burglary, at least, would certainly have qualified as *sariqah* (theft), for which the *hadd* of amputation would have been applied in a *shar'i* system.[7]

In the empire as a whole, the Ottoman reformers had brought about a general weakening of the *shari'ah*, and Islamic law was applied in fewer and fewer areas.[8] It will be recalled that when Husayn became Sharif in 1908, he did so as one opposed to the newly restored constitution and as a defender of the *shari'ah*; soon after he became Sharif, evidence suggests, the *hudud* were in use. A.J.B. Wavell, a British traveller, noticed a procession of nineteen thieves; six had been shot, while the remainder had had their right hands cut off.[9]

4 On this leniency, see Haim Gerber, 'Sharia, Kanun and Custom in the Ottoman Law: The Court Records of 17th Century Bursa,' *International Journal of Turkish Studies*, 2 (1981), pp. 131–47: 'We know that large parts of the orthodox *sharia* were hardly ever in use, e.g., the criminal law which involved amputation of limbs and the like.' Indeed, these punishments, except for the death penalty for apostasy, were officially abolished under the Penal Code of 1858; see Noel J. Coulson, *A History of Islamic Law* (Edinburgh University Press, 1964), p. 151.

5 Snouck Hurgronje, *Mekka*, p. 189. Snouck Hurgronje makes the blanket statement (pp. 182–3) that Hanafi *fiqh* was applied in all religious matters and in family matters, but that 'all other matters were decided according to the new secular law (called al-Qanun al-Munif) which replaced the Shar' al-Sherif (Sacred Law).' This seems a bit of an oversimplification, and contributes to the general confusion over the issue.

6 Ochsenwald, *Religion, State*, p. 89.

7 Joseph Schacht, *An Introduction to Islamic Law* (Oxford: Clarendon Press, 1964), p. 180.

8 See the entry '*mahkama*' in *EI²*, and David Dean Commins, *Islamic Reform: Politics and Social Change in Late Ottoman Syria* (New York: Oxford University Press, 1990), p. 13.

9 A.J.B. Wavell, *A Modern Pilgrim in Mecca and a Siege of Sanaa* (London: Constable, 1913), p. 166. Again, although the evidence of the application of the *hudud* in the Hijaz prior

When he began the Revolt, Husayn posed as the defender of Islamic law against the secularizing reforms of the Young Turks. His call was not a national one, as this would have generated little response, but an Islamic call. In his first proclamation, he singled out the changes the empire had instituted in the *shar'i* laws of inheritance (*mirath*): they had established the *mirath nizami*, which gave new-found equality to males and females in inheritance. In general, all the *qawanin* (secular laws) were applied in the Arab lands, but less so in the Hijaz, and the *mirath nizami* not at all.[10] Nonetheless, Husayn cited this *nizam* as one of the reasons for his Revolt, when he accused the Young Turks of having the gall to mock God's word in the Qur'an, where He said that the man's part was twice that of the woman (*'lil-dhakar mitl al-unthayayn'*).[11] With his pretensions to lead the Arab world, opposition to the *mirath nizami* was designed to strike a strong accord among traditionally minded Muslim males in Syria and Iraq.

The Young Turks were perceived all over the Empire as anti-*shar'i*. At home in Anatolia, the counter-revolution of April 1909 took up the slogan 'the *Şeriat* is in danger, we want the *Şeriat!*'[12] In February 1910 the Ministry of Justice wrote the Ministry of Finance with a proposal to reorganize the courts in the Hijaz. When 'Abdallah and the other Hijazi deputies learned this, they wrote to the Grand Vezier that 'the presence of any courts other than the *shari'ah* would be unacceptable in the holy cities of Islam.' Perhaps because of their letter, and the opinion of Talat that the *shari'ah* law was better suited than secular law to Hijazi society, the *shari'ah* courts of the Hijaz remained under the *şeriateyhülislam*, the top religious figure in the Empire.[13] But the threat to the *shari'ah* remained. In 1913 and 1915 the Young Turks

---

to the rise of Husayn is sketchy, the British concern about the increasing use of these punishments by Husayn and the Sharif's oft-stated publication of the fact would seem to indicate that he did apply them more than had been typical previously.

[10] 'When local Ottoman townspeople died, their property was divided according to Qur'anic injunctions, with recourse to a qadi or mufti if necessary' (Ochsenwald, *Religion, Society*, p. 87). Muhammad 'Abd al-Jawad Muhammad, *Al-Tatawwur al-Tashri'i fi al-Mamlakah al-'Arabiyyah al-Sa'udiyyah* (Cairo University Press, 1977), pp. 40–1, also stresses this.

[11] Muhammad, pp. 40–1. The quote is from Surah IV:11.

[12] Bernard Lewis, *The Emergence of Modern Turkey* (Oxford University Press, 1968), p. 215.

[13] Kayali, dissertation, p. 216.

weakened the independence of the *shari'ah* courts by placing them under the authority of the secular Ministry of Justice.[14]

After the Revolt began, Husayn moved to demonstrate his commitment to the *shari'ah*. The Sharif never ceased to emphasize that he abided by it, and British observers found his application of *shar'i* law worthy of note. The fourth issue of *al-Qiblah* carried an announcement that Husayn had ordered the reorganization of the *shari'ah* court in Mecca. Good salaries would be paid to all officials, and the court would be conducted according to religious law. Fees were to be lower than those set by the Ottomans, and officials who charged more than the official rate would be fired.[15]

Husayn established a court of summary justice (*mahkamat al-mawadd al-musta'jilah*) which adjudicated cases that required immediate action, and suits limited to small amounts (a kind of a small-claims court).[16] He also founded a court of castigation (*mahkamat al-ta'zirat al-shar'iyyah*), which dealt with cases that had no specific Qur'anic punishment, such as homicide. In 1917 *Al-Qiblah* recorded a case in which three young men strangled a co-worker. The government arrested them, and they were brought before the court of castigation, which sentenced them to death. The paper said that they were hanged in the public square to the cheers of the crowd.[17]

Foreigners in the Hijaz at this time took notice of changes in the legal situation. Cornwallis of the British Arab Bureau, on his first visit to the Hijaz after the Revolt, wrote that the *shari'ah* was now the only form of law in the land.[18] The director of the Jeddah branch of the Imperial Ottoman Bank (a mostly French-domi-

---

14 Stanford and Ezel Shaw, *History of the Ottoman Empire and Modern Turkey, II, Reform, Revolution, and Republic: The Rise of Modern Turkey, 1808–1975* (Cambridge University Press, 1977), pp. 306–7. Niyazi Berkes, *The Development of Secularism in Turkey* (London: Hurst, 1998 [rpt. of 1964 edition]), pp. 415–16, puts this reform in 1916, but does not indicate whether it came before or after the beginning of the Sharif's Revolt.

15 *Al-Qiblah*, 25 Shawwal 1334 [24 August 1916].

16 *Al-Qiblah*, 27 Safar 1337 [1 December 1918]. In this article, Husayn announced the establishment of such a court in Jeddah. The article noted also that such a court already existed in Mecca.

17 *Al-Qiblah*, 2 Rajab 1335 [23 April 1917]. *Ta'zir* refers to punishments for which there is no prescription in the Qur'an; the sentence in thus carried out at the discretion of the *qadi*.

18 FO 371/2781/236299, Cornwallis note for Residency, 31 October 1916, enclosed in McMahon to Grey, 13 November 1916.

nated Anglo-French concern) wrote to his superiors expressing his fear that the *shar'i* prohibition on interest would damage the branch's profits.[19] Lawrence, possibly overstating the case, wrote: 'The Turkish civil code has been abolished. In the towns the cadis administer the undiluted Sharia, and in the tribes matters are still to be settled by tribal law, with final reference to [Husayn]. [He] intends, when there is time, to extend the principle and scope of the Sherif to cover modern difficulties of trade and exchange!'[20]

The carrying out of the *hudud* was something of which Husayn was quite proud. For instance, in 1918, four men imprisoned in Yanbu' made an escape but were caught. The organizer of the escape, who had been imprisoned on Husayn's orders, received the *hadd* of having both a hand and a foot amputated. *Al-Qiblah* noted that this was the first time this type of *hadd* had been applied in the Hijaz, and therefore the people were happy that the *shar'iah* was being put to use against serious criminals.[21] The British were shocked, but refrained from making any official protest. Wilson, who discussed the incident with Husayn informally, noted that the act 'created a good deal of divers criticism on the part of the nobles of Jeddah.' Husayn's reply was that this *hadd* was the punishment laid down for rebellion or acts against public security or against the government by the *shari'ah*.[22]

Foreign observers noted that the *hudud* were applied with particular fervor during the *hajj*, as Husayn wished to impress the *hujjaj* with his Islamic zeal.[23] An incident was reported in *al-Qiblah* in 1923 under the headline, 'Applying the *Hudud al-Shar'iyyah.*' The paper said that two pickpockets had been caught working one of the pilgrimage caravans. They were brought to Mecca, where

---

19 FO 371/2781/199283, T. Aboucassem, director, Jeddah branch of the Imperial Ottoman Bank, to London office of bank, 18 September 1916. The bank was actually never allowed to reopen its Jeddah branch, because Husayn rightly suspected it of being under hostile French control, and the British opposed it for the same reason.

20 *AB*, no. 32, 26 November 1916.

21 *Al-Qiblah*, 27 Sha'ban 1336 [6 June 1918].

22 FO 686/38, General Notes on Conversations with King Hussein on [sic] Jeddah on 2, 3 and 4 June, 1918, by Wilson, 6 June 1918.

23 FO 686/28, Jeddah Report, 11–30 August 1922; FO 371/8943/E 2478, Pilgrimage Report, 1922, enclosed in Marshall to Curzon, no. 11, 31 January 1923; FO 371/10006/E 289, Report on the Economic Conditions in the Hedjaz by Vice-Consul L.S. Grafftey-Smith, enclosed in Bullard to Curzon, no. 12, Overseas Trade, 31 October 1923.

the *hadd* was applied as the crowd chanted the Qur'anic passage, '*al-sariq wal-sariqah fa-qta'u aydiyahuma*' ('As for the thief, both male and female, cut off their hands').[24]

In late February 1917, the French mission received a letter from a Hashimite official stating that the government would no longer tolerate the importation of alcoholic beverages. The French would, however, be allowed a small amount for personal use, as long as the customs officials were informed when it was brought into the Hijaz.[25] A few days later, *al-Qiblah* trumpeted the new policy as evidence of the Sharif's concern for the *shari'ah* (so as not to upset the merchants, it was announced that all stocks of alcoholic beverages would be purchased by the government).[26]

Acts of unlawful intercourse were apparently also a problem. Writing in May 1920, the British agent in Mecca, Ihsanullah, reported that Husayn was 'greatly grieved [about] the daily spreading of adulteration in the holy city, and ... that during the last month twenty-three ... virgin girls [were] found [to be] pregnant.' Ihsanullah noted a case wherein an adulterer from the Jiyad quarter of Mecca had been arrested and jailed. The woman, he added, was sent to jail, 'where she [would] remain forever.' 'Indecent women,' of whom Ihsanullah noted 150 in Mecca, were incarcerated in a special prison.[27]

In another case, *al-Qiblah* reported that a court had sentenced some wine drinkers to the *hadd* of lashes. After the sentence had been carried out, the offenders were drafted into the army or sent to work on the railway.[28] Reporting from Mecca, British representative Captain Ajab Khan noted the puritanical streak in Mecca's administration:

Liquors, Music, Gramophones, singing and dancing are prohibited to the public. A certain Sheikh of a 'Hara' [quarter] was recently reported for illicit distilling of 'Aruck' at his house for his own use[.] [O]n searching his house, distilling apparatus was found and captured[,] and

---

[24] *Al-Qiblah*, 31 May 1923. The verse is from V:37. For another such incident, see FO 686/26, Extracts from Report from Agent – Mecca, enclosed in Jeddah Report, 10 May 1920.

[25] MAE, Djeddah (consulat), carton no. 529, 27 February 1917.

[26] *al-Qiblah*, 14 Jamadi al-Ula 1335 [7 March 1917]. In 1919, *al-Qiblah* wrote that Indian newspapers had praised Husayn for this policy (2 Rajab 1337 [2 April 1919]).

[27] FO 682/12, Ihsanullah to British Agent, Jeddah, 19 May 1920.

[28] *Al-Qiblah*, 15 Sha'ban 1337 [15 May 1919].

without any further trial, all the distilling pottery was flung at the head of the defaulting Sheikh and an award of 80 lashes was also inflicted on him.

According to Ajab Khan, flogging was

the ... favourite punishment with the officials ... and ... very often applied. The method of flogging [was] very simple. The convicted person [was] laid on the ground, back upwards, in public, and to hold him down two men [sat] on his neck and one on his legs while two men, one on each side, carr[ied] out the flogging. Amputation [was] also resorted to in a most cruel way.[29]

Historically, some Muslim jurists viewed the use of cannabis as a crime, but the state's reaction to it has varied, perhaps because, as Rosenthal reasons, it was not barred by 'the authority of express statements creditable to the very highest religious sources.'[30] In punishing sellers, however, Husayn followed the strictest interpretation of the jurists, and outlawed the sale of hashish in Mecca. Shipments were confiscated, and the dealers were fined and imprisoned. (This resulted, wrote Ajab Khan, in lowering the quality of the herb available in the holy city.) Hashish was sometimes sold by the most well-known of the élite: in 1920, for instance, a large quantity was found in the house of Muhammad al-Shayba, of the family which held the keys to the Ka'ba. Only Shayba's high status saved him from being imprisoned.[31]

After the capture of Medina in January 1919, *al-Qiblah* made a point of warning that sitting in the city's coffee houses and running shops and government offices during prayer time would no longer be tolerated. From now on, said the paper, everyone must go to the mosque.[32] Captain Zia, the Turkish officer who had been sent to negotiate the surrender of Medina, told the British that Husayn was unfit to run 'civilized' areas, '[W]itness his ruthless application of effete Koranic punishments, such as [the] cutting

---

[29] FO 686/12, Intelligence Report up to 29.2.20, Captain Ajab Khan (Mecca). Eighty lashes is the prescribed *hadd* for drinking wine (Schacht, p. 179).

[30] See Franz Rosenthal, *The Herb: Hashish versus Medieval Muslim Society* (Leiden: Brill, 1971).

[31] FO 686/12, unidentified intelligence agent in Mecca [Nasirudin?] to British Agent (Jeddah), no. 79, 6 August 1920. The term used in this report is 'grass,' and I assume that *hashish* is the substance intended, particularly since the Arabic for weeds or grass is *hashish*.

[32] *Al-Qiblah*, 15 Sha'ban 1337 [15 May 1919].

off of hands and feet for minor offences;' Zia said; 'such action has already gone far to alienate all intelligent Moslem opinion outside of Hejaz.'[33]

The commercial court of Jeddah, which had tried cases in the 1890s and early 1900s,[34] was not restored immediately after the Revolt. But in late 1919 Husayn had an altercation with a Dutch merchant and wanted to try him for slander. When he discovered he had no court in which to try the man, he reactivated the commercial court.[35] 'Abdallah wrote to the British representative, saying that the new court would be under the 'known ways of dealing in commercial law.'[36] *Al-Qiblah* announced the formation of the court (*mahkamah tijariyyah*), which would have six members and a chairman. It would adjudicate cases in which one of the litigants was a foreigner who did not want to be tried in a *shar'i* court.[37]

The commercial court was chaired by Qasim Zaynal, nephew of the *qa'im maqam* of Jeddah and a partner in the most important business house in the Hijaz, Haji Zaynal 'Ali Rida. British Vice-Consul Grafftey-Smith, when asked by the Department of Overseas Trade to report on the difficulties encountered by foreign firms seeking legal action against their agents in the Hijaz, noted that Qasim Zaynal had been heard on more than one occasion to remark that Husayn himself instructed him on the procedure to follow in each case. In fact, Grafftey-Smith had been involved with the New York-based Singer Manufacturing Company, which had claims against their agents in Mecca and Medina. When its representative, a British subject, was stonewalled by the court, Grafftey-Smith appealed to Husayn, who issued his own decision, the content of which demonstrated that he was very familiar with all the particulars of the case.[38]

Although Husayn hoped, by making use of the *shari'ah*, to tap into Islamic legitimacy at the very moment he was rebelling against

---

33 FO 371/4166/21996, Interview with Captain Zia, sent from Constantinople by the Turks to negotiate the surrender of Medina, 19 January 1919, enclosed in Cheetham to FO, no. 39, 24 January 1919.

34 Ochsenwald, *Religion, State*, pp. 84–90.

35 FO 686/26, Intelligence and Political Summary, 21.11.19–1.12.19, 1 December 1919.

36 FO 686/26, Intelligence and Political Report, 1.12.19–11.12.19, 11 December 1919.

37 *Al-Qiblah*, 20 November 1919.

38 FO 371/8954/E 5926, L.A Grafftey-Smith, Vice-Consul, Acting British Agent and Consul, to Comptroller General, Department of Overseas Trade, Overseas Trade no. 5, 8 May 1923.

the legitimate Muslim sovereign, it appears that his strategy was a failure. The use of the *hudud* was not widely supported, and, as will be seen, his unjust accusations against people and the general harshness of his régime must have bred alienatation among the Hijazi population.

The armed forces[39]

Recruiting a regular army. An army can be a means of coercion, in other words, of enforcing the state's will at home, and of exporting it beyond its borders. Husayn, familiar with tribal vicissitudes, realized from the beginning that he could not rely solely on recruits from tribal groups and was convinced that he had to develop a regular, standing army. Quite early in the Revolt, in his contacts with the British he became insistent that they provide him with trained Muslim troops and with artillery, and he withdrew earlier objections to employing Christians in his army. In late June 1916, Husayn informed the British that he wanted to establish an Arab army of 30,000, the core composed of Hijazis and strengthened by non-Hijazi Arab officers. In early August, it was reported that he had begun the voluntary recruitment of a standing army, acquiring 1,000 men in the first three days.[40] In early December, Husayn informed Storrs that he intended to institute compulsory service in the Hijaz.[41] There is in fact no independent evidence of either such large initial success or systematic compulsory service (indeed, avoiding the latter in Ottoman times was considered, along with not having to pay taxes, as one of the primary benefits of living in the Hijaz).

The British were sympathetic to Husayn's need for trained officers, and their first candidate to head the new Hashimite Arab army was the Egyptian, 'Aziz 'Ali al-Masri, proposed by Faruqi, Husayn's representative in Cairo.[42] 'Aziz was a problematic choice; he hesitated to accept the appointment, supporting a Turco-Arab

---

[39] In this section I have often drawn on Eliezer Tauber's extensive research in *Arab Movements*, pp. 83–153. Reference should be made to Tauber where no reference is given here.

[40] *AB*, no. 13, 1 August 1916.

[41] *AB*, no. 35, 20 December 1916.

[42] 'Aziz 'Ali al-Masri was the leader and founder of *al-'Ahd*. In 1914 he was sentenced to death by the Ottomans but received amnesty after Kitchener's intervention. See Tauber, *Arab Movements*, pp. 83–100.

empire and not Arab separatism, and he suspected that Husayn was interested solely in the independence of the Hijaz. Faruqi worked to sway both al-Masri and Husayn, as did Nuri al-Sa'id, a former Arab Ottoman officer serving with the Revolt. When 'Aziz came to the Hijaz in September to assess the situation, he told Husayn that the Arabs should seek autonomy within the Ottoman Empire, and should work to prevent hostilities between Britain and the Ottomans. He even suggested that Husayn not give up his relations with Istanbul. Despite his need for trained officers, Husayn was suspicious of all who might be of help, and, considering that the Revolt had already begun, 'Aziz's suggestions must have seemed treacherous, if not bizarre. Nevertheless, the British pressed Husayn, and al-Masri was appointed Chief of the General Staff of the Hashimite Arab Army in September 1916.

'Aziz, based at Rabigh, was not delegated any real authority by the suspicious Hashimites, but immediately began operational plans which would effectively make him independent of Sharifian influence. 'Abdallah told the British that Husayn harbored suspicions against anyone who had been active in the CUP, as al-Masri had. Most probably realizing that 'Aziz could contribute to the Revolt's military might, and wanting to please the British, Husayn retained 'Aziz. The British again pressed him, and, despite his misgivings, the Sharif appointed 'Aziz Minister of War with an independent budget, on 14 December 1916.

Consistent with his desire to reach an accommodation with the Ottomans, 'Aziz acted perfidiously during an attempted attack on Medina in January 1917. Although there were several versions of this incident, it was clear to all that 'Aziz had acted treacherously. He was removed from his post and sent back to Egypt in February 1917. Given his behavior, wrote Hashimite historian Sulaiman Mousa, 'we may ... consider him fortunate to have escaped so lightly.'[43] A young Egyptian officer, Mahmud al-Qaysuni, took over as Minister of War while Ja'far al-'Askari, a former Ottoman officer from Iraq, took over as commander of the Revolt.

The al-Masri affair did not bode well for relations between the Hashimites and those who were supposed to form the basis of a

[43] Suleiman Mousa, 'The Role of Syrians And Iraqis in the Arab Revolt,' *Middle East Forum* 43 (1967), pp. 5–17 (quote on p. 9).

regular army; problems surrounded its mobilization from the start. Most of the regular soldiers and officers were either Iraqis or Syrians who had served in the Ottoman armed forces and had either been taken prisoner or deserted to Entente lines. It soon became clear, as the British scoured the POW camps of India, Egypt, and Iraq, that these men were not terribly enthusiastic about serving in the Hashimite Army. Many had doubts about serving with Christian powers against the legitimate Muslim sovereign of the day. Moreover, there were some who feared possible reprisals against family still living within Ottoman territory. To many, it seemed safer to stay in the camps.

Faruqi spent a lot of time in Egypt trying to convince soldiers to come to the Hijaz. The first group, which arrived in the Hijaz on 1 August 1916, caused a crisis when it was discovered that they were not prepared to fight for Husayn. Only Nuri al-Sa'id, a few other officers, and some enlisted men agreed to stay.

The first truly successful group, composed of 25 officers and 222 enlisted men, left Bombay for the Hijaz on 16 September 1916. Two months later, another shipment of 90 officers and 2,100 enlisted left for the Hijaz, only to balk when they anchored off Rabigh. After much cajoling, twenty-seven men and six officers agreed to debark. The last attempt at recruitment was carried out in February 1917 in Egypt by Fawzi al-Bakri and Fu'ad al-Khatib. Husayn, having been burned before, was not satisfied with the men they had chosen, and the British also expressed their lack of confidence. Thus ended the effort to create a standing army by recruiting outside the Hijaz.

Instruction. Realizing the need for home-grown officers and soldiers, Husayn announced in *al-Qiblah* in December 1916 the founding of a military academy in Mecca. Its first commander was a Syrian officer, Shukri al-Shurbaji, a member of the Arab nationalist organization *al-Fatat*, who had deserted to the Russian lines at Kermanshah in August 1916.[44] The academy was composed of two parts: an officers' candidate school, and a barracks for the training of enlisted men. The school for officers was located in the

---

[44] *Al-Qiblah*, 11 Safar 1335 [6 December 1916]; Tauber, *Arab Movements*, p. 111. Brigadier Syed Ali el-Edroos, *The Hashimite Arab Army, 1908–1979: An Appreciation and Analysis of Military Operations* (Amman: Publishing Committee, 1980), pp. 55–193, has his name as Shurani.

center of town in a complex owned by Husayn, and had fifty candidates, all of whom were the sons of Meccan notables. Their uniform was khaki, after the English model; their salary was 100 Turkish piasters a month, and they were armed with French rifles. Military instruction was carried out under the supervision of Shurbaji and three Syrian NCOs, employing German and Ottoman methods. The candidates drilled twice daily, for a total of three hours, and Husayn made sure that each day his officers heard guest lecturers speak on several subjects, ranging from history and geography to Arabic and Islamic theology. The school session had no predetermined length. A student graduated when he had passed a certain examination, whenever that might be, thereafter receiving the rank of second lieutenant.

The school for enlisted men was located in an old Ottoman barracks on the outskirts of Mecca. Qaysuni, the young Egyptian-born Minister of War, had his quarters there. Numbering at the time about 350 men, the soldiers were drawn from a more diverse pool than the officers: they included Meccans, bedouin, Medinans and Yemenis. Their uniform was a long tunic, white for dress and khaki for exercises, worn belted over the clothes. They wore sandals and were armed with French rifles. Their daily ration was 750 grams of bread, some butter, and a few handfuls of legumes. According to Lt. Col. Cousse, commandant of the French military mission in the Hijaz, disciplinary measures were brutal: the primary punishment was a beating. Hijazis formed the plurality of officers who trained the troops: five Hijazis, two Egyptians, one Turk, one French-Algerian, one Syrian and one Baghdadi. Cousse was disturbed by the school's inconsistent military training. Infantry instruction was carried out according to Egyptian procedure, artillery courses were taught by the Ottoman method, and machine gun units were modelled on their French counterparts. Cousse wrote that Qaysuni did not have the right personality to run the academy. The Egyptian was too tough on the bedouin, who should have been handled with more tact, thought Cousse. Qaysuni was hated by the former Ottoman officers, who considered him inferior, and despised by the Hijazis. Moreover, he was unable to demand the necessary funds and supplies from Husayn, whom he treated with *'une obséquiosité et d'une timidité toute égyptiennes.'* Husayn himself, who visited the school often, was stingy with the ammunition needed for maneuvers, doling it out case by case. Cousse concluded on an optimistic note, however: despite all the school's problems, it yielded a few hundred soldiers and officers, who, while rough at the edges (*dégrossis*), were more obedient than the prisoners who had previously constituted the bulk of the regulars.[45]

Order of battle. From periodic reports and the work of Tauber, it is possible to reach a general estimate of the order of battle (distribution of forces) of the Sharifian Army. As Table 5.1 shows, most of the regulars must have been Hijazis, as their total number far exceeds that of former soldiers in the Ottoman army who had agreed to fight. (The bedouin component ebbed and flowed unpredictably and was therefore not measurable.) Yet in Faysal's and 'Ali's armies the regulars reached into the thousands; they could not have been provided by the military academy in Mecca. The conclusion, therefore, is that most regular soldiers were pressed into service by Husayn. One British report noted that 'Abdallah's regular army was made up of 'the dregs of Meccan society.'[46]

Hashimite sources, of course, give a different picture. In November 1918 *al-Qiblah* announced the reorganization of the armed forces. On paper, it seemed like a serious attempt at state building, a reorganization of the command structure that would distribute responsibility so that the army would be more efficient and more powerful. The army would have additional departments (*da'irah*): GHQ, ordnance, military justice, and health. It would be structured as an army corps (*mu'askar*), divided as follows: there would be two infantry divisions (*firqah*), each having cavalry, artillery and machine-gun units; each division would have two brigades (*liwa'*); each brigade would have four battalions (*katibah*); each battalion would have four companies (*saff*); each company would have six platoons (*qism*); and each platoon would be made up of six sections (*juz*), composed of twenty soldiers each. The announcement listed the ranks of officers for each unit, as well as additional attached forces. This structure, according to the announcement, yielded a

---

[45] SHAT, 7 N 2138, Centre d'instruction militaire de la Mecque, Le Chef de Bataillon, Commandant p.i. la Mission Militaire Française en Egypte [Cousse], 24 January 1918.

[46] *AB*, no. 80, 26 January 1918.

Table 5.1. THE ARMIES OF THE ARAB REVOLT

	Faysal's army		'Ali's army		'Abdallah's army		Zayd's army	
	Reg.	Irreg.	Reg.	Irreg.	Reg.	Irreg.	Reg.	Irreg.
Beginning of Revolt				10,000				
July 1916				30,000				
Sept. 1916		6,000		8–9,000		6–7,000		6,000
Nov. 1916		5,000		2–5,000		5,000		
Dec. 1916		8–9,000		8,000		4,000		
June 1917	1,673		1,375	5–10,000	104	5,000	610	1,500
Aug. 1917	2,000							
Nov. 1917	3,000		2,000				1,500	
Dec. 1917	4,000						Joined Faysal	
Jan. 1918	4,500		3,000		4–500			
Apr. 1918	8,000	10,000		7,000				
Sept. 1918	8,000	20,000						

Source: Eliezer Tauber, *The Arab Movements in World War I* (London: Cass, 1993).

total of 47,414 men under arms.[47] This was far greater than the total number of soldiers in Husayn's army, as may be seen from Table 5.1. There is, in any case, no independent verification that such a structure actually existed.

Husayn divided his armed forces into 'armies' led by his four sons, although Zayd commanded his army for a short period only. Faysal's army played a role in the Hijaz proper only until the capture of 'Aqabah in the summer of 1917, when his forces were removed from Husayn's immediate influence. We have very little information on the composition of the regulars in 'Ali and

---

[47] *Al-Qiblah*, 2 Safar 1337 [16 November 1918]. This structure shows that Husayn attempted to build his army, at least on paper, based on a combination of British, Ottoman, and Egyptian formations. In addition to the names he gives the units which are cited herein, he also mentions Egyptian and Turkish names for the formations. Thus *mu'askar*, it is noted, is what 'in the east in known as *ordu* [Turkish], and in the European countries is known as army corps or corps d'armée.' It is also not clear from the text in *al-Qiblah* if Husayn is including in his army the army of Faysal, which was at the time – November 1918 – in Damascus. The structure is presented as that of the 'Army of the Arab Hashimite State' [*Jund al-Dawlah al-'Arabiyyah al-Hashimiyyah*].

'Abdallah's armies. Aside from Syrians and Iraqis, local components were Hijazi volunteers, men from the Bisha and the 'Uqayl,
or those forced into service by Husayn. The Bisha and the 'Uqayl
constituted relatively small corporate organizations which had a
special relationship with the state. The Bisha, who were of the
Shahran, were described in the *Arab Bulletin* (probably by Lawrence) as 'the most reliable of the Emir's immediate adherents,
form[ing] the nucleus of his standing force, and serv[ing] as his
police.'[48] Brémond wrote that the Bisha were the best soldiers the
Sharif had, and that this was often the generic name given to regular soldiers.[49] The 'Uqayl, who mostly originated in Najd, have
been described as 'not a tribe but an organization partaking of the
nature of a club or society ... .' They were townfolks and nomads
of the smaller tribes (that is, not Harb or 'Utaybah) who hired
themselves out as guides and mercenaries.[50] These descriptions
suggest that both the Bisha and the 'Uqayl represented a professional military social group or class, and they may have been the
closest to a 'regular' army that Husayn had.

Nevertheless, British officers with 'Ali and 'Abdallah reported
great difficulties in working with both the 'Uqayl and the Bisha,
who were put to use because they had been loyal – when paid well
– to the Sharif in the past. Newcombe wrote bitterly that during
demolition missions against the Hijaz railway the Bisha often
deserted; the 'Uqayl, he said, were timid and refused to go near
the tracks. 'All the difficulties of cutting the line,' lamented
Newcombe, 'come from our own side; the Turks put very few in
our way.'[51] Garland, also involved in the demolition efforts, similarly complained that the 'Uqayl would not follow orders. He had
trained a group of them in Suez – well, he thought, in Suez – but
now 'they have neglected my precise and repeated instructions
deliberately.'[52]

[48] *AB*, no. 41, 6 February 1917.
[49] SHAT, 7 N 2139, Brémond, no. 14, Note sur les tribus des ahl el hedjaz, 17 January 1917.
[50] *GA*, pp. 133–134.
[51] FO 686/2, Report by Lt.-Col. Newcombe, 12 March 1917. See also *AB* no. 46, 30 March 1917; FO 686/6, Report from 28 April–2 May [1917] by Col. Newcombe (quoted); FO 686/6, Colonel Newcombe's Report, 4 May 1917.
[52] FO 686/2, Bimbashi Herbert Garland to Colonel Wilson, 14 August 1917.

The Iraqi and Syrian regulars. Alec Seath Kirkbride, a British intelligence officer who had contact with Faysal's army in the latter days of the Revolt, wrote as follows about the Iraqi officers under Faysal's command:

After having watched [the Iraqis] in action, I came to regard them as the best fighting material amongst the Arabs; they were certainly made of tougher fibre than the Syrians, Lebanese or Palestinians, most of whom seemed to prefer to remain in the safety of a prisoner of war camp once they had got there.[53]

Tauber has closely examined the performance of the army regulars under Faysal's command. He makes a similar assessment of Ja'far al-'Askari, Nuri al-Sa'id and Mawlud Mukhlis, the Iraqi officers who led the regulars, writing that they 'led the Arab forces during the battles, and in fact they were the ones who initiated most of the battles in which the army of the revolt took part.'[54]

In contrast, the assessment of 'Ali's and 'Abdallah's forces by other British and French observers was not charitable. Davenport, who served with 'Ali and 'Abdallah, wrote blistering reports on the Arab regulars. In the midst of an attack, he complained, the Iraqis balked at moving up artillery pieces, and when they did, they stationed them behind a hill to hide from the Turks. They refused to move until the bedouin threatened them with death. In another attack, all of 'Ali's officers claimed they were sick, and eventually deserted him. Davenport wrote that while in 'Abdallah's and 'Ali's camp he was 'pestered ... by the Syrian and Baghdadi parties among the officers, each complaining about the other. The officers have [an] abundance of female society and live in considerable luxury ... They hold fancy ranks without regard to their competence.'[55] He accused the officers of being cowards and of purposely delaying the taking of Medina in order to maintain enormous stipends. They falsified expenses, Davenport complained, and stole stores which they then reported as not having arrived.[56]

---

[53] Sir Alec Kirkbride, *An Awakening: The Arab Campaign 1917–1918* (Tavistock, England: University Press of America, 1971), p. 12.

[54] Tauber, *The Arab Movements*, p. 132.

[55] *AB*, no. 95, 2 July 1918.

[56] FO 686/52, Davenport to Bassett, Jeddah, 25 April 1918, enclosed in Bassett to Director, Arab Bureau, 2 [?] May 1918.

All the armies were affected by the distrust between the Iraqi and Syrian personnel and between them and Husayn. The Syrians resented the fact that most of the officers were Iraqis, particularly since a major goal of the Revolt was the liberation of Syria. Jealousy was intense; a British officer reported that the 'hostility between the Syrians and the Baghdadis [was] very marked. The Baghdadis evidently hate everybody but themselves and are only out for making money.'[57]

In 'Ali's army, the Iraqi officers created a committee to ensure that they and not the Syrians received promotions. The Iraqis complained that men of similar status or length of service in 'Abdallah's and Faysal's army were colonels or even generals. These Iraqi officers were of the poorest quality, wrote Capitaine Depui, the French officer assigned to 'Ali's army; one officer was a *'nullité parmi les nullités,'* while another *'ne sait par quel bout prendre un canon.'* The members of the Iraqi committee demanded a one-third raise in salary in mid-1917; their commander, the Benghazian Nuri al-Kuwayri, was ordered by 'Ali to make them behave. Kuwayri had some success in restoring order, but it was short-lived, as his efforts earned him the enmity of the Iraqis, who convinced 'Ali to remove him from his position. Kuwayri appealed to Husayn, who reinstated him, but he finally left his command in March 1919, despite Husayn's offer to make him commandant of Mecca. Kuwayri did not want to work with Qaysuni, whom no one seemed to like.[58]

The situation was not much better in 'Abdallah's army. On 23 September 1917, a group of Syrian officers beat up the Iraqi commander of his contingent of regulars. The officers threatened to resign if they were forced to obey the Iraqis.[59] There were similar problems in Faysal's army.

If one looks at the army from a Hashimite state-building perspective, the animosity between the Iraqis and Syrian regulars on the one hand, and the Hashimites on the other, was an even

57 Quoted in Tauber, *Arab Movements*, p. 136.
58 SHAT, 17 N 498, Mission Militaire Française d'Egypte, Chef de Bataillon Cousse, Djeddah, No 117A, 14 April 1918, enclosing Extrait d'un Rapport du Capitaine Depui, no. 29, 24 March 1918, sur l'état de la colonne Ali et la formation d'un comité factieux Baghdadien. See also FO 686/52, Nuri el Kueri to Hussein, 17 Sha'ban 1336 [27 May 1918]; Brémond, pp. 228–9.
59 Brémond, pp. 205–6.

greater problem than that between the Iraqis and the Syrians. As will be recalled, Husayn was suspicious of the Iraqis and Syrians from the beginning, and had resisted drafting them. He needed their expertise and wanted to portray his Revolt as an all-Arab effort, but he distrusted them completely. Since most of the officers were Iraqis, Husayn felt the most threatened by them. He thus told Wilson that he particularly distrusted the Baghdadis, and asked the British representative to have his officers forward reports on them.[60] One British official noted correctly that the Syrian officers had not 'been attracted to his service from any feelings of veneration for the Grand Shereef himself... Their ambition is a Syria ruled by Syrians.'[61]

Conflicts between the Hashimites and the Iraqi and Syrian soldiers abounded during the Revolt and afterwards. A statement made by Mark Sykes in December 1917, suggesting that Syria would go to the French, led some officers at 'Aqabah to reject Faysal's authority. Husayn sent the Iraqi 'Ali Jawdat al-Ayyubi back to Egypt at one point, and he resented Nuri al-Sa'id for what he saw as engaging more in politics than in soldiering.

Severe insubordination of their officers was a recurrent difficulty for Husayn's sons. In November 1916 an Iraqi officer in 'Ali's column hit a Hijazi who refused to follow orders. When 'Ali ordered the Iraqi confined, other officers resigned in protest. In 1917 Joyce wrote that operations were carried out not because of 'Ali's initiative, but because of his officers', and that the Amir's control of his officers was weak.[62] In October 1918 an officer in Zayd's force refused to obey orders to move north from Ma'an; Zayd's memoirs contain a telling if somewhat disingenuous account of the problem:

Some call for *wataniyyah* and *mahabbah* [patriotism], but they are far from it. A man is ordered to go to his *watan*, to see members of his *jins* [race, nation] ... after his *watan* has been liberated from the enemy. He avoids it. And he had originally [joined the army] to regain the *watan* by war and to sacrifice his soul. This is incomprehensible.[63]

[60] FO 371/3381/146256, Wilson, Interviews with King Hussein at Jeddah on 17 July 1918.
[61] Quoted in Tauber, *The Arab Movements*, p. 140.
[62] *AB*, no. 54, 22 June 1917.
[63] Entry for 3 October 1918, in Sulayman Musa (ed.) *Al-Thawrah al-'Arabiyyah al-Kubra: Al-Harb fi al-Urdunn, 1917–1918 – Mudhakkirat al-Amir Zayd* (Amman: n.p., 1976), pp. 129–30.

Zayd claimed not to understand, but the Iraqi and Syrian soldiers bridled under their Hashimite overlords because they did not see themselves as subservient. Their behavior provoked an impractical response – officers were transferred among the various armies. This strategy, of course, would not have been conducive to the efficient running of the Hashimite armed forces, and it might well have increased the officers' antipathy for their Hashimite commanders.

In the first months of the Revolt two Egyptian artillery batteries came to the Hijaz at Husayn's request. The Egyptian commander, 'Ali Bey Sa'id, refused to take orders from Husayn, who wanted him and his troops to proceed to Medina to assist in the siege. 'Ali Bey said that he did not want to expose his short-range guns to the long-range Ottoman artillery there. It was necessary for Wingate to chastise the commander and remind him that he was under the direct orders of Husayn. But 'Ali Bey was right, for when his guns finally engaged the Ottomans, they had to withdraw because they were outranged. The commander complained bitterly about Faysal's and Husayn's suspicion of the Egyptians, who, he said, were ordered about with little purpose.[64]

As for Qaysuni, the Egyptian-born Minister of War, Davenport reported that the officers hated him 'so much that there is a danger of him coming to an untimely end from their intrigues.'[65] The Syrians and the Iraqis continuously submitted petitions against him, but the feelings appear to have been mutual. It was reported in 1918 that 'when Northern Army Officers visit Mecca [Qaysuni] has a habit of tearing off their badges of rank.'[66] Husayn complained that although he liked Qaysuni,[67] he was too young. The king's distrust was so severe, that he felt no Arab officers were

---

[64] WP 138/12/19, Sirdar (Erkowit) to Draper (Port Sudan), no. 997, 19 July 1916, for Pearson in Jeddah, to relay to 'Ali Bey Sa'id, commander of the Egyptian artillery battery; WP 138/12/20–21, Sirdar, Erkowit, to Arbur, Cairo, no. 998, 19 July 1916; *AB*, no. 11, 17 July 1916; WP 143/7/40–42, Opinion, expressed privately, by an Egyptian officer, who returned recently from the Hejaz, 25 November 1916.

[65] FO 686/52, Davenport to Bassett, Jeddah, 25 April 1918, enclosed in Bassett to Director, Arab Bureau, 2 [?] May 1918.

[66] Quoted in Tauber, *The Arab Movements*, p. 146. This practice of Qaysuni was probably related to the fact that he did not recognize the ranks of the Northern Army since they were not approved by him or Husayn.

[67] This affection for Qaysuni was probably the result of the sycophantic qualities the Egyptian officer displayed (see above).

suitable to replace Qaysuni. If no acceptable Muslim could be found, he said, he would even accept a British Minister of War.[68]

Such conflicts showed the strong local identification of the various components of the regular Hashimite armed forces, to the detriment of unified action. There seemed to be little sense of a unity of purpose, as Husayn had not succeeded in imbuing his troops with the needed *esprit de corps*. Zayd's lament reflected as much.

A problem of priorities: Medina or Ibn Saud? 'Abdallah, who was protecting the eastern flank of the Hashimite state, was more concerned about Ibn Saud than capturing Medina. After Lawrence visited him in Wadi 'Ays in mid-1917, he reported that the Amir had no intention of cutting the railway north of the town. He observed that 'Abdallah and the approximately 3,000 'Utaybah with him were uninterested in the war. Both Ibn Saud and 'Abdallah wanted control over the 'Utaybah and the latter even dressed as if he was one of them: he wore a girdle of thorns (a *brim* or *barim*) around his midriff which was 'supposed to confine the belly to reasonable limits, [and he] encouraged insects [to live] in his hair, as was the Ateiba custom.' He paid the tribe to stay on his side, and they spent all day in camp, Lawrence said, playing practical jokes, eating, and sleeping.[69]

'Abdallah's lack of progress annoyed the British, who complained about him to Faysal. It was clear that the 'Utaybah did not fight the Ottomans because 'Abdallah was not interested in having them do so. Faysal answered that his brother was 'taking no part in the war against the Turks, because his whole heart, his head, and all his resources are engaged in the problems of Nejd.' According to Faysal, 'Abdallah was 'daily confirming' his hold on the 'Utaybah. 'Without the Ateiba ibn Saud [could] take the Hejaz,' he stressed. He concluded, 'Abdullah is fighting all our battles,

---

68 FO 371/3381/146256, Wilson, Interviews with King Hussein at Jeddah on 17 July 1918.

69 FO 686/6, part 2, T. E. Lawrence (Wedj), to Colonel Wilson, 16 April 1917, also in *AB*, no. 51, 23 May 1917; see also Wilson, *Lawrence*, pp. 386–7.' 'Abdallah and his friends spent much of their time plaguing one Muhammad Hasan, stabbing him with thorns and setting him on fire.' 'Abdallah used him for rifle practice, shooting a coffee pot off the top of his head at twenty yards.

and if he has no leisure to campaign against the railway meanwhile, he should not be judged too harshly.'[70]

By late 1918 it was apparent to all those serving with 'Abdallah that when Medina fell he would move to Khurmah to deal with the Wahhabi supporters there. His men were clamoring for demobilization. They had no contract with Husayn, they told him, and did not want to go with 'Abdallah to Khurmah. It had been reported that 'Abdallah was well aware of the situation, and therefore planned to take only the Syrian and Iraqi officers with him, not the rank and file (he most probably did count on the 'Utaybah). Captain H. Garland of the Egyptian Army wrote that the officers did not want to go either, but nonetheless many did; 'Abdallah must have paid them handsomely. The list of casualties at the Battle of Turabah (May 1919), included many Syrian and Iraqi officers.[71]

The situation with 'Ali was no better: his Iraqi officers were not particularly interested in fighting. During an attack on 13 November 1917, they chose 'prudently' to remain 3 to 4 kilometers behind the action, saying that they did not have enough cannons, that it was difficult to advance in the mountains, and that the animals were tired. In a January 1918 attack the officers claimed that their animals were incapable of advancing the three kilometers over easy territory to engage the enemy, although they were capable of retreating twenty-five kilometers to their home base. Depui noted that the Iraqis did not hide their pro-Ottoman sentiments. On several occasions they expressed sympathy with the Turks, referred to them as *shuhada* (martyrs), and asked the French Muslim officers if they intended to fight *'leurs frères musulmans.'*[72]

In April 1918 British officer Davenport said that 'Ali's and 'Abdallah's Iraqi officers were actually delaying the fall of Medina

---

[70] *AB*, no. 73, 24 December 1917, quoting a report by Lawrence; see also Kedourie, 'Surrender,' pp. 280–1.

[71] *AB*, no. 108, 11 January 1919; FO 882/7, private note by Captain H. Garland, undated [probably late November 1918], quoted in Elie Kedourie, 'The Surrender of Medina, January 1919,' in *idem., Islam and the Modern World and Other Studies* (New York: Holt, Rinehart and Winston, 1980) p. 296. For the list of the dead Syrian and Iraqi officers, see FO 686/18, 'List of Officers and Men of Baghdad and Syria killed at Tarabah,' enclosed in Minister of War Kaisuni to British Agent, 30 July 1919.

[72] SHAT, 17 N 498, Mission Militaire Française d'Egypte, Chef de Bataillon Cousse, Djeddah, no. 117A, 14 April 1918, enclosing 'Extrait d'un Rapport du Capitaine Depui, no. 29, 24 March 1918, sur l'état de la colonne Ali et la formation d'un comité factieux Baghdadien'; Brémond, p. 228.

not only because they were pro-Ottoman, but because they wanted to continue receiving their enormous stipends. When Medina finally fell, he remarked, they would go to Baghdad and trade with all the money they had made.[73]

There seems to have been no qualitative improvement in the regular army after the First World War. One British official reported that paying the Iraqi soldiers was a waste of money: 'All the Baghdadi officers that I have seen are dirty, idle, disloyal and useless.'[74] In 1920 British observers reported mass desertions and mutinies because of the lack of payment.[75] While the French were fighting the Syrians that summer, Syrian officers in Husayn's army approached the French mission in Jeddah. They had not been paid, and did not intend to fight Ibn Saud. The officers wanted to know the attitude of the mission should they desert and claim its protection. 'I understand that they have been told that they will receive protection and repatriation,' wrote the British representative.[76]

Military officers in Ta'if, which soon became the center of the eastern front against Ibn Saud, tried to resign, but Husayn would not accept their resignations. As a result, many obtained medical statements about their poor health; these were ignored. The officers in Ta'if complained of arrears in pay, lack of advancement, and humiliation.[77]

From information on salaries to parts of his army, we can get an indication of certain Sharifian priorities and the resulting problems. Internal security was essential for the pilgrimage, Husayn's biggest money-maker and a major source of his legitimacy. Thus keeping the tribes happy often came at the expense of any offensive capability against Ibn Saud. According to one report, certain

---

[73] FO 686/52, Davenport to Bassett, Jeddah, 25 April, enclosed in Bassett to Director, Arab Bureau, 2 [May?] 1918.

[74] FO 686/26, Intelligence and Political Summary, 21.11.19–1.12.19, 1 December 1919.

[75] FO 686/26, Political Report, 22 April –1 May 1920, 1 May 1920, enclosing Extract from Report from Agent (Mecca), 29 April 1920; FO 696/26, Extract from Mecca Report 29 May 1920; FO 686/26, Jeddah Report to 5 November 1920.

[76] FO 686/26, Political Report, 22 June–2 July 1920.

[77] FO 686/12, Nasiruddin (Jeddah) to British Agent, 10 September 1920. For example, there was the case of the officer in charge of the cannons fired on the 'Id. As the King entertained guests, he waited for the guns to be fired. When it turned out that he could not hear them (it was reported that the guests were noisy), the officer was thrown in jail because the King believed that the guns were not loud enough.

tribesmen were being paid £5 a month, while regular soldiers were receiving much less.[78] In October 1920, wrote the British Agent, Husayn began large-scale recruiting of bedouin. Leading shaykhs were summoned and asked how many 'volunteers' they could produce; the shaykh would name improbably high numbers, and the Sharif gave them money to keep their men at the ready.[79] In the fall of 1920 the British Agent reported that Meccans who had enlisted at the beginning of the Revolt and had been released were now being forcibly re-enlisted.[80] Moreover, orders were given to the shaykhs of Jeddah's four quarters to produce sixty men each.[81]

As the Saudi threat grew stronger in 1924, Husayn made an effort to recruit soldiers from abroad. On 12 June *al-Qiblah* published an official announcement to 'the many people of the *Haramayn* and the Muslim regions' who wanted to volunteer for the 'Arab Army' (*al-Jaysh al-'Arabi*). The announcement mentioned the length of service (three years), rules for advancement, and benefits should the volunteer die in combat.[82] The move seemed quite straightforward, official, and state-like, but it belied Husayn's serious troubles. He could no longer mobilize significant numbers of bedouin to fight for him, the *fallahin* from the area between Mecca and Ta'if often deserted with their rifles, and most of the townsmen refused to volunteer. According to British Agent Reader Bullard, the result was that most of the Hijazi army was by this time made up mostly of extremely poor black men, who were often pressed into service by Husayn.[83]

Ta'if fell to the Wahhabis on 9 September in a rout. The complete mediocrity of Husayn's army was exposed in the battle, when the commander made the strategic error of abandoning

78 FO 686/26, Jeddah Report 20–30 September, 1920.
79 FO 686/26, Abstract from Mecca Reports 23 September–10 October [1920], enclosed in Jeddah Report 1–10 October 1920.
80 FO 686/26, Jeddah Report 1–10 October 1920.
81 FO 686/26, Jeddah Report 10– 20 October 1920.
82 *Al-Qiblah*, 12 June 1924.
83 E.C. Hodgkin (ed.), *Two Kings in Arabia: Sir Reader Bullard's Letters from Jeddah* (Reading, England: Ithaca Press, 1993), henceforth *Bullard*, letters dated 8 June and 15 September 1924 (This collection is a selection of Bullard's reports and letters to England. Both the reports and letters are incomplete, and there is no indication to whom the letters were addressed.) Many blacks in the Hijaz were destitute men who had remained there after coming across from west Africa for the *hajj*.

Ta'if's fortifications to face the Wahhabis at Wadi Muharram, on the outskirts of the town. Bullard reported that the few tribal elements in the army were of little use, and the regular army, 'which is regular only in the sense of being regularly done out of its pay and rations,' was completely demoralized. After desertions and deaths, 'Ali was left with only fifty men to defend the road from Ta'if to Mecca.[84]

Husayn abdicated in favor of 'Ali on 6 October, and 'Ali retreated to Jeddah before the Wahhabis entered Mecca on 18 October 1924. In November 'Ali obtained three airplanes from England, with a Russian pilot named Shirokoff. Bullard described the Hijazi 'Air Force':

As he [Shirokoff] refuses to fly over enemy territory at less than 9,000 or 10,000 feet and as his observer is a one-eyed officer who always wears dark glasses when he goes up, it is not believed that the reports brought back are of great value. Mr Shirokoff is constantly being pressed by the Army Commander, Tahsin Pasha, to drop bombs on supposed enemy concentrations, but has so far refused. There are no aeroplane bombs in the country. Tahsin Pasha wanted Mr Shirokoff to drop hand grenades, and was with difficulty persuaded that if they didn't blow the machine to pieces they would burst before reaching the ground. He then proposed that shells should be dropped, and himself made an experiment with two, but neither exploded … He receives a salary of 60 pounds sterling gold a month, a bottle of whisky a day, and as he supplements this quite inadequate ration by heavy purchases and by drinking at the expense of his admirers, he may one day reach the point of exhilaration at which the prospect of dropping explosives on Mecca will cease to appear objectionable.[85]

'Ali apparently had enough money to recruit forces to hold out at Jeddah. Some Palestinian and Egyptians joined the army, but in February 1925 it was reported that they had not been paid and had accordingly mutinied. In March they began to leave the Hijaz, but in May 'Ali forbade them to do so. The British government intervened on their behalf. Still able to scrape some money together, 'Ali held out in Jeddah until the end of 1926; the 'death rattle' – as Bullard put it – for the Hashimite Kingdom of the Hijaz was sounded in June when about forty Palestinian troops marched

---

[84] *Bullard*, letter of 28 September 1924; Joseph Kostiner, *The Making*, pp. 66–7.
[85] FO 686/29, Bullard to FO, no. 118, enclosing Report for the period 20 November–11 December 1924.

into the British Agency garden, handed over their rifles, and asked for repatriation.[86] Both the army, and thus the kingdom, had given up the ghost.

In two key mechanisms of coercion, the administration of justice and the armed forces, Husayn failed to develop effective methods. In administering justice, his use of the Islamic *hudud*, which was designed to show his Muslim credentials, served only to alienate his subjects rather than contribute to some kind of unifying ideology based on a strict implementation of the *shari'ah*. Husayn also failed to establish a regular army for the Hashimite Kingdom of the Hijaz. The most dynamic force, that of Faysal, was no longer under his control after the summer of 1917; instead, it was squandered on Syrian ambitions, and was later to stay in Syria itself. He did not therefore have the tools needed by the state both for internal coercion and for defending against enemies from without. While initially funds from the British allowed him to raise tribal levies, the cutback in the British subsidy and his own later financial mismanagement did not allow him to keep tribal payments at a level to which the bedouin had become accustomed. This led to desertion and perfidy. Hijazi townsmen did not support the army and those drafted were of a poor quality; this was in contrast to Ibn Saud's army, where townsmen played an important role first as soldiers and then as financial backers.[87] As there had been no conscription in the Hijaz, Husayn believed he needed the expertise of the Iraqi and Syrian enlisted men and officers, but these also turned out to be of questionable quality. On an ideological level, some of them may have believed in the pan-Arab cause, but their constant infighting demonstrated their failure to put this vision into practice. There is also evidence of Husayn's mistrust of those who weren't Hijazi, which raised doubt about Husayn's own commitment to pan-Arabism, or at least his suspicion of those not close to him. Out of this amalgam, Husayn was unable to create the *esprit de corps* necessary for a true fighting army. He lacked the statecraft, the skills necessary to generalize his interests to that of the army, and, indeed, the entire population of the Hijaz.

---

[86] *Bullard*, pp. 87–8, 91–2, 102–5; FO 371/10808, Bullard to FO, no. 29, 22 May 1925.

[87] See Tim Niblock, 'Social Structure and the Development of the Saudi Arabian Political System' in Tim Niblock (ed.), *State, Society and Economy in Saudi Arabia* (London: Croom Helm, 1982), pp. 75–105.

Moreover, his ambitions, which went beyond the Hijaz, led him to neglect this important matter. Ibn Saud, on the other hand, was able to engineer a constellation whereby the interests of his state and of society (in this case, his army) were closely identified in the minds of the populace. When the Wahhabis came calling, their fighting men were driven by the ideology of radical *tawhid*, which to Husayn's great misfortune, proved a more compelling motivating factor than any call to Arab unity or loyalty to the House of Hashim could provide.

6

THE POLITICS OF DECLINING SUBSIDIES
AND REVENUE EXTRACTION

A general note on government finance

An analysis of Hashimite government finances is problematic, as official budget figures were published only once as far as this researcher could tell, and in the sketchiest of forms.[1] Despite the limited information about the government's expenditures, British Vice-Consul Grafftey-Smith surmised that its income was quite large, especially revenues from the pilgrimage, and therefore there must have been a substantial credit in Husayn's coffers. Government salaries were extremely low, and he estimated that the entire expenditure in Mecca did not exceed £1,200 a month. Until 1923 all income came directly to Husayn, but thereafter went through the Ministry of Finance. Yet even this seemingly constructive step in the direction of state- and institution-building was only honored in the breech. When Husayn wanted funds, he would simply ask the Minister of Finance for them. If the latter did not have them, he made good out of his own pocket.[2] Thus, estimations of revenue are quite difficult, and should be regarded simply as indications of magnitude.

Finance: revenue extraction[3]

The British subsidy. With the initiation of the Revolt in 1916 and the end of Ottoman subsidies, the British stepped in to make up

[1] *Al-Qiblah*, 25 Rabi' al-Thani 1336 [6 February 1918]. In 1919, Allenby, the High Commissioner in Egypt, forwarded to the FO an 'approximate estimate of monthly expenditure for administration in the Hedjaz.' Totalling £99,900, this budget was also quite sketchy (T1/12425/51473/20218, Allenby to FO, no. 670, 29 April 1919).

[2] FO 371/10006/E 289, Report on Economic and Financial Conditions in the Hedjaz by Vice-Consul Grafftey-Smith, enclosed in Bullard to Curzon, no. 12, 31 July 1923.

the loss of funds. Their subsidy was for many years the major source of Husayn's income, and marked the greatest change in the nature of Sharifian revenues.[4]

The British subsidy was initially of an indeterminate nature and amount, there having been little expectation of supporting Husayn to the degree that later proved necessary. In fact, when Storrs made his way to the Hijaz on 28 May 1916, he had with him only £10,000 in gold, an infusion earmarked for 'Abdallah and apparently requested before the Revolt. Indeed, the £50,000 that Husayn had requested in February had still not been approved by London. On 29 May Cairo received permission to give Husayn the money if and when the uprising took place and was confirmed. Zayd assured Storrs on 6 June 1916 that the Revolt was under way in Medina, and Storrs asked his superiors that the £50,000, as well as another £20,000 which had already been requested, be sent to Husayn.[5] This was the start of the Hijaz's financial dependence on Great Britain, and getting approval for funds and administering them would become increasingly complicated as events progressed.

It was essential to Husayn that the money keep coming. As Sharif Shakir, 'Abdallah's lieutenant, asked Ibn 'Urayfan, Husayn's messenger: 'Do the English not see that if the Sherif is not able to redeem his money promises to the Arabs, he will be a liar proved and lose his honour before them? Then where will be success?' In a letter handed to Storrs during his trip, Husayn made

---

[3] On the importance of revenue extraction in state formation, see Jill Crystal, *Oil and Politics in the Gulf: Rulers and Merchants in Kuwait and Qatar* (Cambridge University Press, p. xii).

[4] FO 686/90, Note by Faysal for Marshall, transmitted by Rustom Haider, undated, probably late 1919; *AB* ,108, 11 January 1919, note by D.[avid] G.[eorge] H.[ogarth]; T1/12425/51473/11227, Hejaz Finance, Unofficial Note by Colonel Laurence [sic], undated, stamped by the Treasury 13 March 1919.

[5] FO 371/2773/122968, McMahon to Grey, no. 141, 15 June 1916, Storrs' report on his mission to the Hijaz (also in Storrs, pp. 180–188); T1/12016/35047/18697/16, McMahon to FO, no. 388, 24 May 1916; ibid., McMahon to FO, 28 May 1916; ibid., FO to McMahon, no. 426, 29 May 1916; ibid., FO to McMahon, no. 431, 30 May 1916; ibid., McMahon to FO, no. 436, 8 June 1916; ibid., McMahon to FO, 11 June 1916; there is an indication that some funds were transferred earlier; see WP, 136/2/9–11, Clayton to Wingate, 4 February 1916, where Clayton writes of the Sharif accepting £20,000 or £30,000 from the British (the handwriting is unclear with respect to the sum; Wilson, *Abdullah*, p. 27, mentions that £13,000 was paid to 'Abdallah as 'seed money' in the spring of 1916, before the Revolt). In any case, tracing exact amounts of subventions to the Hashimites is extremely difficult, if not impossible.

it clear that there would have to be a major commitment on the part of the British:

In order that the nations may be attracted to us and cherish good feelings towards us, it is necessary that the monthly and annual allowances should be maintained as well as the expenses of the Haram el-Sherif (Kaaba) and its servants as well as the civil and military administration: [sic] also to start a capital of 130 [sic – perhaps referring to thousands] monthly to be handed to us until the establishment of the Government and the assumption of its administration.[6]

The letter also included requests for more arms and provisions. The point was well understood by McMahon, who reported as follows: 'Until [the] Haj is resumed [the] main source of [the] Shereef's resources is dry and he will require constant subsidies. He has recently asked us to continue [the] payments made to him by [the] Ottoman Government for [the] Holy Cities.'[7]

Once the rising was confirmed, the Cairo-based pro-Husayn lobby urged London to undertake a systematic subvention of the budding Hashimite regime. Clayton was in London at the time and served as point man. In late June Husayn came forward with a proposal for a monthly subsidy of £125,000 in gold a month.[8] For the British, this monthly sum was staggering, equivalent to the 1991 purchasing power of £3,607,100, and several-fold more than the funds received by Husayn from the Ottomans (see Chapter 1). Calculated annually, in terms of British governmental expenditures, it was equal to 5.19 per cent of the army and ordnance outlay for 1915 and to the entire yearly outlay in 1916 for colonial, consular, and foreign affairs.[9] Such a request could not be handled

---

6 FO 371/2773, McMahon to Grey, no. 141, 16 June 1916, Storrs' report, appended letter of Husayn, undated.

7 FO 371/2773, McMahon to Grey, no. 141, 16 June 1916, Storrs' report; T1/12016/35047/18697/16, McMahon to FO, no. 444, 11 June 1916.

8 T1/12016/35047/18697/16, McMahon to FO, no. 517, 30 June 1916.

9 The purchasing power of 1916 pounds sterling was calculated in 1991 terms on the basis of the British Composite Commodity Price Index in John J. McCusker, *How Much is That in Real Money? A Historical Price Index for Use as a Deflator of Money Values in the Economy of the United States* (Worcester: American Antiquarian Society, 1992), p.337. McCusker cautions – and the author concurs – that 'such calculation is better considered as hypothetical rather than as definitive' (p. 313). Budget figures are from B.R. Mitchell, *British Historical Statistics* (Cambridge: Cambridge University Press, 1988), pp. 590–1. No figures for military expenditures are given by Mitchell for the years 1916–1919, as these payments were made by votes of credit and not itemized; the

on an *ad hoc* basis, and on 6 July it was brought before the War Committee, which, despite Clayton's advocacy, agreed only to £50,000 per month. McMahon despatched the sum immediately but argued that it would not be enough, emphasizing that in addition to war expenses Husayn must replace the personal subsidy from the Ottomans, pay for the upkeep of shrines and maintain safe travel routes. All this, wrote McMahon, came at a time when trade was nearly at a standstill. He added that he would impress on Husayn the importance of 'satisfactory arrangements for the pilgrimage.' Sir Reginald Wingate, the Sirdar in Sudan, wrote from Khartoum, adding: 'We have encouraged establishment of an independent Arab Kingdom and this cannot take shape without considerable financial assistance which might be regularised by informing the Shereef that it was the intention of His Majesty's Government eventually to consider these advances as loans on which interests might be paid.'

The War Committee then reconvened on 11 July and approved the subsidy of £125,000 a month, for the next four months.[10] McMahon wrote to Husayn informing him of the approval of this sum, but Wilson held up the letter's delivery, and urged instead that the subsidy be given for one year. 'I am convinced,' wrote Wilson, '[that] in the Sherif we are backing the right horse and he will probably eventually be recognized Khalif of Islam.' McMahon endorsed the idea, and the FO agreed that the subsidy could continue at £125 000 a month 'for the present.'[11]

---

figure for 1915 is thus given instead. On wartime budgeting, see Gerd Hardach, *The First World War, 1914–1918* (Harmondsworth: Pelican, 1987), pp. 151–2. The following is given in order to provide the reader with additional indicators of the value of the sum at the time: In 1916 the average price of 4 lbs of bread in London was only 9 pence; in 1912, 5.8 pence (B.R. Mitchell, *Abstract of British Historical Statistics* [Cambridge, UK: Cambridge University Press, 1962], p. 498). In 1912 in Damascus (the closest year for which statistics are available), bread could be had for only 3 Turkish piasters a loaf (Charles Issawi, *The Fertile Crescent, 1800–1914: A Documentary Economic History* [New York: Oxford University Press, 1988], p. 428).

10 T1/12016/35067/18697/16: Extracts from the Proceedings of the War Committee, Thursday July 6, 1916, FO to McMahon, no. 549, 6 July 1916; McMahon to FO, no. 559, 10 July 1916; McMahon to FO, no. 560, 10 July 1916, forwarding Sirdar's no. 925, 10 July 1916; Extract from the Proceedings of the War Committee, July 11, 1916; FO to McMahon, no. 570, 12 July 1916. Sirdar was the designation of the Commander-in-Chief of the Egyptian and Sudanese armies.

11 The Treasury apparently continued to believe that it had authorized the £125,000 for four months only, while the FO had essentially made it indefinite by using the words

Husayn thanked McMahon for the monthly payment, but let him know in no uncertain terms that even this would be insufficient. 'Abdallah requested and received a further £10,000.[12] In February 1917, after the capture of Wajh, and needing to make additional payments to tribes, Husayn requested that his subsidy be increased by £75,000 a month. Again, Wilson was his advocate, writing to London and enclosing in his letter an explanation from Husayn's adviser, Fu'ad al-Khatib. Even allowing for exaggeration, al-Khatib's letter gives us an indication of how Husayn distributed the subsidy. According to al-Khatib, the monthly Ottoman subsidy of £80,000 had been used for payments to tribes, to *ashraf*, to *'ulama*, to 'the servants of the *Haram*' (this was a very broad category including everyone in the *hajj* service industry), and payments to the *Haram* itself (for maintenance). Al-Khatib remarked that people were now receiving payments who had received nothing under the Turks. To maintain their support, he had to maintain the flow of money from his coffers. He had established a whole new administration which employed more officials than in the past: '[Their] salaries were made big,' Khatib stressed, 'in order to attract [them] and prevent them from robbery and bribe taking.' Moreover, because it was wartime, the tribes and the army needed more money than they otherwise would, and the families of those killed in battle were being compensated, according to tribal tradition, on the principle of a *diyyah*, or blood price. Finally, added al-Khatib, Husayn had to use much of his own money for the various expenditures, because he did not have access to his private revenue in Turkey and Iraq.[13]

'for the present.' WP, 138/15/2, McMahon to Grey, no. 176, 25 July 25, enclosing letter to Husayn of same date – the letter embodying the correction can be found in FO 686/47, dated 25 July but sent on 18 August 1916; WP, 138/2/73, Wilson to Arbur, W. 21, 8 August 1916, repeated to Governor General of the Sudan; FO 371/2774/160155, McMahon to FO, no. 691, 14 August 1916; FO 371/2774/160155, FO to McMahon, no. 678, 15 August 1916. It is interesting that in his telegram to McMahon, Wilson essentially endorsed the Sharif's claim to the Caliphate. Perhaps it was a logical assumption giving Kitchener's thinking. Confusingly, however, McMahon substituted the puzzling formulation of 'he will probably eventually be recognized Shereef of Islam' when transmitting Wilson's telegram to the FO.

12 FO 686/47, Sherif to High Commissioner, 25 August 1916; T1/12016/35047/29208/16: McMahon to FO, no. 942, 29 October 1916; Treasury Office Minute, 15 November 1916; Treasury Office to FO, no. 29208, 20 November 1916.

13 FO 686/47, Wilson to Director, Arab Bureau, 22 February 1917, enclosing note by Fu'ad al-Khatib, dated 18 February 1917. Fu'ad's estimate of income – £960,000 a year

Husayn marshalled other factors in favor of his demands. He accused the British of having promised but failed to cut the Hijaz railway, and he argued that the failure had unnecessarily length-ened the campaign and made it more expensive. 'We were sure according to our plans,' he wrote in March 1917, 'that our fight[ers] would be by now in the vicinity of Damascus.' The British, he argued, should be pleased to extend funds to him, as his movement would 'cause the Moslems to be cheerful and happy and [would] multiply their inclinations towards Great Britain which [would be] worth millions and millions of money.'[14]

Wilson again proposed an increase in Husayn's subsidy, to £200,000 a month, and noted that Husayn wanted £225,000 a month after the fall of Medina. Quoting Fu'ad, he argued that the Arab Government 'must be in a position to show itself a greater 'Dowla' [state, or dynasty] than the Turkish Government. This can only be done at the present juncture by outbidding our ene-mies.' When McMahon withheld the proposal from London, waiting for an account of how the money would be spent, Husayn angrily insisted that he was 'not playing tricks.' The account was eventually provided in the briefest of terms, but Wilson's advo-cacy swayed McMahon and the FO, which approved the increase sometime between April and June 1917.[15]

No sooner had the increase been approved than McMahon dis-covered that Egypt's gold supply was low. When he contacted the FO and asked for £500,000 in gold, he was confronted with the general shortage of gold.[16] As a result, the British proposed that

---

– is significantly larger than the amount received in Ottoman times (see Chapter 1).

[14] FO 686/47, Hussein to British Agent, 27 March 1917; see also FO 687/47, Sherif to High Commissioner, 25 August 1916.

[15] FO 686/34, Wilson to Director, Arab Bureau, no. 9/20/28, 29 March 1917; FO 686/47, Fu'ad El Khatib to Wilson, no. 424, 8 Jamadi al-Thani 1335 [31 March 1917]; FO 686/47, telephone message from Sherif to Wilson Pasha, 31 March 1917, enclosed in Wilson to Director, Arab Bureau, no. 9/20/29, 1 April 1917; FO 686/47, High Commissioner to FO, no. 404, 10 April 1917. I could not locate official sanction of the raise to £200,000 monthly and to £225,000 for five months after the fall of Medina, but in FO 686/47, High Commissioner to FO, no. 645, 18 July 1917, McMahon refers to the increase as a *fait accompli*.

[16] On the shortage of gold during the First World War as a result of hoarding, problems of production and the dangers of shipping and concurrent insurance costs, see Hardach, particularly Chapter 6 on currency and finance.

Husayn take silver instead, as well as Egyptian pound notes and Indian rupee notes, a suggestion that was greeted with intense condemnation. The Hashimite administration wrote to Wilson: 'Paper money will assuredly cause bad effect, make people attribute to us worse things than they attribute to Turks and our enemies will thus find a way of saying all sorts of things against us.' Wilson therefore disparaged substitution for gold in communicating with his superiors. The FO wired McMahon that despite Egypt's reduced reserves, its gold would have to be used; barring that, said the FO, perhaps Husayn could be persuaded to take the subsidy in kind. McMahon was adamant that sending commodities was impossible, as Egypt did not have enough for herself. He wrote: '[I]t must be understood that short of stopping payments altogether they must be made in gold' and asked the FO to reconsider.[17]

At this stage, London had another idea: perhaps Husayn could be persuaded to accept commodities at values 'fixed against subsidy at a sufficiently low rate to enable him to retail them to his subjects at a profit to himself.' London did not understand the difficulties of executing such a scheme, but Wilson did, noting that it would put Husayn in direct competition with the very merchants he sought to woo. Moreover, it might flood the market and thus become self-defeating. It would also deprive him of his 10 per cent customs duty. Finally, Wilson stressed that the tribes wanted only gold, because they were used to the British gold sovereigns.[18] Wilson was nevertheless instructed to offer Husayn at a 'favourable opportunity' a proposal that would give him a monopoly on the sale of rice, flour and sugar.[19] In late September, he proposed to Husayn that he take the offered monopoly; the British would help by preventing the export of these commodities from India to the Hijaz, except through official Hashimite channels. Britain would undertake to fix the value of the goods at a rate which

17 FO 686/47, High Commissioner to FO, no. 645, 18 June 1917; FO 686/47, Wilson to Arbur, no. W 1216, 13 July 1917; FO 686/47, Arbur to Wilson, no. AB 970, 15 July 1917; FO 686/47, HC to FO, no. 754, 18 July 1917.

18 686/47, FO to High Commissioner, no. 822, 18 August 1917; FO 686/47, Wilson to Arbur, no. W 1444, 31 August 1917.

19 FO 686/47, Cornwallis, Director, Arab Bureau to Wilson, no. 103/2469, 10 September 1917.

would enable Husayn to make a profit, while taking into account the customs duty that he would lose.[20]

Oddly, although Husayn was dissatisfied with the British proposal, he advanced his own proposal for what seems to have been a similar arrangement, whereby he would establish a 'commercial company' made up of leading merchants but really run by himself.[21] On 15 October 1917 Husayn gave the British Agent a list of goods ordered by the company from India, but it appears that Husayn was more interested in the monopoly *per se* rather than the goods sent by the British as payment in kind for the subsidy. The Hashimite government later attempted to take and sell rice and barley supplied by the British for the Hashimite armies, a step to which the British representative, Bassett, objected strongly.[22]

Husayn continued to lobby for a raise to £225,000, effective immediately and before the fall of Medina, claiming that his sons needed the money to pay the bedouin. Wilson began to be suspicious that Husayn's sons were either hoarding or wasting the money that had already been provided. He wrote that 'Abdallah 'spends all he gets in the most extravagant manner, for his idea of bliss seems to be for the moment, a comfortable camp with all creature comforts and sufficient gold to ladle out indiscriminately to all and sundry, after the manner of seigneur.' Faysal often wrote to Wilson begging for more money, prompting the latter to suspect that the king was scheming to create a direct provision of funds to Faysal, calculating that his advance was so important to the British in Palestine that they would not let it fail. In October 1917, it seems to come as a surprise to Wilson that the premise underlying the British subsidy was indeed impractical: subsidizing all the tribes who came in, he wrote, 'if led to its logical conclusion would mean that the British Government through King Hussein would have to subsidize or pay the vast majority of Arabs in central and northern Arabia which would run into millions of pounds.'[23]

---

[20] FO 686/47, Wilson to King of Hedjaz, no. 12/C, 24 September 1917.

[21] FO 686/48, Sherif Hussein to Colonel Wilson, 15 El Higga 1335 [12 October 1917], enclosed in Wilson to Director, Arab Bureau, no. 12/D.1, 12 October 1917.

[22] FO 686/48, Bassett to Under Secretary of State for Foreign Affairs, 29 December 1917.

[23] FO 686/48, Wilson to Director, Arab Bureau, 12 October 1917; FO 686/47, Sherif Faisal to Colonel Wilson, undated, approximately September 1917; FO 686/48, Faisal to Wilson Pasha, 11 October 1917.

Seemingly without realizing it, the British had fundamentally changed the economy of the Hijaz, so that instead of achieving tribal loyalty, they had created a growing demand for further monies. In late October Wilson wrote to the Director of the Arab Bureau: 'This subsidizing of Sheikhs is most expensive, but another source of trouble is that – in spite of numerous protests on my part at the time – too high rates of pay were issued to the Arabs at the beginning of the revolt and it is not possible to reduce them now without causing widespread discontent.'[24] London pressed on the issue of rupee notes as a substitute for at least £5,000. Husayn claimed that he could not give such notes to the tribes, and Wilson countered that he could use them to pay officials and others in Mecca and Jeddah: they would be glad to 'change them to gold before one day passed [because] merchants want[ed] notes.' As the current exchange rate was 14½ rupees to the sovereign, Wilson recommended that the notes be provided to Husayn at the rate of 15 rupees to the sovereign, thereby giving the Sharif a small profit.[25] Wilson also lobbied the Arab Bureau to increase the subsidy to £300,000 per month. He argued passionately that the 'investment was eminently sound and dirt cheap at the price.'[26]

The High Commissioner picked up on Wilson's argument. In early November 1917 he asked that the subsidy be raised to £225,000, effective immediately, even though Medina had yet to be taken. Despite Husayn's mismanagement, he argued, the increase was fully justified in the light of Faysal's contributions, and it would be a shame to 'lose the full fruits of a policy which [had] fully justified itself both from a military, political, and financial point of view.' His clinching argument revealed an understanding of Husayn's aspirations and their limitations:

[I]t is undesirable on political grounds that the King of the Hejaz should be placed in a position to argue that the cost of Emir Feisul's operations and of any Arab movements which may eventuate in Syria has fallen mainly upon him. It will greatly strengthen his claims for a preponderating voice in any eventual settlement of that area and thus

---

24 FO 686/48, Wilson to Director, Arab Bureau, 21 October 1917. Perhaps such protests were made orally; this researcher's explorations found no record of them.
25 FO 686/48, Wilson to Director, Arab Bureau, no. 12/C, 16 October 1917; FO 686/48, Wilson Pasha to King of Hedjaz, 19 October 1917.
26 FO 686/48, Wilson to Director, Arab Bureau, 21 October 1917.

handicap us and still more our French allies. The progress of the revolt has shown very clearly that the King of the Hejaz is not likely to put up any form of Government which would be acceptable in Syria, either to Christians or Moslems, and it appears improbable that such personal aspirations as he may have in that area can ever be realized. Emir Feisul is regarded by many Syrians as the possible head of a Syrian Arab state but ... a ... Sherifian Government ... in Syria can never be more than nominally under Meccan control or suzerainty. In due course the King of the Hejaz will discover this for himself and he probably has a fairly shrewd idea of it even now, but it would appear inadvisable to throw upon him the bulk of the expenditure incurred in liberating a country in which he has but little chance of realising his aspirations to the full.[27]

The increase to £225,000 was approved some time soon after the High Commissioner's request and authorized to begin in January 1918 for five months.[28]

Meanwhile, the problem of the availability of gold had been temporarily resolved. Faysal and Zayd received gold directly. As for the Hijaz proper, a complicated system was devised for maintaining the continued circulation of gold within it, essentially preventing its export. Merchants who had previously paid for Indian and Egyptian imports with gold were now issued drafts on the Bombay branch of the National Bank of India by the British firm of Gellatly, Hankey and Company in Jeddah. They could then use these drafts to pay for goods in India and Egypt. The gold paid into the Bombay branch by the British Government in exchange for the drafts was handed over to the British Agent at Jeddah and used for the next month's subsidy. In this manner, gold remained in the Hijaz. The final adjustment was made between the FO and the Indian Government, the latter recouping the Bank at Bombay. In Egypt a similar arrangement was made for drafts on the National Bank at Cairo.[29]

In July 1918 the subsidy was reduced from £225,000 to £220,000, as planned. Almost immediately, the armies – particularly Faysal's forces – were weakened by desertions (mostly 'Utaybah). Faysal

[27] FO 686/48, High Commissioner to FO, no. 1200, 2 November 1917.
[28] See FO 686/48, Hussein to High Commissioner, 31 December 1917, where Husayn notes that Hogarth and Philby informed him of the raise. See also WO 158/630, Wingate, BACOS, to C-in-C, Adv. GHQ, no. 632. Memorandum, 27 June 1918.
[29] *AB*, no.75, 3 January 1918.

wrote Husayn that he had no money to give to the powerful al-Ruwallah chiefs:

NURI SHAALAN and NAWWAF have come to GAFR to meet us tomorrow. ZEID and your slave are going there. I regret we have no money, a deficiency which has spoiled and will spoil all our plans. Unless during the next six days you can send us our subsidy and what Y[our]M[ajesty] promised our difficulty will be great.

Husayn's commercial company scheme failed at about the same time, and when another gold crisis occurred, High Commissioner Wingate realized that if he could not organize gold from other sources, he would have to deplete Egypt's supplies. He did look elsewhere, notably to Australia, with little success. Husayn's August subsidy had to be pieced together 'with help from the [local] banks,' a process that delayed the subsidy's arrival and caused further shrinkage of the armies.[30]

After the 30 October 1918 Armistice of Mudros, which ended the conflict between the Entente and the Ottoman Empire, London (particularly the Treasury), tired of advancing huge sums to the Hijaz without having a true accounting of their distribution, considered a substantial cut in the subsidy, to £120,000 a month. This figure may have been prompted by Husayn's comments to Wilson that he anticipated 'a large reduction' in the subsidy after the fall of Medina, and that he intended to reduce bedouin grants to pre-war levels.[31]

At the post-war Paris Peace Conference, Lawrence, who thought little of Husayn and 'Abdallah, played up Faysal's contribution to the war effort. Treasury representative in Paris Dudley Ward gullibly reported a long conversation with Lawrence ('the man primarily responsible for the Hedjaz Campaign'), in which Lawrence told him that 'Abdullah has recently bought

---

[30] T1/12253/49625/20984/18, Wingate to FO, no. 857, 23 May 1918; WO 158/619/50, Bassett to Arbur, W. 480, 28 July 1918; FO 686/39, Feisal to King, 5 August 1918, relayed to King by Bassett on 7 August 1918; WO 158/630, Hedgehog, Cairo, to GHQ, no. G.H. 129, 6 July 1918; WO 158/630, Chief, Egypforce to Troopers, London, no. EA 1555, 9 August 1918. On the desertion of the 'Utaybah Husayn remarked that they did not like the northern climate and were therefore being sent back for service in the Hijaz. Another reason may have been that they were attracted by 'Abdallah, who was recruiting 'Utaybah members to fight Ibn Saud.

[31] *AB*, no. 108, 11 January 1919, note by D[avid] G[eorge] H[ogarth] on Hejaz Supplies and Subsidies.

150 thoroughbred Arab horses at maximum prices and has a bath every day in eau-de-Cologne.' It was rather unfair, wrote Ward, 'that [British] taxpayers should supply funds for [such things].'[32] As a result of this information, the Treasury finally authorized a reduction to £120,000 (exclusive of £80,000 for Faysal), but this did not actually come into effect until February 1919; the Treasury promised further decreases. Wingate seemed resigned to the reduction, but, with the Ottoman Empire no more, suggested hopefully that the *awqaf* which once flowed to the *haramayn* from various parts of the empire become the property of the Hijaz.[33]

British officials who dealt with Husayn pleaded that any further reduction be done gradually, given 'Abdallah's efforts against Ibn Saud and continued payments to tribes.[34] Correspondence flowed between Cairo, the FO, and the Treasury. Allenby, in Cairo, believed that a serious reduction in the subsidy would give the wrong signal to Ibn Saud, who also received a subsidy. Sanction was obtained for a continued subsidy of £100,000 to Husayn through April 1919, but when he was approached about a further reduction to £80,000 beginning in May, he at last presented an accounting of his expenses, which totalled £99,900 a month. When he threatened to resign from office if his subsidy were cut, Allenby recommended that the subsidy remain at £100,000 a month.[35]

---

32 T1/12425/51473, Memorandum by Mr Dudley Ward, no date, probably early January 1919. In a later communication to the Treasury, Lawrence further denigrated Hijazi needs for funds. Speaking of 'Abdallah, he wrote that nearly half of the subsidy to the Hijaz was spent in 'bribing certain tribes of West-Central Arabia not to desert (or oppose) the Sherif; and I have never believed the results justified the expenditure of a sixpence.' Gold, he wrote, was often used for jewelry by 'Abdallah, who 'keeps a field goldsmith hard at work doing swords and daggers for months' (T1/12425/51473/11227/19, Hejaz Finance, Unofficial Note by Colonel Lawrence). Lawrence did quite a job on the Treasury officials in Paris. One Armitage-Smith noted that he discussed reducing the Hijaz subsidy with 'Col. Laurence (Emir and Major-General in the Army of Hedjaz)' (T1/12425/51473, note by A[rmitage]-S[mith], British Delegation, Paris, to Barstow, 16 May 1919).

33 T1/12425/51473/3823/19: FO to Wingate, no. 52, 10 January 1919; Wingate to FO, no. 93, 16 January 1919; FO to Treasury, no. 10420/W/44, 22 January 1919; Treasury to FO, no. 3823/19, 6 February 1919; FO to Cheetham, Cairo, no. 191, 11 February 1919.

34 T1/12425/51473/10981/19, Cheetham to FO, no. 350, 7 March 1919.

35 T1/12425/51473/113574/19, FO to Cheetham, no. 360, 20 March 1919; T1/12425/51473/13983, Allenby to FO, no. 441, 26 March 1919; T1/12425/51473/14402/19, FO to Allenby, no. 394, 29 March 1919; FO 686/59, Curzon to Balfour, 2 April 1919;

The Treasury instead proposed a reduction to £75,000 in August and September 1919, to £50,000 in October, and to £25,000 in November, after which the subsidy would stop. Allenby feared a disaster during the pilgrimage if this plan were followed, and the FO was concerned that the scheme would destroy British dominance in the Hijaz *vis-à-vis* the other powers who were still negotiation in Paris. In any case, Cheetham forwarded £100,000 for August and September, on his own authority. After all was said and done, the Treasury agreed to retroactively sanction the £100,000 for September, but decided that further payments could be no more than £75,000 for October, £50,000 for November, and £25,000 for December 1919.[36] Owing again to low supplies of gold, the payments were made in rupee notes beginning in September 1919.[37] Husayn, wanting gold (he forbade its export from the Hijaz), for a while refused to accept the subsidy in rupee notes.[38]

General financial mismanagement, Husayn's refusal to reach an agreement with Ibn Saud and problems with the pilgrimage caused a flagging in the FO's desire to come to Husayn's aid with huge amounts of cash. Moreover, Husayn was funding Faysal and Zayd in Syria, who were by now working against the interests of Britain's ally, France. The FO wrote to him that if he thought that he could afford to send money to Syria, then he had more than he needed. The British told him that Faysal would now have to approach the French for money, as the subsidy was intended for the Hijaz only. Rather than lose whatever subsidy was left, he undertook to keep the money in the Hijaz.[39]

T1/12425/51473/20218/19, FO to Treasury, no. 65980/me/44, 5 May 1919; FO 371/4189/65980, Allenby to FO, no. 669, 29 April 1919; T1/12425/51473/20218, Allenby to FO, no. 670, 29 April 1919.

36 FO 371/4189/120105, Treasury to FO, 23 August 1919, minute on same by H.W. Young, 25 August 1919; T1/12425/51473/39707/19, Cheetham to FO, no. 1335, 6 September 1919; T1/12425/51473/39849. FO to Treasury, no. 126832/ME/44A, 13 September 1919; T1/12425/51473/3949/19, Treasury to FO, 18 September 1919; T1/12425/51473/41009/19, Treasury to FO, 20 September 1919.

37 FO 371/4147/156998, no. 1645, Allenby to FO, 30 November 1919.

38 FO 686/26, Intelligence Summary 1.10.19–12.10.19; Intelligence and Political Report 11.10.19–21.10.19. Announcements forbidding the export of gold were published in *al-Qiblah*, no. 4, 11 October 1920; The British Agent reported that the Salamah family, pilots in the Jeddah harbor, were arrested and fined for gold smuggling, although he believed that they would soon be pardoned since 'many notables in Jeddah are involved in this gold smuggling' (FO 686/27, Jeddah Report 21.6.21–10.7.21).

At the beginning of 1920, Allenby asked that the subsidy continue until a settlement with the Ottoman Empire had been concluded. The Treasury agreed only to wait for the report of a Muslim financial expert whom Allenby would send to examine Husayn's finances (on the expert's report, see below), but it did sanction continuing the subsidy at a mere £25,000 a month, to April 1920.[40]

Husayn did not cooperate with Allenby's financial expert, but Allenby insisted on maintaining the subsidy at 250,000 rupees a month (about £25,000 at the time, May 1920), citing the prevention of a Wahhabi advance and the safety of the pilgrimage. These arguments did not sit well with the Treasury, which had awaited the report of the financial adviser and received nothing. Privately, Treasury officials believed that neither the FO nor Allenby 'felt any concern about the waste of public money in the Middle East', and that subsidizing competing rulers was an unconscionable drain on the public purse. The Treasury wrote to the FO that it did 'not consider that it is possible to defend the expenditure of further public money on these subsidies before it had been decided to which chieftain and in what measure HMG is to lend support.' It refused to accede to Allenby's request, and the question was laid before the Cabinet.[41] In a memorandum to that body, the FO argued that a continued subsidy of £30,000 a month was a necessity to assure the continuance and security of the pilgrimage, the 'special position' of Britain in Arabia then being negotiated in Paris, and the prevention of a Wahhabi victory, which would

---

39 FO 686/26, Garland, Arab Bureau, to British Agent (Jeddah), no. 34/16/4671, 19 November 1919; FO 686/42, Garland, Arab Bureau, to British Agent (Jeddah), 28 November 1919; FO 686/42, British Agent (Jeddah) to King, 30 November 1919. In late December 1919, the French reported that a train had arrived in Damascus from the Hijaz with a large shipment of arms (FO 686/26, Intelligence Report by Brémond, 31 December 1919).

40 FO 371/4189/151682, Allenby to FO, no. 1578, 13 November 1919; T1/12425/51473/51473, FO to Treasury, 1 December 1919, and Treasury to FO, 8 December 1919; T1/12580/22433, unsigned Treasury memorandum to Sir J. Tilley, undated (probably April 1920).

41 T1/12580/22433, Allenby to FO, no. 440, 5 May, 1920, and attached Treasury minutes; T1/12580/22433/22102/20, Treasury to FO, 18 June 1920; FO 371/5062/E 7835, FO to Allenby, no. 634, 10 July 1920. Allenby's and the FO's insistence on propping up Husayn stemmed from a sense of previous obligation, bureaucratic opposition to the India Office, which supported Ibn Saud, and a general feeling of fear should the *Haramayn* fall to the Wahhabis.

probably close the holy places to many Muslims. The last of these points was being advanced by Faysal in Paris. The FO maintained that since Husayn had agreed (under threat of the loss of his subsidy) to meet Ibn Saud, the subsidy should be granted. Allenby added his voice, stressing that the British had a moral obligation to Husayn to replace the financial and administrative resources that had existed prior to the war, to preserve order and maintain local government. Since Britain was likely to have difficulty with the Arabs with respect to Syria and Palestine, it was essential that in Arabia it re-establish its 'good name for disinterestedness and sympathy with Moslem races.'[42]

The Sharif eventually refused to see Ibn Saud, but a Najdi delegation did go and was well received by the King. The Foreign Office decided to add two additional conditions to the subsidy: that Husayn should spend all the money locally and that he sign the Treaty of Peace with Turkey. This course of action was approved by the Treasury. The FO told Cairo that £10,000 could be paid on acceptance of the conditions, the remaining £20,000 to be paid when they had been ratified.[43]

The Treaty with Turkey (finalized by the Powers at San Remo, on 20 August 1920 – but never ratified by Turkey) established mandates for territories Husayn regarded as belonging to him, although it did recognize the Hijaz as an independent state. The treaty remained a sticking point. Matters were complicated by the fact that Husayn had not been told of the Treasury's intention of eventually doing away with his subsidy; he considered that some payments had been incomplete and that that money was now owed to him.

Husayn refused the conditions, however, and London began to examine its policy of subsidies to Arab rulers. The British Agent in

[42] FO 406/44/ E 8300, Foreign Office Memorandum (circulated to Cabinet, July 19, 1920), 13 July 1920, attaching Allenby to Curzon, no. 559, 28 May 1920. See also FO 371/5962/E 8026, FO to Allenby, 13 July 1920. Husayn argued that the separation of the Hijaz from Palestine, Syria and Iraq would rob the Hijaz, which could not exist as a separate country.

[43] FO 371/5063/E 9671, Scott (Alexandria) to FO, no. 816, 9 August 1920; FO 371/5063/E 9983: minutes by Curzon and others; FO to Treasury, no. E 9983/9/44, 19 August 1920; FO to Scott (Cairo), no. 746, 20 August 1920; FO 371/5063/ E 10787, Minutes; FO 371/5063/ E 11225, Minutes, and Treasury to FO, 10 September 1920, FO to Treasury, 15 September 1920; FO 371/5064/E 11854, FO to Scott (Cairo), no. 835, 28 September 1920.

Jeddah argued that at present Ibn Saud was receiving a subsidy, while Husayn was receiving nothing, and that Husayn was again threatening to resign as a result.[44]

Husayn never gave in. British officials eventually recognized that Ibn Saud and Husayn should be subsidized equally, but the King, with his vision of himself at the helm of a post-Ottoman Islamic polity, refused to sign the treaty, which would have affirmed the League of Nations mandates. Personal negotiation by Lawrence in July 1921 for a bilateral treaty between Britain and the Hijaz yielded nothing, despite Lawrence's offering him an advance of 80,000 rupees – about £5,000 – as a *douceur*. Further negotiations in 1923 with Husayn's representative in London were just as fruitless, and the subsidy was never renewed.[45] Husayn's view throughout was that the subsidy was his due as an ally, and especially as one to whom promises had not been kept.[46]

Taxation and customs. Under the Ottomans, Hijazis had enjoyed an essentially tax-exempt status. It was a point of Islamic pride for the sultan-caliphs to contribute to the Hijaz, rather than tax it. After the Young Turk revolution, attempts at taxation in the Hijaz were greeted with protests. It will be recalled that when in

---

[44] FO 686/19, British Agent (Jeddah) to Curzon, no. 16, 6 February 1921; FO 371/6238/E 2606, British Agent (Jeddah), to FO, no. 25, 21 February 1921.

[45] The tribulations of the subsidy question from 1920/1923 are summarized in FO 371/8937/E 2693, Cabinet, Committee on Iraq, Payment of Subsidies to Arabian Chiefs, Memorandum by the Middle East Department, Colonial Office, 8 March 1923. Further details may be found in: FO 371/6238/E 15722, Memorandum by Colonel Cornwallis on the Future Policy of His Majesty's Government with regard to Subsidies to Chiefs of the Arabian Peninsula, 16 December 1920; FO 371/6240/E 6989, Fifth Meeting of the Political Committee [the 'Cairo Conference'], 16 March 1921; FO 371/6240/E 6373, Colonial Office, Middle East Committee, Minutes of Meeting on 20 May 1921; FO 371/7721/E 2358, minutes on Parliamentary Question by Lord Raglan, 28 February 1922. For two opposing scholarly views of the negotiations for an Anglo–Hashimite treaty, see Yehoshua Porath, 'The Palestinians and the Negotiations for the British–Hijazi Treaty, 1920–1925,' *Asian and African Studies* 8 (1972), pp. 20–48; and Suleiman Mousa, 'A Matter of Principle: King Husayn of the Hijaz and the Arabs of Palestine,' *International Journal of Middle Eastern Studies* 9 (1978), pp. 183–94.

[46] In order to complete the subsidy picture, it should be noted that the French also gave Husayn a subsidy and various presents. In 1916 they amounted to FF 1.35m.; in 1917: FF1m.; for 1918 they proposed giving him FF 976,000 (MAE, Hedjaz, 3 May 1918, Subside au Chérif de la Mecque; T1/12253/49625/27463/18, GOC, Egypt to WO, no. 1756, 8 July 1918; T1/12253/49625/29947/, FO to WO, no. 939, 29 July 1918).

October 1909 the Ottomans tried to enforce a cemetery tax, the result was a riot. It will also be remembered that during the Ottoman period the Sharifate was a state within a state and that Husayn taxed some of the tribes. Following the Revolt, he continued this complex policy of tribal taxation.

When Egyptian financial expert Sani Lackany proposed to 'Abdallah in February 1920 that a house tax in Mecca might be in order, the amir replied that 'the Hashemite Government dared not at present face the discontent which fresh taxation would be sure to arouse.'[47] Nevertheless, with the lowering of the subsidy in 1920, Husayn imposed in Mecca a slight tax for burying the dead.[48] He then took the unprecedented step of imposing wider taxes. The first indications that this was to begin in earnest came in September 1921:[49] he imposed a tax on every package – personal or commercial – leaving Jeddah; a post-customs tax on all packages entering Jeddah; and a tax on water brought into Jeddah from wells outside the city – the only source of supply – to be stored in underground reservoirs (the amount depended on the size of the cistern). The British Agent remarked, 'The king appears to have become, as a result of the new charges, more feared and better hated than ever by his people.'[50] In February 1922 it was reported that Husayn had introduced a new way of mobilizing funds: all shopkeepers, peddlers and auctioneers were ordered to find someone to attest to and guarantee their financial solvency and professional character. To validate the document of guarantee, Husayn assessed a charge.[51]

Husayn's economic relations with the tribes began on a traditional footing, but came to be fundamentally altered by the British subsidy. Prior to the Revolt, Husayn seems to have collected taxes or tribute from the weaker tribes, for example, from the sedentary Bani Malik in the mountains near Lith. They were not a fighting tribe, and British records note that they were 'devoted to the King

47 FO 686/26, Lackany [probably Laqqani] notes on activities of 15 February 1920.
48 FO 686/12, Report by Captain Mian Nasir-ud-din Ahmad for the period ending 9 August 1920; FO 686/28, Jeddah Report 1–20 January 1922.
49 FO 686/74, Lawrence (Jeddah), to Prodrome (London) 19 September 1921.
50 FO 686/28, Jeddah Report, 1–20 January 1922.
51 FO 686/28, Jeddah Report 11–28 February 1922. For further on these taxes, see al-Rashid, vol. 1, pp. 99–100, Note no. 103, Local Taxes Increased in the Hedjaz, US Consul (Aden), 27 March 1923.

of Hejaz and pay him taxes.' On the other hand, the Harb, as the name may imply, was a fighting tribe, and '[paid Husayn] tribute only when it suit[ed] them.'[52] The taxing of Qasim and of the 'Utaybah by the Wahhabis formed a bone of contention with Ibn Saud. In August 1917, *al-Qiblah* announced ceremoniously that the bedouin of the Juhaynah tribe as well as other tribes in the northern areas of Wajh and 'Aqabah were freed from giving the Sharif part of their date crop until the end of the war, an indication that these tribes had previously given tribute to Husayn.[53] During the Ottoman period, the major tribes were primarily accustomed to receiving subsidies during the Ottoman period in order to safe-guard the pilgrimage. Husayn continued this largely distributive policy, enlarging it many-fold with the British subsidy. When he determined that certain tribes were no longer needed for expan-sion, he either stopped subsidizing them or radically reduced their subsidy. It is also doubtful whether he could have continued the subsidy at the levels to which they had become accustomed by the British. The result, as discussed earlier, was an inflation of the price of tribal loyalty, a factor which would have fatal implications for the Hashimite state when the Saudi challenge grew stronger.

The Revolt wrought a major in change in the role of customs duties in the Hijaz as revenue now accrued directly to Husayn, for the first time since 1841.[54] The duty usually assessed on imported goods at Jeddah averaged 10 per cent. Apparently just prior to the Revolt, the Ottomans had collected close to 11 per cent (8 per cent for the Ottoman treasury and 3 per cent for the Ottoman Public Debt). Lawrence reported in November 1916 that there was a 10 per cent *ad valorem* customs tax on imports, but it is clear that this figure was eventually raised. Reports from 1923 showed that it was much higher, averaging about 27 per cent. Theoretically, cus-toms were assessed *ad valorem* based on the invoice, but in practice samples of merchandise were taken into the Jeddah *suq*, sold to the highest bidder, and the customs assessed accordingly. As the Brit-ish Vice Consul noted, such a practice was largely responsible for the high cost of living in Jeddah, and it raised the price of imported goods. All customs were payable only in gold.

---

[52] *HH*, p. 46; 39.
[53] *Al-Qiblah*, 2 Dhu al-Qa'da 1335 [19 August 1917].
[54] See Ochsenwald, *Religion, State*, p. 177.

When particularly pressed for money, Husayn did not hesitate to assess customs on a pilgrim's personal effects. Thus, during the 1922 *hajj*, the 'very clothes the pilgrims were wearing, if they were adjudged new by the customs authorities, were taxed, and on several occasions the tax charged was 50 per cent of the cost of the article.'[55]

Customs was a source of significant income not only for the Sharif, but also for the officials involved. Grafftey-Smith cited several examples of hugely over-valued assessments, the proceeds from which went into the pockets of officials. The Director of Customs himself was an importer, and the Governor of Jeddah was one of the largest merchants in the Hijaz. Conditions reportedly greatly improved after the British Agent and Consul, W. E. Marshall, lodged a protest with Husayn.

It was impossible to get an accurate assessment of customs revenues. In 1923 Grafftey-Smith, while cautious, cited 'one qualified to judge' who valued it at £40,000 gold a month. When it was rumored in 1923 that the customs would be farmed out, the mooted fee was that amount.[56]

Camel hire and licenses. The most widely known and accepted tax in the Hijaz was the Sharif's tax (*koshan*) on camel hire, primarily on the Jeddah–Mecca road, but also on camel traffic between Yanbu' and Medina, Mecca and Medina, and Mecca and 'Arafat. During the 1910 *hajj*, the tax had been relatively low.[57] It remained the prerogative of the Sharif in the new régime, and as a gesture on the occasion of the first pilgrimage after the Revolt Husayn announced its reduction,[58] but the tax increased steadily after this.[59]

---

55 FO 371/8943/E 2478, Pilgrimage Report, 1922, enclosed in Marshall to Curzon, no. 11, 31 January 1923.

56 SHAT, Brémond to Minister of Defense, no. 53, 19 March 1917; *AB*, no. 32, 26 November 1916; FO 882/12, Pearson (Jeddah), to Cornwallis (Cairo), 27 February 1917; FO 371/10006/E 289, Report on Economic and Financial Conditions in the Hedjaz by Vice-Consul Grafftey-Smith, enclosed in Bullard to Curzon, no. 12, 31 July 1923. In mid-1919, Allenby estimated customs income at a much lower level – £15 000 a month (T1/12425/51473/20218); FO 371/8943/E 2478, Pilgrimage Report, 1922 enclosed in Marshall to Curzon, no. 11, 31 January 1923.

57 FO 195/2376, The Hajj Report for 1910–1911, S. Abdur Rahman, Vice-Consul, 30 April 1911.

58 L/P&S/10/586 Arabian Report by Sir Mark Sykes, 25 July 1916; FO 882/15, Draft Communiqué, The Pilgrimage of 1916.

59 FO 371/4194/38756, Pilgrimage 1918, Captain W.P. Cochrane, enclosed in Cheetham to Curzon, no. 80, 19 February 1919; FO 371/5094/E 15806, Report on the Hadj

Bullard wrote that in 1924 Husayn enforced a policy whereby pilgrims were forced to hire more camels than the weight of their luggage warranted. If the camel drivers did not comply, they were penalized. Husayn was therefore able to greatly increase his tax revenues.[60]

Husayn also had an income from the issuing of licenses. The position of the head of guilds was usually hereditary, though theoretically dependent upon government approval. All members of guilds paid a *kafalah* (guarantee) tax to the government. It was collected annually by the shaykh of each guild, who was allowed to keep 10 per cent for himself.[61]

Personal wealth. British officials believed that Husayn had amassed considerable personal wealth. According to a report by Storrs in 1915, Husayn's family property in Egypt amounted to about 6,300 *feddans*, 5,000 of which had been a gift from Muhammad 'Ali, 2,000 of those being constituted as *waqf* and administered by the Sharif. Husayn had numerous other properties in the Hijaz.[62] Bullard wrote in 1924, 'I have come to the conclusion that this is the truth about King Hussein's finances: he has a considerable nest egg, laid probably during the golden days of the subsidy, and he spends on ordinary expenditure less than he receives.'[63]

Forced loans and fines. To gain additional revenue Husayn frequently forced wealthy individuals to lend him money. According to Grafftey-Smith, most merchants of Jeddah, Mecca and Medina were creditors of the government; should they refuse to become such, 'unpleasant consequences' entailed. Repayment was promised, but remitted only in the rarest of cases.[64]

(Pilgrimage) for the year 1338 A.H., i.e., 1920 A.D, by Captain Nasiruddin Ahmed, 8 October 1920, enclosed in Allenby to Curzon, no. 1327, 4 December 1920; FO 686/27, Jeddah Report 11–20 May 1921; FO 686/28, Jeddah Report 1–20 January 1922; FO 371/10006/E 289, Report on Economic and Financial Conditions in the Hedjaz by Vice-Consul Grafftey-Smith, enclosed in Bullard to Curzon, no. 12, 31 July 1923.

60 FO 371/10812/E 1779, Pilgrimage Report, 1924, enclosed in Bullard to Chamberlain, no. 15, 27 February 1925.
61 FO 371/10006/E 289, Report on Economic and Financial Conditions in the Hedjaz by Vice-Consul Grafftey-Smith, enclosed in Bullard to Curzon, no. 12, 31 July 1923.
62 WP, 135/6/21–22, Sherif of Mecca, by R. Storrs, 22 November 1915. The holdings in Egypt are also mentioned in the letter from Bullard, cited in the next note.
63 FO 686/137, Bullard to Lt. Col. W. Dent, Air Headquarters, Baghdad, 19 June 1924.

A regular source of income was to arbitrarily set the rate of exchange, then fine the money-changers who 'violated' the order.[65] For example, in late 1923 it was reported that Husayn had fined money-changers who did not trade at the official rate of 7 majidi to the pound sterling. But, noted the British Agent, he himself forced them to exchange for him £3,000 into silver at the rate of 13 majidi to the pound, even though the market rate was just under 13.[66] This practice did much to alienate merchant support for Husayn.

Projects and concessions. Husayn was a ruler with a foot in both centuries. While insisting on receiving the subsidy he regarded as his, he was not unaware of the fact that the Hijaz had to modernize and diversify its methods of income production beyond the subsidy and the capriciousness of the pilgrimage. Yet there was a gap between this intellectual understanding of the problem and the realization that efficient, rational steps had to be taken to solve it.

In 1922, the British Chancery at Jeddah forwarded some rocks to its counterpart in Alexandria. They were accompanied by the following letter:

Dear Chancery: By this mail we are forwarding to you two bags containing stones. This is not an attempt at humour but a response to King Hussein's request that we might have these stones examined, and, if the examiner thinks fit, reported upon ... All Hashemite geese are swans, and all Hejaz mica is gold; perhaps you will in due course let us know what these weighty hopes are – or are not.

After having the rocks assayed, Egypt replied in September 1922 that the rocks were volcanic in origin and contained no minerals of commercial value.[67]

The British mocking of Husayn's 'gold fever,' while typical of their attitude towards him by this time, was entirely misplaced; Husayn's belief that the Hijaz held gold was not. Many Muslims believed that God not only had blessed the Hijaz by choosing to

64 FO 371/10006/E 289, Report on Economic and Financial Conditions in the Hedjaz by Vice-Consul Grafftey-Smith, enclosed in Bullard to Curzon, no. 12, 31 July 1923.

65 FO 371/10006/E 289, Report on Economic and Financial Conditions in the Hedjaz by Vice-Consul Grafftey-Smith, enclosed in Bullard to Curzon, no. 12, 31 July 1923.

66 FO 686/28, Jeddah Report 30 November–31 December 1923.

67 FO 141/812/14741: Jeddah Chancery to Residency (Alexandria), undated; Residency (Ramleh), to Marshall, 1 September 1922.

reveal His word in Mecca, but also had blessed it with riches, notably gold, which had once been mined in the Hijaz, according to the historians Ahmad ibn 'Ali al-Maqrizi (d. 1442) and Abu al-Hasan 'Ali al-Mas'udi (d. 928).[68] Husayn probably knew of certain bedouin oral traditions concerning gold deposits and was certainly aware of a place named Mahd al-Dhahab ('cradle of gold'), located east of Mecca and Medina. He had high hopes, therefore, of finding gold, and in an interview with Wilson in 1918 stated that two to four 'dinkems' of pure gold had recently been obtained in trial crushings from a piece of quartz about the size of a football. Meccan goldsmiths, Husayn added, had assayed the gold at 24 carats.[69]

The Hijaz attracted carpetbaggers interested in gaining various concessions. In early 1920 Lieutenant (later Major) Harry St Clair Garrood asked the Arab Bureau in Cairo for permission to enter into a concessionary agreement with Husayn involving oil exploration in the Hijaz. Garrood had served with British demolition parties operating alongside 'Abdallah in 1918 and had been Acting British Agent in Jeddah for a short time in 1919.[70] Cornwallis of the Arab Bureau said that there was no objection to Garrood's efforts – as long as they had no official connection with Britain. Major Charles Edwin Vickery, Garrood's successor in Jeddah, therefore interceded with Husayn on Garrood's behalf, asking that the concession be entertained as a personal favor to himself; it was granted in May 1920.[71] Private correspondence between

[68] M. Casanova, *Une Mine d'Or au Hidjaz*, offprint of *Bulletin de la Section Géographique* (Paris: Imprimerie National, 1920), found in the archives of the Royal Geographical Society, London.

[69] FO 371/3381/146256, Wilson, Interviews with King Hussein at Jeddah on 17 July 1918. The British never seriously explored the possibility of gold in the Hijaz, and Husayn was not able to carry off such exploration himself. It is ironic, therefore, that in 1932 the American engineer K. S. Twitchell, who was in the employ of Charles Crane (of King–Crane Commission fame), confirmed the availability of commercial values of gold ore at Mahd al-Dhahab. It took over fifty years for the Saudis to officially open the mine, and in 1989 the first ore was processed (K. S. Twitchell, *Saudi Arabia: With an Account of the Development of Its Natural Resources* [Princeton University Press, 1947], p. 147; Saudi Press Agency, 30 April 1983; *British Broadcasting Corporation: Summary of World Broadcasts*, 2 May 1983; *Economist Intelligence Unit Country Profile: Saudi Arabia, 1992–93*, p. 19).

[70] For his activities with 'Abdallah see *AB*, no. 88, 7 May 1918, no. 95, 2 July 1918, and no. 98, 23 July 1917; for his short stint in Jeddah, see his Jeddah Report of 11 September 1919 in FO 686/26.

Garrood and Husayn between 1921 and 1923 shows clearly that despite having the concession, Garrood was never allowed to carry out his explorations. Husayn apparently expected him to use his influence with the British on his behalf and against Ibn Saud. It also seems that Garrood himself ran into some financial difficulties.[72]

In late 1916 Husayn tried to avail himself of French expertise in developing his economy. The Sharif knew that he had one readily available important commodity, the wool and skins left over from the sacrifices of sheep by tens of thousands of pilgrims.[73] The idea was to develop a tannery and other projects in the Mecca valley. This was the one French project (for others, see Chapter 3) to which the British seemed not to have objected, even though Sykes suspected that Brémond had approached Husayn rather than vice versa. In any event, the French could find no suitable Muslim to oversee the operation, and it was abandoned.[74]

The French believed that they had not exhausted the possibility of gaining some commercial advantage in the Hijaz, and in February 1917 the French government teamed up with the merchant house of Hauet and Bayart to explore the possibilities of skin and wool exports from the Hijaz. A mission sent to the Hijaz was defined as '*strictement privé*,' although French officials noted its importance for the national interest and put themselves at the mission's disposal.

Headed by one V. Bellet the mission arrived in Jeddah on 25 March 1917. Bellet immediately discovered a harsh reality of the Hijazi economy: that, to a great extent, it was controlled by Husayn, who had forbidden the export of skins by anyone but the Hijazi '*maison Hassan Sabban frères*.' Bellet thus wrote to his principals about the '*impossibilité pour nous lutter contre un monopole*.' He explained how the system worked. After the sacrifice, the animals

[71] See the correspondence on the concession in FO 686/72, and the note that the concession was granted in FO 686/26, Political Report, 22.5.20–1.6.20.

[72] For access to this correspondence I thank Jeffery Rudd, who located Garrood's heirs, obtained copies of the documents and translated them.

[73] It was reported in the *AB*, no. 33, 4 December 1916, that the price of sheepskins had fallen to almost one-half of their 1914 price, thus probably making them quite attractive to the French.

[74] MAE, Hedjaz, vol. 1707, contains the correspondence on this subject; Sykes' minute is in FO 371/2783/228575, commenting on a request from the French Chargé d'Affaires, French Embassy (London), 4 November 1916.

were left on the ground. Men of the Sabban firm, acting as agents of the municipality, buried the carcasses. To defray their costs, they were allowed to sell the skins. The Sabban family had fifty such agents, and it can be assumed that the Sabbans paid Husayn for the privilege. Bellet concluded that the French could not compete against such a system.

In April 1917 Husayn announced a new national project: a tannery. It would manufacture shoes of all kinds for men and women and would use local hides. This would provide work, and the products would be sold at low prices. For this reason, noted *al-Qiblah*, the export of hides was forbidden.[75] When the French discovered that their military experienced a shortage of skins, Husayn indicated to Brémond that he would sell them what they needed. Encouraged by this bit of loosening the French, together with La Maison Bayart, made another attempt at the export of skins and wool. Bayart's representative, a North African Muslim, arrived in Jeddah on 4 September 1917, entered into negotiations with Ibrahim Sabban at the French Mission, and after a short while was informed that Husayn would permit the export of 50,000–60,000 skins. Husayn nevertheless eventually prohibited this activity, probably because of the tannery.[76]

At times Husayn seemed to have a dim realization that improving the lot of the pilgrims could help him financially, but projects to that end were invariably more tied up with gaining political advantages from the British. Thus, in 1923, he entered into a concessionary agreement with the Middle East Development Corporation for the development of a Jeddah–Mecca railway. In letters to Sir T. Royden and Lord Inchcape, the concessionaires, Husayn regaled them with the history of his relations with, and abandonment by, the British. It was clear that he wanted Royden and Inchcape to lobby on his behalf (not an uncommon request from foreign governments who have relations with firms of another country). It was heavily intimated that the concession was conditional upon the success of their lobbying efforts.[77]

---

[75] *Al-Qiblah*, 10 Jamadi al-Thani 1335 [2 April 1917].

[76] This section is based on the correspondence in MAE, Hedjaz, vol. 1705.

[77] FO 371/8950/E 6359: Sir T. Royden, Cunard Steamship Line (London) to Sir Eyre Crowe (FO), 15 June 1923, enclosing two letters from Husayn to Lord Inchcape, one undated, the other dated August 1922. The Cunard Steamship Line stood to gain handsomely from conveying pilgrims not only to Jeddah but all the way to Mecca by

In an attempt at a centralized economy, and in line with Husayn's desire to force dependence on the state's central authority, the National Company (*al-sharikah al-wataniyyah*) was formed. According to *al-Qiblah*, the company was established as a national enterprise for the betterment of the Arabs and would sell products at lower than market value.[78] It will be recalled also that the idea for the company had originated with the British. When certain goods – such as cereals and rice – were scarce, the company confiscated imports at Jeddah even though customs had been paid by the merchants, and it sold them at a high price. When prices were low, or when there was a large stock in the National Company's stores, these and other goods were returned to the merchants.[79] This company was in direct competition with local merchants and thus undermined their support for Husayn.

During his stay in the Hijaz in February 1920, financial expert Lackany noted that while exporting hides would be a good idea, their export could be restricted by Husayn, who, at a moment's notice, could claim that they were being requisitioned by the army.[80] In the same month the establishment of the 'National Hide Company' was announced.[81] According to the British Agent, it was well known in the Hijaz that the company was 'a partnership between His Majesty and the Kaimakam of Jeddah with a royal monopoly for the purchase and export of hides.'[82] The King also established a shipping company. In about January 1922 the shaykhs of the various guilds were summoned to the King, who 'asked' them how many shares (at £5 gold each) they could pawn off on their members.[83]

In an August 1918 article extolling Hashimite industry, *al-Qiblah* mentioned the recent opening of a soap factory and a textile factory in Mecca.[84] In July 1920, it announced the founding

---

rail. The text of the actual concession is in FO 371/E 6930/248/91.

[78] *Al-Qiblah*, 30 Dhu al-Qa'dah 1335 [16 September 1917]; 11 Rabi' al-Awwal 1336 [24 December 1917]; 22 Rabi' al-Thani 1336 [3 February 1918].

[79] FO 371/10006/E 289, Report on Economic and Financial Conditions in the Hedjaz by Vice-Consul Grafftey-Smith, enclosed in Bullard to Curzon, no. 12, 31 July 1923.

[80] FO 686/26, Lackany notes for 14.2.20.

[81] *Al-Qiblah*, no. 359, 19 February 1920.

[82] FO 686/26, Intelligence and Political Report 21.2.20–2.3.20.

[83] FO 686/26, Political Report 13.6.20–22.6.20; FO 686/27, Jeddah Report 1–10 December 1921; FO 686/28, Jeddah Report 1–20 January 1922.

[84] *Al-Qiblah*, no. 210, 22 Dhu al-Qa'dah 1336 [28 August 1918].

of another national company called *Jam'iyyat al-Ta'sis lil-Mashari'
al-'Umraniyyah fi al-Hijaz* for building projects. Its first project was
to manufacture ships, and – incredibly – cars. Major merchants
headed up these projects: Muhammad Tawil, Inspector of the
Registrar; Muhammad Salah Banajah, chairman of the Chamber
of Commerce; 'Ali Salamah of the family of harbor pilots; Tahir
al-Dabbagh, chair of the treasury (*al-amwal*); and others.[85]

Financial management in the Hijaz: the Lackany mission. The question of the currency in use was a crucial one for the Hijazi economy. It affected both trade and the relationship between Husayn
and the major merchants. In much of the world at that time there
was a move away from the gold standard. Because the tribes liked
to be paid in gold, Husayn wanted to keep it in use. Moreover, like
many people, he seems to have believed that it held 'real' value, in
other words, that it held its value and could always be counted on
to do so.

Before the First World War, large sums of Indian currency had
been brought into the country by pilgrims. Imports were paid for
largely with this currency, effectively returning it to India. With
the outbreak of the War and the consequent drop in pilgrimage
traffic, a gold shortage developed as Hijazi merchants had to pay
for Indian and Egyptian goods with what little gold there was, and
there was much hoarding as well.[86] Husayn kept his accounts in
Turkish piasters (a silver currency; in October 1919, the exchange
rate was 112 Turkish piasters to the gold pound sterling), yet
accepted payment only in gold; wholesale merchants did the
same.[87]

In January 1920 Husayn, seeing that the British were determined to issue his subsidy in rupees instead of gold, tried to force
the merchants of Jeddah to accept the rupee as the only legal
tender. When they balked at the rate of 8½ rupees to the pound
sterling – the rate at which the British had granted his subsidy – he
agreed to a rate of 14 rupees to the pound. He had the merchants
write to the British Agent to that effect and promise to carry out
their trade in rupees, both notes and silver. A similar commitment

[85] *Al-Qiblah*, no. 401, 19 July 1920.
[86] *AB*, no. 40, 29 January 1917.
[87] FO 686/51, Notes on Hedjaz Currency written in Jeddah 4 October 1919 by Messrs
Gellatly Hankey and Company.

was published in *al-Qiblah*. On the face of this, it seemed a kind of accommodation between two competing social forces, the state and the merchants, with the accommodation on Husayn's side and clearly at his expense. The merchants would see his willingness to help them, and, to the British, he could say that he was reforming his economy. It is difficult to determine just what Husayn personally gained by this arrangement. The British Agent in Jeddah speculated that he simply wanted to acquire more gold and the higher rate was an incentive to merchants to take the rupee, even though it entailed a loss.[88]

Other developments illustrate some interesting aspects of the capability of Husayn's state in areas away from the center of power, Mecca. Cowling, the representative of Gellatly, Hankey and Company, wrote to the British Agent:

While merchants are glad to receive Rupees at 14 to Sterling they are by no means ready to pay out at this rate. We may tell you in confidence that as soon as HM [Husayn] left Jeddah his orders in this direction were at once ignored. As an instance of this we may say that if one pound sterling is to-day taken into the Suk it will be found impossible to obtain Rupees 14 change for same. The person applied to will either state that he has no Rupees or offer from Rupees 13 to 13 and one half for the Gold pound Sterling.

He cautioned that the net effect of all this was that gold remained the real basis of the country's currency system, with all the difficulties that entailed, including the deflation of the British subsidy.[89] In Mecca, Husayn had the law enforcement apparatus to bring about compliance, while Jeddah, a major port only 54 kilometers away from Mecca, seemed to be more on the periphery and not subject to coercive measures.

The British view was that Husayn was entitled to set any exchange rate that he liked, although he would have to bear the consequences. That Husayn did not understand what he was doing by fixing the exchange rate at 14 rupees to the pound sterling is indicated by his complaints to the British soon afterwards. In January 1920 he protested to the High Commissioner that the

---

[88] FO 686/26, Political and Intelligence Report for ten days ending 22 January 1920; FO 686/51, Abdallah Ali Riza, Kaimakam, Jeddah, to British Agent, 13 January 1920; FO 686/51, Cowling (Gellatly, Hankey and Co.), to British Agent, 20 January 1920; *al-Qiblah*, no. 349, 15 January 1920.

[89] FO 686/51, Cowling [Gellatly, Hankey and Co.] to British Agent, 20 January 1920.

rupee was inflated at a value above that at which he received his subsidy. He was then dourly advised to let the rupee circulate at the value it was sent to him. The British Agent told 'Abdallah that Husayn's policy deflated the value of his subsidy and that HMG might 'consider that his subsidy is still too high and might yet reduce it.'[90]

Meanwhile, Cowling's suspicions about the continued use of gold were confirmed. In early February, *al-Qiblah* announced that pilgrims had to bring gold or silver with them – no notes would be accepted. The British representative in Mecca reported that the government was accepting only gold or silver in payment for all manner of services.[91]

With real fear that this policy would have a devastating effect on both the pilgrimage and the Hijazi economy, the British forced upon Husayn – as a condition of any subsidy whatsoever – a Muslim financial expert. Both the King and 'Abdallah were very reluctant, viewing the prospect as interference in their internal affairs. When the British Agent stated explicitly that Husayn's subsidy depended on it, Husayn conceded.[92]

Sani Lackany (probably Laqqani), an expert in financial affairs for the Egyptian Government, arrived in the Hijaz in February 1920 to examine the kingdom's finances; Lackany's notes and report shed light on its financial management. According to Lackany, Husayn took the entire subsidy into his private coffers, from whence it was dispensed – in consultation with his wife. Particularly in the army's case, disbursement was often made very late, as Husayn would feign illness on pay day.

Lackany met many obstacles during his research. Husayn resented his coming and did not make financial records available; he refused to listen to Lackany's pleading on the gold issue. According to Lackany the king was full of modernizing ideas such as founding an agricultural school and setting up a scientific organization for research and exploration. There was a scientific committee for the improvement of public works, such as wells and

90 FO 686/51: High Commissioner to King Hussein, 20 January 1920; Assistant British Agent to Abdallah, 23 January 1920.
91 FO 86/12, Nasiruddin, Mecca, to British Agent, 8 February 1920, citing *al-Qiblah* of 7 February 1920.
92 FO 686/26 Political and Intelligence Report for ten days ending 22 January 1920.

water plants; Husayn showed Lackany diagrams for water plants and wells designed by the committee. Lackany wrote:

The King's designs in this direction bid fair to be an expensive game. His excess zeal in certain respects affords a remarkable contrast to his conservatism in others. He is just as forward looking in starting an agricultural school a generation before the time that such an institution is ever likely to be of any use ... [But the] Mecca water supply – a potential source of infection – is relegated to oblivion at the very time when expenditure to the point of extravagance is cheerfully borne when it is incurred by the Regular Army.[93]

Lackany believed that Husayn would eventually open up his records. He tried to tempt 'Abdallah with a peek at the budget of the Egyptian Ministry of Awqaf, saying that he was anxious to make Egyptian pious donations devoted to the *Haramayn* available on a more liberal basis than before. 'Abdallah did not take the hint, and Lackany was forced to confront him point blank about Husayn's records. The amir was very concerned, saying that he could not relay such a request for fear that Husayn would resign. The whole episode seemed somewhat surrealistic to Lackany, who related a strange occurrence. In attempting to gain access to the accounts, he asked the Minister of Awqaf – a Turk – for a record of the some 6,300,000 lbs of wheat consigned annually to the Hijaz from Egypt:

'Effendem Hojaj Sheria,' [came the reply]. What kind of Hojaj Sheria? I asked. 'Effendem Hojaj Sheria.' Where, how? 'Effendem Hojaj Sheria' was the invariable reply which the man kept repeating parrot-like to all and sundry enquiries. So much did he get on the Emir's ['Abdallah's] nerves that he asked him what the devil he was talking about.[94]

This Turkish means 'Sir, the pilgrims, sharia.' It is complete nonsense, and either the minister was so scared of Husayn that he was struck dumb by Lackany's request or he was feigning insanity so as not to comply.

93 FO 686/26, notes by Lackany for 14 February 1920.
94 FO 686/51, British Agent to Director, Arab Bureau, Financial Mission of Sani Effendi Lackany, 13 March 1920. Lackany's notes on his meetings with the King and 'Abdallah in February 1920 are in FO 686/13 and FO 686/26; his final report is in FO 371/5258/E 5671, attached to Allenby to FO, no. 520, 19 May 1920. The distribution of wheat from Egypt was apparently an established institution. In *al-Qiblah*, no. 422, 5 October 1920, an announcement was made to all those holding chits for a wheat ration to come to the main granary in Mecca.

Both the British Agent and Lackany recommended that Husayn be instructed to adopt the rupee as his official currency; Allenby demurred, as did the FO, for fear of being perceived as interfering in Husayn's internal affairs. One British official minuted, 'It is obviously impossible to induce King Hussein to make the change while he is in his present mood ... and thus the Hedjaz itself is the principal loser from the King's antiquated theories of political economy.'[95] Contrary to all advice, but in keeping with his aspirations, Husayn eventually issued his own currency (see Chapter 6).

The financial system operating in the Hijaz under Husayn was primarily one of intense revenue distribution, not extraction. The Ottomans, caretakers of a vast empire, could afford to run such a system; extraction came from places other than the Hijaz. But a distributive system was not tenable once the Hijaz achieved independence and was cut off from the Ottoman state's financial umbilical cord. Husayn believed that he could solve this problem by establishing his suzerainty over other Arab lands; they would provide extraction, and he would distribute in the Hijaz. But when this did not come about Husayn tried the various and sundry money-making projects detailed above, which all failed miserably. His taxation efforts foundered on a lack of tradition of taxation in the Hijaz, and his inability to establish a high enough degree of legitimacy that would make taxation possible.

The British subsidy fundamentally altered the economy of the Hijaz, putting an unpredecented large amount of cash in Husayn's hands. Husayn's tribal confederacy was based on these funds, and not on additional attraction factors and foci of loyalty and solidarity. As will be seen, this lack of cohesion was one of the crucial factors which led to Husayn's downfall. Unlike Ibn Saud, who was charismatic and had a powerful religious message, Husayn based his chieftaincy on the British subsidy, without creating additional attraction factors and foci of loyalty and solidarity. Instead of engendering personal, dynastic, religious or ethnic loyalty, he relied solely on British monetary and political support.

95 FO 686/51, British Agent to Arab Bureau, 28 February 1920; FO 371/5258/E 5671, Allenby to FO, no. 520, 19 May 1920; FO 686/51, FO to Allenby, 10 June 1920.

Husayn's major failure, probably the result of incompetence and blind ambition, was that he did not properly invest in the infrastructure of the one money-making export the Hijaz had – the *hajj*. For this effort, he could have counted on British help and on aid from Muslim countries. Without doing that, and without the resources, say, of Saudi Arabia, the economy of Husayn's Hijaz was bound, it seems, to fail.

7

SOCIETY AND
STATE FORMATION
IN THE HASHIMITE KINGDOM
OF ARABIA

'The local fortune tellers and soothsayers have predicted the King's death on July 25th. If it comes true they are not likely to be in want for the rest of their lives.'[1] (report by British Agent, Jeddah, July 1920)

As Husayn set out to build his state, which was, in his view, to be the legitimate successor polity to the Ottoman Empire, he used mechanisms of coercion and revenue extraction. Coalition building is also an important component of state formation.[2] This is often accomplished on two levels. The first is the delicate task of giving potential coalition partners – the élites – a stake in the state by some kind of attenuated power-sharing and/or granting access to the resources of the state. The second is on the discursive level, by putting forth an ideology, often through education and symbols, that is somehow inclusive of the élites and/or legitimizing of the ruler.

The structure of Hijazi society on the eve of the Sharif's succession has been discussed in Chapter 1. Husayn's rule was too short for any significant social change to take place; the extant social structures continued during the period under discussion. Our task in this chapter, therefore, is to discuss the role, if any, society played in Hijazi state formation. As will be demonstrated, Husayn failed to integrate the élites into the new states, a shortcoming which had disastrous consequences.

[1] FO 686/26, Political Report 22.6.20–2.7.20.
[2] See Crystal, p. xii.

Façade and fealty: alienating the Hijazi élite, 1916–1924

The urban élite. Like many modern states in formation, Husayn set up a formal administrative apparatus which was intended to give his new state the look of one capable of replacing the Ottoman Empire. Many key notables received positions in this framework, but, as will be shown, it remained a façade with no power, and the administration remained centralized in the extreme. Husayn's first government, announced in October 1916, was composed as follows:

Prime Minister (*Ra'is al-Wukala*)	Amir 'Ali ibn Husayn
Minister of Foreign Affairs	Amir 'Abdallah ibn Husayn
Minister of Interior	Amir Faysal ibn Husayn

Minister of Justice,
    Deputy Prime Minister,
    Hanafi *mufti, Qadi al-Quda*
	'Abdallah Sarraj

Minister of War	Sa'id 'Ali Pasha

Minister of Public Works,
    Shaykh al-Mutawwifin of
    Javanese pilgrims
	Yusuf ibn Salim Qattan

Minister of *Awqaf* and Director of the *Haram*	Muhammad Amin al-Makki
Minister of Finance, merchant	Ahmad Banajah
Minister of Education *mutawwif*, reader in the *Haram*	'Ali Makki [Maliki?]

Husayn also constituted a Council of Notables (*Majlis al-Shuyukh*) on the same occasion:

Shaykh Muhammad Salih al-Shayba, President
    Keeper of Keys to Ka'ba
Sayyid 'Abdallah bin Muhammad Salih al-Zawawi
    Shafi'i *Mufti*, Vice-President
Shaykh Muhammad 'Abid
    Maliki *Mufti*
Shaykh 'Abd al-Qadir ibn 'Ali al-Shayba (assumed Keeper of Keys
    position on death of Muhammad in September 1917)

Sayyid 'Ali ibn 'Alawi al-Saqqaf
   Shaykh or *Naqib al-Sadat*
Shaykh 'Abdallah ibn Zaynal 'Ali Rida,
   merchant, head of Jeddah Chamber of Commerce
Shaykh 'Ali ibn 'Abdun al-Sharbasi,
   merchant
Shaykh Abu Bakr ibn Muhammad Khuqayr,
   'Alim
Sharif Hamza ibn 'Abdallah al-Fa'ar,
   head of the *ashraf* of the Barqah 'Utaybah
Sharif Fitim [Fitil?] ibn Muhsin
Sharif Sulayman ibn Ahmad ibn Sa'id
Sharif Nasir ibn Shakir
Shaykh 'Abdin Husayn,
   'Alim
Sayyid Ibrahim 'Ali[3]

At first glance it is clear that, at least on paper, Husayn attempted
to strike a balance in the *Majlis al-Shuyukh* between the *'ulama*, the
ashraf, merchants and tribal forces. In the government, he
included his own sons, *'ulama*, and merchants. Yet all the sources
point to his refusal to delegate responsibility, his extreme centralization, and his cruelty to those who opposed him. The façade
was, however, maintained, and every so often *al-Qiblah* would
announce that a meeting had taken place.[4]
   Many of those appointed to these positions were the objects of
such a high degree of ridicule in British reports that it is probable
that they were not well respected in Hijazi society either. For

---

[3] This list of members of the first government and the *Majlis al-Shuyukh* is drawn from
   AB, no. 27, 26 October; no. 28, 1 November 1916; FO 371/2782/21297, McMahon to
   Grey, 20 October 1916; Hanadi Yusuf Ghawanimah, *Al-Mamlakah al-Hashimiyyah
   al-Hijaziyyah* (Amman: Dar al-Fikr lil-Nashr wal-Tawzi', 1989), pp. 81–84. It should
   be noted that some sources have slightly different names holding various positions.
   Other sources used here are the personality profiles by Benazzouz in SHAT, 7 N 2139,
   1916–1917; FO 882/20, J.W.A. Young, Mecca Personalities; FO 882/20, J.W.A. Young,
   Jeddah Personalities.
[4] For example, *al-Qiblah*: 28 Rabi' al-Thani 1336 [10 February 1918]; 7 Jamadi al-Ula
   1336 [17 February 1918]; 14 Jamadi al-Ula 1336 [24 February 1918]; no. 204, 1 Dhu
   al-Qa'dah 1336 [7 August 1918]; no. 257, 16 Jamadi al-Ula 1337 [16 February 1919].

example, the Minister of Public Works had begun his life as a servant to a *qahwaji* (coffee-house owner). He was widely known to be ignorant, reported in one source (quoting an Egyptian newspaper) as one who was unable to distinguish between an 'alif' and a telegraph pole; Husayn made him President of the Mecca municipality. In 'enlightened circles,' one French North African wrote, he was considered a parvenu.[5] The Minister of Finance, of the important Banajah merchant family, was well known 'for his peculiarly immoral nature' and for the strange way of walking he had cultivated when performing the *tawaf* (circumambulation of the Ka'ba).[6]

Why did Husayn appoint such people? We can only surmise. Perhaps he tried to coopt certain families and social groups, while at the same time not appointing anyone who could serve as a focus of opposition. Of course, we must also not ignore the possibility of simple incompetence on Husayn's part.

Although giving positions to several of the Hijazi élite, it was clear from the very beginning of the Revolt that Husayn had no intention of granting them a serious role in government. Instead, he chose Syrians – whom he distrusted – and a few unsavory locals who were not respected and who acted on Husayn's and their own whims.

It became apparent soon after the Revolt broke out in June 1916 that Husayn had not succeeded in coopting or otherwise gaining the support of the urban élite. Lawrence noted in late January 1917 that while at the outbreak of the Revolt the townsmen supported the Sharif because he was able to get British subsidies and end the blockade of the Hijaz (see Chapter 2), they now

saw signs of danger and uncertainty in the future and their loyalty was tempered accordingly. They began to doubt how far it was possible that the Sherif could establish any permanent independence; many of the leading families, dependent on Turkish pensions, doubted how long the Sherif could go on paying them, now that the Turks had gone ... To this must be added an emotion common probably to all in varying degrees,

---

5 J.W.A. Young, 'A Little to the East: The Experience of an Anglo-Egyptian Official, 1985–1925' (henceforth, Young, 'Experience'), Middle East Centre, St Antony's College, Oxford; SHAT, 7 N 2139, Benazzouz (Mecca), Cheikh Youssef Guettan, Ministre des Travaux Publics, 14 January 1917.

6 Young, 'Experience;' SHAT, 7 N 2139, Benazzouz (Jeddah), Cheikh Ahmed Benadja, Ministre des Finance, 2 March 1917; Young, Mecca Personalities.

namely, a half-conscious regret in assisting at what might be a fatal blow to the unity of Moslem power so long represented before the world by Turkey.

Although Lawrence ended on an optimistic note about the Sharif's abilities to control the opposition, his initial assessment proved to be the correct one.[7]

British reports were practically unanimous in describing the opposition of the élite to Husayn, usually phrasing this as 'pro-Turk' or later, 'pro-Wahhabi.' The Hijazi élite simply wanted to stay out of Husayn's way, and this directed their behavior until the Wahhabi victory at Turabah in May 1919. From that point until the bitter end, the élite made its views quite clear, in confidence, to anyone who would listen. The British Agent reported in early 1920 that the élite of Jeddah, without any 'organized scheme, form part of a very strong clique against Hussein and the present regime. They would like to see the King [replaced] with Ali and Abdallah.'[8] A similar report later in the year stressed that the leading notables and merchants of Jeddah 'reflect general opinion in praying for [Husayn's] speedy death. They would infinitely prefer to return to the rule of the Turks … The situation, therefore, is that a Sherif sits on the throne of Hedjaz, hated and dreaded by his subjects, with whom it is literally impossible to work or even to regard as a sane man.'[9]

The residents of Jeddah were particularly open with the British Agent. In mid-1920 the Mayor (probably *Ra'is al-Baladiyyah*) approached him stressing that he had the promise of sixty signatures to a petition requesting that the King be removed immediately, if the Agent approved. He reported that all sorts of petitions were coming in asking for HMG to take over customs and the policing of Jeddah.[10] With the fall of Faysal's kingdom in Syria in the summer of 1920, 'the flight of the Emir and the termination of Sherifian rule [was] hailed with great satisfaction, which the leading notables and merchants have difficulty concealing.'[11] Captain Nasiruddin Ahmed reported from Mecca in early 1921 that while no Muslim wished to see the Wahhabis in charge of the *Haramayn*,

---

[7] *AB*, no. 41, 6 February 1917.

[8] FO 686/26, Intelligence and Political Report, for ten days ending 21 February 1920.

[9] FO 686/26, Political Report 1–12 June 1920.

[10] FO 686/26, Local News 13–22 June 1920.

[11] FO 686/26, Political Report 1–10 August 1920.

the 'present feeling is that even a Jew, let alone Ibn Saud, would be a relief.'[12]

The *Amir al-Hajj* of the Egyptian pilgrimage reported in 1922 that as a result of Husayn's levies on the merchants, the conditions of the inhabitants were miserable. 'Nobody could say that he is content or satisfied with the policy of the Government and the treatment of the people. Everyone of them wishes from the bottom of his heart that the present Government is changed or overthrown. Nobody dares to show or express his feeling for fear of the king who is considered by all to be despotic and oppressive to the last extremity. He kills anybody he likes to kill, casts into prison anybody who falls [out of] favor and seizes the property of any man without pity and he seems to have no fear of God.'[13]

From the beginning it was clear that Husayn's government was over-centralized in the extreme. He trusted few people, and therefore did not delegate authority. A British Agent in Mecca, Agub Khan, reported that

the King has centralized all the authority in himself, and even orders for trivial things have to be orally received from him ... The so called Ministers are only nominal and are mere executants of the King's will, and they do not possess the initiative, power or courage of even expressing their views. In name there exists everything requisite for a state, but in reality there is nothing and the King's will is the law of the country.[14]

Not did only this alienate people who thought they should have a place in the government, but it made for extremely poor functioning. British officials often remarked on the 'absurdity' of the King trying to do everything himself, 'down to the pettiest and minute matters.' He had, wrote British Agent Vickery, 'no aptitude for governing.'[15]

Husayn's most common method of punishment was the 'Qabu,' his dungeon under the Sharifian palace in Mecca. This was a deep

---

12 FO 686/27, Report by Captain Nasiruddin Ahmed (Mecca), 10 January 1921.

13 FO 371/7717/E 10447, Lewa Mabrouk Pasha Fahmi, Notes on my visit to the Hedjaz as Emir el Haj in 1340 (1922 AD) submitted to His Lordship the Field Marshal Lord Allenby, High Commissioner in Egypt, 19 September 1922, enclosed in Allenby to FO, no. 756, 22 September 1922.

14 FO 686/12, Captain Agub Khan (Cairo) to Arab Bureau, 10 April 1920.

15 FO 686/30, Wilson to Arbur, 11 October 1917; FO 686/36, Wilson to Arbur, 12 October 1917; FO 686/18, Record of conversation with 'Abdallah, 12–15 July 1919; FO 686/26, Batten, Appendix to Report 20 September 1920; *NOME*, no. 2, 30 January 1920.

underground cell into which the king's enemies were deposited, with little regard for the offense: they were often thrown in there and left to rot, fettered and without food. In 1920 several merchants of Mecca were thrown in the dungeon for not exchanging gold at the rate fixed by the Sharif. Young reported that in the Qabu

sanitary arrangements did not exist. The prisoner was supplied only with water, and for further sustenance he depended upon help from friends outside. Extreme cases had been known in which the prisoner had been chained to a board on the ground, his legs fastened near or wide apart according to the severity of the punishment, in which condition he could neither change his clothes nor rise from the ground, nor make any movement except the movement of his hands waving them day and night to keep off the pestilential mosquitoes. Thus he lay surrounded by filth until his torture was terminated by release or more often death.

Few apparently came out alive. Amin al-Rihani, a Leba-nese–American traveller, wrote that one 'often hears it in Jeddah – [w]hen a man is called to Mecca by His Majesty, he makes his will.'[16] To this of, course, must be added the various *hudud* described in Chapter 4, which, far from aiding Husayn's search for Islamic legitimacy, only threw the fear of God into the inhabit-ants of the Hijaz, who were not known for their religiosity.

Husayn's alienation of the élite must have also been surely caused by his practice of publicly humiliating his opponents. Young wrote that prominent notables who angered Husayn were enlisted by the King in the register of the *qayadah*, 'the lowest class of men and boys in Mecca who were employed in dancing and entertainments.' Each one was forced to don a special cap and placed under the control of the *shaykh* of the *qayadah*. A similar practice had existed in nineteenth-century Egypt.[17]

---

[16] FO 686/12, Nasiruddin Ahmed (Mecca) to British Agent, 25 October 1920; FO 371/7715/E 10447, Mabrouk Pasha Fahmi, Notes on my visit to the Hedjaz as Emir el Haj in 1340 (1922 AD) submitted to His Lordship the Field Marshal Lord Allenby, High Commissioner in Egypt, 19 September 1922; al-Rashid, 1, Report on Arabia from Mr Amin Rihani, enclosed in Consul Edward Groth (Beirut), to Secretary of State, 27 October 1923; Young, 'Experience,' p. 7.

[17] Young, 'Experience,' p. 8. The word *qawwad* also refers to a pimp. Toledano records that one of the worst punishments that could be inflicted on the Egyptian élite was to force them to wear the clothes of the *fallah*, known as *libda wa-za'abut* – *State and Society in Mid-Nineteenth Century Egypt* (Cambridge University Press, 1990), pp. 162–3; the *libda* was a felt skullcap, while the *za'abut* was a woolen robe with a low neckline).

Probably the greatest contributory factors to the alienation of the merchant élite were Husayn's practices of forced loans, not paying for goods, and controlling the exchange rate. The leading ammunition merchant of Mecca, one 'Abd al-Khayr, was forced to pay a loan to Husayn; after doing so, Husayn demanded another, and when he declared he could not pay, Husayn threw him in the Qabu; while he was there, the King looted his stores. In November 1922 Husayn ordered the merchants of Mecca to pay him £15,000. In 1923 it was reported that financial transactions were becoming daily more chaotic. Because of Husayn's control of exchange rates, it was nearly impossible to send gold from town to town, as it was subject to confiscation. Bills in Jeddah could no longer be settled by draft, as these were liable to a premium of 3–4 Turkish piasters per £1. This had the effect of raising prices and cutting profit margins.[18]

In Mecca, Husayn upset the *ashraf* in late 1920 and early 1921 when he decided to widen the streets of the markets. The *ashraf* owned a great deal of property in the area, and protested strongly. It was apparently around this time that many notables began to contact Ibn Saud for relief, and it was reported that they had been given to understand that there would be no massacres or robbery if they kept indoors.[19] This development illustrated the chieftaincy's temporary nature; once the leader disappointed, the élite began to transfer its loyalty elsewhere.

Like all merchants, leading men such as Muhammad Husayn Nasif and 'Abdallah 'Ali Rida of Jeddah lost quite a lot of money on account of the King. Nasif was known for his Salafi sympathies and natural inclination towards Ibn Saud (see Chapter 1). While as agent for many *ashraf* Husayn could not get rid of him entirely, he forced several loans out of the man. Nasif was a major informant for both the British and the French, requesting protection and even citizenship from them. It was reported that the King had nearly ruined him, and that he had 'been bled almost white by forced loans.'[20]

18   FO 686/28: Jeddah Report 1–10 March 1922; Jeddah Report 1–30 November 1922; Jeddah Report 1–28 February 1923.

19   FO 686/12: Ihsanullah (Mecca) to British Agent, 19 December 1920, 29 December 1920; Nasiruddin Ahmed (Mecca) to British Agent, 9 January 1921.

20   L/P&S/12/217, P 2507, Arab Personalities, enclosed in Consul Stonehewer-Bird (Jeddah) to Chamberlain, no. 60, 20 April 1928; MAE, AH 24, Depui (Paris) to

Husayn behaved in a similar fashion to the prominent 'Ali Rida family. Although he appointed 'Abdallah 'Ali Rida, head of the Jeddah Chamber of Commerce, as *qa'im maqam* of the coastal town, Husayn probably thought this would allow him to look to Rida for funds. Rida was probably the richest man in Jeddah, and the king took quite a bit of money from him. Since he was opposed to Husayn, he was often cited in reports as being a Turkophile or pro-Wahhabi. 'Abdallah's brother and family patriarch Zaynal, as well as his nephew Muhammad 'Ali also suffered at the hands of Husayn. The latter had established several schools (see Chapter 1), and they were his pride and joy. Before the War, they had been at a high-school level, but since then Husayn had not let him bring in teachers from overseas, so they had fallen to a primary-school level.[21] He must surely have been disappointed and resentful.

As noted above, the Jeddah élite were in constant contact with the British Agent. Vickery reported: 'I must say ... that the Kaimakam, Rais Baladia and all the leading merchants of Jeddah convey at once to me all the private orders of the King; they detest him and are very anxious for British occupation.'[22] In one conversation, 'Abdallah 'Ali Rida poured out his heart to the British Agent. He pointed out that the state of affairs was simply appalling, 'the administration drifted from bad to worse and the King is not only unpopular but absolutely hated, being entirely in the hands of a little gang of so-called advisers who are the worst specimens of scoundrels one could think of.' If the people of the Hijaz 'do not stir,' concluded the British Agent, 'it is only from sheer fear.'[23]

In another example of a policy which alienated the local élite, the *ayal al-harat* (see Chapter 1) were pressed into the army, and they feared that fate more than imprisonment.[24] It will be recalled

Minister of Foreign Affairs, 28 September 1924; SHAT, 7 N 2139, Benazzouz (Jeddah), Note sur Mohammed Nacif, intendant du Malik à Djeddah, 23 June 1917; Young, Jeddah Personalities; FO 371/4144/1181, Wilson to Arbur, 4 December 1918.

21 L/P&S/12/217, P 2507, Arab Personalities, enclosed in Consul Stonehewer-Bird (Jeddah) to Chamberlain, no. 60, 20 April 1928; MAE, AH 24, Depui (Paris) to Minister of Foreign Affairs, 28 September 1924; Young, Jeddah Personalities.

22 FO 371/5092/E 6979, Extracts from report dated 27 May 1920 by Colonel C.E. Vickery.

23 FO 686/26, Intelligence and Political Report for ten days ending 1 February 1920.

24 FO 882/23, Ihsanullah (Mecca) to British Agent, no. 25, 19 May 1920.

that in Ottoman times they were often considered neighborhood heroes; they were usually let off quite easily, and even when imprisoned were brought sweets and had visitors who stayed for hours drinking tea.

Instead of integrating the élite into the administration, Husayn relied on several Syrians and some particularly unsavory local characters, those referred to by 'Abdallah 'Ali Rida above. Two of the Syrians chosen by Husayn, Fu'ad al-Khatib and Muhibb al-Din al-Khatib of the Damascus élite,[25] were active in the pre-war Arab movement and had previously served the British. Fu'ad had worked for the Sudan Government, and had been 'employed temporarily' as a British intelligence agent. It seems that it was he who suggested to the Arab Bureau that Husayn establish *al-Qiblah*, and wrote a detailed memorandum describing the physical needs of the paper and what should be its propaganda goals. He arrived in early August 1916 to edit the paper, along with Muhibb al-Din, serving both as under-secretary of foreign affairs and as the Hijazi representative in Cairo. Fu'ad had many conversations with British officials in Jeddah, in which he sought sympathy for Husayn, and a more pro-Arab policy in order that he should not be tarred with the British brush. The King himself suspected Fu'ad of being a British agent, although it is unclear whether after 1916 he was acting in that capacity. In August 1918, Husayn stated that Faysal suspected Khatib of sedition, and Husayn had him removed from Cairo over the sincere objections of the British. Fu'ad ended up in Damascus, working for Faysal, thus Faysal's accusation of sedition may have been a ruse to get him out of Husayn's service, with which Fu'ad had expressed dissatisfaction. In general Husayn did not trust the Syrians who worked for him, although he trusted them more than local Hijazis.[26]

25 On Muhibb al-Din, see William Cleveland, 'The Role of Islam as Political Ideology in the First World War,' in *National and International Politics in the Middle East: Essays in Honor of Elie Kedourie* (London: Cass, 1986), pp. 84–101.

26 Tauber, *Emergence*, p. 237; *AB*, no. 37, 4 January 1917; Tauber, *Arab Movements*, pp. 104, 137; *HH*, p. 64; FO 882/14: Fuad El-Khatib to Clayton, 19 July 1916; Deedes to Clayton, 19 July 1916; Clayton to Private Secretary, Khartoum, 25 July 1916; Cornwallis to Clayton, 5 August 1916; FO 882/3, Statement on Hedjaz taken from Fuad Eff. El Khatib, 1917; FO 882/12, Fu'ad al-Khatib to Wilson, 20 April 1917; FO 371/3383, Hogarth's 'Extracts from Notes of Conversations with King Hussein,' undated, enclosed in Wingate to Balfour, 27 January 1918; FO 686/30, Bassett to Arbur, 8 September 1918; FO 686/30, Basset to Arbur, 8 September 1918; FO 686/30,

Muhibb al-Din al-Khatib was a writer and an early activist in the Arab nationalist societies. He served the British as a drago-man in Hudaydah, Yemen, from 1908–1909, and went to Iraq in October 1914 as a British agent and on behalf of the Decentral-ization Party in order to incite Muslims to revolt against the Ottomans. He arrived with Fu'ad to serve as editor of *al-Qiblah* in August 1916. Husayn harnessed Muhibb al-Din's consider-able literary skills, and he and 'Abdallah must have surely appre-ciated his brand of Arab nationalism, which glorified the Arab within Islam. He wrote several articles in *al-Qiblah*, including one titled 'How We Can Serve Our Country.' Al-Khatib defined the task of the government, which was to defend against outside threats, carry out justice, safeguard human rights, and push for progress; what was for the good of the individual was for the good of the entire people, and *vice versa*, wrote al-Khatib. The people should all do their part, from the merchant who provides quality goods at reasonable prices, to the artisan who must strive for the best, he concluded. But this ideal was far removed from the state of affairs in the Hijaz. Not only the British decried Husayn's government; Muhibb al-Din painted a picture of the King as 'a nervous, small-minded man with no capacity for objectivity and no knowledge of military matters.' The sources conflict on when Muhibb al-Din actually left Husayn's service, either in October 1917 or later, but by 1919 he was working for Faysal in Damascus.[27]

While Syrians handled the ideological organ and engaged in high policy, Husayn appointed some particularly unsavory char-acters to look after his interests in Jeddah and Mecca. In the former, Husayn appointed Sharif Muhsin ibn Mansur al-Karimi

draft of letter from High Commissioner to King Husayn, undated, but from mid-September 1918; FO 686/39, Wilson to King of Hedjaz, 9 September 1918; FO 686/30, Bassett to Arbur, 8 November 1918. By 1924, Fu'ad was back in the Hijaz, acting as 'Ali's foreign secretary. Bullard reported that he suffered from his connection with the Sudan, as many regarded him as a British agent (Bullard, pp. 70, 75).

27 Muhammad 'Abd al-Rahman Burj, *Muhibb al-Din al-Khatib wa-Dawruhu fi al-Harakah al-'Arabiyyah, 1906–1920* (Cairo[?]: al-Hay'ah al-Misriyyah al-'Ammah lil-Kitab, 1990; Tauber, *Arab Movements*, pp. 17–18, 139; Tauber, *Emergence*, pp. 44–50, 93, 122, 133–4; *al-Qiblah*, 22 Rabi' al-Thani 1335 [14 February 1917]; FO 195/2320, Robertson (Hodeidah) to Monahan (Jeddah), 25 March 1909; SHAT, 7 N 2139, Benazzouz (Mecca), Mohib-ed-Dine el Khatib, 1 December 1916; Nimrod Hurvitz, 'Muhibb al-Din al-Khatib's Semitic Wave Theory and Pan Arabism,' *MES* 29 (1993), pp. 118–34.

of the Masruh Harb, who was often designated *Amir al-Harb*.'[28]
He had led a force which attacked the Ottomans in Jeddah when
the Revolt broke out, and plundered the Ottoman treasury.
Muhsin handed out judgments against those who offended him
or whom he suspected of being against the Sharif; these included
flogging, slashing about the head with a sword, and branding the
offender's tongue with a red-hot iron rod. Along with his servant
Ahmad Hijazi, he was greatly feared by the merchant community,
from whom he took protection money for goods going to Mecca;
it was said of Muhsin by the notables that when 'we think of him
our loins tremble.'[29]

In Mecca, Husayn appointed Ibrahim Ramil as Chief of Police.
Ramil was a purveyor of cakes until the *qa'im maqam* called him to
his office and informed him that he had been appointed to the
lofty post. This caused a scandal among the notables, as Ramil was
well known as a fence and a loan-shark. Completely illiterate,
Ramil eventually endeared himself to some of the notables by
being tough on the poor while ignoring the infractions of the rich.
He arrested people arbitrarily, including one notable whom he
detained when he heard that he read foreign newspapers, and
therefore must be an intriguer.[30]

It would seem that Husayn should have been able to count on his
sons for support. He appointed them to positions in the government,
but, except for 'Abdallah, they were otherwise occupied during and
after the Revolt. Over time, much distrust developed between
Husayn and his sons, until he eventually alienated them all.

The first one to be alienated was Faysal, a process which probably began in 1918, over Husayn's mistrust of the Syrian and
Baghdadi officers in his son's entourage. In August, Allenby presented Faysal's general, the Iraqi Ja'far al-'Askari, with the British
Companion of the Most Distinguished Order of Saint Michael

---

[28] Goldie noted that the Harb confederation were ruled by a council of *mashayikh* of the
various tribal sections. While the amir of the tribe was nominated by the Sharif, the
'Emirate of the tribe is a nominal office only, and in the councils the hold carries no
more power than the other members. He is, however, the mouthpiece of the council
in negotiations' (*AB*, no. 114, 30 August 1919). It appears, however, that Muhsin acted
more for the king than for the tribes.

[29] Young, Jeddah Personalities; *HH*, pp. 68–69.

[30] SHAT, 7 N 2139, Benazzouz (Mecca), Bramin Ramil, Directeur de la police à la
Mecque, 13 January 1917; Young, 'The Experience'; this notable was 'Ali Hijazi, a
small merchant of Mecca (Young, Mecca Personalities).

and Saint George (CMG) decoration in a ceremony with all military honors. Ja'far had been given the position of Commander in Chief of the Northern Arab Army by Faysal in 1917, although Husayn had never approved it. The following day, Husayn published a proclamation in *al-Qiblah*, announcing that Ja'far was simply in charge of one of the sections of the Northern Arab Army. Ja'far promptly resigned, as did all the Syrian and Iraqi officers. Faysal was forced to resign also, and did so on 29 August, resulting in the suspension of military operations. The High Commissioner, Allenby and Wilson set about trying to get a retraction from the King. But instead, Husayn telegraphed abusive messages, including one to Zayd in which he called Faysal a traitor and put the former in charge. However, since the messages passed through British radio operators, Lawrence corrupted or deleted offending passages. On 4 September, a message arrived which was a half-hearted apology and a retraction, as well as a repetition of the charges against Ja'far and Faysal. Lawrence suppressed the last part, and took it to Faysal, effectively ending the crisis.[31]

By the end of 1918, Faysal seems to have become disillusioned with his father. Although he appeared in Paris in early 1919 for the Peace Conference as the representative of the Hijaz, this was because the Hijaz was already more or less accepted as an independent state, which he wished to use as a *fait accompli* to attach to Syria. He put forth claims to Syria, Iraq, Najd and Yemen. With respect to Syria, he was willing to accept only technical advice; as for Iraq, he stated that the Arab Government there 'would have to be buttressed by the men and material resources of a great foreign Power;' concerning Palestine, he accepted an 'effective superposition of a great trustee.' In a meeting with British officials in London on 27 December 1918, following a meeting with Zionist leader Chaim Weizmann two weeks earlier, and cognizant of the need for Jewish support for his claims on Syria, Faysal actually admitted the 'moral claims of the Zionists,' and stated that it would ill become the Arabs 'to make difficulties over a question of which they regard the British Government as the best judges.' He

---

[31] *AB*, no. 101, 27 August; no. 104, 24 September 1917; FO 686/39, Wilson to HH the King of Hedjaz, 9 September 1919; FO 686/26, Davenport (Wejh) to GSO, Hedjaz Operations (Cairo), 13 September 1919; Tauber, *Arab Movements*, pp. 140–4; Wilson, *Lawrence*, pp. 539–42; *SPW*, pp. 576–9.

concluded that 'the interests of the Arab inhabitants may safely be left in the hands of the British Government.' Moreover, he was told officially that if France insisted on its rights under Sykes–Picot, 'Great Britain would not be in a position to refuse.'[32] Thus, although speaking in the name of his father, he had already acquiesced on Palestine – a position which Husayn certainly did not support – and was wavering with respect to the other areas.

Faysal, nevertheless, did argue his father's case against the Wahhabis, and even sent Husayn arms from Damascus, although he appears to have failed to raise troops.[33] But the agreement reached by Faysal in late 1919 and early 1920 to allow partial French tutelage over Syria earned him a public repudiation by his father.[34] In March, Faysal was proclaimed King of Greater Syria, with no role for Husayn ('Abdallah was offered the throne of Iraq). Later that same month, a mission arrived from Syria led by Fu'ad al-Khatib to try to patch up relations between Faysal and Husayn, but the latter refused to recognize his son as King of Syria.[35]

In February 1921 Husayn confided to the British Agent his jealousy of Faysal. While Faysal had been chosen to attend the Peace Conference, complained Husayn, he himself was forbidden to go to London. Husayn said that Faysal was 'no better than a gramophone, repeating the last words he had heard, and had no claim to speak with authority.' When the British Agent reminded the King that Faysal was his chosen representative it 'merely drew from him a snort of contempt.'[36]

Although no love was lost between father and son, Faysal, fearing the implication in Iraq of a Wahhabi victory, lobbied hard with the British there on behalf of the Hijaz, despite what he referred to as 'the mad obstinacy of his father which has alienated his subjects

32 FO 608/92, Feisal, Territorial Claim of the Government of the Hejaz, 29 January 1919 (this document was written with the help of Lawrence; see Wilson, *Lawrence*, p. 595); FO 371/4162/605, Interview with Sherif Feisal, 27 December 1918;
33 FO 686/17, Arbur to Wilson, no. AB 808, transmitting Zayd to king, 14 June 1919; SHAT, 16 N 2302, Picot (Beirut) to MAE, no. 1043, 20 July 1919; FO 686/26 (French document in British files), Brémond, Renseignements, 31 December 1919.
34 Khoury, *Urban Notables*, pp. 89–91; FO 882/22, Extract of a Letter from Emir Feisal to Lord Allenby, no. 195 S., 11 February 1920; FO 371/5062/E 5347, Scott (for Allenby) to Curzon, no. 503, 16 May 1920.
35 FO 686/26, Political and Intelligence Report 12–22 March 1920.
36 FO 686/27, Jeddah Report 1– 20 February 1921.

as well as hostilized [sic] his neighbours.'[37] When in March 1924 Husayn had himself declared Caliph, Faysal suppressed the Reuters report announcing the fact.[38]

Relations with 'Abdallah were more complex. He was the most vocal proponent of his father's ambitions, but after the son's defeat at Turabah their relations deteriorated markedly. In late October or early November 1919 'Abdallah told the British Agent in Jeddah that he had practically been pensioned off, as Husayn had taken control of his work and he was Foreign Minister in name only: 'He was very depressed about it and held forth at length on the vanities and futilities of the world.' It was reported that Husayn now gave 'Abdallah no money, and in his will had left everything to his wife, the mother of Zayd, who in any case controlled a great deal of Husayn's wealth.[39]

Husayn no longer trusted 'Abdallah, and in early 1920 the latter and 'Ali expressed to the British Agent that they were ashamed of their father. 'By Allah,' exclaimed 'Abdallah, 'that man is really mad, and if he cannot rule and take advice, and that other coward will not rule [he referred to 'Ali], I myself will take the throne and rule the country and administer it properly.'[40] According to a British operative in Mecca, 'Abdallah was extremely out of sorts that Husayn did not listen to him, and was jealous that his younger brother Faysal at least had a throne. Since 'Abdallah had been proclaimed King of Iraq in March 1920, Husayn sent him to Cairo in May, where he said that 'Abdallah was now his representative at the Peace Conference, and would speak on behalf of Syria and Iraq, as he had repudiated Faysal. But since the mandates had been awarded at San Remo in April, the British did not recognize 'Abdallah as King of Iraq or as Husayn's spokesman for Syria, as that was up to the French.[41]

By now realizing that he had no future in the Hijaz, and having heard rumors by September 1920 that the British were to put

---

37 FO 371/7713/E 5412, High Commissioner for Iraq to the Secretary of State for the Colonies, no. 364, 23 May 1922.

38 FO 371/10217, CO to FO, no. 11939/24, 13 March 1924.

39 FO 686/26: Political and Intelligence Report 26 October–21 November 1919; Intelligence Report 22 March–1 April 1920; FO 686/12, Captain Agub Khan (Cairo) to Arab Bureau, 10 April 1920.

40 FO 686/26, Vickery to Director, Arab Bureau, 11 January 1920; FO 686/26, Jeddah Report 10–20 September 1920.

41 FO 686/12, Captain Agub Khan (Cairo) to Arab Bureau, 10 April 1920; FO 371/5062/E 5374, Scott (for Allenby) to Curzon, no. 503, 16 May 1920;

Faysal on the throne of Iraq instead of himself, 'Abdallah decided to assert himself. Ostensibly heading for Syria in response to nationalists gathered in Amman, he set himself up in Transjordan. His parting shot was a raid on the whole balance of the Jeddah customs, where he made off with £70,000, and yet another forced loan from the merchants, which amounted to £20,000. When finally set up as amir of Transjordan in 1923, 'Abdallah was helpful to Husayn's Caliphal ambitions, and even attempted to recruit men and send arms for the Hijazi army to fight against Ibn Saud in 1924, although he was prevented from doing so by the British.[42] Of course, as was the case with Faysal, this was probably more out of a fear of Wahhabi threats to Transjordan and Iraq than out of filial loyalty.

Finally, Husayn did not seem to have had a good relationship with his eldest son, 'Ali, although British reports noted that he was more afraid of and more obedient to his father than any of the other brothers. Fu'ad al-Khatib told Vice-Consul Grafftey-Smith that 'Ali had spoken to him seriously in 1921 of leading a movement against the King, 'whose intransigent personal animosities are recognised by his sons to be obstacles to the progress of the Arab cause.' In late 1922, 'Ali was reported to be opposed to his father's policy towards Ibn Saud and his generally aggressive mien, which had isolated him from the rest of the world. Husayn was also withholding money from 'Ali, who was attempting to govern Medina.[43]

Husayn was unable to bring the urban élite over to his side. There were three main causes for their alienation: Husayn's inability to govern properly and delegate authority; his fleecing of the merchants and other notables; and his inability to control the tribes, which wrought havoc on the settled population and reduced the pilgrimage (see Table 7.1, p. 200).

---

[42] Acting British Consul Major Batten wrote: 'The Emir recently stated that Feisal appears to be "our man now" .... He is obviously hurt, and he has referred more than once to his being the only son of the three elder brothers with no prospects, in spite of the part he played in the War and subsequently' (FO 686/26, Jeddah Report 10–20 September 1920); FO 686/26, Jeddah Report 10–20 October 1920; FO 371/10016/E 10891, CO to FO, no. 52883/24, 4 December 1924; FO 371/10807/E 11, CO to FO, no. 59811/24, 31 December 1924; Wilson, *King Abdullah*, pp. 42–51.

[43] FO 371/6239/E 5816, Report by Secret Intelligence Service, no. 210, 18 May 1921; FO 686/28, Jeddah Report, 1–10 March 1922; FO 686/28, Jeddah Report 1–30 November 1922.

The tribal élite. As noted earlier, the British subsidy to Husayn fundamentally altered the economy of the Hijaz. This change particularly affected the tribes, who had become accustomed to receiving a massive influx of British sovereigns, thus inflating the price of tribal loyalty. When British funding began to dry up, Husayn began to cut back tribal subventions, a policy which – when combined with the appeal of the Wahhabis – eventually lost him all tribal support.

As Sharif of Mecca, Husayn's starting point with the tribes of the Hijaz was quite good. He was at the top of the Sharifal pyramid, and as such enjoyed a basic respect from the tribes. Lawrence reported that the property of the *ashraf*, if it was marked with the Sharifal *wasm* (brand), was in theory and to a large extent in practice exempt from confiscation during tribal raiding. Moreover, their blood price was usually four times higher than that of non-*ashraf*, an often useful deterrent.[44] Finally, it will be remembered from Chapter 3 that he had succeeded in making alliances with the tribes in common cause against the Hijaz railway.

The problems in the subsidization of the tribes became apparent not too long after the occupation of 'Aqabah in the summer of 1917. Wilson remarked that the policy was

most expensive, but another source of trouble is that – in spite of numerous protests on my part at the time – too high rates of pay were issued to the Arabs at the beginning of the revolt and it is not possible to reduce them now without causing widespread discontent.[45]

Even though in the fall of October 1917 the British subsidy was still going strong, Husayn began to pull back on subsidies to tribes he believed he no longer needed in order to continue the Revolt north of 'Aqabah. These were the tribes of central and southern Hijaz, and his fatal mistake was in taking their support for granted. Thus the British officer Davenport reported on discontent among the key Harb tribe: their pay was many months overdue, and they had little food, which had in any case become quite expensive. Under the Ottomans, the bedouin had redress when overcharged,

---

[44] FO 686/6, Lawrence (Wejh) to Wilson, Notes, 26 April 1917.
[45] FO 686/48, Wilson to Director, Arab Bureau, 21 October 1917; it should be remembered that about this time Ibn Saud began to become a threat to the tribes of the Hijaz, particularly the 'Utaybah and some of the Harb; this aspect of the undermining of Sharifian influence among the tribes is covered in Chapter 7.

Table 7.1. HAJJ ARRIVAL FIGURES, 1907–1925[a]

Year	By sea	By land	Total
1907			250,000[b]
1908	68,000	105,000	173,000[c]
1909	67,901[d]		
1910	90,051		200,000[e]
1911	90,000	27,000	117,000[b]
1912	100,000	200,000	300,000[b]
1913	96,924[f]		
1914	56,855[g]		
1915			NA
1916	6,800[g]		
1917	7,936[g]		60,000[g]
1918	7,133[h]		44,000[h]
1919	22,174[i]		70–75,000[j]
1920	58,584[k]		80,000[k]
1921	57,255[l]		
1922	56,319[m]		65,000[m]
1923	75,221[n]		100,000[n]
1924	92,707[o]		150,000[o]
1925	2,352[p]		

[a] David Long cautions against the unreliability of pilgrimage statistics, particularly previous to and including the period covered in the present study. Even bearing in mind his own caveat, he does present the statistics, although does not give sources for the period covered here. (David Long, *The Hajj Today: A Survey of the Contemporary Muslim Pilgrimage* [Albany: SUNY Press, 1979], pp. 125). Ochsenwald, who gives statistics from 1853–1908, also cautions that they should be taken only as 'very rough indications.' (Ochsenwald, Religion, p. 61). In this table, statistics for both land arrivals (where obtainable) and sea arrivals are given. They both should be treated as indications, although those for sea arrivals are closer to being accurate, as the British officials from whose reports these statistics are drawn apparently had access to passenger lists.

[b] Long, p. 127.

[c] Ochsenwald, *Religion*, p. 61.

[d] FO 685/3, Haj Report for Year 1908–1909, by Vice-Consul Mohammad Husayn, 19 May 1909, enclosed in Monahan to Lowther, no. 24, 21 May 1909.

[e] FO 195/2376, The Hajj Report for 1919–1911, S Abdur Rahman, Vice-Consul, 30 April 1911.

[f] FO 368/1438, The Haj Report for year of 1913/14, S Abdurrahhman, Acting British Consul, 25 December 1914.

g FO 371/3052/243933, Pilgrimage 1917, Captain W.P. Cochrane. 21 November 1917, enclosed in Wilson to Wingate, no. Ref. 20, 27 November 1917.

h FO 371/4194/38756, Pilgrimage 1918, Captain W.P. Cochrane, enclosed in Cheetham to Curzon, no. 80, 19 February 1919.

i FO 371/4195/167339, Pilgrimage 1919, by Major W.E. Marshall, MC, RAMC, enclosed in Allenby to Curzon, no. 631, 17 December 1919.

j FO 371/4195/167322, Extracts from a Report on the Pilgrimage 1919, by Lt. Col. Vickery, CMG, DSO, British Agent, Jeddah, enclosed in Allenby to Curzon, no. 618, 16 December 1919.

k FO 371/5094/E 15166, Report by Major W.E. Marshall, RAMC, on the Pilgrimage, 1920, 10 October 1920, enclosed in Allenby to Curzon, no. 1282, 22 November 1920.

l FO 371/7709/E 1120, Pilgrimage Report 1921, enclosed in Marshall to Curzon, 30 January 1922.

m FO 371/8943/E 2478, Pilgrimage Report 1922, enclosed in Marshall to Curzon, 31 January 1923.

n FO 371/9999/E 25, Pilgrimage Report 1923, enclosed in Bullard to Curzon, no. 100, 18 December 1923.

o FO 371/10812/E 1779, Pilgrimage Report 1924, Bullard to Chamberlain, no. 15, 27 February 1925.

p FO 371/10814, Pilgrimage 1925, M. Yaseen Khan, Indian Pilgrimage Officer, Rabigh, 21 August 1925.

---

an agent told Davenport, but now the Sharif let the merchants of Mecca and Jeddah run wild. The Harb were thus about ready to desert; although the *mashayikh* themselves were loyal, they could no longer control their people on promises and 'Inshalla Bukra [tommorow, God willing],' wrote Davenport.[46] This disaffection seems to have first manifested itself sometime in October, when a band of Hawazim Harb robbed a party led by a French Muslim officer and two *ashraf* three days out of Yanbu'. They declared that they would do the same to everyone until their claims were satisfied by Husayn. Husayn Mubarak (Zubayd Harb) of Rabigh, in hiding somewhere, was bribing some of the Masruh Harb with money provided by the Ottomans.[47] In January 1918, an agent reported extreme dissatisfaction among both the Hawazim and Ahamidah Harb, since they had not received the pay due to them from the Syrian and Egyptian *mahmal*s. As a strong signal to the

---

46 FO 686/48, Davenport to Bassett, 14 October 1917, enclosed in Wilson to Director, Arab Bureau, 21 October 1917.

47 *AB*, no. 67, 30 October 1917. Mubarak, the recalcitrant *shaykh* of Rabigh, was ordered after the war to live near Mecca. In November 1919, he was murdered. According to the British Agent, 'it is said that this act was done at the instigation of the king' (FO 686/26, British Agent to Director, Arab Bureau, 2 December 1919).

King, when the latter was in Jeddah the Bishr (of the Masruh Harb) raided a caravan on the Mecca–Jeddah road; they had been to ʿAli, who had refused them money. When the King returned to Mecca the next day, he did so not by the direct route, but by an indirect northern route: Wilson posited that Husayn may have already been unsure of his very own safety on the main road.[48] By the end of February, Davenport was reporting that nearly all the Juhaynah had disappeared from ʿAbdallah's forces, and were said to be hostile.[49] In March, it was reported that Sharif Muhsin had demanded that the Muʿabbad and the Baladiyyah tribes, who were responsible for protecting the road, hand over 800 camels. They refused because they had not been paid, and the King put six of them in jail. During the same month, reports grew more frequent that the tribes around Wajh were becoming less loyal.[50]

There were more and more reports as the year wore on that the Harb were openly defying the King. In response, the King had begun to prevent the Muʿabbad and Bishr from purchasing food in Jeddah, an age-old tactic used by amirs to put pressure on tribes by denying them access to food and markets for their goods. The Muʿabbad and Bishr thus threatened to raid Jeddah itself. Goldie concluded that the ʿHarb confederation is openly defying the authority of the King, and with the exception of the Weld Mohammed who are still loyal and whose dira is in the vicinity of Medina … the Kabyles of this confederation are now looking towards Nejd for protection.' By April 1918, it was reported finally that most of the Harb had left the Sharifian cause.[51]

It appears that from 1918 onwards, tribal chaos reigned in the Hijaz. Less than two years after the beginning of the Revolt, despite massive funding and an excellent opening hand, Husayn's greediness and inability to counter Wahhabi propaganda were taking their toll. For half of 1918 the subsidy was at its highest – £225,000 a month – being reduced to £200,000 only in July; from February 1919 it was reduced to £120,000 and later to £100,000

---

48 FO 686/10, Wilson to Director, Arab Bureau, 31 January 1918, enclosing reports from MN, 21, 24 January 1918; FO 686/10, from MN, 10 March 1918.

49 WO 158/634, Bassett to Arbur, no. W. 537, 26 February 1918.

50 FO 686/10, from MN, 10 March 1918; FO 686/49, Bassett to Director, Arab Bureau, 21 March 1918.

51 FO 686/6, Ruhi, 9 March 1918; FO 686/10, Ruhi, 9 March 1918; *AB*, no. 84, 7 April 1918; FO 686/10, Goldie to Wilson, 11 February 1918.

until October, when it began to drop significantly. Thus when the subsidy was at its highest, Husayn was not distributing it to the tribes, and was instead trying to control them by regulating access to markets. It is therefore doubtful that even without a reduction he would have paid them.

At the end of 1919, it was reported that 'the tribes do what they like.' 'Ali was afraid to go to Medina, of which he was supposed to be the amir.[52] From 1920, the Jeddah–Mecca road itself was not regarded as safe; in February it was noted that the government mail had been attacked on the road three times in the last three weeks. A caravan of stores for the government had also been plundered by the 'Utaybah near Bahra.[53]

For the British Agent, this was evidence of the change wrought by the British subsidy: 'During the war the Bedu were well paid and well fed – at our expense – now they have reverted to conditions as regards food and money which are worse than those before the war.' With Husayn preventing them from purchasing anything more than small amounts of food, they had simply resorted to their former livelihood, which was raiding.[54] Husayn apparently kept the bedouin on the verge of starvation, so that they would have to keep coming into town and a closer eye could be kept on them. British operative Nasiruddin Ahmed wrote from Jeddah that 'there has been a large influx of half famished, sick and insufficiently clad Bedous of both sexes into Mecca. The sight was too pitiable [sic] for words.'[55] The situation was made worse by the conflict with the Wahhabis, as Husayn also prohibited Najdi markets to Hijazi bedouin.[56] 1920 witnessed increased reports of a total breakdown of order in the Hijaz, and reports reflected the fear of the urban population that the bedouin were out of control. In Mecca itself, murders and violence were said to be a common occurrence, as the bedouin perpetrators went unpunished.[57]

52 FO 686/26, Political and Intelligence Report 21–31 December 1919. On the special circumstances in Medina, see below.
53 FO 686/26, Political and Intelligence Report for ten days ending 1 February 1920; *NOME*, no. 3, 1 April 1920.
54 FO 686/26, Political and Intelligence Report 21 February–3 March 1920.
55 FO 686/26, Extract from Mecca Report 29 May 1920; FO 686/12, Nasiruddin Ahmed (Jeddah) to British Agent, 24 July 1921; FO 686/28, Jeddah Report 1–30 April 1923.
56 FO 686/12, Intelligence Report by Captain Agab Khan (Mecca), 17 March 1920.
57 FO 686/12, Intelligence Report by Captain Agab Khan (Mecca), 9 March 1920.

In a bid to get the pilgrimage caravan safely to Medina, Husayn gathered representatives of the Harb in Mecca in April 1920 and reportedly paid them handsomely.[58] However, an indication of how unsure Husayn was of his standing among the tribes was seen when he hedged his bet by sending some 1400 pilgrims by ship from Jeddah to Yanbu' (and then by land to Medina), instead of overland directly from Mecca to Medina.[59] A major caravan of mostly Indian pilgrims which left Jeddah for Medina in late July 1920 was attacked, harassed and robbed along the entire route. Stragglers were picked off, as in the case of one Haji Khanjan Mirdha of Bengal, who 'went out to answer the call of nature, but did not return.'[60] In the same month, the Juhaynah attacked the coastal town of Umm Lajj, driving out the *qa'im maqam* and other government employees.[61] Before the Revolt, according to one British informant, the *ashraf* had such control that even a slave of one of them accompanying a caravan was enough to protect it. But now the bedouin did not respect the *ashraf*, and if a *sharif* was not accompanied by many heavily armed men, the bedouin would attack the caravan.[62] The situation did not improve the next year, when about sixty people were killed on the way between Mecca and Medina and Medina and Yanbu'. Many were held up in Medina for thirty-three days. Similar problems on the route to Medina plagued the Hashimites to the very end.[63] This reality did not prevent *al-Qiblah* from publishing articles praising the security afforded the *hujjaj* in the Hijaz.[64]

The dilemmas of the tribes of the Hijaz in the latter part of Hashimite rule were exemplified by the case of several Billi *mashayikh* from the coastal region between Yanbu' and 'Aqabah. In January 1924 a representative of the Billi, one Muhammad al-'Arabi, exploited Husayn's absence from the Hijaz (he was on his

58 FO 686/12: Ihsanullah (Mecca) to British Agent, 17 April, 29 May 1920; *NOME*, no. 4, 24 May 1920.
59 FO 686/26, Political Report , 22 June–2 July 1920.
60 FO 371/5094/E 15801, Allenby to Curzon, no. 1322, 3 December 1920, enclosing Note from Batten to HC, 17 November 1920, enclosing Petition from Hajee Mod. Ghulam Hassan Khan and other Hajees, undated.
61 FO 686/27, Jeddah Report 21–30 January 1921.
62 FO 686/12, Ihsanullah (Mecca) to British Agent, 14 April 1921.
63 FO 686/27, Jeddah Report 11–30 October 1921; FO 686/28, Jeddah Report 31 August–30 September 1922.
64 *Al-Qiblah*, 29 March 1923.

way to Amman to have himself proclaimed Caliph) by sneaking off to Cairo in order to seek British aid. He said that his people were being threatened by the Wahhabis, while King Husayn was not only unable to protect them, 'but his government was cruel and rapacious in the extreme.' If Britain would give the Billi support in funds and ammunition, they would kill Husayn or confine his influence to a small zone around Mecca. He hinted to the British that Husayn need not necessarily return from his present journey.[65] By the end of Husayn's reign, the tribal élites' animosity towards him seems to have been fairly pervasive.

Symbols, state education and social cohesion

Like other nascent states, Husayn attempted to use state education and national symbols in an effort to bring about social cohesion. The idea was to inculcate ideas and promote symbols which appealed to the general populace, causing them to identify with the state.

Symbols. Husayn gave his state the standard symbols: first a flag, then stamps, and finally coins in 1923, the latter several months before he declared himself caliph.

The flag of Husayn's kingdom was a red chevron with three horizontal stripes: black, white, and green. Black was for the 'Abbasids, white for the Umayyads, green for the Shi'ah of 'Ali, and red was for the *ashraf* of Mecca. It appears that Mark Sykes himself designed the flag; our sources are not only Sykes' biographer, but Husayn himself. During one of his conversations with Wilson touting his ambitions and his belief that Britain supported them, he told the British Agent that his national flag was the Arab national flag, and had been designed by a British official, Mark Sykes; the flag symbolized Hashimite rule over the Arabs. As a result, he was entitled to rule over the Arab world.[66] Husayn also

---

[65] FO 406/53/E 666: Kerr (Cairo) to Curzon, no. 32, 13 January 1924, enclosing Memorandum by R. Furness, Oriental Secretary, 11 January 1924; MacDonald to Allenby, 24 January 1924. Al-'Arabi was given no aid by the British, who remained neutral.

[66] Shane Leslie, *Mark Sykes, His Life and Letters* (London: Cassell, 1923), p. 280; Kedourie, *Anglo-Arab Labyrinth*, p. 198, citing FO 141/679, file 4088/17, Wilson, 5 June 1918. Arnold Rabbow, *Div-Lexicon Politischer Symbole* (Munich: Deutscher Taschenbuch Verlag, 1970), pp. 179–80. According to Khayriyyah Qasimiyyah, *al-'Alam al-Filastini* (Beirut: PLO, Markaz al-Abhath, 'Abhath Filastiniyyah' series, no. 21, 1970), Sykes

established two decorations utilizing these colors: the Order of the *Nahdah* (revival) and the Order of the *Istiqlal* (independence); the former was for those who actually participated in the Revolt. Both had five classes, with a special 'in brilliante' first class for heads of state.[67]

It is unclear just on whose initiative Hijazi postage stamps were printed. According to Storrs it was his idea, although the diplomatic record shows that McMahon had telegraphed the FO that 'Shereef requests to be provided with issue of postage stamps.' In either case, both parties had an interest in showing Sharifian independence from the Ottomans, and stamps were an oft-used indication of independence. Husayn's first designs were rejected by the British as not good enough (they were of monuments in the Hijaz), and they set Lawrence, then an intelligence officer in the Survey Department of Egypt, the task of redesigning them. The designs finally chosen were of calligraphy and abstract geometrical motifs based on monuments in Cairo. The central motif in all the stamps was the calligraphed *Makkah al-Mukarramah* (Mecca the Revered), and they bore the simple legend 'Hijaz Mail' (*Barid Hijazi*). Contemporary observers pronounced the stamps beautifully designed and executed. Husayn was proud of his stamps, and often publicized international reaction to them.[68]

The above holds true for stamps issued from 1916–1917. There are no signs of greater ambition in them, and the legend *Barid Hijazi* was quite limiting for the 'King of the Arab Lands.' Terms such as 'government,' 'state,' 'Arab' and 'Hashimite' were conspicuously absent. But after 1921, with his ambitions clipped by the British, Husayn issued stamps that were more in keeping with his far-reaching goals: these stamps carried the legends 'al-Hukumah al-'Arabiyyah al-Hashimiyyah' (the Hashimite Arab Government). Finally, in 1924, he issued stamps with a gold overprint,

---

was not responsible for creating the flag: she cited in this respect Muhibb al-Din al-Khatib, who said that the three horizontal stripes were created by *al-Fatat*; Husayn only added the red chevron.

67 FO 686/143, Bullard to FO, 28 February 1925.

68 FO 371/2774/148524, McMahon to FO, no. 639, 30 July 1916; Ami Ayalon, 'The Hashemites, T.E. Lawrence, and the Postage Stamps of the Hijaz,' in Asher Susser/ Aryeh Shmuelevitz (eds), *The Hashemites in the Modern Arab World: Essays in Honour of the late Professor Uriel Dann* (London: Cass, 1995), pp. 15–30; ; *al-Qiblah*, 7 Shawwal 1335 [26 July 1917].

'*Tidhkar al-Khilafah*' (Commemorating the Caliphate), in honor of his assumption of the title.

Similarly, Husayn began issuing coins by simply overstriking Ottoman, Egyptian, and Austrian Maria Theresa thaler coins with the logo *al-Hijaz*. It was not until September 1923, a few months before he assumed the caliphate, that Husayn actually minted his own coins, with a decidedly more royal flavor. These carried, *inter alia*, the following logos: 'Hashimite Arab Government' (*al-Hukumah al-'Arabiyyah al-Hashimiyyah*; 'Struck at Mecca the Revered, Capital of the Arab Government'; and 'Husayn bin 'Ali, Reviver of the Arab Lands' (*Nahid bil-Bilad al-'Arabiyyah*). Most of the coins were in bronze and silver, while the highest denomination, one *dinar*, was gold. They were all dated with the year of Husayn's accession, AH 1334, and with the regnal year, 8 (a few were minted with the ninth regnal year).[69]

Bullard wrote that Husayn wanted his coins to replace the Turkish piasters in circulation. He sent eight donkey-loads of the coins to Jeddah, and town criers informed the public that anyone who criticized or laughed at the new coins would be hanged or have his tongue cut out. Husayn had not produced enough of the coins, remarked Bullard, and they soon disappeared from circulation.[70] A few 'gold' coins were also produced, and Bullard sent some of these to the Royal Mint to be assayed. It reported back in November 1923 that one of the coins rang dumb, the other well, and concluded that they were probably manufactured from melted down Turkish gold lire, and would therefore be regarded as unfit by any European mint.[71]

Education. Education did not truly become the province of the state until major educational reforms were instituted in the Ottoman Empire in 1869, and in the Hijaz in particular in 1874, with the establishment of the first Rushdiyyah school. Up to 1908, there were apparently four Ibtida'iyyah schools, four Rushdiyyahs and

---

69 *Al-Qiblah*, 20 September 1923; Chester Krause and Clifford Mishler, *1995 Standard Edition of World Coins* (White Plains, NY: Krause Publications, 1994), pp. 1797–1800; Tim Browder, 'Coinage of Hejaz Kingdom,' *Numismatic Scrapbook Magazine* 26 (1960), pp. 3489–96. I wish to thank Dr Michael Bates of the American Numismatic Society for these numismatic references.

70 Bullard, pp. 11–12.

71 FO 686/51, Comptroller General of Department of Overseas Trade to British Vice-Consul, 12 November 1923; Bullard, pp. 13–14.

one I'dadiyyah, all concentrated in Jeddah, Mecca, Medina and Yanbu'. But these schools were attended mostly by the children of Ottoman Turkish officials, as they were considered alien by most of the Hijazi population. Instead, many attended other formal and informal Islamic educational institutions.[72] The Sharif had little if any role in education during the Ottoman period, education being either in private hands or in the Ottoman state schools.[73]

But after the Revolt Sharif Husayn seems to have devoted much effort to education. He had spent time in Istanbul and had apparently absorbed a positive attitude towards modern schooling. As noted above, he established a Ministry of Education. He seems not to have liked the private Falah schools supported by the 'Ali Rida family, and endeavored to put modern education under the authority of the state. Our main source on education under Husayn, Saudi researcher Abdullatif Abdullah Dohaish, exhibits a very positive attitude towards Husayn's efforts. From 1916 to 1919, notes Dohaish, Husayn opened several secular elementary, intermediate and secondary schools in Mecca, Jeddah, Medina and other towns, replacing the Ottoman ones. An agricultural school and military academy were also established, and several textbooks printed. Teachers were either local or recruited from Syria. Graduation ceremonies were held, and dignitaries attended. Dohaish assesses that Sharifian educational efforts were 'successful within [their] limits' when compared with the earlier Ottoman schools, which were aimed at Turkification. Considering the large number of pupils enrolled, stresses Dohaish, his achievements 'can only be described as impressive.'[74]

---

72 Ochsenwald, *Religion, Society*, p. 78; Dohaish; FO 195/1514, Abdur Razzack (Jeddah), Report on the Educational Establishments in the Hedjaz, 14 September 1885; and Ma'oz, p. 241. See also FO 195/1514, Report on Education within the Consular Districts of Damascus, printed in Issawi' *Fertile Crescent*, pp. 67–70. There was some educational reform in the Ottoman Empire which began in the reign of Sultan Mehmet II (1808–39), mostly in medical and military training. Rushdiyyah (modern government secondary [higher primary? – see Dohaish, p. 64]) schools began to be established in Turkey proper in 1846, in Aleppo in the 1850s and in Damascus in the early 1860s, but major reform dates from 1869, with the proclamation of the Ottoman Law for the Regulation of Public and Private Institutions. This legislation established four grades of schools: Ibtida'iyyah (lower primary), Rushdiyyah (higher primary), I'dadiyyah (lower secondary), and Sultaniyyah (higher secondary).

73 Dohaish, *passim.*; FO 195/1514, Abdur Razzack (Jeddah), Report of the Educational Establishments in the Hedjaz, 14 September 1885. State involvement in education during this period was limited to Ottoman initiatives; see below.

With respect to increased student numbers, in 1885 there were reportedly only eighty-four pupils enrolled in the Ottoman secular schools, a figure which increased slightly to 149 in 1902. In contrast, in 1917 there were close to 500 students in Jeddah and Mecca alone.[75]

Dohaish notes that the schools differed from the traditional *kuttab* in that they had a defined period of study, introduction of subject matter was progressive, and the classroom was Western in style, with the pupils sitting in rows in front of a blackboard, instead of being in an informal circle around the teacher. More importantly, the schools' curricula included many modern subjects, such as geometry, science, arithmetic and book-keeping.[76] Unfortunately, Dohaish does not go into the curriculum content in areas such as history, which would have allowed us to assess attempts at the inculcation of the Hashimite view of Arab nationalism and Husayn's ambitions.

Husayn was quite proud of his educational accomplishments. *Al-Qiblah* was chock-full of announcements and articles on education, and news of school openings packed the paper.[77] In an article in 1916, Husayn stated that the goals of the new schools were to create people to fill administrative posts.[78] As we have seen, this was not carried out in practice. On the first anniversary of the Revolt, *al-Qiblah* made a point of stressing that under the Ottomans the Arabs received a poor education, in order that they should not take good positions away from Turks. But since the Revolt, wrote the newspaper, the King had made education a top priority and as a result significant progress had been made.[79]

It appears, therefore, that while we might find it difficult to credit Husayn with much progress during his tenure, the sphere of education constitutes an exception.

---

[74] Dohaish, pp. 210, 244.

[75] Dohaish, pp. 210–11.

[76] Dohaish, pp. 215, 220–2.

[77] See, for example, *al-Qiblah*: 8 Safar 1335 [2 December 1916]; 11 Safar 1335 [6 December 1916]; 4 Jamadi al-Ula 1335 [25 February 1917]; 18 Shawwal 1335 [6 August 1917]; 28 Shawwal 1335 [16 August 1917]; 16 Dhu al-Qa'dah 1335 [2 September 1917].

[78] *Al-Qiblah*, 1 Safar 1335 [26 November 1916].

[79] *Al-Qiblah*, 2 Dhu al-Qa'dah 1335 [19 August 1917].

The abandonment of the Hashimites: the Hijazi urban and tribal élite from the fall of Ta'if to the fall of Jeddah, September 1924–December 1925

By the time Ta'if fell in early September 1924, it was already clear that Husayn had entirely alienated both the urban and tribal élite. What remains to be told, therefore, is the story of the élite's struggle to maintain and increase its power in the closing months of the Hashimite regime and the onset of the Saudi one.

The fall of Ta'if was greeted in Jeddah with 'hardly concealed delight.' While hitherto the Jeddah élite, it was reported, had concealed their hate of Husayn under an 'effusive servility,' the news from Ta'if led them 'to talk treason boldly.' Even after the Wahhabi atrocities at Ta'if became known, Bullard reported that the event roused nearly universal enthusiasm; Husayn had obviously failed to ensure that the élite identified themselves with his cause. The struggle between Ibn Saud and Husayn was viewed by the élite as a personal rather than a national one, and therefore its primary value in the eyes of the notables was that it furnished an opportunity to be rid of Husayn.[80]

A counterattack in late September failed miserably.[81] Husayn's appeal to the British for aid was rejected in no uncertain terms, in a message that distanced his former allies from him once and for all:

In reply to Your Majesty's telegram No. 111, a summary of which I duly communicated to His Majesty's Government, I am instructed by His Majesty's Prime Minister and Secretary of State for Foreign Affairs to convey to Your Majesty the following reply: His Majesty's Government have never wavered from their policy of assisting in every possible way to promote peace and good fellowship amongst the various rulers of the Arabs. At the same time they adhere to their traditional policy of non-interference in religious matters and do not propose to be entangled in any struggle for the holy places of Islam which may be entered upon by the independent rulers of Arabia. Should such a struggle take place they intend to confine their efforts to an attempt to safeguard so far as

---

80 FO 371/10014/E 8654, The Capture of Taif, Bullard to MacDonald, no. 95, 21 September 1924. The Wahhabis at Ta'if massacred an estimated 500–800 non-combatants, with the British Agent giving a more conservative figure of about 200. The residents of Ta'if were pillaged, all their money and jewelry were taken, and many were left with nothing but their underclothes.
81 FO 371/10014/E 8315, Bullard to FO, no. 65, 27 September 1924.

this is practicable such of His Majesty's Moslem subjects and of the Moslems under his protection as may be in the Hejaz. Only in the event of both contending parties spontaneously asking for the good offices of His Majesty's Government to assist them to settle their differences by peaceful arrangement would His Majesty's Government be prepared to undertake such a task. They attempted it last winter at [the] Koweit Conference but in vain, the failure being largely due to Your Majesty's delay in agreeing to send a representative. This is the end of the message which I have to convey to your Majesty.[82]

Two of the leading merchants of Jeddah, the *ra'is al-baladiyyah* and the *qa'im maqam* approached Bullard, asking for British protection or mandate over the Hijaz. Bullard replied in the style of the message quoted above, and they were indignant. As far as the Hijaz élite were concerned, he remarked, under the Turks they did not have to worry about their own safety, and could go about their business; along came the British, and replaced the Ottomans with a far more oppressive government, which left them defenseless. With the failure of 'Ali's counterattack on Ta'if ('Ali had scraped together a force of Hadhramawtis and *ayal al-harat*, but had no powerful tribes with him), civil government in Mecca disintegrated. Most of the élite fled to Jeddah, often on foot. The Jeddah and Mecca notables, gathered together in Jeddah, began to talk openly of deposing King Husayn, who remained in the palace with some slaves and Syrian soldiers.[83]

On 3 October 1924, 'Ali arrived in Jeddah and summoned a meeting of the notables. He told them that he came on behalf of Husayn, who was ready to abdicate if they wished. After discussion, they sent the King a telegram asking him to abdicate in favor of 'Ali. But the King, in a last fit of obstinacy, announced that he would give up the throne to anyone but 'Ali; 'Ali, it appeared would not assume the throne anyway, because he feared he would be King for only a few days. As a result, a crowd of notables converged on the British Agency, demanding protection. Bullard sent them packing, and they returned to 'Ali, who finally agreed to assume office on 4 October. Some prominent dignitaries were involved in these negotiations, including Sulayman Qabil, 'Abdallah 'Ali Rida, Salih ibn Abu Bakr Shatta, and Muhammad Shalhut [or Shalhub], who signed themselves in the correspon-

[82] FO 686/21, Bullard to His Majesty King Hussein, no. 15, 29 September 1924.
[83] Bullard, p. 60.

dence as 'the delegates of the entire Hijazi people.' On the same day, the *Qadi al-Quda*, 'Abdallah ibn 'Abd al-Rahman al-Sarraj, sent this telegram to the foreign legations:

Following upon the abdication of His Majesty King Hussein, the nation has recognized his Highness the Amir Ali as constitutional King of the Hejaz only (*malik dusturi 'ala al-Hijaz faqat*).[84]

In other words, 'Ali was neither caliph nor king of the Arab lands. On 4 October, several of these notables, along with Muhammad Nasif, 'Abd al-Ra'uf Sabban, Qasim ibn Zaynal 'Ali Rida, Muhammad Tahir al-Dabbagh[85] and others, constituted themselves as the 'Hijazi Patriotic Party of Jeddah' (*al-Hizb al-Watani al-Hijazi bi-Jiddah*). They sought some kind of rudimentary constitutional régime, with absolutely no pretensions outside the Hijaz. In a telegram to Muslim leaders and newspapers throughout the world, the party declared that they had compelled Husayn to abdicate, 'and to betake himself to anywhere he likes to live.' 'Ali had been chosen King of the Hijaz only, and was under a constitutional government, as long as he abided by the decision of the Islamic world concerning the holy places. The message ended with an appeal to Muslims to help the Hijaz, and to facilitate negotiations with Ibn Saud.[86]

Two other documents found in the British archives demonstrate that notables intended the Hijaz to make a *volte-face* from Husayn's policies. Instead of the Hijaz spearheading an 'Arab Revolt' with Islamic overtones, they now referred to the 'Hijazi nation' (*al-ummah al-Hijaziyyah*), represented by this party of notables who had taken the affairs of 'their beloved country' (*watanihim al-mahbubb*) into 'their own hands' in order that it be led by good leaders. The party referred to itself as 'empowered by their nation' (*bi-niyabat ummatihim*), and implored the *ummah Hijaziyyah* to be patient and put its faith in them. The nation was called upon to help the party extricate the country (*bilad*) from its present catastrophe as a 'religious and patriotic duty' (*al-wajib*

---

84 FO 371/10015/E 9344, Bullard to MacDonald, no. 99, 11 October 1924. This document contains the translations of the correspondence between the notables, the British, and Husayn. The Arabic originals along with French translation are to be found in MAE, Djeddah (ambassade), carton no. 13.

85 Dabbagh went on to become 'Ali's Minister of Finance (Philby, 'The Fall of Mecca,' *Daily Telegraph*, 13 February 1925).

86 FO 371/10015/E 9344, Bullard to MacDonald, no. 99, 11 October 1924.

al-dini wal-watani). The party constitution *(nizam al-hizb)* stressed that it would work for a 'legitimate and representative government' *(hukumah shar'iyyah niyabiyyah).*[87]

'Ali and what was left of his army abandoned Mecca on 14 October; Husayn left Jeddah on the same day. His parting shot was a letter to Sarraj, protesting that the government of the Hijaz was to be limited to the Hijaz proper, and 'the institution of a constitutional government whereby the precepts of the Qu'ran and the traditions of the prophet are set at nought even in the holy places and replaced by a secular code.'[88]

On the face of it, this new-found expressed local patriotism was remarkable when it is considered that the idea of a *watan* (at least in the Arab sense) was practically non-existent in the Hijaz before the war.[89] But now, with their interests deeply threatened, the notables adopted an entirely new ideology: Hijazi patriotism. This idea did have some roots in a feeling of Hijazi superiority because of the presence of the *Haramayn*, and freedom from taxes and conscription, but it took the Wahhabi threat to bring it out in a fairly coherent ideological platform.[90]

This group of notables thus appears to have had two main concerns. First, it appealed to local patriotism and interests, abandoning any role for the Hijaz beyond its traditional role under the Ottomans. Completely sickened by Husayn's authoritarian form of government and system of forced loans, it sought as its second concern to assure a degree of representation for the populace of the Hijaz, led by itself. In this, it put forward a policy that was the reverse of Husayn's. They would have gladly returned to their situation under Ottoman rule, but with that gone, this seemed the best choice.

Bullard seemed to think that the new party was actually in a minority, as a much stronger group did not want to commit the

---

[87] FO 371/10015/E 9344, Bullard to MacDonald, no. 99, 11 October 1924; FO 686/90, two documents in Arabic entitled *Al-Hizb al-Watani al-Hijazi bi-Jiddah.*

[88] FO 686/29, Jeddah Report for 11–20 October 1924; FO 686/90, ex–King Hussein to the Acting Prime Minister of the Hejaz, 14 October 1924.

[89] William Ochsenwald, 'Arab Nationalism in the Hijaz.'

[90] In a similar yet different vein, Philip Khoury demonstrates how the notables of Damascus executed an ideological about face – from Ottomanism to Arabism – following the entrance of Sharifian and British forces in 1918 (*Urban Notables and Arab Nationalism: The Politics of Damascus 1860–1920* (Cambridge University Press, 1983), pp. 73, 77.

country to continued support of the Hashimites. He assessed that even 'Ali's supporters would sacrifice him if he refused to follow their advice or was displeasing to Ibn Saud. But, Bullard concluded, 'Ali was likely to go along with his supporters as he was 'as weak and irresolute as his father is obstinate and determined.'[91]

In early November, Bullard reported that the party had ceased to exist, and that statements issued after that in its name were false. The party was formed to bring about the abdication of Husayn, and it had originally included nearly all the important men of Jeddah together with many notables who had fled from Mecca. It remained united until 'Ali refused to abdicate. When this happened, Director of Customs Tawil went over to 'Ali with some other supporters, and all the rest resigned. Since then, all messages were from Tawil only, who was now in reality governor of Jeddah, coopted by 'Ali.[92]

As the notables gathered in Jeddah, they waited to see how the Wahhabis in Mecca would behave. Once they saw that no repeat of the Ta'if massacre took place, they were convinced that the best policy would be to surrender to Ibn Saud. Extremely conciliatory communications from the Saudis reinforced this feeling. Ibn Saud addressed a letter to the people of Jeddah and Mecca which arrived in Jeddah on 16 October. He promised them that their lives and property would be safe, and that he would not treat them in a displeasing manner or do anything contrary to the law. Ibn Saud also wrote that he would make the country safe for pilgrims. Perhaps most importantly, the Wahhabi leader promised the notables of the Hijaz that he would not 'treat them as vassals, but with advice, security and comfort.' Nothing would be done, concluded Ibn Saud, which would injure them or their honor.[93] The contrast with Husayn's behavior must have been quite apparent to all.

A delegation from Jeddah went to Mecca in late October, and met with Khalid ibn Mansur ibn al-Lu'ayy, the amir of Khurmah and Ibn Saud's general. Khalid offered handsome terms, promising to leave the notables of Jeddah alone, not to send troops, and to let the town govern itself, stipulating only that they seize 'Ali or force him to leave the country. If they failed to do so, warned

[91] FO 371/10015/E 9344, Bullard to MacDonald, no. 99, 11 October 1924.
[92] FO 371/10016/E 10783, Jeddah Report 31 October–8 November 1924.
[93] FO 686/29, Jeddah Report 11–20 October 1924; letter (proclamation) from Ibn Saud to the people of Jeddah and Mecca, 20 September 1924.

Khalid, Jeddah would meet the same fate as Ta'if. But 'Ali refused, as by this time he had assembled about him a small coterie of Syrian and Iraqi soldiers, whom he apparently paid handsomely. Moreover, he was receiving financial encouragement from Husayn and 'Abdallah.[94]

'Ali arrested four of the leaders of this delegation, who were, in essence, an anti-Hashimite faction of the élite. Although sentenced to death, imprisonment, or exile, 'Ali pardoned them in order to avoid making trouble for himself. Therefore, Bullard concluded, anti-Hashimite agitation among the élite had died down.[95] After they were released, these men became the nucleus of a 'peace at any price' party, who were in opposition to the military officers and other pro-'Ali notables.[96]

The danger to Jeddah remained, as Ibn Saud threatened to attack if they did not hand over 'Ali. Ibn Saud could have attacked any time after he captured Mecca, but probably refrained from doing so due to the presence of foreign consuls and the fear that his followers would get out of hand.[97]

'Ali, for his part, could continue to hold out, as he was supplied from the sea, funded by his father and 'Abdallah, and the Wahhabis were only shelling sporadically. Soldiers often threatened mutiny, but 'Ali was able to head them off with a payment of £10,000 which arrived from Husayn, part of the Hijazi treasury which he had taken with him.[98]

---

[94] FO 686/29, Jeddah Report, 21–30 October 1924. There was another reason that 'Ali might have been holding on so tightly to his throne. As early as August 1924, even before the fall of Ta'if, the Egyptians began to look for a foothold in the Hijaz, in accordance with King Fu'ad's caliphal aspirations. Egyptian interest came at the end of several years of conflict between Egypt and the Hijaz, which culminated in July 1924 with Husayn cutting Fu'ad's name out of the *kiswa*. In the fall of 1925, 'Ali would offer Fu'ad what amounted to an Egyptian religious protectorate over the Hijaz, and even implied giving him the caliphate, in exchange for financial assistance (see FO 686/29, Jeddah Report 31 July–30 August 1924; FO 371/10007/E 7062, Thomas Spring-Rice to Clark Kerr, no. 870, 21 August 1924; FO 371/10014/E 8831, Kerr [Cairo] to FO, no. 330, 11 October 1924; Martin Kramer, 'Shaykh Maraghi's Mission to the Hijaz, 1925,' *AAS* 16 [1982], pp. 121–36). Hijazi–Egyptian relations deserve fuller treatment in another study.

[95] FO 371/10016/E 10783, Jeddah Report for 31 October–8 November 1924.

[96] FO 371/10807/E 945, Philby in the *Daily Telegraph*, 14 February 1925.

[97] FO 686/29: Jeddah Report 20 November–11 December 1924; Jeddah Report 12–30 December 1924.

But this was not enough money to keep things running, and 'Ali and Faysal approached the British for a loan. Fu'ad al-Khatib, who had returned from Syria to work for 'Ali as Foreign Minister, even sent a letter to foreign consuls threatening to impose forced loans on their subjects. When Faysal in Iraq offered to secure the loan against Hijazi customs receipts, he was curtly informed that London did not consider that a good investment.[99]

In March 1925, 'Ali finally attempted an attack to break the Wahhabi siege, but the Hijazi troops did not acquit themselves well. They 'appeared to have not heart for the work,' wrote Bullard, 'and this is borne out by the fact that a high proportion of the wounds received are in the discrete rather than the valiant portions of the body viz. the back and buttocks.'[100]

In July and August, with little money left, 'Ali resorted to his father's old tricks and began to extort money from the Jeddah merchants. Sums gained in this manner, together with funds from Husayn, allowed him to pay his troops for a bit longer.[101]

Meanwhile, factional quarreling between notables broke out in Jeddah. Muhammad al-Tawil and Sayyid Fadl al-Saqqaf (the king's secretary) on the one hand, and Fu'ad al-Khatib on the other, fought over Fu'ad giving permission to foreign subjects living in Jeddah to go to Wahhabi-controlled Mecca where living was cheaper. The first faction believed that this would give encouragement to Ibn Saud. The fight developed into a propaganda war, mostly via the pasting of proclamations on walls at night.[102]

By October, it was clear that the end was finally near. The soldiers and bedouin had taken to selling their government-issue ammunition in the market to raise money to buy food. Small parties deserted to the Wahhabis.[103] On 17 November, tribal troops broke into open revolt in Jeddah, as did Syrian troops and the palace guard on 19 November, although all were temporarily pac-

---

[98] FO 686/29, Jeddah Report 11–28 February 1924. In April, another £20 000 was sent by Husayn from 'Aqabah, heading off another mutiny (FO 686/29, Jeddah Report 12–30 April 1925).

[99] See correspondence on this issue from March to October 1925 in FO 686/140.

[100] FO 686/29, Jeddah Report 12–19 March 1925.

[101] FO 686/29, Jeddah Report 21 July–10 August 1925.

[102] FO 686/29, Jeddah Report 21 July–10 August 1925; FO 371/10812, proceedings of H.M.S. *Clematis*, 24 August 1925.

[103] FO 686/29, Jeddah Report 29 September–29 October 1925.

ified with promises of pay.[104] Medina capitulated on 5 December, making 'Ali's position impossible.

'Ali's promises earned him a few weeks' grace, but on 6 December a major mutiny broke out among the Syrian and Palestinian soldiers, who barricaded themselves in a mosque. A few days later, members of the Hijazi élite and Harb bedouin, representing about three-quarters of 'Ali's total forces, sent a message to Ibn Saud offering their submission and asking for instructions.[105]

'Ali finally approached the Acting British Consul, Jordan, to ask him to mediate his submission to Ibn Saud. He officially abdicated on 19 December, and was allowed by Ibn Saud to leave the Hijaz, which he did aboard the HMS *Clematis* on the next day. Ibn Saud entered Jeddah on 23 December.[106] In his farewell proclamation, 'Ali expressed his sincere feelings that he had only been guided by what was best for the nation. He left the government in the hand of the *qa'im maqam*, 'Abdallah 'Ali Rida, and asked all officials to remain at their posts.[107]

As for the tribal élite during this final period, after the furore around the fall of Ta'if had died down, those near Jeddah no longer had reason to pillage as 'Ali abandoned Husayn's foolish policy of blockading food supplies, and they were allowed to buy provisions freely. But Sharif Muhsin's Masruh Harb, acting on behalf of 'Ali, began to rob those going from Jeddah to Medina in order to prevent support for Ibn Saud. In revenge, Wahhabi tribes raided Muhsin's properties in the fertile Wadi Fatimah. Most of the Harb were by now not supporting the Hashimites, as they were afraid of the Wahhabis. By December 1924, 'Ali had practically no tribal support whatsoever.[108]

---

104 FO 371/10810/E 7167, Acting British Consul to FO, no. 163, 19 November 1925.
105 FO 371/10810: E 7505, Acting British Consul to FO, no. 173, 6 December 1925; E 7557, Acting British Consul to FO, no. 175, 7 December 1925; FO 686/25, Acting British Consul to FO, 11 December 1925.
106 FO 371/10810: E 7758, Acting British Consul to FO, no. 185, 14 December 1925; E 8066, Acting British Consul to FO, no. 192, 24 December 1925; FO 686/92, Ibn Saud to British Agent, 17 December 1925; Acting British Agent to FO, 19 December 1925; FO 686/29, Jeddah Report, 28 November– 31 December 1925.
107 FO 686/92, Proclamation by 'Ali, undated.
108 FO 371/10015/E 9344, Bullard to MacDonald, no. 99, 11 October 1924; FO 686/29, Jeddah Report 21–30 October 1924; FO 371/10016/E 10783, Jeddah Report 31 October–8 November 1924; FO 686/29, Jeddah Report 9–19 November 1924; FO 686/29, Jeddah Report 20 November–11 December 1924; FO 686/29, Jeddah Report

And what of Husayn, Caliph and King of the Arab Lands? Ibn Saud had rightly assessed that one of the main causes preventing the surrender of 'Ali was the constant influx of money from Husayn in 'Aqabah, where the ex-king had been holed up since he left Jeddah. In mid-May 1925, he stated that the prolongation of the war was the result of the presence of Husayn in 'Aqabah, and that he had forces which would soon move on that town to eject him. This threat caused a stir in London, for it had not yet been decided officially that Transjordan – which was under British control – included 'Aqabah in its borders. It was decided to officially include 'Aqabah in Transjordan in order, *inter alia*, to force Husayn out. The ex-King and Caliph was therefore unceremoniously removed from 'Aqabah to Cyprus, thus ending the controversy with Ibn Saud, and sending Husayn into an ignominious non-Arab exile.[109]

The failure of state capabilities on the periphery: the case of Medina

As was noted in Chapter 2, Medina was not always well controlled from Mecca, and in fact in the late Ottoman period was administered directly from Istanbul, a development made possible by the completion of the Hijaz railway. One of the ways of assessing state capability is to look at the periphery, rather than the center.[110] It therefore seems worthwhile to examine the ability of Husayn to extend his state to Medina, which was, after all, the second of the *Haramayn*.

Although Medina did not fall until early 1919, the situation which obtained there between 1916 and 1919 still merits examination, as it will be seen that its inhabitants were far from being predisposed to Sharifian rule. Like many towns in the Hijaz, Medina lived in fear of marauding tribesmen; the notables had enjoyed a good life under the Ottoman régime, and felt relatively safe. Thus when the Revolt opened,[111] they feared being overwhelmed by the bedouin and were reported to be resisting. 'The townspeople are accustomed to taking the part of the Turk against

11–29 August 1925.

[109] FO 371/10808/E 2858, Bullard to FO, no. 76, 17 May 1925; on Husayn in 'Aqabah, see the voluminous correspondence in FO 371/10809.

[110] See Migdal, p. 182.

[111] It will be recalled that the Revolt was opened by Faysal among the tribes in the outskirts of Medina.

the Arabs [that is, the bedouin – author], and fight hard,' noted a contributor to the *Arab Bulletin.* [112]

A revealing report by Miralai Sadiq Bey Yahya of the Egyptian army, who was sent to help in the surrender of Medina, illustrates for us the conditions during the administration of the Ottoman General, Fakhri Pasha. As has been shown, Husayn oppressed the merchants and higher classes in Mecca and Jeddah, taking their property and forcing loans. Yet, perhaps surprisingly, Fakhri, who was under siege, treated the Medinans quite well. No buildings were razed or confiscated for military purposes without a committee of local notables assessing their value and the owner being compensated. Fakhri encouraged residents to emigrate to Syria, and their property was locked up and looked after. Detailed lists of confiscated property and stores were kept for payment after the war, and some even received payment before it had ended. Even luggage left behind at the railway station was tagged and kept in storage or forwarded to the owners. Moreover, to increase food supplies, Fakhri bought 6,000 kilos of wheat which were planted on the outskirts of the city; the blades grew wonderfully to a height of ten inches.

Thus when Husayn's men entered Medina, the local élite were quite apprehensive, as they had heard about the situation in Jeddah and Mecca. They confided their fears to Sadiq Bey:

They showed that they are not satisfied and view the future with alarm and doubt, fearing the bad treatment which will appear in future and that they will not enjoy their personal freedom and the security of their property and money, and that there will be no justice or equality, nor rest or respect for anybody. They also stated that they have enjoyed justice and equality under the Turkish reign. Each of them used to drive in his carriage in Medina in perfect freedom and safety and the Turkish Government collected no taxes from the natives except the very small tax collected by the Municipality for town cleaning.

The élite of Medina were not to be disabused of their assessment of Sharifian rule. First, upon the arrival of the Arab forces, their animals promptly made short work of the wheat Fakhri planted for the citizens of Medina. After 'Abdallah entered the town on 10 January 1919, many of his bedouin proceeded to loot the very houses of absentee residents which Fakhri had so closely guarded.

[112] *AB*, no. 6, 23 June 1916.

Sadiq Bey estimated that only about one-eighth of the homes escaped this pillaging, in which 'Abdallah's Syrian and Baghdadi officers also participated. 'The natives lost during the first twelve days after the surrender more than they had lost during the last two years when Fakhri was at Medina,' lamented Sadiq Bey.[113]

Apparently, soon after its liberation, Sharif Shahhat ibn 'Ali, who, it will be recalled from Chapter 2, had represented Husayn's interests in Medina, took over the town; Husayn had no choice but to appoint him *qa'im maqam*. He had previously opposed the Ottomans on Husayn's behalf, but was now opposing the Sharif. In fact, it appears that Shahhat had established his own little chieftaincy in and about Medina, similar to that established by another sharif – Khalid – in Khurmah.[114] Shahhat and his brother Nasir were from a lesser branch of the *ashraf*, the Husaynis. Nasir felt that he had not been rewarded properly for the role he played in the war. On occasion, Nasir had sounded out the British Agent 'very guardedly' as to HMG's attitude should Ibn Saud attack King Husayn or anyone revolt against him. For months, Shahhat – who enjoyed considerable support from the tribes – terrorized the town; disorder and pillaging were the order of the day.[115]

'Ali had entered Medina on 2 February, but apparently did not stay for long; by the end of 1919, it was reported that he was afraid to return to the town, as the way was blocked by recalcitrant tribes angered at Husayn, and the Harb had already held him up once. He eventually reached Medina in mid-February 1920, after having taken a circuitous route to avoid tribes that were lying in wait for him.[116] Upon his arrival 'Ali dismissed Shahhat, replacing

---

113 FO 686/57, Report on Medina by El Miralai Sadik Bey Yehia, DSO, Egyptian army, 10 February 1919. See also Elie Kedourie, 'The Surrender of Medina, January 1919', in Elie Kedourie (ed.), *Islam in the Modern World and Other Studies* (New York: Holt Rinehart and Winston, 1980), pp. 277–96. S. Tanvir Wasti has a fascinating account, based on an Ottoman eyewitness source, of life in Medina – which he perceptively terms a 'city-state' – during the Hashimite siege ('The Defense of Medina, 1916–1919,' *MES* 27 [1994], pp. 642–53.)

114 Indeed, Medina had a tradition of being a separate, Shi'i emirate from Mecca, until early Ottoman times. Even after the advent of the Ottomans, it was never entirely subjugated (see Ende, pp. 272–81).

115 See Kedourie,'Surrender;' FO 371/6234/E 1139, Jeddah Report 1–10 January 1921.

116 FO 686/26, Intelligence and Political Report 11–21 October 1919; Intelligence and Political Report 21–31 December 1919; Intelligence and Political Report for ten days ending 1 February 1920; Intelligence and Political Report for ten days ending 21 February 1920.

him with one Mansur ibn Ahmad as *qa'im maqam*. But Shahhat began to use his influence among the tribes to make 'Ali's life and that of the town miserable. In early April, it was reported that one Shaykh Ibn 'Umayr complained to 'Ali of non-payment. Having received nothing, he raised his standard under the walls of Medina and fired at some of the gendarmerie. Later that month, when al-Hanakiyyah (north-east of Medina) was raided by followers of Ibn Saud, 'Ali ordered Shahhat to attack them, but Shahhat audaciously refused, reportedly saying that he did not wish to repeat what had happened at Khurmah! Various sections of the Harb were constantly threatening Medina, firing on 'Ali's supporters on the outskirts of the city.[117]

'Ali was thus in a bind. Shahhat was treacherous, but his influence with the surrounding tribes made his support essential. He was therefore reluctantly reinstated by 'Ali in May.[118] But this had little effect, if any. Daylight robberies in the town became a regular occurrence, and bedouin kept up desultory fire on 'Ali's installations in town in order to extract money from him. It was reported that he began to emulate his father's tactics, forcing loans out of local merchants and landowners. In the course of a Friday sermon when Husayn's name was mentioned, one got up and said that Husayn 'had long ago died and gone to Hell, [so] why mention his name.' The gentleman was promptly apprehended and hanged. People in Medina, it was said, believed that no one had been hanged there for 200 years.[119] After 'Ali left Medina in August 1920, it was reported that Shahhat was in open revolt, and would not allow 'Ali to return.[120]

It will be remembered that residents of the Hijaz were often the beneficiaries of gifts of grain sent from Egypt. The Hashimites could not make this up during the war, and when it was resumed, 'Ali commandeered the Medina supply, doling it out slowly. As a result, prices rose, and raids were reported at the end of 1920 to be

---

[117] FO 686/12, Intelligence Report by Captain Agab Khan (Mecca), 9 March 1920; Intelligence Report from Agent at Mecca, 8 April 1920; FO 686/26 Report 22 April–1 May 1920.

[118] FO 686/26, 11–21 May 1920.

[119] FO 686/12, Report by Mian Nasir-ud-din Ahmed (Mecca) for the period ending 29 July 1920.

[120] FO 686/26, Jeddah Report 20–31 August 1920; FO 686/12, Report by Capt. Nasir-ud-din Ahmed (Mecca) for period ending 31 August 1920.

taking place right up to the walls, making it impossible for pilgrims to visit shrines in the vicinity.[121] The town residents thus lived in fear of the bedouin. Ihsanullah reported that merchants had no protection from the government, and had instead to rely on a '*halif*' (ally) from the surrounding tribes.[122]

By early 1921 it was clear that Shahhat was defying Husayn. It was reported by the British Agent that 'Medina ... is now practically independent of the King and under Sharif Shahaat.' Shahhat was ordered to Mecca, but refused to come, and also refused to hand over thirty individuals whom the King had ordered arrested. He was posing as the champion of the Medinans against the authority of Mecca, and had gained support from the populace, who no doubt were well aware of Husayn's despotic tendencies.[123]

In an effort to clip Shahhat's wings, 'Ali returned to Medina in February 1922. He also wanted to regain control over tribes in vicinity that were pro-Ibn Saud. Nevertheless, his mission was a failure, and Fu'ad al-Khatib informed the British Agent that 'Ali had wired Husayn that he could not be held responsible for the safety of pilgrim traffic to Medina. In mid-year, it was reported that some of 'Ali's officers were selling arms and ammunition from government arsenals to the bedouin. In October, there was an explosion at the main ammunition depot in the town; according to reports, Shahhat had been acting as an intermediary in these transactions, and the explosion was purposely set so that deficiencies in the ammunition and arms would not be discovered.[124]

Meanwhile, 'Ali imprisoned merchants who refused to pay forced loans. He also set up a hated prison similar to that of Husayn; after a short stay, merchants usually paid up. Shahhat played the role of defending the prisoners, and worked for their release. The merchants were further hurt by the lack of security on the roads. The few pilgrims who actually made it to Medina

---

121 FO 686/12, Nasiruddin Ahmed, news report 29 September 1920; FO 686/26, Jeddah Report 20–30 November 1920.

122 FO 686/12, Ihsanullah (Mecca) to British Agent, 29 November 1920.

123 FO 686/27: Jeddah Report 1–10 January 1921; Jeddah Report 11–31 July 1921; FO 686/28, Jeddah Report 21 January–10 February 1922.

124 FO 686/28: Jeddah Report 11–28 February 1922; Jeddah Report 11–31 March 1922; Jeddah Report 1–31 October 1923; Jeddah Report 1–30 November 1922; FO 371/8938/E 4642, Memorandum – Attitude of the Hedjaz Arabs towards Turkey, undated, stamped 8 May 1923.

had less money to spend once there, and most had been robbed on the way.[125]

In early 1923, Husayn was successful in luring Shahhat to Mecca by promising him that he would be involved in conveying the Ottoman ex-Sultan to Medina. Although it was reported that 'few expect him to return alive,' he did. As the year drew to a close, it was clear to observers that the Medinans, like most Hijazis, were hopeful of a Saudi victory to rid them of Hashimite oppression.[126]

In 1924 Shahhat was reported to be running circles around 'Ali, entirely ignoring his orders, and trading with Ibn Saud. Husayn, passing through Medina on his way to Transjordan, did all he could to alienate the Medinans. He refused to pass through a special gate that had been decorated in his honor, and instead of distributing any largesse, he saved it for those who would proclaim him Caliph in Transjordan.[127]

It seems absolutely clear, therefore, that Husayn proved incapable of extending his rule to Medina, the second most important city in his realm. It was indicative of the lack of state capability in the Hijazi periphery, and the inability of the Hashimite regime to entirely replace its Ottoman predecessor.

The Saudi comparison

A brief look at the way in which Ibn Saud engaged in generally successful coalition building after he took over the Hijaz points up the errors of Husayn's ways.[128] Ibn Saud's successes are all the more remarkable when it is remembered that he was not even from the Hijaz. Unlike Husayn, Ibn Saud developed a bureaucracy with the strategic purpose of bolstering the state. It will be remembered that it was the alienated notables of the Hijaz who facilitated the entrance of Ibn Saud into the main Hijazi cities. He allowed them to maintain their social position, did not oppress them, and even institutionalized their leadership by constituting a *majlis ahli* and later a *majlis al-shura*. The *'ulama* of the Hijaz were absorbed into Ibn Saud's new judicial system; familiar names of

---

125 FO 686/28, Jeddah Report 1–31 October 1922.
126 FO 686/28, Jeddah Report 28 September –31 October 1923.
127 FO 686/28, Jeddah Report 1–31 March 1923; FO 686/29, Jeddah Report 1–29 January 1924.
128 This section is informed by Kostiner, *The Making*, pp. 100–117.

prominent *'ulama* of the Hashimite period are found in the sources after the Saudi conquest, such as Abu Bakr Khukayr, Majid Kurdi, 'Abd al-Rahman al-Zawawi, and 'Abd al-'Aziz al-'Atiqi. Both the Nasif and 'Ali Rida families continued to be prominent; scions of the former entered the army and held high positions in the Saudi–funded international Islamic bureaucracy, while the descendants of the latter formed one of the Kingdom's largest commercial conglomerates. But Ibn Saud was smart enough not to rely entirely on the local aristocracy, and brought many foreign officials into senior posts in the bureaucracy. His relations with the notables of the Hijaz were not always smooth, as they often resented the foreigners and the financial burden that the Hijaz had to bear supporting the poorer region of Najd, but Ibn Saud was able to maneuver well amongst them.

As for the tribal elements, here Ibn Saud was initially less successful. Both Najdi and Hijazi tribesmen were not integrated into the new, emerging bureaucracy in the Hijaz. The *Ikhwan* developed into an opposition, embodying a conservative lobby that did not like Ibn Saud's attempt at modern state formation. Eventually, they revolted, and Ibn Saud finally overcame them in 1930.

As a result of Husayn's lack of leadership the administration in the Hijaz was quite poor, most notables had little stake in his régime, and simply kept their heads down until Husayn left the scene. His methods of government were so draconian as to alienate any jot of support that he might have been able to gain. Successful chieftaincies, though often *ad hoc* in nature, usually centered on a connection to the personality of a charismatic leader. Ibn Saud succeeded in this in Najd, but Husayn had failed in the Hijaz. The élite did not identify with him personally, let alone the state and Hashimite ideology.

Husayn's attempts at internal consolidation were a total failure. Preoccupied with grander aspirations, he seemed to pay little or no attention to social cohesion at home. His methods of government alienated all, urban and tribal. He did not integrate the élite into his administration, choosing instead to take officials who further alienated the élite. The tribal and urban élite were dealt out of state-building entirely; instead of involving them, he oppressed them socially and financially. He did not develop a new élite with a connection to the state; the new élite of the Arab Revolt was that which formed around Faysal in Damascus. He was inept at forming the coalitions and personal relationships necessary to stay in power. It was not until Ibn Saud came along that the urban and tribal élite of the Hijaz eventually came to have a stake in state building. By then, of course, it was too late for the Hashimite Kingdom of the Hijaz.

8

PURSUING AMBITIONS AFTER THE REVOLT, 1917–1924

'[In] pursuit of a phantom kingdom never to be realized' (H. St John B. Philby, *Indian Government*, 1918)[1]

After Faysal put his forces under the command of Allenby following the capture of 'Aqabah in July 1917, the Arab Revolt effectively ended in the Hijaz. Hashimite forces still surrounded the Ottoman army in Medina, but they were not pressing home the advantage. Instead, Husayn was concerned with the growing encroachment of Ibn Saud, who threatened to undermine not just his grander plans of a caliphate but even his own rule in the Hijaz. As the Revolt drew to a close, Husayn pressed the British to clarify their policy on his borders. Was he to be King of the Hijaz only and not of Syria (including Lebanon and Palestine), Iraq, and the Arabian Peninsula itself? Husayn's home territory, the Hijaz, could not survive economically without these lands. And what of the caliphate?

It is clear that at times, for fear of antagonizing Husayn, the British actually encouraged his hopes.[2] For instance, in mid-1918, when Husayn sent a note to Wilson explaining why he signed his correspondence 'King of the Arab Countries,' Wilson, replying 'privately,' stressed that 'I personally believe that after this war the world will see some new titles appear and some old titles disappear but first we must entirely defeat our enemies before such matters

---

[1] Harry St John Bridger Philby, Diary of Najd Mission, vol. 1, p. 339, Philby Papers, St Antony's College, Oxford.

[2] Jeffery Rudd has admirably demonstrated how British fears of disabusing Husayn of his ambitions materially contributed to their continuation ('Abdullah bin al-Husayn: The Making of an Arab Political Leader,' unpublished PhD dissertation, SOAS, 1993).

can be usefully discussed.'[3] Wilson no doubt assumed that by designating the communication as 'private,' it be would understood as personal and unofficial. It is unlikely, however, that Husayn received the letter in that spirit. For the Sharif, it was a tantalizing promise of greater things to come, if only he would wait until after the war.

It also seems clear (see Chapter 2) that Husayn aspired to the caliphate in its traditional meaning, as a temporal and spiritual office. Personal ambition aside, it appears that he was earnestly motivated – out of guilt, perhaps – to replace the Ottoman Empire with a similar Arab-led Muslim empire. From the end of the war in the Hijaz until he declared himself caliph in 1924, Husayn consistently maintained these aspirations.

The general lines of Husayn's vision gave concern to the British. A few weeks after the November 1917 Balfour Declaration, Wingate noted in a worried tone that it was plainly 'evident that King Hussein has in no degree abated his original pretensions concerning Syria and apparently still nourishes the illusion that through the good offices of His Majesty's Government he may be installed, at any rate nominally, as overlord of [a] greater part of the country.' Wingate concluded that it was worthwhile 'as an immediate opportunist [sic] policy' to 'encourage' Husayn's 'belief that an Arab State or Confederacy has been created of which he is Moslem overlord'; otherwise he might abdicate.[4]

Wilson and Kinahan Cornwallis of the Arab Bureau had a series of conversations with 'Abdallah in December 1917, in which we first see some changes in Husayn's vision, probably as a result of the British pressure to come to an accommodation with Ibn Saud, Husayn's realization that he could not control the Wahhabi movement, and the British refusal to support his ambitions in Syria and Iraq. In these conversations, 'Abdallah told Cornwallis that 'peace and unity could only be attained in Arabia by the grant of full internal independence to the different ruling chiefs, who in their turn [would have to] recognize the suzerainty of the King of the Arabs.' According to Cornwallis, 'Abdallah was willing to have his father be overlord over 'strong and friendly rulers,' while Husayn, he suspected, 'would prefer a collection of puppet rulers with

---

3 FO 686/9, Hussein to Wilson, received on 18 June 1918, and Wilson to Hussein, Private, 20 June 1918. The British addressed him as 'King of the Hijaz.'

4 FO 371/3054/228069, Wingate to FO, no. 1286, 29 November 1917.

himself as the one strong man.'[5] It seems that this was the first time the Hashimites began to outwardly advocate a policy of over-lordship, which the British and Husayn were to call 'suzerainty,' or *'ri'asah.'*

'Abdallah also told Cornwallis to relay to Wingate confiden-tially that the real reason for his coming to Jeddah was to discuss with Cornwallis and Wilson the possibility of proclaiming his father caliph. As long as the Ottoman Sultan held the title, there could be no real independence for the Arabs, he stressed; his father was the most fitting candidate, and his assumption of the office would bring Arab rulers over to his side. When Cornwallis reminded 'Abdallah that the King once claimed that he had no wish to become caliph, 'Abdallah replied that this was customary – the decision had to be made for him by others.[6]

Worried about Husayn's possible reactions to the Balfour Dec-laration and Jemal Pasha's public revelation of the Sykes–Picot Agreement in a speech in Beirut in December, the British sent the Arab Bureau's D.G. Hogarth to Husayn. Jemal had branded Husayn a traitor to Islam;[7] Husayn believed that his defense against the accusation must be his becoming the sultan-caliph. Husayn had convinced himself that this was possible; as he saw it, the British would play along. Iraq would eventually be his, after a temporary British occupation, for which he would be compen-sated financially. Syria would be his, too, as the French position in Syria would be like that of Britain in Iraq. Hogarth had ten meet-ings with Husayn in January 1918, reporting later that 'the King barely touched on Mesopotamia and neither said nor asked any-thing of importance about the future of either Baghdad or Basra.'

While the British may have found this omission puzzling, in the light of Husayn's goals, Husayn no doubt assumed that they would be his. This belief was inadvertently encouraged by Hogarth, who 'was careful to let these questions ... alone.'

What Hogarth told Husayn was so vague as to leave him confi-dent that his ambitions would be fulfilled. Hogarth read him the Foreign Office formula later known as the 'Hogarth Message':

---

5 FO 686/14, Cornwallis to Clayton, 9 December 1917; *AB*, no. 76, 13 January 1918.

6 FO 883/13, Director, Arab Bureau, to High Commissioner, 3 January 1918.

7 See Rudd, p. 146, for Jamal Pasha's remarks about Husayn and Sykes–Picot.

The Entente Powers are determined that the Arab race shall be given full opportunity of once again forming a nation in the world. That this can only be achieved by the Arabs themselves uniting, and that Great Britain and her Allies will pursue a policy with this ultimate unity in view.

The message also included assurances that the Muslim holy places in Palestine would have a 'special régime.' The first part of the message did little to dampen Husayn's ambitions; after all, wrote Hogarth himself, Husayn regarded Arab unity as 'synonymous with his own Kingship,' and as 'a means to his personal aggrandizement.' 'Great Britain has planted a tree and it is natural that she will look after it until it grows and bears fruit,' wrote the King to the High Commissioner afterwards. As for the statement on Palestine, Husayn surely must have seen this as British deference to him as representing Muslims. Husayn believed that after the war he would get what was due to him. Hogarth inadvertently reinforced Husayn's misunderstanding of the Husayn–McMahon correspondence by calling the letters 'agreements' which 'safeguard[ed] the interests of our Allies and especially France.' Husayn laughed off this British deference to French interests while making a reference to Fashoda in Sudan, where in 1898 Kitchener had faced down French troops as Britain asserted its colonial interests in the upper Nile Valley.[8]

Hogarth was impressed with Husayn's determination that another Muslim power must replace the Ottoman Empire. But Mecca had to lead; it could never take second place, stressed Husayn. In his report Hogarth wrote:

He is born to rule, but, probably, not to rule much farther than his eyes can see. If he is ever to be King of an Arab Nation, that nation must be a federation of sovereign states with local autonomy so complete, that his shadowy suzerainty will stand simply for a symbol of unity and accord.[9]

The erroneous European conception of the caliphate – as an office bereft of temporal power – seems to have underlain this assessment. It thus allowed Hogarth practically to endorse such a 'suzerainty.'

---

8 FO 371/3383/25577, D[avid] G[eorge] H[ogarth], 'Report on Mission to Jeddah,' 15 January 1918, and Hussein to High Commissioner, 31 December 1917, both enclosed in Wingate to Balfour, no. 15, 27 January 1918; Rudd, pp. 146–7. For the Fashoda incident, see Thomas Pakenham, *The Scramble for Africa, 1876–1912* (London: Abacus, 1992), pp. 547–54.

9 *AB*, no. 77, 27 January 1918.

All the British officials connected with the Arab Bureau put forth the suzerainty idea from late December 1917 until well into 1918. Wingate supported a British policy which would make the King '*primus inter pares* with the other Arabian Chiefs.' Clayton proposed a 'Suzerain authority' in which HMG 'would welcome King Hussein as Suzerain.' Hogarth, Wilson and Cornwallis issued similar endorsements.[10]

At a meeting of experts on Arab affairs in Cairo on 23 March 1918, it was generally agreed that no Arabs would accept Husayn as their 'temporal overlord.' Sir Percy Cox voiced his approval of the idea of *primus inter pares*, on the understanding that such a policy refer to the religious and not the temporal supremacy of Husayn.[11] Clayton also began to see the wisdom of having Husayn as a figurehead of 'a series of states loosely bound together in a confederation of which the King of the Hejaz would be the – at least nominal – head.'[12]

As Husayn recognized his limits towards the end of 1917, particularly his failure to get the British to recognize him as King of the Arabs and to force other Arabs to accept him in that capacity, he seems to have gradually dropped his insistence on this title and to have developed the suzerainty policy.[13] Thus, Husayn's policy dovetailed with British views, although he may well have hoped that the British would eventually enforce his broader view of suzerainty.

In a series of conversations with Wilson, stretching from late May to November 1918, Husayn elaborated on his plan. In early June, Husayn's forces sustained a serious defeat at Khurmah (see Chapter 9), which forced him to become more specific about his suzerainty plan. 'As the Ottoman Empire will be destroyed,' Husayn told Wilson in June, 'it is essential that there must be a large and independent Moslem Government in its place and a

[10] Daniel Silverfarb, 'The British Government and the Khurmah Dispute, 1918–1919,' *Arabian Studies* 5 (1979), pp. 37–60. For more on the British view of Husayn as *primus inter pares*, see *AB*, no. 77, 27 January 1918. It should not be forgotten that these officials developed the suzerainty idea also as a way of protecting Husayn from Ibn Saud.

[11] FO 371/3407/70822, Account of a Meeting held at the Residency at 6 p.m. on 23 March 1918.

[12] FO 882/3, Clayton to Wilson, 6 May 1918, cited in Colman, p. 252.

[13] Colman, pp. 252–8.

united Arabia is the obvious Government indicated.'[14] As suzerain, he would be the substitute. In the Arabian Peninsula, the amirs would maintain rule in their families and appoint their own officials. He would give each amir a *firman* 'saying that the rule of the country would be entirely in his hands as long as he continued his work properly; if he did badly he might be [removed] … Emirs would appoint Governors, inflict taxation, etc., without reference to the Overlord and in fact would have complete Home Rule.' None of them would pay tribute.

The Suzerain would interfere only in conflicts between regions or larger tribal matters. Husayn gave two examples. First, if some Hijazis went to Najd and committed a crime, Husayn would ask Ibn Saud to swear a religious oath that it was so; the Hijaz government would pay the fine imposed, and the Hijazis would be dealt with on their return to the Hijaz. Second, if an entire town or tribe complained to the suzerain, 'the latter would deal with the matter.' But the amirs would have to acknowledge Husayn as their 'overlord.' When Wilson reminded Husayn that HMG had treaties with the Idrisi and Ibn Saud, he remarked that Britain need only tell them to join the confederation and they would. As for Syria and Iraq, where, he acknowledged, he did not know the local customs, the people could form their own government and solve all local issues. Since the Arabian chiefs would pay no tribute, Syria and Iraq would provide income for the upkeep of the *Haramayn*.

Wilson concluded as a result of these conversations that Husayn had interpreted the correspondence with HMG to mean that it accepted him as overlord. Moreover, 'to [the British] approval of an Arab Caliphate if one is set up the King attaches a far wider meaning than [HMG] ever intended, as he includes Temporal as well as Spiritual power in the term Caliphate.'[15]

On 18 July 1918, Husayn, reported Wilson, had told him that he considered England to have promised 'the revival of the Arab

---

[14] FO 686/38, Notes of conversations with King Hussein on 31 May, 1 and 2 June, enclosed in Wilson to Wingate, 5 June 1918.

[15] *Ibid*. It is perhaps ironic that just a few months later, the *AB* serialized a translation of Alfonso Nallino's 'Appunti sulla natura del "Califfato" in genere e sul persunto "Califfato Ottomano",' where Nallino attacks just such European misconceptions of the caliphate. See *AB*, no. 101, 27 August 1918; no. 102, 3 September 1918; and no. 104, 24 September 1918.

Caliphate and a United Arabia under his ... suzerainty ('taht Riasaty' [sic]).' The borders encompassed the whole of 'Geziret el Arab' with certain reservations concerning Basra and other regions bordering the Persian Gulf. Wilson asked Husayn what he meant by the term *Jazirat al-'Arab* (which usually means Arabia or the Arabian Peninsula); Husayn replied that the term was synonymous with *al-Bilad al-'Arabiyyah* (the Arab Lands), over which he had already declared himself king. He begged Wilson to give him an official assurance, privately, that at a peace conference Britain would adopt this policy; otherwise, he would not be able to continue in office.[16]

In November, well after his defeat at Khurmah, Husayn presented Wilson with a twelve-point program, written mostly with reference to Ibn Saud, although the principles were to apply to other amirs. Husayn would rule a *markaz*, or central government; the amirs would be ruled by the Qur'an and the Sunna, along with the common law laid down by each amir, whose power was to be 'more than that of a vali and [less than] that of independent Emirs.' Most important,

the Emir of Nejd has ... no right to negotiate with any other power regarding anything whatever because such rights [are]one of the prerogatives of the Merkaz [Central Government] and ... [matters] should be referred to it and should be done through it and must be approved by it.

Husayn noted further that Najd would have no representation abroad and that the *markaz* would be responsible for the protection and the external affairs of Najd. As for tribal matters, in addition to dispersing the *ikhwan hujar* (the military enclaves of Ibn Saud's most fanatic followers – see below), Husayn's scheme aimed at assuring tribal harmony by demanding that Ibn Saud give Hijazi tribes access to Najdi markets and pasture lands.[17]

Husayn's program was based on his experience as a leader of a typical Arabian tribal confederacy or chieftaincy. It would encompass all of the Fertile Crescent and the Arabian Peninsula, with

16 FO 686/9, Wilson, 19 July 1918, Interview with King Hussein at British Agency, Jeddah, on 18 July, 1918. On Husayn's unusual use of the term *Jazirat al-'Arab*, see below.
17 FO 686/40, Husayn to Wilson, 21 November 1918, enclosures no. 1 and no. 2 in Wilson to Wingate, 24 November 1918.

Husayn as chieftain; responsibility for internal affairs would be delegated, but he would be the primary ruler and any independence of the amirs was to be quite limited. With his sons in Syria and Iraq, Husayn probably reasoned that he would be able to contain Ibn Saud and eventually destroy him.[18]

Throughout the entire period under examination, neither Husayn nor 'Abdallah relented on the issue of the caliphate. *Al-Qiblah* consistently raised the topic, although Husayn was always careful to put the words in the mouth of an outsider. Thus in October 1917 *al-Qiblah* published an article on the 'Golden Age of al-Husayn' signed by an Egyptian – *'khadim al-dawlah al-Hashimiyyah'* (servant of the Hashimite dynasty) – one Ahmad Farid Rifa'i. He wrote that if anyone were worthy of being the successor of the Prophet, it was the Hashimite *'imam'* from Quraysh.[19] In early January 1918 Husayn wrote to the British representative Bassett, reminding him that McMahon had written that 'Great Britain wishes that the Arab Caliphate should be re-established. Upon such foundations has the Arab movement been built.' Husayn stressed his awareness that Great Britain had not promised the caliphate to him specifically, but, he said, once it had chosen him as the leader of the Arab movement, 'it became incumbent upon me to serve her good aspirations and the welfare of the Arabs religiously as well as nationally.'[20]

Al-Qiblah reported that on the occasion of awarding a prize at a school in Jeddah, Husayn was referred to as *amir al-mu'minin*.[21] In late 1918 *al-Qiblah* published an ostensible protest by Husayn against those who wrote letters to the paper using this title. This belonged properly only to the Caliph, protested Husayn.[22] Simply bringing up the subject, whether such letters were sent to the newspaper or not, was intended to show Muslim support for the Hashimite Caliphate.

---

18 See Colman, p. 297. For more on the suzerainty plan, see Joshua Teitelbaum, 'Sharif Husayn ibn Ali and the Hashemite Vision of the Post-Ottoman Order: From Chieftaincy to Suzerainty,' *MES* 34 (1998), pp. 103–22.

19 *Al-Qiblah*, 1 Muharram 1336 [17 October 1917].

20 FO 882/13, Hussein to Bassett, 21 January 1918.

21 FO 686/6, Bassett to Director, Arbor, 20 August 1918.

22 *Al-Qiblah*, no. 237, 5 Rabi' al-Ula 1337 [8 December 1918]; the point was made repeatedly (see, for example, no. 309, 24 Dhu al-Qa'dah 1337 [17 August 1919], and no. 323, 16 October 1919).

Husayn lost no chance to show the British how much support he had among Arabs, and he would bring up certain issues in an attempt to force them into a decision. For instance, in March 1919 he presented the British with a petition from 'the people of Nablus' asking him to rule them. This petition was the subject of several letters.[23] Husayn wrote giving orders to various tribal leaders (*mashayikh*) in Iraq.[24] When the British called him on this, Husayn asked how he should respond to the entreaties from Mesopotamia. In a reply worthy of 'Sir Humphrey' in the BBC's 1980s television series *Yes, Minister,* the British Agent in Jeddah was instructed to inform Husayn that

[I]nasmuch as most of the King's correspondents from other parts of Arabia seem to be malcontents or persons desiring to obtain financial aid, [the] King would seem well advised to confine his replies – where any reply at all is sent – to a courteous acknowledgement with, parhaps [sic], an expression of his general interest in the welfare of the various Arab peoples.[25]

In mid-1919, the British were presented with a letter from twenty-five Yemeni leaders, addressing Husayn as *amir al-mu'minin* and as 'the Khalifa of his great-grandfather – the lord of all apostles – the protector of the City of God ... the King of Arab Kings ... Grand Suzerain.'[26] Having had enough of this, the British Agent remarked to Husayn that the use of the term *amir al-mu'minin* as one of his titles was poor judgment. In response Husayn referred to the

High Commissioner's exalted letters at the beginning of our negotiations (in 1915) regarding the clause in which he remarks that Great Britain's intention is to restore the Arab Caliphate; and your Excellency [the British Agent, Jeddah] now says: 'Do not write Emir-el-Muminin!'[27]

---

23   FO 686/30, exchange of letters, beginning 20 March 1919, between British representative Bassett and Sadaqa, assistant under-secretary for foreign affairs. On 6 January 1919, *al-Qiblah* published a *bay'ah* (oath of fealty) of the 'residents of Jaffa' proclaiming loyalty to Husayn.

24   FO 686/10, Gertrude Bell, Baghdad, for Civil Commissioner, in Charge Iraq Section, Arab Bureau, to Director, Arab Bureau, 25 October 1918.

25   Captain Mackintosh, Acting Director, Arab Bureau, to British Agent, Jeddah, no. 114/6/9622, 31 December 1918.

26   FO 686/10, Letter to Husayn from twenty-five Yemeni shaykhs, 24 June 1919.

27   FO 371/10217/E 2298, W. J. Childs, Great Britain, King Hussein of the Hedjaz and the Caliphate: Memorandum on British commitments to King Hussein, 12 March 1924.

When Faysal was proclaimed King of Syria and 'Abdallah of Iraq, Husayn reminded the British that they had, in his eyes, committed HMG to Arab independence, and recognizing a caliph 'of noble stock' once approved by the Arabs.[28] Husayn held on tenaciously to these perceived British promises.

In April 1920 in Cairo, 'Abdallah gave an illuminating interview to a correspondent for *The Times*. He argued that the Hijaz should lead the independent 'Jeziret-el-Arab,' in which he included the Arabian Peninsula, Syria, and Mesopotamia, with each of those lands remaining 'internally independent.' From the rest of the interview, it is clear that he saw his family as the overall head of this combined polity, himself in Iraq and Faysal in Syria. He argued against the Turkish claim to the caliphate; the man who would be caliph must meet four conditions, he maintained: he must have descent from Quraysh; he must possess the *Haramayn*; he must hold *Abwab* [gates] *al-Haramayn*, in other words, Damascus and the routes from Mesopotamia to the *Haramayn*; and he must have 'adequate temporal power to maintain his position.' It was the latter, he stressed, that was the most important of these conditions.[29] Here, then, was the argument for a Hashimite Caliphate, or suzerainty, with temporal as well as spiritual powers. 'Abdallah continued to canvass support for his father's caliphate. During a speech in May 1923 celebrating the (conditional) British recognition of Transjordanian independence, the loyal son paid tribute to Husayn as *amir al-mu'minin*.[30]

Husayn, frustrated by the British and seeing the fulfilment of his ambitions fade, attempted to revive them with the 'Arabian Peninsula Conference' – *Mu'tamar Jazirat al-'Arab*. First established in August 1922, the conference held its second session in Mecca in August 1923. It included 'representatives' of Syria, Iraq, Palestine, Yemen, Hijaz and the Hadramawt. In one of its proclamations, the 'Executive Committee' addressed all the amirs of Arabia, calling for unity and a common political agenda: all political bodies should affiliate with the conference. The only practical call in the proclamation was for the boycott of all British, French, and Jewish goods, and for the replacement of these with products

---

[28] FO 686/42, Abdullah to British Agent, no. 97, 24 March 1920.

[29] FO 371/5187/E 3996, clipping from *The Times*, undated, but datelined Cairo, 28 April 1920.

[30] *Al-Qiblah*, no. 695, 14 June 1923.

made in the Arab countries. The Executive Committee called for a meeting in the following year, 1924, but it never took place.[31]

We have noted that Husayn adjusted his terminology to the changing reality of his strategic position. The terms *al-jazirah*, *al-jazirah al-'arabiyyah*, and *jazirat al-'arab* were used synonymously with *al-bilad a-'arabiyyah* or *bilad al-'arab*. In 1916 he had declared himself *Malik al-Bilad al-'Arabiyyah*, not *Malik al-Jazirah al-'Arabiyyah*. In standard Arabic usage, the terms using the word *jazirah* are coterminous with the English 'Arabia' (older usage) and 'Arabian Peninsula,' while the expressions using the word *bilad* connote the meaning of 'the Arab lands' or 'land of the Arabs.'

Husayn received delegations from the Arab world while in Transjordan in 1924, issuing a royal decree that they henceforth be designated 'delegations of Arabia' (*wufud al-jazirah*), instead of signifying their real place of origin, such as Palestine or Syria.[32] Why did Husayn use the term *jazirah* in such an unusual fashion? The classic lexicon *Lisan al-'Arab* gives several uses of the term in Arabic literature; some include Iraq by mentioning the Tigris and the Euphrates, and Syria by implication, as the Tigris goes through northern Syria.[33] It should be remembered that 'Abdallah

---

31 On the 'Arabia Conference' see the following: MAE, Le Caire (Ambassade), carton no. 131, informant (signature illegible) to Henri Gaillard (Cairo), in English, 27 October 1923; *al-Qiblah*, no. 708, 5 August 1923; no. 737, 10 November 1923; FO 686/28, Jeddah Report, 28 September–31 October 1923; *OM* 2 (1922), pp. 291–2; *OM* 3 (1923), pp. 447–51. See also Kramer, *Islam Assembled*, p. 82.

32 *Al-Qiblah*, no. 757, 24 January 1924. See also *al-Qiblah*, no. 443, 23 December 1920, which notes that Husayn's Revolt was not the '*al-nahda al-Hijaziyyah*,' but rather the '*al-nahda al-'Arabiyyah*'; its goal was to join the Arabs in 'an independent Arab community in Arabia' (*jam'iyyah 'Arabiyyah mustaqillah fi al-Jazirah*). It is clear from the article that Syria and Iraq – 'whose borders are well known'– are included in the '*Jazirah*.'

33 Muhammad ibn al-Mukarram ibn Manzur, *Lisan al-'Arab*, 1 (first edition, Cairo, 1883–90, edition used is published by Dar al-Ma'arif, n.p., n.d.) pp. 613–14. Among the Khilafatists, the term seems to have been first used in January 1920, in a petition drawn up by Muhammad Ali for presentation to the viceroy. They stressed that the Caliph had to maintain his temporal authority over the '*jazirat al-arab* ... which includes all Arab lands' (Minault, p. 86). In a later period, there were two newspapers called *Jazirat al-'Arab* and *al-Jazirah al-'Arabiyyah* in the Arab world. The former was a Hashimite weekly published in Amman in 1927, while the latter was a daily and then a weekly which moved from Damascus to Amman in 1939, and appeared until the mid-1950s (Ami Ayalon, *The Press in the Arab Middle East: A History* [New York: Oxford University Press, 1995], p. 102); they did not deal solely with affairs in the Arabian Peninsula.

joined Rashid Rida's Society of the Arab Association while in Egypt in 1914. Rida's organization wanted to unite the independent amirs of the Arabian Peninsula in order to form a 'union between the Arabian Peninsula and the Ottoman Arab provinces' (*ittihad Jazirat al-'Arab bil-wilayat al-'Arabiyyah al-'Uthmaniyyah*). This 'Arab Empire' was to be headed by the Sharif of Mecca, as Caliph.[34] In other words, by 1914 the idea of *Jazirat al-'Arab* as a political unit was in vogue, with both a wide and a narrow meaning.

The term *Jazirat al-'Arab*, as employed by Husayn in 1924, although not unheard of, was nonetheless unusual. Threatened by Ibn Saud, the only other serious contender in the *Jazirah*, Husayn may have wanted his rule over the Peninsula to seem a *fait accompli* (which it was not); with this known entity as the basic political unit, he may have thought he could go on to join the other parts of the Arab world to *Jazirat al-'Arab*. The British complained during this period about Husayn's mental state, and it is easy to imagine that he believed, perhaps desperately, that his actions would induce others to do as he wished and *be* as he wished. It is impossible otherwise to explain how he could demand that delegations from Palestine and Syria be called *wufud al-jazirah*.

Hashimites, Kemalists, and the Ottoman Caliph: maneuvering for the advantage

We must turn our attention to an aspect of Husayn's caliphal ambitions that we have not yet considered: his relations with the fledgling national régime of Mustafa Kemal in Turkey.[35] In the summer and fall of 1920, both opposed the British. Whitehall had supported a Greek occupation of parts of Anatolia and had forced the humiliating Treaty of Sèvres on the Ottoman government. In September, the Arab Bureau received reports that Husayn had contacted Kemal, and the British representative in Jeddah confirmed that Hashimite–Turkish nationalist relations were widely discussed in Mecca. A new biweekly,

---

34 *Al-Manar*, 28 June 1919, p. 203; Tauber, *Emergence*, pp. 114–15.
35 For further details on this, see Joshua Teitelbaum, ' "Taking Back" the Caliphate: Sharif Husayn, Mustafa Kemal, and the Ottoman Caliphate,' *Die Welt des Islams* 40 (2000), pp. 412–24.

al-Falah, ran the headline, 'Mustafa Kemal Swears Allegiance to King Husayn,' while *al-Qiblah* ran an official denial of such a development.[36]

In November 1920 the British Secret Intelligence Service – the SIS – reported that the idea of abolishing the Sultanate was being discussed in Islamic circles in Switzerland. Many supported Husayn for the Caliphate, the SIS believed, and such was the prevailing opinion among Turks in Switzerland.[37] There were other incidents and reports that supported the possibility of a Hashimite–Kemalist entente. 'Abdallah was reported to have met a Kemalist envoy near Azraq in northern Transjordan in December 1920, and in the same month a Turkish officer arrived in Mecca for talks with Husayn.[38]

In January 1921 British Agent Captain Nasiruddin reported from Mecca that 'a message [was] said to have come' from 'Abdallah, saying that he was in contact with the Kemalists, and that contacts were under way for the Caliphate to be offered to Husayn in exchange for declaring open hostilities against the Allies. Batten, Acting British Agent in Jeddah, was inclined to discount an open *rapprochement* between the King and Mustafa Kemal, but hedged that the 'possibility must however be still kept in view.'[39]

It is unlikely that any solid agreement was reached between Kemal and Husayn. The British Agent assessed in 1920 that communications had passed between the two, since Husayn considered himself aggrieved by the British and may well have wanted to

36 FO 686/26 Jeddah Report 20–30 September, 1920; FO 686/12, Confidential Report by Captain Mian Nasir-ud-din Ahmad, Mecca, for period ending 19 September, 1920; FO 686/12, Ihsanullah to Batten, 26 September 1920. British spies in Istanbul reported contacts between Faysal and Jemal Pasha in the summer of 1919; the reports were considered reliable. H.W. Young minuted that 'as soon as he realizes that he is to be abandoned to the French, he will naturally turn to the Turks' (FO 371/4233/115573, Calthorpe [Constantinople] to Curzon, no. M. 1100, 1 August 1919, enclosing report from Intelligence Officer [b] Constantinople to GHQ, no. I.C. 517, 24 July 1919; minute by Young, 14 August 1919.)

37 FO 371/5058/E 14781, Secret Intelligence Service, Political Report, 23 November 1920.

38 FO 371/5177, British Agent (Jeddah), to FO, no. 410, 14 December 1920; FO 686/12, Ihsanullah (Mecca), to British Agent (Jeddah), 18 December 1920.

39 FO 686/12, Mecca Report to 1 January 1921 by Captain Nasiruddin, Mecca, 19 January 1921; FO 686/27, Jeddah Report 11–20 January 1921.

keep his options open, but he was not so reckless as to confront the only Power in a position to help him.[40]

On 1 November 1922 the Turkish Grand National Assembly voted to separate the caliphate from the sultanate, abolishing the latter and removing from the Ottomans all temporal powers. The Assembly noted that the Caliphate would remain in the Ottoman house, but the state would choose the member of the house who was worthy and fitting in learning and character.[41] *Al-Qiblah* issued a special edition on 12 November in which Husayn announced that the reigning Sultan-Caliph, Mehmet Vahdettin VI, had asked for British protection. Husayn extended an invitation to the Sultan to come to the Hijaz,[42] and on 17 November it was reported that he had fled on a British warship. The Assembly promptly deposed Vahdettin, electing Abdulmecid as Caliph.[43] The Şeyh-ul-Islam, Mustafa Sabri, arrived in the Hijaz on 5 December; the ex-Sultan did so in the second week of January 1923.[44]

The action of the National Assembly met with bitter criticism in the pages of *al-Qiblah*; mostly quoting other papers, it decried the removal of temporal power from the caliph as entirely against Islam. The new Caliph, Abdulmecid, who – some papers said – had distinguished himself in poetry and painting, was compared with the early Arab caliphs, who had distinguished themselves by strictly following God's law.[45] It was left to the readers of *al-Qiblah* to infer just which modern leader followed in the path of the Rashidun. The paper reported Vahdettin's movements as he left Malta and then Port Said, and arrived in Jeddah[46] accompanied by much pomp and circumstance. *Al-Qiblah* went out of its way to describe the magnificence of the royal welcome enjoyed by the deposed Sultan.[47] Upon his arrival in Mecca, reported the paper on 22 January 1923, the Sultan put on the *ihram* (pilgrim garb), and performed the *tawaf* and other rituals.[48]

---

40 FO 686/26, Jeddah Report 1–10 October 1920.

41 Bernard Lewis, *The Emergence of Modern Turkey* (Oxford University Press, 1969) pp. 257–9.

42 FO 686/28, Jeddah Report 1–30, 1–30 November 1922.

43 Lewis, p. 259.

44 FO 686/123, Curzon, Lausanne, to British Agent, Jeddah, 20 November 1922; FO 686/28, Jeddah Report 1–31 December 1922; and Jeddah Report 1–31 January 1923.

45 *Al-Qiblah*, no. 651, 8 January; no. 656, 25 January; no. 657, 29 January 1923.

46 *Al-Qiblah*, no. 651, 8 January; no. 652, 11 January; no. 653, 15 January 1923.

47 *Al-Qiblah*, no. 653, 15 January 1923.

48 *Al-Qiblah*, no. 655, 22 January 1923.

The reason for Husayn's sudden hospitality was the same as for his tentative negotiations with the Kemalists: he hoped to have the caliphate bestowed upon him. The first concrete indication of this was in a conversation between Dr Naji al-Asil, Hijaz representative in London, and E.C. Forbes Adam of the Foreign Office on 12 January 1923 in Lausanne. Asil said that Husayn would try to persuade an international delegation of *hujjaj* to petition him during the *hajj* to take the office upon himself. The ex-Sultan would then come forward and offer Husayn the caliphate, 'thus reversing voluntarily the forced seizure of the Caliphate by Sultan Selim I in 1517 from the last Arab Caliph.'[49]

Vahdettin, however, was satisfied with neither the spiritual experiences of Mecca nor the salubrious mountain air of Ta'if; he informed the British representative that he wanted to leave for either Haifa or Cyprus. Husayn did not hide his contempt for a Muslim leader who would abandon the Hijaz for other parts. Husayn could not prevail upon Vahdettin to stay; he left in May 1923 for Switzerland.[50]

Husayn had not been successful in persuading Vahdettin to endorse his being caliph. Grafftey-Smith, Acting British Agent in Jeddah, reported that he had a copy of an intriguing document published in Turkish and in Arabic, a manifesto in which the ex-Caliph apologized for his actions from the date of his accession, attacked the Kemalists for tampering with the caliphate, and expressed effusive gratitude to Husayn. But Vahdettin had not signed the manifesto, and all copies were immediately withdrawn from circulation. It appears that the document had been prepared for Vahdettin, but that he refused to sign it.[51]

During the Lausanne conference, on 1 or 2 February 1923, a secret meeting held at the Hotel Cecil in the rooms of the Egyptian delegation was observed by an agent of the British SIS. Present were Husayn's representative, Naji al-Asil, Shakib Arslan, Nuri Sa'id, Ja'far al-'Askari, Isma'il Sidqi, Ahmad Lutfi Bey and two Indian nationalists. Asil stated that he was autho-

49 FO 371/9135/E 601, Forbes Adam to Curzon, 12 January 1923.
50 FO 686/28, Jeddah Report 1–31 March1923; Jeddah Report 1–30 April 1923; Jeddah Report 1–29 May 1923.
51 FO 686/28, Jeddah Report 1–30 April 1923. According to a report in *The Times*, Vahdettin did sent a telegraph of support to Husayn when he proclaimed himself caliph (see below; FO 371/10217/E 2276, clipping from *The Times*, 13 March 1924).

rized to propose that if Turkey were prepared to recognized Husayn 'as king of all the Arabian Peninsula,' Husayn 'would undertake to use all his influence in Arabia to befriend Turkey against England and would in fact be quite prepared to enter into an offensive and defensive alliance with her.' Al-'Askari seconded the motion and offered the support of Iraq, which would abandon its treaty with Britain if Turkey would recognize Arab independence. Another probable condition was that Turkey give up its claim to Mosul.

Asil, Arslan, the two Indian activists, and Syrian nationalist Ihsan al-Jabri went to see the Turkish representative to the Lausanne Conference, General Ismet Pasha, on 4 February. They repeated Asil's proposal, to which Ismet replied that Turkey would recognize the independence of 'Arabia,' but could recognize Husayn as king of such an entity only if the Arabs themselves did so. While not willing to discuss Mosul, he was prepared to recognize the independence of Mesopotamia. He appealed to Husayn to forget all enmity with Turkey and to unite with it against Britain. The British agent SW/1 confirmed that further communication between Turkey and Husayn occurred later that month.[52]

Taking the Caliphate

In June 1923, Husayn announced that a delegate of the anti-British Central Caliphate ('Khilafat') Committee, Maulvi Qayyamul Din Abdul Bari, would soon visit the Hijaz.[53] In November,

---

52 FO 371/8937/E 4075, Secret negotiations during the Lausanne Conference, 27 March 1923, enclosed in M[alcolm] W[oolcombe], SIS Section Ia, to Oliphant, 28 March 1923. It should be noted that Forbes Adam, who was in constant contact with Asil in Lausanne, minuted that he had been made aware of these meetings by Asil and Ja'far, who had 'pulled the legs' of the Indian activists. He had therefore, concluded Forbes Adam, considered the affair 'too farcical' to report it. In reply the SIS defended the extreme reliability of agent SW/1, and countered Forbes Adam by stating that Naji was a double-dealing intriguer, who wanted to ensure that the British did not believe any reports they might get about such meetings (minutes by Forbes Adam, 29 March 1923, and by Malcolm Woolcombe, 18 April 1923, in FO 371/8937/E 4075).

53 *Al-Qiblah*, no. 693, 7 June 1923. Abdul Bari and the Ali brothers formed the *Anjuma-i Khudda-i Ka'ba* (Association of Servants of the Ka'ba) in May 1913 to protect the *Haramayn* from non-Muslim aggression. It supported the importance of Ottoman–Arab unity for that cause, and wanted the Ottomans to remain neutral during the war. During the war itself, many leaders were interned for being anti-British (and therefore anti-Husayn). The Khilafat movement developed after the

Husayn received a telegram from Shawkat and Muhammad Ali, the Khilafatist leaders, in which they called for prayers for the independence of '*Jazirat al-'Arab.*' Such support was significant for Husayn in his quest for the Caliphate, because many Indian Muslims still retained animosity towards him for his Revolt against the Ottomans.[54]

As early as March 1923, reports began to appear that Husayn was planning a trip to northern and southern Syria.[55] He arrived in Transjordan in January 1924. Husayn had significant support from some Palestinians,[56] and 'Abdallah was already established in Transjordan. Husayn's travel northwards was accompanied by a steady flow of announcements in *al-Qiblah*, detailing his progress and the rousing reception he received in each location, each of which was deemed so wonderful as to be beyond written description.[57] Perhaps he meant the trip to demonstrate to the British that he had support beyond the Hijaz, and it may have been preparatory to his having himself declared caliph.

The build-up in the reportage continued, as Husayn distributed £580 in gold to 'Christians, Jews and Arabs' in Jerusalem.[58] Indeed, his two months' visit relegated 'Abdallah to a secondary role, as delegations from Palestine, Lebanon, Syria, and Egypt, as well as British officials and a Zionist delegation went to see Husayn in Amman.[59]

Probably the most striking evidence of the connection between the visit to Transjordan and the planned assumption of the caliphate was an article in *al-Qiblah* on 11 February 1924. The headline read, 'The Caliphate and the Arabs: The Faith of the Arab *Ummah* in His Majesty the Savior, His Defense of Its Rights.' The enthu-

---

war as a mass movement in order to maintain the Ottoman Empire and protect the caliphate. It claimed that India's Muslims owed political loyalty to the Ottoman Caliph. In 1924, the movement split into pro-Husayn and pro-Ibn Saud factions. See Jacob Landau, *The Politics of Pan-Islam: Ideology and Organization* (Oxford: Clarendon Press, 1990); Gail Minault,*The Khilafat Movement: Religious Symbolism and Political Mobilization in India* (New York: Columbia University Press, 1982).

54 *Al-Qiblah*, no. 737, 15 November 1923; Jeddah Report, 1–29 November 1923.

55 *Al-Qiblah*, no. 671, 19 March 1923.

56 On Palestinian support for Husayn in 1922–3, see Kramer, *Islam Assembled*, pp. 82–3.

57 *Al-Qiblah*, no. 752, 7 January; no. 754, 14 January; no. 755, 17 January; no. 756, 21 January; no. 757, 24 January; no. 761, 7 February 1924.

58 *Al-Qiblah*, no. 760, 4 February 1924.

59 Wilson, *Abdullah*, p. 79.

siastic reception was pointed to as support received by Husayn in
Transjordan, whose populace hoped for the return of the caliphate, and the newspaper reported Husayn's promise to 'do his
utmost to establish the caliphate.'[60]

On 3 March 1924, while Husayn was still in Transjordan, the
Turks abolished the caliphate. Four days later, Herbert Samuel,
British High Commissioner in Palestine, received the following
from 'Abdallah:

In consequence of the abolition of the Caliphate by Turkish
Government leaders of Moslem religious opinion have been obliged to
come to a decision regarding the Caliphate. Numberless telegrams of
allegiance to King Hussein as Emir el–Musninin [sic] have been
received from all Arab countries, and especially from Holy Places of
Mecca and Medina universally recognising him as Caliph. King Hussein
has therefore accepted the position of Caliph.[61]

Husayn had finally done the deed, after years of preparation. The
official announcement came from Shunah, 'Abdallah's winter
camp:

The step taken by the Ankara Government towards this honorable office
has led the religious authorities in the *haramayn al-sharifayn* and the
al-Aqsa Mosque and neighboring countries ... to surprise us and compel
us to accept the Great Imamate (*al-imamah al-kubra*) and the Grand
Caliphate (*al-Khilafah al-'uzmah*) ... Almighty God knows that our sole
object is to serve Islam and my people the inhabitants of Arabia
(*al-Jazirah*) in particular, and the Muslims in general.

The newly self-proclaimed Caliph concluded by inviting sub-
scriptions for the maintenance of the deposed Ottoman House.[62]

In mid-March 1924, both Husayn and 'Abdallah gave interviews to a correspondent for the *Manchester Guardian*. The king
told the reporter that the caliphate had been 'thrust upon me.' He
continued:

From everywhere they come to me and say: 'Islam must have a Khalif to
protect it, and the Khalifate must not be allowed to die out. You are the

60 *Al-Qiblah*, no. 762, 11 February 1924.
61 FO 307/10217/E 2187, High Commissioner for Palestine to Secretary of State for the
Colonies, no. 86, 7 March 1924.
62 Husayn's Caliphate Proclamation, 11 March 1924, in 'Abdallah, *Mudhakkirati*, pp.
197–200; see also FO 371/10212/E 2608, Fu'ad El Khatib, Foreign Minister Hashemite
Arabic Government (Shunneh, Amman) to FO, 13 March 1924.

only Prince competent to fill it. Your are the independent ruler of a great Moslem and Arab State. In your charge are the Holy Cities. You are of the tribe of Koreish. Your orthodoxy and zeal for the true faith are beyond all question. You are an Arab of the Arabs.'

'Abdallah was more joyful:

They [the Turks] have rendered the greatest possible service to the Arabs. I feel like sending a telegram thanking Mustafa Kemal. The Khalifate is an Arab institution. The Prophet was an Arab, the Koran is in Arabic, the Holy Places are in Arabia, and the Khalif should be an Arab of the tribe of Koreish ... Now the Khalifate has come back to Arabia.[63]

The reaction to Husayn's assumption of the caliphate was mixed.[64] If we are to believe *al-Qiblah*, the reception was fervent and overwhelming in the Hijaz itself. The issue of 6 March 1924 describes the *bayʿah* given to Husayn by the people of Mecca the day before in the Haram, and the letters of support sent by Meccan *ʿulama*. Similar ceremonies were held in Taʾif and Jeddah. The same issued carried an item on the abolishing of the caliphate by the Turkish National Assembly, as well as an interesting account of the reasons behind Husayn's assumption of the caliphate. Entitled 'The Caliphate and the Arabs: A General Overview,' the article developed Husayn's view of the centrality of the *Jazirah* in Islamic history; when the Arabs ran their own affairs 'in their *Jazirah*' (*fī Jaziratihim*), the paper explained, Islam was at its zenith and there was loyalty to the caliphate; it therefore followed that the 'existence of [a] mighty, independent Arab state in the *Jazirah*, which guards the Caliphate, is a necessity for the preservation of Islam, its strength, and the *shariʿah*.'[65]

    Bullard, on the other hand, had a typically more jaded view of the reception accorded Husayn's proclamation:

63 FO 371/10217/E 2286, clipping from the *Manchester Guardian*, 13 March 1924.
64 It seems that it was not 'uncompromisingly hostile,' as maintained by Kramer (*Islam Assembled*, p. 83). For more details and hundreds of documents on Husayn's assumption of the caliphate, see the following: Muhammad ʿAdnan al-Bakhit (ed.), *Wathaʾiq Hashimiyya, vol. 7 – Awraq ʿAbdallah bin al-Husayn: al-Husayn bin ʿAli wal-Bayʿah bil-Khilafah, 1924* (Amman: Jamʿiyyat Al al-Bayt, 1996); Muhammad Yunis al-ʿAbadi, *Al-Rihlah al-Mulukiyyah al-Hashimiyyah* (Amman: Ministry of Culture, 1996); Nidal Daʾud al-Muʾmini, *Al-Sharif Husayn bin ʿAli wal-Khilafah* (Amman: Lajnat Taʾrikh al-Urdunn, 1996).
65 *Al-Qiblah*, no. 769, 6 March 1924.

In point of fact the Hejaz is much surprised by the decision. What really happened, it would appear, was that King Hussein first stage managed at Amman a request that he should accept the Caliphate and then telegraphed to Mecca ordering the Prime Minister (the Grand Qadi ['Abdallah Sarraj]) to work up a similar demand there. The instructions were obeyed, and a demand secured from people who would as ready have proposed ... that relativity or bimetallism should become the state religion. Jeddah was taken completely by surprise by the summons to the Government building and the announcement by the qaimaqam that His Majesty King Hussein had accepted the Caliphate. The announcement was listened to without enthusiasm, and a speech from a young Syrian, ending with 'Long Live the Caliph Hussein', was received in dead silence. The Jeddah people are greatly depressed. The assumption of the Turkish Caliphate has given a check to the hope that had hitherto sustained them that sooner or later the Turks would recover the Hejaz and the nightmare reign of Hussein I would come to an end.[66]

On Friday 7 March 1924, several mosques in Damascus, Aleppo, and Beirut, offered prayers for Husayn as caliph. (Just how much of this support was to be attributed to anti-French sentiment must be surmised.) The Syrian periodicals *Alif-Ba* and *al-Nahdah* published articles in favor of Husayn's caliphate. In Egypt, however, there was general disapproval among the populace of Husayn's action, and High Commissioner Allenby reported that many seemed to favor King Fu'ad.[67] *Al-Qiblah* published *bay'ahs* from all over Iraq, not only Baghdad and Mosul but also Najaf and Karbala.[68]

In Haifa the British district governor assessed that while Christians and Muslims had been 'agreeably impressed' by Husayn, support for his caliphate was 'more opportune than cordial,' mostly because of Husayn's inability to intervene effectively on

---

66 FO 371/10006/E 3356, Jeddah Report 1–29 March 1924.

67 FO 371/10217: E 2131, Consul-General (Beirut) to FO, no. 3, 9 March 1924; E 2663, Smart (Damascus) to FO, no. 10, 10 March; E 2230, Allenby (Cairo) to FO, no. 64, 11 March; E 2213, Russell (Aleppo) to FO, no. 2, 11 March; E 2660, Russell (Aleppo) to FO, no. 41, 11 March; E 2678, Russell (Aleppo) to FO, no. 43, 12 March 1924; *al-Qiblah*, no. 771, 13 March 1924.

68 *Al-Qiblah*, no. 772, 17 March; no. 774, 24 March; no. 775, 27 March; no. 802, 7 July 1924. In this context it is worth noting some of Husayn and 'Abdallah's pretensions also to rule over Shi'i Muslims. Jeffery Rudd has collected a bizarre series of British references to the supposed Shi'i nature of the Hashimites and has shown that the idea was planted by Husayn. It was later used to justify proposing 'Abdallah to rule Iraq and after that to justify Faysal's actually doing so (see Rudd, pp. 170–1; 178–9; 184–91).

behalf of Palestinian Arabs. In Jaffa as well as Nablus he was acclaimed as caliph. In Majdal a notable addressed an assembly in support of Abdulmecid, 'ignoring the intimation of assistance from the King.' As a delegation from Transjordan left the town it was abused with cries of 'Down with King Husain! Long life to Abdel Majid!'; in Gaza, the Mufti prayed for Husayn as caliph and was subsequently threatened with a beating if were to do so again.[69]

Over the course of months, *al-Qiblah* carried various and assorted *bay'ah*s from the Arab and Muslim world, including India and even Liberia. Many had probably been paid for by Husayn or arranged through the pilgrim guides. Bullard commented that the names of many 'were no more distinctive than John Brown.' The telegraph office would not accept any telegram to Husayn unless it was addressed to 'His Majesty Commander of the Believers [*Amir al-Mu'minin*],' so anyone needing to communicate with him was mentioned in the pages of *al-Qiblah* as having given a *bay'ah*. The swearings of fealty reached a degree of absurdity, with one recognizing Husayn as caliph 'in the name of 5 million Moslems of the Malay Peninsula.' Bullard was present when some Bahrainis asked the governor of Jeddah to thank Husayn for offering to bring them from Jeddah to Mecca by car. Wrote the bemused Bullard, 'The Governor turns to the telephone and shouts: "They thank His Majesty the Commander of the Believers." Recognition!'[70]

As far as can be determined, Indian Muslim activists were divided on Husayn's assumption of the caliphate. Husayn was quite aware of this and published articles in *al-Qiblah* stating that 'most' Indian Muslims supported his caliphate and that more were coming around all the time in a 'reversal of opinions' (*inqilab afkar*), as they began to understand that 'the love of the Arabs was a matter of faith ' (*hubb al-'Arab min al-iman*).[71] In a letter to the president (*ra'is*) of the Khilafat Committee, 'Abdallah Sarraj of Mecca stressed that a part of the Hijaz railway was now fully functioning,

---

69 FO 371/10102/E 3865: District Governor Symes (Haifa) to Chief Secretary, 28 March; Headquarters (Gaza) to Assistant Secretary, 29 March 1924; FO 371/10217/E 2276, clipping from *The Times*, 13 March 1924; FO 686/71, High Commissioner (Jerusalem) to British Agent (Jeddah), 13 March 1924.

70 Most issues of *Al-Qiblah* from March to July, 1924 carried these; Bullard, pp. 34–35.

71 *Al-Qiblah*, no. 781, 17 April; no. 788, 19 May; no. 789, 22 May 1924.

thanks to the new caliph.[72] Among the Khilafatists, Abdul Bari sent a telegram of congratulations to Husayn but urged him to seek the approval of a Muslim conference. Other Khilafatists, led by the Ali brothers, condemned Husayn as an instrument of European domination in the Arabian Peninsula.[73]

Wanting to give his caliphate more legitimacy, King Husayn convened a Consultative Council (*majlis shura al-Khilafah*) in March and a Pilgrimage Congress (*mu'tamar al-hajj*) in July 1924.[74] A few days after his return to the Hijaz in late March, Husayn announced the establishment of the Consultative Council. Signifying his vision of a combined spiritual and temporal caliphate, the Council was to advise on both cultural and religious issues as well as on the exploitation of economic resources such as agriculture and industry, all with the goal of developing the Islamic world spiritually and economically.[75]

The Council was composed of thirty-one 'representatives' of the Muslim world, 'elected' by the leading *'ulama* and foreign residents of the *Haramayn*. In Husayn's various proclamations concerning the Council, his terminology is instructive. Mecca was called the *markaz*, to which would be sent, at Husayn's expense, various technicians and teachers charged with carrying out the mandate of the Council. Husayn's return to Mecca was reported as a return to the *markaz*.[76] The new caliph set up the Qadi al-Quda as the chairman of the Council, as a kind of *Shaykh al-Islam*.[77] It will be recalled that Husayn, in his suzerainty plan, envisaged Mecca as being the *markaz* of his polity; such language, so far from reality, was pitifully indicative of the low point to which Husayn had fallen.

The Council reportedly met at least twelve times, on Tuesdays. It published two proclamations, neither of which contained anything more noteworthy than a call to Muslims to observe the Qur'an and the Sunnah and to condemn the Kemalists.[78]

[72] *Al-Qiblah*, no. 782, 21 April 1924.
[73] Minault, p. 206; *Al-Qiblah*, no. 772, 17 March 1924. For another Husayn announcement by Indian Muslims, see *al-Qiblah*, no. 820, 10 September 1924.
[74] Both are discussed in Kramer, *Islam Assembled*, pp. 83–85.
[75] *Al-Qiblah*, no. 776, 31 March 1924.
[76] *Al-Qiblah*, no. 776, 31 March; no. 777, 3 April 1924.
[77] *Al-Qiblah*, 10 April 1924.
[78] *Al-Qiblah*, no. 797, 19 June; FO 686/29, Jeddah Report 30 May–28 June 1924.

Husayn's ambitions to be recognized as caliph finally ended with the Pilgrimage Congress of July 1924. Most of the delegates were Hijazis. Its charter praised the Arabs and their primacy in Islam, stressed that Muslims from all quarters should gather together and understand each other, and called for better education in technical and religious matters.[79] Quite striking was its lack of any reference to the Caliphate. Apparently, a strong bloc of participants resisted Husayn's efforts to be recognized as Caliph in the charter. Bullard observed that 'the jejune nature of the results of the Pilgrimage Conference suggest complete failure.'[80] Two months later, Ta'if fell to the Wahhabis.

[79] The charter is in *Al-Qiblah*, 7 July 1924, and is translated in full in Kramer, *Islam Assembled*, pp. 181–2.

[80] Kramer, *Islam Assembled*, pp. 84–4; FO 371/E 7084, Jeddah Report 29 June–30 July 1924; FO 686/29, Jeddah Report 31 July–30 August 1924.

9

TRIBES AND TERRITORIES

SAUDI THREAT, HASHIMITE RESPONSE, AND SAUDI INVASION, 1917–1925

'Without the Ateibah Ibn Saud can never take the Hejaz.' (Faysal to Lawrence, December 1917[1])

It will be remembered that during the war, 'Abdallah was quite inactive and was, as Faysal explained, keeping one eye on Ibn Saud. After the fall of 'Aqabah in July 1917, the Sharif poured more of his British-supplied gold into mobilizing the 'Utaybah tribe. He was, wrote the Arab Bureau, 'assiduously buying over such Saudi tribesmen from their allegiance as he [could].' Ibn Saud complained about this to the British.[2] After the fall of Medina in January 1919, 'Abdallah's full attention turned to Ibn Saud.

An understanding of tribal dynamics along the seam between the Hijaz and Najd is essential at this point in our discussion. In tribal chieftaincies the 'borders' of states were defined more as a function of which tribal groups were part of which chieftaincy than as a defined geographical demarcation. Yet even the tribal groups themselves had no sharp dividing lines but rather defined their own territories – their *dirah*s – as the areas in which they were settled or wandered. The battle between Husayn and Ibn Saud can therefore best be understood if looked on as a struggle between competing tribal chieftaincies for the loyalty of certain tribes, primarily the 'Utaybah.

The 'Utaybah have been described as the 'most powerful tribe in

---

[1] *AB*, no. 73, 24 December 1917.
[2] Goldberg, pp. 155–6.

central Arabia, strong in arms and great camel breeders.'[3] They were divided into two main groups (in Arabic, *batn*), al-Ruqah and Barqah; the former lived mostly in the Hijaz, the latter mostly towards Najd. Their *dirah* thus straddled Najd and Hijaz. While the Arab Revolt raged in the Hijaz, 'Abdallah seems to have controlled most of the 'Utaybah, particularly the al-Ruqah. But around the end of 1917 and the beginning of 1918, the tide began to turn. 'Abdallah told Cornwallis of the Arab Bureau in December 1917 that he 'had gained ground [with the 'Utaybah] during the last year by lavish gifts to their chief sheikhs, [but that] Ibn Saud … had countered with his Wahhabi campaign.'[4] Later, 'Abdallah commented that the tribes were forced to choose between competing tribal confederacies: '[One] thing which induces Arabs to join [the Wahhabis] is their desire for freedom of movement and trade between Hedjaz and Nejd[;] at present a non-Wahabi Ateibi cannot visit a Wahabi Ateibah settlement in Nejd in safety. He must either turn Wahabi or suffer death at the hands of his fellow tribesmen of that persuasion whose guest he is.'[5]

It is likely that the first significant display of Wahhabism to Hijazis in the twentieth century occurred at the pilgrimage of 1917, in September of that year. 'Aqabah had fallen on 6 July: three days later the *Arab Bulletin* printed a letter from 'Abdallah to his father warning him not to let the Wahhabis come on pilgrimage: '[If Ibn Saud] asks for permission for making the pilgrimage, I hope your majesty will not approve.'[6] There is no record of any British pressure on Husayn to let the Najdis come (as there was later), so we must assume that he ignored 'Abdallah's warning of his own will. Husayn's underestimation of Ibn Saud's influence was characteristic, tied as it was to his belief that the British would favor him over his rival.

---

[3] *GA*, p. 348. In general tribal information is taken from among the following five reference texts, which often repeat each other; only when quotations are used will the specific reference be given: Fu'ad Hamzah, *Qalb Jazirat al-'Arab* (Riyadh: Maktabat al-Nasr al-Hadithah, 1968); *AP*; *A Handbook of Arabia*, vol. 1, General, (May, 1916); *HH*; *GA*. Also of interest is 'Atiq bin Ghayth al-Biladi, *Mu'jam Qaba'il al-Hijaz* (Mecca: Dar Makka lil-Nashr wal-Tawzi', 1979).

[3] *AB* no. 76, 13 January 1918.

[4] FO 686/18, Record of conversation with H.H. Amir Abdullah at Jeddah July 1919, conversation of 7 July 1919.

[6] *AB*, no. 56, 9 July 1917. See also FO 686/14, Abdullah's letter to the king 30 August 1917.

The number of Najdi pilgrims was estimated by various sources at between 7,000 and 10,000. The delegation included tribal leaders from Qasim, among them representatives of its two major towns, Buraydah and 'Anayzah. Although gifts were exchanged between Husayn and the leader of the Najdi delegation, Ibn Saud's brother Muhammad, Husayn was afraid that Ibn Saud had sent Wahhabi preachers with the pilgrims. The Hijazi populace was reported to be 'restless,' and Husayn ordered his men to report anyone who mingled with the Najdis.[7] They were the largest contingent from any single location, and British observers termed them 'the most outstanding feature of this year's pilgrimage.'[8]

Of particular note was the presence of tribal leaders from Qasim in the Najdi delegation, a situation surely quite embarrassing for Husayn, who claimed to have their allegiance. He had bragged to Wilson only a few weeks earlier that 'the people of Qasim are serving as soldiers with my sons to the number of 4,000 – the most faithful of our troops.'[9]

It appears that the first recorded foray of the Wahhabi *Ikhwan* against tribes loyal to Husayn was the raid led by Sultan ibn Bijad ibn Humayd (of the 'Utaybah's Barqah *batn*) on Bijad ibn 'Ommeyyad' in December 1917. Bijad ibn Ommeyyad was an 'Utaybi (probably from the al-Ruqah *batn*), and he and his fellow tribesmen sought redress from King Husayn. 'Abdallah treated this incident with gravity.[10]

---

[7] *AB*, no. 73, 16 December 1917; FO 686/14, Ruhi (Mecca) to Wilson, 24 September 1917; FO 371/3408/94497, Report on the Hedjaz Pilgrimage 1917 by an Indian Police officer, enclosed in IO to FO, 27 May 1917.

[8] *AB*, no. 67, 30 October 1917. For a detailed study of the *hajj* in Saudi–Hashimite relations, see my 'Pilgrimage Politics: The *Hajj* and Saudi–Hashemite Rivalry, 1916–1925' in Asher Susser and Aryeh Shmuelevitz (eds), *The Hashemites in the Modern Arab World: Essays in Honour of the late Professor Uriel Dann* (London: Cass, 1995), pp. 65–84.

[9] FO 686/14, Hussein to Wilson, 5 September 1917.

[10] *AB* no. 76, 13 January 1918; FO 371/3056/242193, Wingate to FO, no. 1388, 23 December 1917. Bijad had been the leader of the *Ikhwan hijrah* of al-Ghatghat – located about 80 kilometers south-west of Riyadh – since 1913. This *hijrah*, writes Habib, was like a beacon flashing the message of a revived Islam towards the Hijaz (John Habib, *Ibn Sa'ud's Warriors of Islam: The Ikhwan of Najd and Their Role in the Creation of the Saudi Kingdom, 1910–1930* [Leiden: E.J. Brill, 1978], pp. 56–8.) Most important, it belonged to the 'Utaybah. Habib, in passing, notes by name several branches (*fakhdh*) of the 'Utaybah living in al-Ghatghat (p.71). It is apparent from an examination of the

Because the Hashimite chieftaincy was competing with the rising Saudi chieftaincy, British officials in Cairo were worried about the potential for conflict between the two and began to search for a legalistic solution to 'the border' between the Hijaz and Najd. The Hashimites played to the British desire. Advancing the suzerainty plan, 'Abdallah also drew British attention to the 'treaty' between Ibn Saud and that had resulted from the latter's foray into Qasim in 1910;[11] it stipulated that Ibn Saud would not tax the 'Utaybah and that Qasim should pay tribute to Mecca. 'Abdallah admitted that no payment had been received and that the agreement had lapsed because Husayn had been satisfied with the mere acknowledgement of his rights.[12] In conversations with Hogarth in January 1918 Husayn was asked not to claim the 'Utaybah in Najd territory; Hogarth reported that, at first acquiescing, Husayn eventually insisted that 'Qasim [was] really with himself as well as all Ateibah.'[13]

In early 1918 the British reported increasing tension betweens the two protagonists over the allegiance of the 'Utaybah and Qasim. 'Abdallah was believed to be plotting in Qasim. When Husayn wrote to Fuhayd ibn Mu'ammar, known as the 'amir' of Buraydah, that Qasimi merchants and tribesmen were forbidden access to Hijazi markets, and to Sultan ibn Bijad ibn Humayd of the 'Utaybah with another demand, Fuhayd and Sultan forwarded the letters, unanswered, to Ibn Saud, who then complained to the British that the Sharif was writing to his officials.[14]

Husayn also began to imprison people he believed sympathetic to Ibn Saud. Of particular concern to Ibn Saud were the sons of one Salih Fadl, a personal friend who was a native of 'Unayzah in Qasim but who resided in Medina. His sons, who lived in Jeddah,

Gazetteers that they were all from the Barqah section of the tribe. This attack was later known in diplomatic correspondence as the 'Ghatghat affair.' 'Ommeyyad' is perhaps the Arabic name Umid.

11 On this, see Chapter 2.
12 FO 686/14, Arbur to Bassett, Cornwallis for Hogarth in Jeddah, 10 January 1918; FO 686/14, Cornwallis (Abu Markha) to Clayton, 9 December 1917; *AB*, no. 76, 13 January 1918. The Hashimites, although asked, never produced a copy of the 'treaty' – an omission that further undermined their case in British eyes.
13 FO 371/3383/25577, Hogarth, Report on Mission to Jeddah, 15 January 1918, enclosed in Wingate to Balfour, no. 15, 27 January 1918.
14 FO 686/15, Note of Meeting Held at Residency (Cairo), 21 January 1918; FO 686/15, Philby (with Ibn Saud at Shaib Shauki) to Bassett (Jeddah or Cairo), 15 April 1918.

were imprisoned in Mecca and their property was confiscated. Fadl wrote to 'Abdallah asking that his sons be sent to him, as he had escaped from Medina and was on his way to 'Unayzah. Instead, 'Abdallah sent men after Fadl, and they plundered his party. Fadl eventually reached Ibn Saud, who communicated with Husayn on behalf of Fadl's sons. He was refused. A British official familiar with tribal affairs in Arabia noted that such behavior was considered to be an act of war.[15]

The significance of Wadi Subay'[16]

Meanwhile, trouble was brewing in the village of Khurma in Wadi Subay'. The wadi runs on an approximate southwest–northeast axis east of Ta'if. In the south of the wadi is Turabah (about 144 kilometers from Ta'if), the last major settlement on a southern road between Hijaz and Najd. From Turabah it is an easy ascent to Ta'if, and from Ta'if an equally easy descent into Mecca itself. In the north is Khurmah (about 200 kilometers from Ta'if), which is not far from the Ta'if–Najd road. As it was the first settled area west of the Najd desert, whoever controlled Wadi Subay' was a potential threat to Ta'if and hence the entire Hijaz. The wadi itself and the surrounding area formed a fertile territory between southern Hijaz and Najd, as did its tributary, Wadi Khurmah.

The region was populated predominantly by the large 'Utaybah tribe (Ruqah section), and by the smaller Buqum and Subay' tribes. The Buqum were centered around Turabah and were mostly nomadic. They numbered about 500 tents. The Subay' had a large settled population, a large portion of which was spread throughout Najd. The nomads amongst them wandered as far as the Summan steppe and eastern Tuwayq, and they comprised about 1,000 tents. Those Subay' who lived in the wadi were loyal to the Sharif, while the rest, the larger part living outside the region, were loyal to Ibn Saud.

---

[15] FO 686/6, Report by MN, 12 March 1917; FO 686/15, Captain H. Goldie (Jeddah), Note on the situation at Wadi Khurma; FO 686/15, Philby (with Ibn Saud at Shaib Shauki) to Bassett (Cairo or Jeddah), 15 April 1917. Fadl's sons were finally released in October 1918 (FO 686/16, Bassett to Arbur, 3 October 1918).

[16] This concerns the episode known to students of Saudi Arabia colloquially as 'Khurmah and Turabah'; it is called here Wadi Subay' (it goes by that name in its northern reaches and by Wadi Turabah in the south) because a topographical approach to this issue makes for a better understanding of its complexities.

It appears, though, that many of the wadi were now turning to Ibn Saud. As Philby wrote:

The influence of the Meccan Government has always been somewhat restricted by the Wahhabi sympathies of a considerable section of the inhabitants, and also by the familiar Arab preference for authority remote – where authority must be conceded – in this case that of Nejd, the town of Turabah being only 160 kilometres distant from Mecca.[17]

The town of Khurmah was populated mostly by settled Subay', but the amir of Khurmah was Khalid ibn Mansur Ibn Luw'ayy, a sharif of the Ruqah section of the stronger 'Utaybah. Khalid had converted to Wahhabism in 1914 and adopted the unique garb of the *Ikhwan*. The amirate of Khurmah seems to have been in Khalid's family for many years, nominally loyal to Mecca but in reality quite independent. (Indeed, the position of the Ibn Luw'ayy family in Khurmah suggests the existence of smaller tribal polities situated between major chieftaincies. Medina often constituted a similar polity.)

The first obvious sign of tension appears to have surrounded Khalid's visit to Mecca in late 1916. Whether he came to congratulate Husayn on his proclamation as King of the Arab Lands, or whether he was summoned, is not clear. In any case, Husayn, surprised that he appeared wearing the garb and beard of the Wahhabi *Ikhwan*, put Khalid under house arrest. Upon his release, 'Abdallah requested that he come to Wadi 'Ays, where Wilson saw him in April 1917. 'Abdallah probably thought that after Khalid's imprisonment he could finagle his support, but when Khalid quarrelled with one of 'Abdallah's men, he was disgruntled because 'Abdallah merely imprisoned the man. Husayn then sent an *'alim* – Shaykh al-Zawawi of the Shafi'i *madhhab* – to Khurmah to counter Wahhabi influence, but al-Zawawi was rejected by the locals, as was a tax collector sent in 1918.[18] The conflict was also given voice from the Saudi side. In

---

17 *AB*, no. 104, 24 September 1918.

18 Information on the history and human and physical geography of Wadi Subay' is taken from the following primary and secondary sources: FO 686/15: Note by Captain H. Goldie on Khurma, 7 September 1918; FO 686/16: History of Khurma, H. Ruhi (Jeddah), 3 October 1918; Wilson to Wingate, no. 20/6/1919, 16 January 1919, enclosing statement by an Alim at Mecca, and statement by Yassin Bey Ibn Hassan, an old Turkish official; *AB*: no. 104, 24 September 1918; no. 112, 24 June 1919; no. 113, 17 July 1919; no. 114, 30 August 1919; FO 406/41: Allenby to Curzon, no. 269, 11 June 1919, enclosing Note by Captain Garland of the Arab Bureau, on the Khurma Dispute between King Hussein and Ibn Saud, 4 June 1919; FO 371/4162/605, Interview with Sherif Feisal (at the India Office),

November 1917 Ibn Saud told the British Political Resident in
Kuwait, Colonel Hamilton, that Husayn was using the British subsidies to attract Ibn Saud's 'Utaybah and Harb, as well as many townsmen from Qasim. But even Ibn Saud realized that the tide might be
turning. Hamilton wrote that Ibn Saud told him 'with manifest ela-
tion that the Barqah section of the Ateibah had been converted [as] a
body to the Ikhwan.'[19]

It was in mid-May 1918 that the British became aware of how
serious the problem at Khurmah was for Husayn. He had received
an upsetting letter from Khalid declaring that he now had joined
Ibn Saud.[20] Husayn complained that Ibn Saud was 'transgressing'
against the 'Utaybah; when the British representative hesitated
and asked for more details Husayn replied that he now had a force
on its way to Khurmah.[21] Husayn expected British help not only
because he believed that he was to rule over Ibn Saud after the war
but because the British had a treaty with the Wahhabi leader. He
expected that the British would control him.

Husayn (and Faysal) had on occasion expressed a fear of the
Wahhabi message and the *Ikhwan*, but he had not yet seen how
fearless Ibn Saud's forces could be and was still overconfident. In
early June 1918, Husayn despatched a force headed by Sharif
Hamud ibn Zayd ibn Fawwaz; his forces were soundly defeated,
suffering twenty-eight dead. His artillery had been in poor repair,
but Husayn, in a characteristic underestimation, had told his Minister of War, Qaysuni, that the condition of the pieces did 'not
matter as long as [the artillery pieces] showed smoke to frighten
the Arabs.'[22]

The defeat of Hamud was a shock to Husayn, and about this
time the British began to report problems with the his mental
state. Wilson reported that he was nervous and tired and that 'his

27 December 1918; FO 882/13, H. Goldie (Yanbo), Notes regarding Wadi Khurma, 13
August 1918; L/P&S/18/B 308, Arabia: The Nejd–Hejaz Feud, January 1918, Kostiner,
diss., pp. 38–40; Goldrup, pp. 308–318; Habib, pp. 87–102.

19 *AB*, no. 92, 11 June 1918.
20 FO 686/15, Captain H. Goldie (Jeddah), Note on the situation at Wadi Khurma, 19
June 1918.
21 FO 686/15, Hussein to British Agent, 13 May; Bassett to Husayn, 14 May; Husayn to
British Agent, undated; *AB* no. 91, 4 June 1918.
22 FO 686/15, Captain H. Goldie (Jeddah), Note on the situation at Wadi Khurma 19
June 1918.

... state of mind might lead him to a nervous breakdown or ill-considered action.'[23] With good reason, Husayn doubted British commitments to him and to an Arab union, and he begged Wilson to assure him privately that after the war this union would be HMG's policy.[24]

On 13 June another force of eighty-two men with two machine-guns, again headed by Sharif Hamud, was despatched from Mecca to the Khurmah area. About the same time or slightly later, Husayn ordered Shakir ibn Zayd to proceed from Wadi 'Ays with a much larger force. The British were worried lest the conflict between Ibn Saud and Husayn explode and undermine the war effort. When Wilson probed Husayn for Shakir's intentions, he replied that Shakir would not go beyond Khurmah and was interested only in capturing or killing the rebel Khalid. Shakir, argued Husayn, was the amir of the 'Utaybah, and his personal influence was expected to have excellent results. Husayn claimed that he was not interested in making trouble for Ibn Saud – if he were, he bragged, all he had to do was to send Shakir to Qasim, 'and at a word [he]could have the whole of Qasim in revolt' against Ibn Saud. Wilson supported this thesis about Shakir and in general agreed that Husayn should be allowed to put down the rebellion.[25]

Husayn was again underestimating the pull of the Wahhabi *da'wah*, as well as overestimating the influence of Shakir. In fact Shakir, despite his dress and behavior, was not of the 'Utaybah in any real sense and had little influence among them. But for Husayn, it was absolutely imperative to put down the Khurmah revolt; not doing so could easily affect his rule in the Hijaz proper, where the rest of the 'Utaybah and perhaps even the essential Harb might also revolt at the display of such weakness. On 17 July 1918, Husayn issued a warning to the residents of Khurmah, who had 'listened to the seductions of Khaled ibn Mansur,' and he attacked aspects of Wahhabi teachings. Proclaimed Husayn, 'God

---

23 FO 686/9, Hussein to British Agent, 26 June 1918; FO 371/3389/121208, Wingate to FO, no. 1055, 9 July 1918.

24 FO 686/10, Wilson to Arbur, no. W.428, 18 July 1918.

25 *AB*, no. 95, 2 July 1918; WO 158/619, Note by Major Cornwallis (Director, Arab Bureau, Cairo) 18 July 1918; FO 686/9, Interview with King Hussein on 20 July 1918; FO 686/10: Wilson to Arbur, W. 428, 18 July; Wilson to Arbur, W. 435, W. 437, 20 July 1918; Wilson to Joyce (Akaba), no. W. 439/120, 21 July 1918.

has placed [Khurmah] under my authority in spite of your will or the will of Khalid,' and 'you and [he] bear allegiance to me.'[26]

British officials went into high gear to prevent a confrontation at Khurmah. Wilson's conversations had been intended to accomplish just that, but Husayn was beside himself with anxiety. Wilson pressed him about Shakir's intentions, eliciting a very emotional response. Husayn struck the settee on which he was sitting and swore by the honor of his family 'that he would not stir from his seat until his resignation had been accepted by His Majesty's Government.'[27]

Not trusting that Shakir would limit himself to Khurmah, the FO moved to head off an escalation. Bassett informed Husayn that 'His Majesty's Government would view with grave disfavour any action by either party or their followers liable to aggravate or to provoke hostilities.' A similar message had been sent to Ibn Saud. Husayn's response was again to suggest his resignation: 'I should also like [HMG] to point out the place which she may think best for me to live in'[28] – threats to resign were to become an enduring pattern.[29] The British responded with flattery and protestations of loyalty and said, 'There are, God willing, many years of happiness and prosperity in store for [you] in which to enjoy the fruits of the work.'[30] When Bassett suggested that Husayn write Ibn Saud a conciliatory letter, Husayn replied that he had already written offering to have his son Zayd marry one of Ibn Saud's daughters, but that the Najdi had refused.[31]

---

26 FO 686/13, Sherifian warning, 17 July 1917; Goldrup, p. 310.
27 FO 686/18, Wilson to Arbur, no. W. 780, 20 July 1918, citing his own no. 669 of 23 June 1918; FO 686/9, Wilson, Interview with King Hussein on 20 July 1918, dated 21 July 1918.
28 FO 686/10, Arbur to Bassett, no. AB. 982, 24 July 1918; FO 686/10, Hussein to British Agent, 28 July 1918.
29 In November 1919, Vickery, who had replaced Wilson, actually accepted the king's resignation after one of these fits of pique. Husayn was flabbergasted and exclaimed, ' "What, you accept, you accept my resignation," and fell back on the sofa pulling his beard' (FO 686/26, Intelligence and Political Report 26 October–21 November 1919). In contrast, Cornwallis wrote of Wilson's gullibility when dealing with Husayn, but noted that 'his transparent honesty & shall we whisper stupidity avail where another man's cleverness would fail' (Clayton Papers, 470/7/17–18, Cornwallis, Jeddah, to General [Clayton], 28 November 1917).
30 FO 686/10, Arbur to Bassett, no. AB. 036, 3 August 1918.
31 FO 686/10: Bassett to Husayn, 4 August; Bassett to Arbur, no. W. 539, 8 August 1918, relaying Husayn's reply. For a record of this offer, see FO 686/37, Wilson to Director,

But Husayn and 'Abdallah were building up to a confrontation at Khurmah. Although Shakir was taking his time gathering support, 'Abdallah was writing to chieftains, probably 'Utaybah, calling Ibn Saud a rebel and saying that he intended his forces to move to the Shudhub wells which were one day east of Khurmah (in other words, well into territory claimed by Ibn Saud). There he would form a great tribal gathering. Husayn did not deny that 'Abdallah sent the letters and in fact stressed that it was his right to do so.[32]

Sometime during the summer of 1918, Husayn became more desperate as a result of the encroachment of Ibn Saud and the lack of firm British commitments. Regarding the latter, Clayton and Wingate, fearing what Husayn might do, lobbied hard for a definite private commitment to Husayn on the 'suzerainty' policy.[33] Things were going from bad to worse for Husayn at home. Shakir, Husayn's vaunted 'amir' of the 'Utaybah, who had been encamped on the Mecca–Khurmah road since July, failed to entice that tribe over to him. British officers in Yanbu' reported that many 'Utaybah, including several of the shaykhs who had initially complained to Husayn about the raid of Sultan ibn Bijad, were deserting from 'Abdallah, Faysal, and 'Ali and going over to Ibn Saud. The people of Ta'if reportedly showed 'signs of nervousness and a desire to move to Mecca.'[34]

At the height of this tension, in August–September 1918, Khalid struck pre-emptively at Shakir. Shakir's force was annihilated, and the Ruqah 'Utaybah who were with him deserted *en*

Arab Bureau, 29 November, enclosing note by Cornwallis, 28 November, on meeting with Wilson and Husayn on 24 November 1917.

[32] FO 686/15: Bassett to King of Hejaz, 21 August; Hussein to British Agent, 22 August 1918.

[33] 'King Hussein is in a state of mind which unless rectified may lead to serious consequences. He may at any moment take action which would involve disastrous effects on our Arab policy' (FO 882/3, Private and Secret Note, circulated in Cairo by Clayton, dated 8 September 1918; FO 882/3, Memorandum by Clayton, 2 September 1918; FO 371/3384/183342, Wingate to Balfour, no. 219, 21 September 1918, enclosed in Papers relating to King Hussein's version of his Agreements with His Majesty's Government, Eastern Department, FO, 5 November 1918). FO policy on Husayn was fiercely opposed by the pro-Ibn Saud India Office; see, for example, Daniel Silverfarb, 'The British Government and the Khurmah Dispute, 1918–1919,' *Arabian Studies*, vol. 5 (1979), pp. 37–60.

[34] WO 158/619: Yenbo to Arbur, no. G 557/20, 27 July 1918; Political, Baghdad, to Arbur, no. 7363, 5 September 1918, reporting observations by Philby, dated 18 August 1918; *AB*: no. 103, 10 September 1918; no. 104, 24 September 1918.

masse to the *Ikhwan*, turning on Shakir and stripping him of all his arms as they left.[35]

Husayn could not let this stand. The Wahhabi movement presented two primary threats: first, the *Ikhwan* themselves challenged the tribal system in the Hijaz, as one of the major aims of the movement was the renunciation of tribal ties in favor of the bonds of brotherhood in the Wahhabi *da'wah* and domicile in the *hujar*.[36] When the British asked Husayn to meet Ibn Saud in mid-September 1918, he replied that first Ibn Saud must be compelled to disband the *Ikhwan*.[37] Second, Faysal told the India Office in late December 1918 that Khurmah, the first village on the western side of the Najd desert, was an outpost of fanaticism in the settled area, a situation which might have been tolerable if confined to the desert. He proposed to lead troops against the forces in Khurmah. (Lawrence, who probably interpreted for Faysal at the meeting, repeated these words practically verbatim as his own in an FO minute.)[38]

Meanwhile, Ibn Saud had furthered his cause by installing a representative (known as a *ma'mur*) at Turabah, which was even closer to Ta'if than Khurmah. The Buqum tribe of Turabah approached the Sharifian forces at 'Ushayrah, asking for relief from the *ma'mur* and the Wahhabi *Ikhwan*.[39]

British officials did their best to restrain Husayn from mounting another attack in Wadi Subay'. Regardless of whether or not he was capable of managing a major offensive at this point, refraining from activity would have caused the tribes to doubt him. While the IO

---

35 Goldrup has this battle occurring at 'Ushayrah on 16 September; Garland has it 'in August' at the Hannu Wells, 26 kilometers *east* of Khurmah (Goldrup, p. 310; FO 406/41/91521, Allenby to Curzon, no. 269, enclosing Note by Captain Garland, of the Arab Bureau, on the Khurma Dispute between King Hussein and Ibn Saud, 4 June 1919); it most probably took place in September at 'Ushayrah, which is about 70 kilometers north and slightly east of Ta'if; FO 686/16, Goldie to Bassett, 17 October 1918; *Al-Qiblah*, no. 216, 30 September, cited in *AB*, no. 107, 6 November 1918.

36 John S. Habib, *Ibn Sa'ud's Warriors of Islam: The Ikhwan of Najd and Their Role in the Creation of the Saudi Kingdom, 1910–1930* (Leiden: E.J. Brill, 1978), pp. 16, 31–2.

37 FO 686/16, Hussein to Acting British Agent, 18 September 1918; see also FO 686/40, Husayn to British Agent, 21 November 1918, enclosed in Wilson to Wingate, 22 November 1918.

38 FO 371/4162/605, Interview with Sherif Feisal (at the IO, 27 December 1918); FO 371/3390/213146, minute by T.E. Lawrence, undated, but written on 31 December 1918 or 1 January 1919.

39 FO 686/16, Goldie to Bassett, 20 October 1918; FO 686/18, Garrood (Jeddah) to Arbur, no. V. 1037, 2 November 1918.

and the FO argued over who should have Khurmah, the appearance
of *Ikhwan* well west of the town was recognized in London as
extremely dangerous to Husayn. On 6 December 1918 he reported
that an *Ikhwan* force had raided a Sharifian base at 'Digadiah' (perhaps Dughaybjah) seventy-two kilometers north of Ta'if, and that
Ibn Bijad was 'advancing towards Mecca.' On 13 December, HMG
decided 'to warn Ibn Saud plainly that if he [did] not … withdraw
all militant Ikhwan now west of Khurmah, his subsidy [would] be
stopped' and the British would feel free to act as necessary for the
maintenance of peace. But India Office officials in Baghdad and
Bahrain used bureaucratic delaying tactics not to forward it immediately to Ibn Saud.[40]

The failures associated with Wadi Subay' began to take their toll
on the essential Harb, as well as the Juhaynah. Captain Goldie
reported from Yanbu' that most of 'the Harb confederation is now
openly defying the authority of the King … and … looking
towards Nejd for protection.' The Harb feared an invasion from
their traditional enemies, the 'Utaybah, many of whom – if not
most – were by now under Ibn Saud's control. They were thus
confronted with two alternatives: either side with the 'Utaybah,
which meant going over to Ibn Saud, or face an 'Utaybi invasion.
This political situation was aggravated by the fact that 'Ali and
'Abdallah were no longer paying these tribal groups the massive
British-supplied sums they had come to expect.[41] In late 1918,
Husayn was thus facing the possibility of losing the loyalty of his
core tribe, largely because of Ibn Saud's absorption of the
'Utaybah. A slow but sure domino effect was beginning. The
Sharif no longer had at his disposal the cohesion-producing
incentives – primarily money – that had ensured tribal loyalty,
whereas Ibn Saud could attract tribes through promises of booty
and expansion, and a movement of religious revival.

With Wingate, Hogarth and Wilson as his lobbyists, Husayn
continued to provide them with evidence of *Ikhwan* aggression
west of Khurmah, notably attacks on the 'Utaybah by Ibn Bijad.
He threatened to resign or to attack Khurmah.[42] The British govern-

40 L/P&S/18/B 308, Arabia: The Nejd–Hejaz Feud.
41 FO 686/10, Captain H. Goldie (Yenbo) to Wilson, 11 February 1919.
42 FO 686/17, Cheetham (Cairo) to FO, no. 252, 17 February 1919; FO 371/4144/29325,
    Cheetham (Cairo) to FO, no. 277, 20 February 1919; Kostiner mentions that in
    December 1918 and January 1919 Shakir 'launched two small scale attacks on Khurma

ment adopted a basically pro-Husayn position, despite remonstrations from the India Office. Policy directives were forwarded from London to India Office officials in Baghdad, but there officials continued to put up bureaucratic obstacles which served to help Ibn Saud. A very firm message was sent to Ibn Saud in March 1919 – with a copy to Husayn – in which HMG threatened his subsidy if he did not remove himself from Khurmah; otherwise, Wahhabism would 'constitute an immediate menace to the safety of the Hejaz, which [the British] are bound to protect from alien aggression from whatever quarter.' A.T. Wilson, the Indian Government's representative in Baghdad, later claimed that this message had been overlooked; Ibn Saud continued to receive his subsidy and was never given the ultimatum.[43]

Yet now, puffed up with assurances that Britain would back him, Husayn met 'Abdallah at 'Ushayrah on 1 April 1919, while tribal representatives gathered; his son had moved there not long after Medina had surrendered on 10 January 1919. Husayn rarely left Mecca, even for Jeddah, and his journey to 'Ushayrah was a pure demonstration of power and confidence. It had a temporary effect. Husayn pardoned those who came in (perhaps 10,000), begging understanding from Husayn, claiming that the *Ikhwan* were vicious and that they had no choice but to support Ibn Saud. He even sent a message to Khalid offering him a pardon if he were to surrender.[44] 'Abdallah, who had written threatening letters to Ibn Saud, now proposed that he make the tribal gesture of sending a family member, both as a hostage and as a gesture of good faith. Ibn Saud might send one of his sons, 'Abdallah urged, to 'guarantee the success of smoothing over the differences between you and my father.'[45]

On or about 20 May 1919, after about a month and a half of rallying tribes, 'Abdallah moved on Turabah, which fell after a short

---

which were easily repulsed'(dissertation, p. 96); in fact there may have been several such skirmishes during this time, perhaps brought about by what is known as 'reconnaissance in force,' whereby probes are made of enemy positions and readiness, with the knowledge that some contact might be made. Such raids put pressure on surrounding tribes to choose sides, lest they risk being attacked themselves.

43 FO 686/17, FO to HC (Cairo), No 323, 12 March 1919; it was not until mid-December 1919 that Wilson deigned to inform HMG that the ultimatum had been 'overlooked' (Silverfarb, 'Khurmah Dispute').

44 *AB*, no. 111, 24 May 1919.

45 Habib, pp. 90–1.

siege. He let his men plunder the place and he executed at least two people.[46] His mood was now bright and his confidence high. Husayn's attitude, strengthened by his mistaken notion that the British had given Ibn Saud an ultimatum, was vividly demonstrated in a letter he sent to 'Abd al-'Aziz on 23 May. The letter opened with 'Abdallah typically referring to himself as 'Ibn *Amir al-Mu'minin* al-Husayn bin 'Ali.'

Perhaps more significant is the missive's evidence of the threat that the *Ikhwan* movement presented to the established sociopolitical order in the Hijaz. While upbraiding Ibn Saud for claiming the Barqah and al-Ruqah sections of the 'Utaybah, 'Abdallah wrote, 'If you seek the welfare of the Muslims, as you claim, then release those whom you ordered to sell their livestock and for whom you built dwellings and go back to your *dirah*.'[47]

While 'Abdallah had been rallying tribes, Khalid had heard of his movements and therefore had allied himself with Ibn Bijad. We have seen earlier that 'Abdallah was no soldier. As Catroux put it, the amir *'était un homme aimable, un bon compagnon de table, un poète fécond en improvisations imagées, mais il n'était point un soldat.'* Having taken Turabah, he ignored the standard procedure of manning a defensive perimeter at night. Moreover, the Baghdadi officer under 'Abdallah's command, wrote Garland, had 'maxims not to allow military duties to interfere with his night's rest.'[48] When Khalid's men struck under the cover of the night of 25–26 May 1919, they overpowered 'Abdallah's hugely superior force.

---

[46] Goldrup, p. 331; Mohamad Almana, *Arabia Unified: A Portrait of Ibn Saud* (London: Hutchinson Benham, 1980), pp. 64–5; Kostiner, diss., p. 98.

[47] 'Abdallah (at Turabah) to Ibn Saud, 23 Sha'ban 1337 [23 May 1919], printed in Salah al-Din al-Mukhtar, *Ta'rikh al-Mamlakah al-'Arabiyyah al-Sa'udiyyah*, vol. 2 (Beirut: Manshurat Dar Maktabat al-Hayat, n.d.), pp. 207–9. Al-Mukhtar interpolates that 'dwellings' refers to the *hujar* built for the above-mentioned tribal sections.

[48] Général Catroux, *Deux Missions en Moyen-Orient (1919–1922)* (Paris: Librairie Plon, 1958), pp. 210–11 (Catroux was the French representative in the Hijaz at the time); FO 406/41/95840, Allenby to Curzon, no. 278, 15 June 1919, enclosing Note by Captain Garland on the Khurma Dispute, 10 June 1919. The motivation of the Iraqi officers with 'Abdallah was very poor before Turabah and may have contributed to the rout (Ibrahim al-Rawi, *Min al-Thawrah al-'Arabiyyah al-Kubra ila al-'Iraq al-Hadith: Dhikriyyat* [Beirut: Maktabat Dar al-Kutub, 1969], p. 132. Al-Rawi was one of the Iraqi officers with 'Abdallah during the war and at Turabah. He claimed that the reason for the low motivation was that once the Turks were defeated, the Iraqis did not wish to fight other Arabs).

At the moment of attack, 'Abdallah's frightened 'Utaybah turned on him, opening fire on his tent. The amir escaped bareheaded and in his nightshirt (or perhaps even *demi nu*, according to Catroux), as did several of the officers. Those officers who were not so lucky were decapitated and their heads impaled on the lances of Khalid's warriors; one of them did not merit even that indignity and was chopped into little bits. 'Abdallah rode off so hastily that he left behind all his money, most of his weapons and stores, as well as his sword, which Khalid took as a prize. As Khalid passed among the bodies he had piled up in what was left of 'Abdallah's tent, he lectured the Sharifian prisoners:

Sachez que je suis l'Emir de La Mecque ... Je suis tolérant ... J'en veux seulement à Hussein et à ses fils que j'espère abattre d'ici peu et purifier ainsi les Lieux Saints. Je vous engage à ne pas me faire la guerre une seconde fois. Je compte faire mon entrée a La Mecque avant le pèlerinage s'il plait à Dieu. Allez l'annoncer au Chérif et à Abdallah qui vient de s'enfuir piteusement.[49]

All told, the Hashimites sustained approximately 250 dead, about seventy of whom were officers.[50]

On 29 May 1919, *al-Qiblah* published an admission of what had happened at Turabah but attributed the disaster to a failure of supplies to reach 'Abdallah.[51] What the newspaper did not reveal, of course, was the panic that ensued after the battle. The Hashimite army, holding just west of the Ta'if–'Ushayrah line, had been reduced to about 400 regulars, a maximum of 1500 tribal levies, and four inferior machine guns and artillery pieces. In Ta'if several Sharifian officials fled in panic, without packing their bags; Mecca was reported to be in a state of great alarm, and the Hashimites had lost all influence over the tribes. The Wahhabis,

---

49 SHAT, 7 N 4183, Catroux to Minister of War, 20 June 1919, enclosing Extraits d'une lettre d'un Ministre Chérifien [probably Qaysuni, Minister of War] à un notable du Djeddah, 16 June 1919; Catroux, p. 210; FO 406/41/95840, Allenby to Curzon, no. 278, 15 June 1919, enclosing Note by Captain Garland on the Khurma Dispute, 10 June 1919. Habib, who based his research primarily on pro-Wahhabi sources, substantiates the reports of the slaughter at Turabah (pp. 92–4).

50 SHAT, 7 N 4183, Catroux to Minister of War, 20 June 1919, enclosing Extraits d'une lettre d'un Ministre Chérifien [probably Qaysuni, Minister of War] à un notable de Djeddah, 16 June 1919; FO 406/41/95840, Allenby to Curzon, no. 278, 15 June 1919, enclosing Note by Captain Garland on the Khurma Dispute, 10 June 1919.

51 *Al-Qiblah*, no. 286, 29 Sha'ban 1337 [29 May 1919].

British representatives reported, were able to move into the Hijaz at any time, and Wilson sent home alarming telegrams about the need to evacuate 11,500 British Indian subjects from Jeddah and Mecca. Ibn Saud, who had entered Turabah, was sternly warned by London to remove his men from Khurmah and Turabah.[52] Truly fearful of a Wahhabi advance, the British, at Husayn's request, sent six warplanes to Jeddah. The idea of sending Muslim troops was discussed in London, but was eventually rejected.[53]

'Abdallah's defeat had a terrible effect on the tribes of the Hijaz. The key Harb confederation was withholding support until they were paid. Stories of *Ikhwan* atrocities spread and probably became increasingly exaggerated, but by mid-June, when a Wahhabi advance had not materialized, a degree of calm returned to the Hijaz. Ibn Saud sent a conciliatory message to the British accepting their offer of arbitration, but he did not withdraw from Khurmah or Turabah.[54]

Husayn wished at this stage, wisely, to press home the advantage. He considered the British planes to be under his command and wanted them to bomb Wahhabi positions. Wilson informed him that they were only for the defense of Mecca and Ta'if. However, he also informed Husayn that if Ibn Saud did not evacuate his forces from Khurmah and Turabah, 'Abd al-'Aziz would be 'an enemy of Great Britain.'[55]

Then, on 17 June, Britain reversed its policy. Disturbed by Husayn's defeat and lack of support at home, it moved from its stalwart pro-Hashimite position. Whereas previously HMG had agreed that Khurmah should be Husayn's without any need for arbitration, it now favored reconciliation. Philby was instructed to

---

52 SHAT, 7 N 4183, Catroux to Minister of War, 20 June 1919, enclosing Extraits d'une lettre d'un Ministre Chérifien [probably Qaysuni, Minster of War] à un notable du Djeddah, 16 June 1919; FO 686/17, Wilson to Arbur, no. W. 586, 8 June 1919; FO 371/4146/86805, Allenby to FO, no. 950, 10 June 1919; FO 686/17, Wilson to Arbur, no. W. 589, 8 June 1919; FO 371/4146/87357, Allenby to FO, no. 953, 11 June 1919; FO 686/17, Official and Urgent Communication from His Britannic Majesty's Government to the Renowned Emir Abd el Aziz Ibn Abderrahman el Feisal el Saud, Emir of Najd, 3 June 1919.

53 FO 686/17, Wilson to Arbur, no. W. 585, 3 June 1919; F0 371/4146, Allenby to FO, no. 962, 12 June 1919; Silverfarb, 'Khurmah Dispute.'

54 FO 686/17, Wilson, Appreciation of the present Khurma situation, 15 June 1919; Silverfarb, 'Khurmah Dispute.'

55 FO 686/17, Wilson to King of Hedjaz, date unclear, but 15 or 16 June 1919.

deliver a message containing the idea of reconciliation to Ibn Saud but was prevented from doing so by Husayn, who rejected arbitration and refused to allow Philby passage through the Hijaz.[56] Ibn Saud informed Wilson that he was heading back to Najd with some of his followers but was not moving out of Khurmah and Turabah.[57]

Husayn's refusal to allow Philby passage through Ta'if angered the British, and when he telephoned Wilson on 25 June 1919, HMG was not receptive to his latest strategy. He now wanted to attack Ibn Saud and finish him off with a strong show of force and bombing by the British planes; he would then go to England in triumph as a guest of King George. If this plan was not accepted he would resign. Husayn's remarks showed how little he appreciated the deterioration in his situation. Wilson, who had probably been Husayn's greatest advocate, spoke harshly to 'Abdallah, telling him that the whole mess was 'due to the unfortunate defeat of [his] Army.' Wilson said, 'We are here in the King's interests and to help him, and I tell you we are tired to death … It is not my fault you have no Army.'[58] The tone of voice of this most stalwart of Husayn's supporters was a telling indication of the change in British attitudes. As primarily urban men, he and 'Abdallah underestimated Ibn Saud and his hold on the tribes; all they believed was needed was a one-off show of force. The British were exasperated, and withdrew their planes from Jeddah.[59]

Ibn Saud demonstrated statesmanship by committing himself not to have a Najdi pilgrimage in 1919 and not to move beyond Khurmah and Turabah.[60] Husayn never reached England; to his chagrin, in November 1919 Ibn Saud's son Faysal was invited to London instead.

The Sharif's rule in the Hijaz was continuously undermined by Wahhabi efforts following the Turabah débâcle. In late July 1919 Goldie reported two incidents, one tribal and the other urban, that

---

56 Silverfarb, 'Khurmah Dispute.'
57 FO 686/17: Abdel Aziz ibn Abel Rahman el Faisal el Saud to Colonel Wilson, 18 June; Wilson to Arbur, no. W. 667, 22 June; Wilson to Arbur, no. W. 669, 23 June 1919; *AB*, no. 112, 24 June 1919; Silverfarb, 'Khurmah Dispute.'
58 FO 686/18, Note of telephonic conversations on 25 June 1919.
59 FO 686/18, High Commissioner to Hussein, relayed in Arbur to Wilson, no. A.B. 909, 15 July 1919.
60 FO 371/4146/115917, Civil Commissioner (Baghdad) to India Office, 5 August, 1919.

showed his waning control. An *Ikhwan* patrol north of Medina made contact with some of 'Ali's regular troops and Harb bedouins. When the Harb saw that the Wahhabis were getting the upper hand, they turned on 'Ali's regulars, killing many of them. Then, in Mecca, Husayn discovered a 'secret society' that was pro-Wahhabi: its members included Sharif Sharaf and his brother, the Maliki Mufti, the Grand Qadi, the entire Shayba family (hereditary keepers of the keys to the Ka'bah), and about twenty others.[61]

The confrontations in Wadi Subay' were a turning point for the British, demonstrating that they had backed the wrong horse. Despite all the funds Britain had poured into the Hijaz, Husayn was unable to keep the loyalty of his tribes.[62] In contrast, Ibn Saud, with a much more modest subsidy, was able to do this very thing with comparative ease; the Wahhabi leader had shown himself to be a statesman who could compromise. To London it appeared that if Ibn Saud had wanted to move into the Hijaz, he could have, but that he refrained out of respect for British wishes.

British exasperation with Husayn was one of the most lasting legacies of this dispute, and it had far-reaching consequences. The Foreign Secretary, Lord Curzon, who wrote short but poignant minutes, noted that he was considering Husayn's 'complete disappearance, not only without apprehension, but even with satisfaction.' For the Secretary, Husayn was a 'pampered and querulous nuisance.' John Shuckburgh of the India Office summed up the British attitude by the end of 1919: 'We…said to him in effect: "Very well; if you won't let us help you in our own way, we wash our hands of you. Settle with the Wahabis as best as you can."'[63] Curzon later said: 'I don't think we shall ever have peace until he has gone. But I do not want to administer the final

---

61 FO 686/18, Major Goldie, Acting British Agent to Director, Arab Bureau, 30 July 1919.

62 'Abdallah lamented, 'I cannot get the Bedouins to face the [*Ikhwan*] enemy, who believe that death is the key to paradise.' This fact was also appreciated by the French, who quoted a Sharifian official who marvelled that the Wahhabis fought '*avec l'espoir de gagner le ciel*' (FO 686/17, ['Abdallah,] A Notification given to H E The Minister of War [Qaysuni], 3 June 1919; SHAT, 7 N 4183, Catroux to Minister of War, 20 June 1919, enclosing Extraits d'une lettre d'un Ministre Chérifien [probably Qaysuni, Minister of War] à un notable de Djeddah, 16 June 1919.) This kind of devotion glared in contrast to the behavior of 'Abdallah, his officers, and the tribes under his command throughout the Revolt and later against Ibn Saud.

63 Silverfarb, 'Khurmah Dispute.'

kick.'[64] The legacy of Wadi Subay', Husayn's refusal to recognize
the British and French mandates, and his shabby treatment of pilgrims, moved the British to assume a 'neutral' policy in the ten-
sions between him and Ibn Saud.[65] Under the circumstances, it
amounted to a pro-Ibn Saud policy.

Interlude: a note on relations with the tribal chieftaincies of Ibn
Rashid of Jabal Shammar and the Idrisi of 'Asir

Other tribal confederacies, of secondary importance, were at work
during this period. One was that of Ibn Rashid, headquartered at
Ha'il in Jabal Shammar; and another was that of the Idrisi in 'Asir.
The former had been supported by the Ottomans, while the latter
had had a treaty with the British since 1915. Husayn's aspirations
and fear of Ibn Saud led him to covet the tribes and territory of
both.

Ibn Rashid, who controlled the Shammar tribe, was in the pay
of the Ottomans for most of the war. This alliance with a weak
central government enabled him to maintain local autonomy.[66] In
fact, the Ottomans were unable to force him into action against
the Sharif during the war. But the British made things increasingly difficult for him by forbidding the Shammar their essential
markets in Kuwait and Iraq.[67] Worried about this, the defection of
some of his tribesmen to Husayn,[68] and the growing strength of
his traditional enemy, Ibn Saud, Ibn Rashid eventually sought an
alliance with the Sharif. The negotiations lasted throughout 1918
and well into 1919, but after the Turabah defeat Husayn hastened
them, and it was 'freely rumoured' that Husayn had given Ibn
Rashid £50,000.[69] *Al-Qiblah* announced that Ibn Rashid had been

---

64 FO 371/5064/E 12144, Minute by Curzon, 6 October 1920.

65 Silverfarb, 'Khurmah Dispute.'

66 Madawi Al Rasheed, *Politics in an Arabian Oasis: The Rashidi Tribal Dynasty* (London:
I.B. Tauris, 1991), p. 217.

67 FO 686/23: Cox (Baghdad) to Arbur, 13 June 1917; Bassett to Fuad El Khatib, 15 June
1917; FO 371/3407/70822, Account of a meeting held at the Residency at 6 p.m. on 23
March 1918.

68 FO 686/10, Major Joyce (Wedj), Intelligence Notes, 10 May 1917.

69 FO 686/23, Davenport (Yanbo) to Jeddah, 17 April 1918; FO 686/23, Bimbashi
Garland (Yanbo) to Bassett 15 September 1918; *AB*, no. 107, 6 November 1919; FO
686/18, Wilson to Arbur, no. W. 724, 9 July 1919; FO 686/18, Hussein to Ibn Rashid,
11 July 1919; FO 686/26, Intelligence and Political Report 11–21 December 1919; Al
Rasheed, pp. 219–220.

invested with the Order of the *Nahdah*, first class, along with some Shammari shaykhs who received a lesser class of that order.[70] But with the Wahhabi capture of Ha'il in 1921, the Rashidi amirate ceased to be.

It will be remembered that early in his rule the Sharif had attacked the Idrisi of 'Asir and in doing so strengthened the small 'A'id chieftaincy in Abha (the 'Ai'd clan were kinsmen of Husayn), which was a bone in the throat of the Idrisi. With British help, the Idrisi had captured the important port of Qunfudhah in 1916, only to be forced from it by the British in favor of the Sharif. These efforts had important tribal issues as their source. The Idrisi was of service to the British during the war, and he enjoyed a subsidy. But as the war drew to an end, the conflict between Husayn and the Idrisi resurfaced. Husayn's aspirations in 'Asir were made clear in a conversation with Wilson in late 1918. The Sharif demanded to be represented at the surrender of the Ottoman garrisons in Yemen and 'Asir, which had been included in the Arab Kingdom that he believed was promised to him; Wilson reminded him of the treaty HMG had with the Idrisi.

In early 1919 Husayn began a concerted effort to intrigue against the Idrisi. He wanted to see Ibn 'A'id kept in place in Abha,[71] no doubt in order to put pressure on the Idrisi via the tribes in the Abha region. Just as Ibn Saud was able to play on the aspirations of a local amir such as Khalid of Khurmah, Husayn used a similar tactic. He received the allegiance of the head of the 'A'id clan, Hasan ibn 'Ali ibn Muhammad, and sent him a case of treasure. Hasan's loyalty, however, was not absolute – he swore fealty to the Idrisi as well.[72]

When the Idrisi fought back by sending emissaries to tribes in northern 'Asir and southern Hijaz, Husayn complained that he now felt surrounded by two threatening movements, that of the Idrisi and that of Ibn Saud. In May 1919 the Sharif sent some officials to Qunfudhah – to the Idrisi's chagrin, since the latter had

70 FO 686/19, excerpt from *al-Qiblah*, no. 401, 18 July 1920.
71 FO/686/40, Wilson to Wingate, 24 November, enclosing Conversation with King at British Agency 12/11/18; *AB*, no. 76. 13 January 1918.
72 *AB*, no. 109 6 February 1919; FO 406/42/63908, Political Resident (Aden), to High Commissioner 9 October 1919. Hasan was probably playing Husayn against the Idrisi (FO 371/4162/27040, Cheetham to Curzon, no. 57, enclosing report by N.W. Clayton, Liaison Officer with the Idrisi, to Resident [Aden], 18 December 1918). Hogarth believed this to be the case (FO 371/4162/50574, Note on Aden despatch S no. C–195 of February 27, 1919, date 7 March 1919).

hoped to have the issue of that port's sovereignty adjudicated after the war.[73]

The tenor of events changed after 'Abdallah's Turabah débâcle. Fearful of Ibn Saud, Husayn made an overture to the Idrisi, who agreed to accept his 'nominal but not effective suzerainty' if the Sharif would grant him Qunfudhah; the Idrisi also agreed to attack Ibn Saud.[74] But Husayn seemed to prefer undermining the Idrisi rather than reaching an alliance with him, although he might have been able to use his help against Ibn Saud. In August, several relatives of Hasan Al 'A'id arrived in Mecca. They returned to Abha in October, with an agent of Husayn, Sharif 'Abdallah ibn Hamza; but upon their arrival, Hasan was deposed by local tribesmen stirred up by the Idrisi. 'Abdallah ibn Hamza fled after his house was bombed, and other members of the Al 'A'id went down to Jizan to ask a pardon for Hasan.[75] Meanwhile, in August, the Idrisi had received a messenger from Ibn Saud.[76]

Ibn Saud considered the area around Abha a fertile ground for Wahhabi propaganda and had sent proselytizers there at the request of members of the Ghamid, Zahran, and Qahtan, who disliked Hasan Al 'A'id's rule. Ibn Saud warned Hasan to leave the tribes alone, and when Hasan told him to mind his own business the Wahhabi amir sent his trusted lieutenant and relative 'Abd a-'Aziz ibn Musa'id ibn Jilawi (Ibn Musa'id) to Abha, which he captured in May 1920. Ibn Musa'id was then authorized to move against the pro-Sharifian Banu Shihr to the south (it will be remembered that 'Abdallah's mother was of that tribe). Hasan was taken back to Riyadh for 're-education', and by July he was back in Abha, supposedly loyal to a new Idrisi–Saudi alliance.[77]

Yet Hasan was still capable of raising a following. It was reported in July 1920 that – still enjoying full Sharifian support – he had attacked Idrisi forces near Abha. Apparently, driven by *Ikhwan* atrocities in Abha, some of the tribes had flocked to the Al

[73] FO 686/16, Wilson to Arbur, no. W. 827, 10 January 1919; *AB*, no. 113, 17 July 1919.

[74] FO 686/18, High Commissioner to FO, no. 1122, 18 July 1919.

[75] *Al-Qiblah*, 1 September 1919; *AB*, no. 113, 17 July 1919; Kostiner, *The Making*, p. 44; FO 406/43/171711: Political Resident (Aden), to HCL, 31 December 1919; Political Resident (Aden), to HCL, 28 February 1919; FO 882/22: Batten (Jeddah) to Arbur, no. V. 46, 10 May 1920; Arbur to British Agent, 13 May 1920.

[76] *Notes on the Middle East* (NOME), no. 1, 7 December 1919. NOME was the successor to the *AB*.

[77] Goldrup, p. 369.

'A'id; the Idrisi himself, by now very concerned about the *Ikhwan*, was having second thoughts about an alliance with Ibn Saud.[78] Husayn took advantage the Idrisi's indecision to attempt a reconciliation with him. When Sayyid Muhammad al-Sanusi, the latter's cousin, was in Mecca on *hajj* in August 1920, Husayn pampered him and implored him to put in a good word with the Idrisi, saying, Ibn Saud is 'the enemy of us all.'[79] The Sanusi returned to 'Asir with conciliatory letters from 'Abdallah and Husayn, but the Idrisi told the British representative that the Sharif was treacherous and could not be trusted; if he were serious, he proclaimed, let him turn over Qunfudhah. He would agree to a treaty with Husayn only if it were guaranteed by the British. In any event, he emphasized, there could be no real peace as long as the Sharif was in power. HMG, while expressing support for an agreement in principle, refused to guarantee it and warned the Idrisi that an alliance which would attack Ibn Saud would be viewed with the greatest of concern.[80]

But the Idrisi was doing poorly in a war with the Imam of Yemen, and he now sought any means of maintaining his rule. He thus began to negotiate both with Husayn and Ibn Saud in mid-1921. Exchanges with the Sharif amounted to little, but he and Ibn Saud signed a document of alliance in about April.[81]

By the summer of 1922, the area around Abha was more an area of conflict between Husayn and Ibn Saud than between Husayn and the Idrisi. Faysal ibn 'Abd al-'Aziz Al Sa'ud entered Abha victoriously in October. Husayn's Banu Shihr fled, as did Hasan ibn

[78] FO 406/44/E 8377, Acting Political Resident (Aden) to Curzon, 2 July 1920; See also letters from Hasan (signed ('Amir of Asir') and his kinsman to Husayn in FO 686/26, Acting British Agent to Director, Arab Bureau, 31 July 1920; FO 371/5148/E 12528, Scott (Cairo) to Curzon, no. 1109, 30 September 1920.

[79] FO 682/12, Report by Captain Mian Nasir-ud-din (Mecca) for the period ending 8 August, 1920; FO 371/5148/E 13108, Resident (Aden) to FO, no. 360 AP, 22 October 1920;

[80] FO 371/5148/E 13233, Political Resident (Aden) to Curzon, no. 26 14 October 1920; FO 686/19, Curzon to British Agent, no. 22, 10 December 1920.

[81] FO 371/7719/E 694: Correspondence between Husayn and the Idrisi, communicated by the Colonial Office, 18 January 1922; E 3836, Colonial Office to FO, 10 April 1922. Later negotiations between Husayn and the Idrisi, carried out by the Arab–American Amin al-Rihani in June 1922, also amounted to nothing; the British did not expect them to, because whereas the Idrisi was 'well intentioned,' the Sharif by this time was being referred to as 'the demented Hussein' (FO 371/7719/E 8402, Communication by Colonial Office, 23 August 1922; and minute by Bentinck, 24 August 1922.)

'A'id. Husayn sent 500 soldiers to support another local amir (Sharif 'Abdallah ibn Hamza al-Fa'ar of Qunfudhah), but the intervention was a total failure. The Saudis eventually caught up with Hasan, who, it was reported, retired in Riyadh on a pension from Ibn Saud.[82] In April 1923 a Hijazi force besieged Abha in order to collect taxes.[83] According to one report the area was actually occupied on behalf of Hasan Ibn 'A'id.[84] But Husayn's government and military were in a shambles, and the force soon withdrew.[85]

The Idrisi died of natural causes in March 1923, and a battle for succession ensued which lasted well into 1924, and even beyond.[86] By then, however, Husayn was no longer a factor.

Relations with both the Idrisi and Ibn Rashid demonstrated the importance of the interactions of smaller tribal confederations with bigger ones. By gaining the loyalty of parts of tribes, opposing rulers could cause much trouble.

From Turabah to Ta'if: the eastern tribes, encroachment and invasion, 1919–1924

The diplomatic history of the relations between Husayn, Ibn Saud, and the British until the fall of Mecca is well-travelled scholarly ground.[87] Our purpose here is to give a short account of the milestones in the development of this triangle as well as to add to our knowledge by demonstrating its implications for Husayn's rule at home in the Hijaz.

Kostiner has drawn our attention to the fact that writers in Arabic have referred to Saudi encroachment in the Hijaz as a *zahf*, or crawling.[88] While it may have been possible soon after Turabah for a Wahhabi invasion to take place, the attack on Ta'if did not occur until September 1924. Ibn Saud had his reasons for taking

---

[82] Kostiner, *The Making*, pp. 53–4; Goldrup, p. 371–2.

[83] Goldrup, p. 372.

[84] FO 371/8953/E 417, Acting British Consul to FO, no. 19, 25 April 1923.

[85] *Al-Qiblah*, no. 686, 10 May 1923.

[86] FO 371/8953: E 3757, Communication from Colonial Office, 12 April 1923; E 5572, Communication from the Colonial Office, 30 May 1923; FO 371/10007/E 11374, Communication from Colonial Office, 15 December 1924.

[87] See, in particular, Gary Troeller, *The Birth of Saudi Arabia: Britain and the Rise of the House of Saud* (London: Cass, 1976), and the more recent Haifa Alangary, *The Struggle for Power in Arabia: Ibn Saud, Hussein, and Great Britain, 1914–1924* (Reading, England: Ithaca Press, 1998).

[88] Kostiner, *The Making*, p. 62.

his time – improved relations with the British and a consolidation of his presence in 'Asir and Jabal Shammar. Also during this period Khalid worked at eroding Husayn's tribal support, initially in the Wadi Subay' area, and soon after in the Hijaz proper. When the invasion came, Husayn had nearly no support.

In September 1919 Husayn's threats to resign and let Ibn Saud take over became more frequent as the latter grew stronger and it became known that the British would not support Husayn's aspirations beyond the Hijaz at the expense of their French allies.[89] Following the visit of the Saudi delegation to London in November 1919, which left a good impression, Wilson was instructed to urge Husayn to meet with Ibn Saud in Cairo, Jeddah, or Aden; if Husayn agreed, he could expected to be invited to London himself. Husayn agreed to meet Ibn Saud in Jeddah,[90] calculating, as the British did not, that he would refuse. The Wahhabi leader countered by demanding that Husayn come himself and offered the venues of Baghdad or Bombay,[91] knowing, of course, that Husayn had not left the Hijaz since the campaign in 'Asir, before the war.

The approaching pilgrimage in August 1920 had become an issue between the two men. Ibn Saud demanded it as his right to make the pilgrimage[92] – and it would be a way of extending the Wahhabi *da'wah* to the Hijaz. For Husayn, allowing Ibn Saud to do so would look like weakness. Significantly, the British took the view that the pilgrimage was an issue of religious freedom, and pressured Husayn to let the Najdis come.

In early May 1920 Ibn Saud and Husayn were invited to a meeting on board a British ship in Aden Harbor. Before the proposed meeting, Husayn was asked to permit the Najdi pilgrimage, Ibn Saud to guarantee the behavior of his subjects, and both 'to maintain the *existing truce* between them over the pilgrimage season.' If these conditions were not met, the two rulers were told,

89 FO 686/26, Political Report on the Hedjaz, 21 September 1919; FO 686/42, FO to Allenby, 15 November 1919.
90 FO 371/5061/E 3916, Secretary's Note, Interdepartmental Conference on Middle Eastern Affairs, undated, covering the period 15 November 1919 to 27 April 1920 (henceforth, Secretary's Note); FO 371/4147/156472, FO to Colonel Wilson, 1 December 1919.
91 Secretary's Note.
92 Secretary's Note.

they could not 'reasonably expect a continuation of financial or other support from His Majesty's Government.'[93]

That was the ultimatum from far-away London; but in reality there was absolutely no 'existing truce' between the protagonists. In November 1919 Ibn Saud's *ma'mur* (representative) at Turabah, Muhammad ibn Ibrahim ibn Sultan, had sent out letters to 'Abdallah's 'Utaybah demanding that they join him with rifles, horses, and camels.[94] On 8 March 1920, forces loyal to Ibn Saud had raided and burned two villages 32 kilometers south-east of Ta'if, killing some of the residents.[95] The following month, it was reported that Khalid's men had occupied al-Hanakiyyah, three days east of Medina on the road to Qasim; a village in the same area headed by Shaykh Ibn Mujid of the Masruh Harb was attacked and looted.[96] These raids had an extremely detrimental effect in the Hijaz, particularly in and around Ta'if. The notables sent their families away, no one was tending the town's famous gardens, and the road to Mecca was considered unsafe despite payments to the surrounding tribes by Sharif Shakir. Trade between the Hijaz and Najd stopped, and prices rose sharply in Mecca. As a result, starvation ensued and people began to die in the streets.[97]

Under these circumstances Husayn was hardly in a concilia-tory mood. His reply to the British ultimatum was a petulant assent to a meeting with Ibn Saud and to a Najdi pilgrimage. Husayn said, 'I will see him but will not talk to him [about] any-thing because I consider it useless.' He did not agree, however, to a specific meeting.[98] Ibn Saud's reply was respectful and to the point; he said that he preferred the Mecca area as the meeting place; the meaning of this was that he would come on *hajj*. He also

---

93 FO 371/5061/E 3798, FO to Allenby, 4 May 1920 (emphasis mine); message delivered to Husayn on 19 May (FO 686/18, British Agent to HM The King, 19 May 1920).

94 FO 868/18, Abdallah to Vickery, 15 November 1919, enclosing letter from Muhammad ibn Ibrahim ibn Sultan to Abdallah ibn Turki and all he sees of the ETEIBA who are with the Sherif, 28 October 1919.

95 Secretary's Note.

96 FO 686/12, Intelligence Report, Captain Ajab Khan (Mecca), 8 April 1920.

97 FO 686/12, Intelligence Report, Captain Ajab Khan (Mecca), 17 March 1920; Intelligence Report, Captain Ajab Khan (Mecca), 28 March 1920; FO 686/12, Intelligence Report, Ihsanullah (Mecca), 8 April 1920; FO 686/26, Report, 22 April–1 May, 1920.

98 FO 686/18, Abdallah to British Agent, 28 May 1920.

stressed that he would observe the truce, although he was not doing so. London sent its endorsement of Ibn Saud's idea to Husayn.[99]

But Husayn grew more intractable by the day. The British Agent believed that Husayn was afraid to leave the Hijaz for fear of a revolt,[100] and in fact Ibn Saud's reach was getting closer and closer. Husayn had good reason to wonder how long the Hijazi populace would remain loyal to him. While these discussions were under way, he reported the Wahhabi occupation of al-Suwayrqiyyah and Safinah, located about halfway between Ta'if and Medina, and asked the British for armored cars and twelve planes.[101] The Sharif also reported that Ibn Saud's *ma'mur* in Turabah had attacked a village only two hours from Ta'if, killing one sharif 'Abdallah.[102] Husayn suggested – with a certain degree of wry obduracy, we might imagine – that the meeting take place in Ibn Saud's territory.[103] He also demanded that the Najdis come by sea when making the pilgrimage to avoid creating internal problems for him as they traversed the Hijaz. Finally, he offered his resignation, as he felt he had been let down by the British government. Allenby viewed this letter as a refusal to meet with Ibn Saud.[104]

Having decided to force Husayn's hand the FO replied to his letter as if it assumed that he had agreed to a Meccan rendezvous. It informed Ibn Saud of this, asking him to take with him a small number of men to the meeting. Husayn was greatly upset by this *fait accompli.*[105] It will be remembered that in mid-1920 Husayn's subsidy was being discussed in London; at this juncture HMG

99 FO 371/5063/E 8912, three letters from Ibn Saud, dated 23 May 1920, enclosed in Political Agent, Bahrain, to Civil Commissioner, Baghdad, no. 155–C, 7 June 1920; FO 371/5062/E 6859, FO to Allenby, no. 556, 21 June 1920.

100 FO 686/26, Political Report 22 June–2 July 19210.

101 FO 371/5062/E 6922, Allenby to FO, no. 604, 20 June 1920. Suwayrqiyyah was the headquarters of Shaykh Furn, chief of the Bani 'Awf, a sub-tribe of the Harb.

102 FO 371/5062/E 6778, Allenby to FO, no. 593, 18 June 1920.

103 FO 686/26, Political Report 22 June–2 July 1920.

104 FO 686/18, King Hussein to British Agent, 26 June 1920; FO 371/5062/E 7499, Allenby to FO, 30 June 1920. These discussions, it should be remembered also took place against the British abandonment of Faysal to the French in Syria in the summer of 1920.

105 FO 371/5062/E 7449: FO to Allenby, no. 600, 2 July; FO to Allenby, no. 601, 2 July (copy of message to Ibn Saud); FO 371/5093/E 9285, King Hussein to British Agent, no. 178, 6 July 1920.

proposed to Husayn that he be given £30,000 for agreeing to the Najdi pilgrimage and a meeting with Ibn Saud. It was hoped, Allenby wrote to Husayn, that he would be as generous as Ibn Saud had been conciliating.[106]

Husayn bridled, calling the offer what it was – a bribe. He absolved himself of all responsibility and again offered his resignation. Ibn Saud could do what he wanted, said Husayn, but 'I will not discuss with him any subject.'[107] In contrast Ibn Saud made the British task easier by sending a small delegation. Also, claiming insufficient time to prepare, he decided not to make the *hajj* himself. The British appreciated the gesture and Ibn Saud was thanked for the 'statesmanlike manner' in which he had dealt with the situation.[108]

The Najdi delegation to the 1920 pilgrimage numbered only thirty-two persons, and was headed by Ahmed Ibn Thunayan, the trusted lieutenant who had accompanied Ibn Saud's son Faysal to London in November 1919. Husayn did not hide his bitterness. He told the British Agent that he had expected more support from HMG, because the Hijaz had fought alongside Britain during the war, while Najd had been a mere spectator – and now the Hijaz was despised and belittled. He told the British Indian Muslims deputed to accompany Thunayan that he had demanded that Britain assure him the *status quo ante*; if this were not forthcoming, Ibn Saud could take over the Hijaz, for all he cared. But negotiations continued, Husayn's sons acting in his stead. 'Abdallah produced a copy of the 1915 Treaty between Britain and Ibn Saud (or perhaps an earlier draft) and pointed to Article 6, which stated that Ibn Saud could not make territorial adjustments without the consent of HMG. 'Ali then produced an Ottoman record book from 1910, showing emoluments of officials from Khurmah and Turabah with those from the Hijaz, an indication, he contended, that the two villages were part of Husayn's territory. During the

---

106 FO 371/5062/E 8300, FO to Allenby, no. 654, 7 July 1920; FO 686/19, Arbur to Marshall, no. A.B. 360, 20 July 1920.

107 FO 686/19, Hussein to British Agent, no. 188, 23 July 1920; FO 686/26, Political Report 1–10 August 1920; FO 686/19, King Hussein to British Agent, no. 196, 31 July 1920.

108 FO 371/5063/E 11854, Ibn Saud to Political Agent, Bahrain, 16 July 1920, enclosed in latter to Civil Commissioner, Baghdad, no. 215–C, 26 July 1920; FO 371/5093/E 9111, Civil Commissioner, Baghdad, no. 9028, to Political Agent, Bahrain, 27 July 1920.

talks, it became clear that Ibn Saud had not given Thunayan authority to negotiate on borders.[109] That being the case, 'Abdallah and Thunayan reached an agreement which amounted only to a truce, with the case to be submitted to the British. 'Abdallah signed for the Hijaz, as his father refused to do so. To the British Agent, the whole episode was illustrative of Husayn's 'obstinacy and chicanery.'[110]

There being no real truce, Khalid, with or without the consent of Ibn Saud, continued to raid in the direction of Ta'if. Husayn reported that no sooner had the Najdi delegation left, than on 20 September Ibn Saud's men from Khurmah and Turabah attacked the tribe of Quraysh only 30 kilometers from Ta'if, killing nine and taking twenty-one camels.[111] In October there was a skirmish at Safinah, a village on the eastern Mecca–Medina road, and the tribes around Medina were reported to be leaning towards Ibn Saud.[112] And, at the end of the year, support for the Saudis was reported to be on the rise among the urban populations of Mecca and Jeddah. Batten wrote that one-half of the 'better class' and one-third of the poor of Jeddah were reported to be in favor of Ibn Saud. While in the outlying areas the motive was fear, in Mecca and Jeddah the motive was 'genuine disgust with malpractices ... and a reaction against the present state of affairs under King Hussein.'[113]

Amir 'Ali, who was responsible for the tribes around Medina, attempted a parley with Khalid at Wadi Liyyah, only about four hours from Ta'if, at the end of 1920 or the beginning of the next year; the village of Liyyah itself was occupied by the Wahhabis.

109 FO 371/5064/E 12125: Hussein to British Agent, no. 212, 1 September 1920; letter to Seyyed Sadik Hassan Khan Sahib and Sheikh Farhan Bey Rahamat, 1 September 1920; Acting British Agent to Director, Arab Bureau, 5 September 1920. Thunayan, by the way, reported that he was not received courteously, as befitting 'our position and that of our Hakim .... We really feel ourselves insulted ... especially when we saw the relations and tribesmen of Bin Rashid and they way the were treated.' (FO 371/5064, Ahmed Al Thenyan to Bin Saud, n.d., probably late September 1920).

110 FO 371/5064/E 12144: Extracts from Report by Major W. Batten, Acting British Agent, Jeddah, for period 1–10 September 1920; Agreement made between Nejd Deputation and King Hussein's Committee, 3 September 1920; FO 686/19, Arbur to Batten, 20 September 1920.

111 FO 686/19, King to Acting British Agent, 24 September 1920.

112 FO 686/12, Nasiruddin Ahmad (Mecca) to Batten, 12, 13 October 1920.

113 FO 686/26, Jeddah Report 11– 20 December 1920.

When 'Ali's lieutenant questioned Khalid about having his forces so close to Ta'if, the latter replied that he now spoke in the name of Sharif Hamzah al-Fa'ar, as well all the 'Utaybah of Sharifs Hamud and even Shakir. They had sworn loyalty to him, and he had come to collect taxes from them. Hamzah, who was subsequently reprimanded by Husayn, protested his innocence, but instructions were given for the destruction of his property in Wadi Liyyah if Khalid moved on Ta'if.

The *ashraf* of Ta'if were by now wavering in their loyalties. By at the latest the beginning of 1921, and most likely even sooner, the 'Utaybah along the border had almost completely gone over to Ibn Saud.[114]

Husayn's growing weakness, and the concurrent growth in Khalid's power, was reflected in an offer reliably reported to the British Agent. Husayn relayed to Khalid that he could be confirmed as amir of Khurmah and given a free hand if he acknowledged Husayn as his suzerain and repudiated Ibn Saud. Here Husayn may have been trying to take advantage of Khalid's dispute with Ibn Saud over his desire to invade the Hijaz immediately. Sharif Sharaf was also reported to be in contact with Khalid.[115]

Ibn Saud's preoccupation with Jabal Shammar seems to have been responsible for a decrease in tribal trouble on the seam between Najd and Hijaz in 1921. Some raiding was reported, which Husayn tried to use to convince the British that he deserved more funds, planes, and armored cars. He absolved himself of responsibility if the Wahhabis came on this year's pilgrimage.[116] He was, however, saved the embarrassment of a Najdi *hajj*, as Ibn Saud was indeed involved in capturing Jabal Shammar's main town, Ha'il, which finally fell in November 1921. Lawrence reported Husayn to be quite agitated over its fall.[117] The British had begged Ibn Saud to put off the pilgrimage, and his decision to

---

114 FO 686/12, Ihsanulla (Mecca) to the British Agent, 1 January 1920; FO 686/27, Jeddah Report 11–20 January 1921.

115 FO 686/27, Jeddah Report 21–30 January 1921; FO 686/93, Lawrence to Prodrome London (Curzon), 2 August 1921.

116 FO 686/27, Jeddah Report 11–20 May 1921; FO 371/6238/E 5693, Marshall to FO, no. 49, 17 May 1921; FO 371/6240/E 5834: Hussein to General Haddad (London), 16 May 1921; Faisal to General Haddad (London), 16 May 1921.

117 FO 686/19, Lawrence to Prodrome, 2 December 1921.

forgo a Najdi *hajj* had the result of increasing his standing in London.[118]

In August Husayn's military position was reported to be extremely weak, but Khalid's distrust of Ibn Saud seemed to prevent what Khalid estimated to be an easy march to Mecca. In October 1921, Sharifian forces acquitted themselves well against Khalid's forces at a location 60 kilometers east of Ta'if.[119]

With the fall of Rashidi-ruled Ha'il in late 1921, Husayn's fear of a Wahhabi thrust at the tribes north and east of Medina intensified. Most ominous was the possibility of a move through al-'Ula to Wajh, on the coast, cutting off a significant part of the northern Hijaz. In an attempt to forestall this development, Husayn began to intrigue with the defeated Muhammad ibn Talal Ibn Rashid, who was under house arrest in Riyadh, by offering him arms. Ibn Saud intercepted their communications, which led Cox, High Commissioner of Iraq, to remark, '[W]e shall never have relief until [Husayn] is eliminated.' When HMG complained to Husayn about his communications with Ibn Rashid, Husayn remonstrated that while Ibn Saud was being given every advantage by London, he was not allowed to make the alliances necessary to defend himself.[120]

Ibn Saud now had the Shammar in the north and was active along the border between the Hijaz and 'Asir in the south and west. In mid-March 1922, Ibn Saud attacked tribes between 'Asir and Hijaz; in May it was reported that the main tribes in this area, Ghamid and Zahran, had gone over to him.[121]

The British still expected Husayn to allow a Najdi pilgrimage in 1922. The Sharif was indignant: he had 'risked his whole existence in those disasters the peril of which was certain and the

---

118 FO 371/6241/E 7664, High Commissioner for Mesopotamia to Bahrain, no. 251, 1 July 1921; FO 371/6242/E 9716, High Commissioner for Mesopotamia to Secretary of State for the Colonies, no. 414, 24 August 1921; FO 371/7711/E 2566, Minute by Carnegie, 8 March 1922.

119 FO 686/93, Lawrence to Prodrome, 2 August 1921; FO 686/27, Jeddah Report 11–30 October 1921.

120 FO 686/19, Acting British Agent to High Commissioner (Baghdad), 13 February 1922; FO 371/7711/E 2249, High Commissioner for Iraq to Secretary of State for the Colonies, no. 154, 27 February 1922; FO 371/7712, Hussein to British Agent, no. 96, 26 April 1922.

121 FO 372/7712/E 3008, Fu'ad [al-Khatib] to FO, no. 14, 18 March 1922; FO/371/7713/E 5137, Marshall (Jeddah) to FO, no. 30, 18 May 1922.

results of which are still unknown,' while he had stood firmly by Great Britain during the evacuation of the Dardanelles and the fall of Kut-al-Amara, 'a grave and dreadful combination of circumstances.' Husayn told the British representative Marshall that he had 'become the victim of my trust and reliance on British honour.'[122] Husayn again offered to let the Najdis come by sea but soon retracted. 'If I hear of the arrival of even a small party of them,' he said, 'I will at once leave Mecca and go down to Jeddah.' Since many of the Ghamid and Zahran had taken refuge in Mecca, he would not be held responsible if they took revenge on the Wahhabis.[123]

When told that the Najdis would have to be allowed to make the pilgrimage, Husayn backpedalled, saying that he would accept villagers but not nomads. He added another impossible condition: he must be provided with four airplanes, to be under his command. He repudiated all responsibility for what might happen to the Najdis if they came.[124]

While Husayn threatened disaster, the British prevailed upon Ibn Saud to limit the size of his contingent, which he agreed to do. To the Foreign Office in London he again appeared to be one who had 'behaved well and ha[d] shown loyalty to His Majesty's Government. Moreover, of all chieftains in Arabia he alone has shown signs of statesmanship.' Husayn, on the other hand, was now viewed by some British officials as being 'practically demented.'[125]

This impression of the faltering Sharif was strengthened by another Hashimite about-face. Ibn Saud agreed that all Najdi pilgrims would be settled villagers, and he asked that his good wishes be sent to Husayn. Husayn was reported to be delighted. About 1800 Najdis made the pilgrimage, and the Hashimites told the British Agent in Jeddah that they gave the Najdis a cordial recep-

---

[122] FO 371/7713/E 6547, Hussein to British Agent, 26 May 1922, enclosed in Marshall to Curzon, no. 48, 11 June 1922.

[123] FO 371/7712/E 4409, Marshall to FO, no. 29, 29 April 1922; FO 371/7712/E 6077, Hussein to British Agent, no. 104, 17 May 1922, enclosed in Marshall to Curzon, no. 38, 22 May 1922.

[124] FO 371/7713/E 5884, Marshall to Curzon, no. 38, 11 June 1922; FO 371/7713/E 6034, Hashimite Acting Foreign Minister to FO, no. 580, 15 June 1922.

[125] FO 371/7713: E 6037, Balfour to Marshall, no. 72, 22 June 1922; E 6881, High Commissioner of Iraq to Secretary of State for the Colonies, 6 July 1922; Troeller, p. 177.

tion, even treating some as royal guests.[126] 'Ali reported that he had
sent a friendly letter to Ibn Saud. However, Ibn Saud reported
otherwise.[127] First, thousands of pounds of gold were confiscated
as the pilgrims left the Hijaz, its export being forbidden. More
seriously, a letter sent to Ibn Saud from Husayn ignored his titles,
demanded the restoration of the Rashidi amirate and the return of
certain villages in Qasim, and called on Ibn Saud to relinquish
control of some tribes. It also proposed an alliance against the
British. Otherwise, wrote Husayn, he would abdicate in Ibn
Saud's favor. The letter was read out to the Najdi pilgrims.[128]

Immediately after the 1922 pilgrimage Wahhabi encroachment
was accelerated. Khalid captured Khaybar, removing a strategic
position on the road to Medina,[129] and in September there were
clashes between Ikhwan and the Sharifians at Ukhaydar.[130]
Husayn refused to sanction the Najdi pilgrimage for 1923 unless
Ibn Saud withdrew (he later relented to allow villagers to come).[131]

In late 1922 the British began plans for a conference (later
known as the Kuwait Conference) which would solve the problems in the region. The British envisioned a trade of territory
among the Hijaz, Najd and Transjordan, whereby 'Aqabah would
go to Transjordan, Kaf and much of Wadi Sirhan would go to Ibn
Saud, and the Hijaz would extend as far north as Mudawwarah.
Most important, Husayn would get Khurma and Turabah. But
such desiderata were kept secret from the protagonists.[132] An indication of British disregard for Husayn was that he was not
informed of this conference until just before it took place, in late

[126] FO 371/7713: E 6881, High Commissioner of Iraq to Secretary of State for the Colonies,
no. 484, 8 July 1922; E 6861, Marshall to FO, no. 41, 10 July 1922; FO 371/7714/E 7601,
Marshall to FO, no. 42, 31 July 1922.
[127] FO 371/7714/E 8629, Marshall to Balfour, no. 61, 10 August 1922; FO 686/28: Jeddah
Report 31 August–30 September 1922; Jeddah Report 11–30 August 1922.
[128] FO 371/8936/E 1363, King Hussein's letter dated 12 August 1922 (apparently
addressed to Musa'id [ibn Suwaylim], the head of the Najdi *hajj* delegation, enclosed
in Imam Sir 'Abdul 'Aziz ibn Sa'ud) to His Excellency Sir Percy Cox, 4 September
1922.
[129] Kostiner, p. 64.
[130] FO 686/28, Jeddah Report 31 August–30 September 1922.
[131] FO 371/8937/E 2420, Hussein to British Agent, no. 487, 30 January 1923; FO
371/8938/E 6605, Secretary of State for Foreign Affairs (Mecca) to British Agent, no.
67, 6 June 1923.
[132] Troeller, p. 201; R/15/1/594, Colonial Office to Resident (Bushire), 8 November
1923.

1923. He was humiliated and reminded the British of the high position he had once held with them as a loyal ally and a spokesman for the Arabs.[133] Husayn made demands which were perfectly logical from his standpoint but which were not to Ibn Saud and the British. First, to reintroduce old players in order to maneuver against Ibn Saud, he demanded the re-establishment of the amirates of 'Asir and Jabal Shammar and the evacuation of Wahhabi forces from those areas. Second, he required the compensation of the Juhaynah and the Billi for the recent raids in the Medina area.[134] When these desiderata were not granted, Husayn refused to be represented at the conference. While these communications took place, 'Ali was preparing to retake Khaybar from the Wahhabis; his column included, according to Bullard, 'guns, ammunition and riff-raff dressed as troops.' 'Ali could obviously no longer count on tribal support, as a successful raid by *Ikhwan* leader Faysal al-Duwaysh near al-'Ula proved.[135] By now, Husayn's position had become so desperate that *al-Qiblah* reported a severe earthquake in Najd to be divine vengeance for the evils of Wahhabism.[136]

The conference opened in mid-December 1923 and lasted until April 1924, but it accomplished nothing on the Hijazi–Najd front. Husayn's presumptuous assumption of the caliphate in March 1924 had put an end to even the slightest hope of a Hashimite–Saudi reconciliation.[137]

The failure of the Kuwait Conference was the signal for Ibn Saud to move. He knew that the British would not stand in his way, and he feared the surrounding 'Hashimite tier' of Iraq, Transjordan, and the Hijaz. Moreover, the restraint imposed by his British subsidy had recently been removed;[138] he was also

---

133 FO 686/135, King Hussein to Bullard (Jeddah), 9 September 1923; FO 686/28, Jeddah Report 1–29 November 1923; FO 371/9997/E 1622, Herbert Samuel (High Commissioner, Palestine) to J.H. Thomas (Secretary of State for the Colonies), 1 February 1924, enclosing Memorandum of the interview with King Husain at Amman on the 21 January 1924.

134 Troeller, p. 200.

135 FO 686/28, Jeddah Report 1–29 November 1923; Troeller, p. 199.

136 *Al-Qiblah*, no. 659, 5 February; no. 661, 12 February 1923.

137 Husayn agreed in February 1924 to send his son Zayd to the conference, but Ibn Saud refused to send his son Faysal, leading Husayn to withdraw his offer (Troeller, pp. 207–211).

138 Kostiner, *The Making*, p. 65.

surely aware of the constant erosion of support for Husayn within the Hijaz itself. It was now time, as Ibn Saud's aide Hafiz Wahbah wrote, to 'turn Hussein's many mistakes to the advantage of Nejd' and to be done with him.[139]

For much of the summer there had been repeated Saudi raids into Hashimite Transjordan and Iraq,[140] perhaps diversionary in nature. These were reported falsely in *al-Qiblah* as great Hashimite victories.[141] 'Ali went out to Ta'if at the end of August in a last-ditch effort to garner support among the local tribes and to head off a Wahhabi attack there. Ibn Saud's force left Riyadh on 1 August 1924, and Ta'if was taken on 5 September. 'Ali retired to 'Arafat.[142] Mecca fell in October without a fight; 'Ali held out in Jeddah until December 1925.

The period from 1917 to 1924 was one without triumph for Husayn. Heading a tribal confederacy built up artificially with a temporary influx of British gold, it was no match for the expanding, dynamic confederacy led by Ibn Saud. His grandiose ambitions, initially cultivated by the British, underwent practically no change as his position weakened. He had no counterbalance to the ideology of the Wahhabi movement, which combined with Ibn Saud's statesmanship towards the British to undermine him completely. The British stood by while Ta'if fell, and from there it was not too long before the '*Amir al-Mu'minin*' was forced to abdicate. Neither of Husayn's sons – one in Transjordan and one in Iraq – gave him shelter. Ater spending most of his exile in the decidedly non-Arab country of Cyprus, Husayn died in Amman in 1931.

---

139 Cited in Kostiner, *The Making*, p. 65.
140 Troeller, p. 217.
141 *Al-Qiblah*, no. 817, 5 September 1924.
142 FO 371/10014, Bullard to McDonald, no. 95, 21 September 1924, enclosing memorandum, The Capture of Taif.

10

CONCLUSIONS

This work has examined a case of failed state formation in the Hijaz, a process which was all the more remarkable given the clearly evident advantages Husayn ibn ʿAli enjoyed at the beginning of the Arab Revolt. The primary reason for the state's collapse was Sharif Husayn's failure to adapt to changing circumstances. These changes presented Husayn with several challenges, and he was not up to them; this was a result of both a lack of leadership qualities and developments that were beyond his control.

The Revolt began as an expanding tribal chieftaincy. Initially, Husayn used the massive British subsidy wisely, and through Faysal was able to throw the Ottomans out of the Hijaz, with the notable exception of Medina, which fell only in 1919. A militant *ʿasabiyyah*, based on previous hatred of the Ottomans, was created among the tribes. Initially, even urban élites supported him.

But after the capture of ʿAqabah in the summer of 1917, the chieftaincy lost its dynamic quality. Husayn did not develop into a charismatic leader like his son, Faysal, nor his nemesis, Ibn Saud. The Hijaz itself became a backwater, as expansion continued north. Facing this challenge, a wiser leader would have turned to consolidating his rule at home in the Hijaz. But for Husayn, the Hijaz was not the focus of his best efforts; instead, blinded by ambition, he devoted his energy to attaining what he believed was his right: ruling much of the Arab world. He therefore ignored the need for a sensible administration in the Hijaz and for creating the social cohesion necessary for state formation. His cruel and over-centralized government succeeded only in alienating the important urban and tribal élites. It seems that Husayn was simply not cut out to rule.

Soon after the capture of ʿAqabah he began to lose control very close to home. Not only did he fail to establish any sort of legitimacy or develop the coercive ability to control such areas as parts of 'Asir, Wadi Subay', and Medina, but he even lost the loyalty of the tribes along the key Jeddah–Mecca road. In these localities chieftains were able to thwart all Hashimite rule, and thus achieve in practice virtually independent status. As one Hijazi minister wrote to a French official: '*Tarabah et Khormah ne constituent plus un Emirat comme auparavant mais on travaille activement à y fonder une sorte d'Etat.*'[1]

In contrast, through assiduous coercion and effective Wahhabi propaganda, using the *da'wah* of preachers to reach all levels of society, Ibn Saud gained adherents to his cause. His was a vigorous, expanding chieftaincy at precisely the time when Husayn's chieftaincy was stagnating, its leader ignoring serious problems at home while fecklessly putting his faith in the British.

As Ibn Saud bore down on the Hijaz, the urban and tribal élites abandoned Husayn. The British feigned neutrality, but such a stance amounted to backing for Ibn Saud, as Husayn had built his entire strategy on British support. The Sharif was left hanging, and the *Haramayn* fell to the Wahhabi chieftaincy.

First and foremost, Husayn's state was a failed chieftaincy. It was a weak state, which did not develop the capabilities 'to penetrate society, regulate social relationships, extract resources, and appropriate resources in determined ways.'[2] The élites maintained their distance from him, and he was unable to extract resources in an effective manner.[3]

Husayn's state, as it competed with other social organizations, failed to provide these competitors with the essential tools of survival that would make them loyal to him. His state therefore had very little social control, a factor which was necessary in order for other social organizations to agree to subordinate their own inclinations to those of the state.[4] Sharif Husayn did not provide the Hijazi élites with these tools; on the contrary, his oppression of them

---

[1] SHAT, 7 N 4183, Catroux to Minister of War, 20 June, enclosing Extraits d'une lettre d'un Ministre Chérifien à un notable de Djeddah, 16 June 1919.

[2] Joel Migdal, *Strong Societies and Weak States: State–Society Relations and State Capabilities in the Third World* (Princeton University Press, 1988), pp. 4–5.

[3] Jill Crystal, in her *Oil and Politics in the Gulf: Rulers and Merchants in Kuwait and Qatar* (Cambridge University Press, 1990), p. xii, also draws our attention to the importance of revenue extraction in state formation.

[4] See Migdal, pp. 22, 27–8.

made it difficult for them to make a living. His mismanagement of the *hajj* made them lose money, and he maneuvered the foreign currency exchange rate to his advantage and to their detriment.

There are three indicators of increasing levels of social control: compliance, participation, and legitimation. Husayn only reached the first, compliance, using the most basic of sanctions, force. This is typical of weak states. In contrast, the strongest states enjoy legitimation, which is 'acceptance, even approbation, of the state's rules of the game, its social control, as true and right.' The state's symbolic configuration is accepted. People approve of the social order demanded by the state. They accept the state's governing myths.[5] Husayn could force merchants to exchange money at rates favorable to him, and he could force loans out of them, but the state he created remained far away from legitimation. Indeed, Husayn's and 'Abdallah's ideas of Arab nationalism were accepted not by the élite of the Hijaz but by a new, mostly non-Hijazi élite that went on to rule Syria and later Iraq. Husayn's 'governing myths' were rejected in the Hijaz. On the other hand, the modern states of the Arabian Peninsula, which successfully travelled the long road from chieftaincy to modern state, did achieve large degrees of legitimation and hence social control, no doubt helped by their oil wealth. Their 'governing myths,' such as the unity of 'Saudi' Arabia, were accepted.

Husayn failed in another key area, that of social cohesion or coalescence. Husayn's state was unable to provide a supra-*'asabiyyah*, an overarching group feeling that was superior to the *'asabiyyah* of other social groups. According to Ibn Khaldun, to build a strong state one must supplement this supra-*'asabiyyah* with *iltiham*, a coalescing of the subordinate groups with the ruling group, a process of 'social integration by and around the ideology professed by the ruling' *'asabiyyah*.[6] Unfortunately for Husayn, most of the Hijazi élite saw his rule as disturbing their special

---

[5] Migdal, pp. 32–3.

[6] This understanding of Ibn Khaldun is developed by Ghassan Salame, ' "Strong" and "Weak" States: A Qualified Return to the *Muqaddimah*' in Giacomo Luciani (ed.), *The Arab State* (Berkeley: University of California Press, 1990), pp. 29–64 (quote on p. 32); see also Eric Davis, 'Theorizing Statecraft and Social Change in Arab Oil-Producing Countries,' in Eric Davis and Nicholas Gavrielides, *Statecraft in the Middle East: Oil, Historical Memory and Popular Culture* (Miami: Florida International University Press, 1991), pp. 1–35. Both Salame and Davis acknowledge their debt to Antonio Gramsci and his concept of 'hegemony.'

status under the Ottomans, and were glad to see him go. In a strictly ideological sense, we could say that Husayn failed to generalize his specific brand of Arab nationalism (the primacy of the Arabs in Islam and the primacy of the Hashimites among the Arabs) into a supra-*'asabiyyah* and make it the central ideology of Hijazi society, a justification for his breaking away from what was until then the legitimate political framework, the Ottoman Empire. The Sharif used the *shari'ah* and other symbols in this regard and propagandized via *al-Qiblah*, but he failed. The Ottoman House had enjoyed this type of supra-*'asabiyyah* in the acceptance of its right to rule among the overwhelming majority of its Muslim subjects.

For a state to be strong, coalitions must be established with important élites. A major tool in achieving coalitions is the fabrication of an ideology and symbols that allow the state to forge 'emotive links with the populace over which it rules.' This forging is often done by a reinterpretation of the past to fit the goals of the state; as Davis terms it 'the construction of a particular form of historical memory.' In this work, we have examined Husayn's feeble attempts at coalition building and his failure to establish the important emotive–ideological links with the residents of the Hijaz – in other words, we have studied the Sharif's poor statecraft.

Husayn had poor leadership qualities. He did not know when to coopt, when to ally, and when to fight various social groups which competed with the state. This activity, done properly, is 'statecraft,' which Davis defines as entailing the 'skills whereby political élites or ruling classes promote state formation.'[7]

In states such as Husayn's where extraction is needed in order to survive,[8] the ability to extract revenue is a good measure of state strength.[9] Husayn's weak state was only at the social control level of compliance, and it had to use coercion to extract revenues. Husayn's state lacked the legitimacy which leads a society to say, 'Yes, the state has a right to extract revenues from us.' State forma-

---

[7] Davis, pp. 12–14.

[8] As opposed to so-called 'rentier states' or distributive states such as the oil countries of the Persian Gulf.

[9] Migdal (p. 171) points to Israel as an example of a very strong state, citing as an indicator the fact that in 1979–80 it extracted 36 per cent of its GDP in taxes, higher than any OECD state.

tion is also enhanced when revenues are effectively collected. Such revenue collection was extremely important in the Hijaz, where Husayn's new state had to find the resources to replace the Ottoman subsidies to which Hijazis had been accustomed for hundreds of years. But Husayn failed to collect effectively.

Husayn's kingdom fared poorly in the periphery, another place where the strength of a state may be measured.[10] The case of the peripherally located semi-independent amirate of Khurma is one example of the Hijaz's lack of state capabilities, but this study has shown that state capabilities were extremely weak even in the important city of Medina, and at times even in Jeddah. Failure stood out particularly in the area of security, where Husayn failed to prevent tribal raiding of pilgrimage traffic. British subsidies had fundamentally changed the economy of the Hijaz, with tribal leaders expecting very high pay. When this was not forthcoming, they resumed their raiding.

Husayn could not reconcile himself to the role of Hijazi tribal potentate which the British eventually wished him to play, and he did not adapt to changes in the region's constellation of power. Confronted with the lack of British commitment to his ambitions, he did not significantly alter his goals. In his view, the British had promised him everything; if they felt an obligation to the French, it was their problem. The same was true for Ibn Saud, Husayn believed: the British gave the Wahhabi chieftain a subsidy – let them halt it and recognize the Sharif as the supreme leader. He thus viewed British attempts at reconciling the two protagonists as a betrayal of trust. He was the heir to the Ottoman Empire, with British consent, he believed. Ibn Saud should therefore be brought to heel.

Husayn failed to make the needed transition – not entirely by his own fault – on the stateness continuum from conquest movement to quasi-modern state, what Nettl has called greater 'stateness.'[11] The expanding, dynamic chieftaincy of the Arab Revolt, fueled by British gold and guns, began in 1916 but really ended with the capture of 'Aqabah in the summer of 1917. After that, the Hijaz became a hinterland, while Faysal continued the movement northwards. British mentions of an Arab Caliphate

[10] On success in the periphery as a measure of state strength, see Migdal, pp. 31–2, 182.
[11] See Nettl.

and Arab unity had fallen on the fertile ground of Husayn's mind; he was more concerned with what he saw as his British-guaranteed ambitions rather than consolidating his rule in the Hijaz.

BIBLIOGRAPHY

PRIVATE AND PUBLIC ARCHIVES

Public Record Office, Kew, London

FO 78 General Correspondence, Turkey
FO 141 Egypt, Embassy and Consular Correspondence
FO 195 Embassy and Consular Archives, General Correspondence to Constantinople
FO 371 General Political Correspondence
FO 406 Confidential Print, Eastern Affairs
FO 424 Confidential Print, Turkey
FO 608 Peace Conference of 1919–1920
FO 685 Jeddah Agency Papers
FO 686 Jeddah Agency Papers
FO 882 Arab Bureau Papers
T 1 Treasury Office
WO 33 Confidential Printed Papers
WO 158 Correspondence and Papers of Military Headquarters

India Office Library and Records, London

L/P&S/10 Departmental Papers, Political and Secret Separate Files
L/P&S/11 Departmental Papers, Political and Secret Annual Files
L/P&S/18 Political and Secret Memoranda
R/15 Persian Gulf Residencies

Ministère de la Défense, Service Historique de l'Armée de Terre, Château de Vincennes, Paris

Sous-Série 4H Les Archives du Levant
Sous-Série 6N Fonds Clémenceau
Sous-Série 7N L'Etat-Major de l'Armée (Section de l'Afrique)
Sous-Série 16N Grand Quartier Général-Théâtres d'Opérations Extérieures
Sous-Série 17N Mission Militaire Française en Egypte (Hedjaz)

289

Ministère des Affaires Etrangères, Archives Diplomatiques, Nantes

Djeddah (légation puis ambassade)
Djeddah (consulat)

Archives du Ministère des Affaires Etrangères, Quai d'Orsay, Paris

Série E Levant, 1918–29
Sous-Série Arabie–Hedjaz
Série Guerre, 1914–18
Sous-Série Affaires Musulmanes (Evènements d'Arabie, Hedjaz)

Middle East Centre, St Antony's College, Oxford

J.W.A. Young manuscript
H. St John Bridger Philby Papers

Sudan Archive, Durham University

Sir Reginald Wingate Papers
Sir Gilbert Clayton Papers

Churchill College, Cambridge

George (Lord) Lloyd Papers

Liddell Hart Centre for Military Archives, King's College London

Viscount Allenby Papers
Akaba (Joyce) Papers

PUBLISHED OFFICIAL DOCUMENTS

Admiralty, Naval Intelligence Division. *Geographical Handbook of Western Arabia and the Red Sea*. London: HMSO, 1946.

Admiralty, Naval Intelligence Division. *A Handbook of Arabia*. London: HMSO, 1920.

Arabian Personalities of the Early Twentieth Century. Cambridge: Oleander Press, 1986. rpt. of internal Arab Bureau publication, Cairo, 1917.

Bakhit, Muhammad 'Adnan (ed). *Watha'iq Hashimiyyah*, vol. 7 – *Awraq Abdallah bin al-Husayn: al-Husayn bin 'Ali wal-Bay'ah bil-Khilafah, 1924*. Amman: Jam'iyat Al al-Bayt, 1996.

Foreign Office, Historical Section. *Peace Handbook*. vol 2: *Arabia*. London: HMSO, 1920.

Gooch, G.P. and Harold Temperley (eds.). *British Documents on the Origins of the War, 1898–1914,* vol. X, Part II: *The Last Years of Peace.* London: HMSO, 1938.

Hogarth, D.G. *The Hejaz before World War I: A Handbook.* Cambridge: Oleander Press, 1978. rpt. of internal Arab Bureau publication, Cairo, 1917.

Lorimer, John. *Gazetteer of the Persian Gulf, Oman, and Central Arabia.* Calcutta: Government Printing House, 1908–15.

Al-Rashid, Ibrahim. *Documents on the History of Saudi Arabia.* Salisbury, NC: Documentary Publications, 1970.

NEWSPAPERS AND PERIODICALS

Al-'Arab
Al-Manar
Oriente Moderno (OM)
Al-Qiblah
Revue du Monde Musulman (RMM)

BOOKS AND UNPUBLISHED THESES

Al-'Abadi, Muhammad Yunis. *Al-Rihlah al-Mulukiyyah al-Hashimiyyah.* Amman: Ministry of Culture, 1996.

'Abdallah ibn al-Husayn. *Mudhakkirati.* Jerusalem: n.p., 1945.

Alangary, Haifa. *The Struggle for Power in Arabia: Ibn Saud, Hussein and Great Britain, 1914–1924.* Reading, UK: Ithaca Press, 1998.

Al-Album al-Hashimi. Amman: Matabi' al-Shams, 1994.

Almana, Muhammad. *Arabia Unified.* London: Hutchinson Benham, 1980.

Alorabi, Abdulrahman. 'The Ottoman Policy in the Hijaz in the Eighteenth Century: A Study of Political and Administrative Developments, 1143–1202 AH/1735–1788 AD.' Unpublished PhD dissertation. University of Utah, 1988.

Altorki, Soraya and Donald Cole. *Arabian Oasis City: The Transformation of 'Unayzah.* Austin: University of Texas Press, 1989.

Al-Amr, Saleh Muhammad. *The Hejaz under Ottoman Rule, 1869–1914: Ottoman Vali, the Sharif of Mecca, and the Growth of British Influence.* Riyadh University Publications, 1978.

Anderson, Lisa. *The State and Social Transformation in Tunisia and Libya, 1830–1980.* Princeton University Press, 1986.

Anscombe, Frederick F. *The Ottoman Gulf: The Creation of Kuwait, Saudi Arabia, and Qatar.* New York: Columbia University Press, 1997.

Antonius, George. *The Arab Awakening.* London: Hamish Hamilton, 1939.

'Arif Ahmad 'Abd al-Ghani. *Ta'rikh Umara' al-Madinah al-Munawwarah*. Damascus: Dar Kinan lil-Tiba'ah wal-Tawzi' wal-Nashr, 1996.

Arnold, Thomas. *The Caliphate*. London: Routledge & Kegan Paul, 1965.

Arthur, George. *Life of Lord Kitchener* vol. 3. New York: Macmillan, 1920.

Ayalon, Ami. *The Press in the Arab Middle East: A History*. New York: Oxford University Press, 1995.

Baker, Randall. *King Husain and the Kingdom of the Hejaz*. Cambridge, UK: Oleander Press, 1979.

Bang, Anne K. *The Idrisi State in 'Asir, 1906–1934: Politics, Religion and Personal Prestige as Statebuilding Factors in Early Twentieth-Century Arabia*. Bergen, Norway: Centre for Middle Eastern and Islamic Studies, 1996.

Al-Batanuni, Muhammad Labib. *Al-Rihlah al-Hijaziyyah*. Cairo: n.p., 1329 (1911).

Batatu, Hanna. *The Old Social Classes and the Revolutionary Movements in Iraq*. Princeton University Press, 1978.

Ben Dor, Gabriel. *State and Conflict in the Middle East*. Boulder, CO: Westview Press, 1983.

Berkes, Niyazi. *The Development of Secularism in Turkey*. London: Hurst, 1998, reprint of 1964 edition.

Al-Biladi, 'Atiq ibn Ghayth. *Mu'jam Qaba'il al-Hijaz*. 3 vols. Mecca: Dar Makka lil-Nashr wal-Tawzi', 1979.

———. *Nasab al-'Arab: Qabilat Harb*. Mecca: Dar Makka lil-Nashr wal-Tawzi', 1984.

Brémond, E. *Le Hedjaz dans la Guerre Mondiale*. Paris: Payot, 1931.

Buchan, John. *Greenmantle*. London: Nelson, 1916.

Bullock, David. *Allenby's War: The Palestine–Arabian Campaigns, 1916–1918* London: Blandford, 1988.

Burckhardt, John Lewis. *Travels in Arabia*. London: Cass, 1968.

Burj, Muhammad 'Abd al-Rahman. *Muhibb al-Din al-Khatib wa-Dawruhu fi al-Harakah al-'Arabiyyah, 1906–1920*. Cairo: al-Hay'ah al-Misriyyah al-'Ammah lil-Kitab, 1990.

Burton, Sir Richard F. *Pilgrimage to al-Madinah and Meccah*. Edited by Isabel Burton. 2 vols. New York: Dover, 1964.

Busch, Cooper Briton. *Britain, India and the Arabs 1914–1921*. Berkeley: University of California Press, 1971.

Catroux, Général. *Deux Missions en Moyen-Orient, 1919–1922*. Paris: Plon, 1958.

Colman, Ronald. 'Revolt in Arabia, 1916–1919: Conflict and Coalition in a Tribal Political System.' Unpublished PhD dissertation, Columbia University, 1976.

Commins, David Dean. *Islamic Reform: Politics and Social Change in Late Ottoman Syria*. New York: Oxford University Press, 1990.

Coulson, Noel J. *A History of Islamic Law*. Edinburgh University Press, 1964.

Crystal, Jill. *Oil and Politics in the Gulf: Rulers and Merchants in Kuwait and Qatar*. Cambridge University Press, 1990.

Dawn, C. Ernest. *From Ottomanism to Arabism: Essays in the Origins of Arab Nationalism*. Urbana: University of Illinois Press, 1973.

De Gaury. *Rulers of Mecca*. London: Harrap, 1951.

Didier, Charles. *Sojourn with the Grand Sherif of Makkah*. Translated by Richard Boulind. Cambridge, UK: Oleander Press, 1985.

Djemal, Pasha. *Memories of a Turkish Statesman 1913–1919*. New York: Arno, 1973.

Dohaish, Abdullah Abdullatif. *History of Education in the Hijaz up to 1925*. Cairo: n.p., 1978.

Donner, Fred. *The Early Islamic Conquests*. Princeton University Press, 1981.

Duguet, Firman. *Le Pèlerinage de La Mecque au point de vue religieux, social et humanitaire*. Paris: Geuthner, 1932.

El-Edroos, Brigadier Syed Ali. *The Hashimite Arab Army, 1908–1979: An Appreciation and Analysis of Military Operations*. Amman: Publishing Committee, 1980.

Eickelman, Dale. *The Middle East: An Anthropological Approach*. Englewood Cliffs, NJ: Prentice-Hall, 1988.

Eldar, Dan. 'Ha-Mediniut ha-Tsarfatit ve-Yahasah la-Leumiyut ha-'Aravit ula-Tziyonut beyn ha-Shanim 1914–1920.' Unpublished PhD dissertation, Tel Aviv University, 1978.

Faroqhi, Suraiya. *Pilgrims and Sultans: The Hajj under the Ottomans, 1517–1683*. London: I.B. Tauris, 1994.

Farmayan, Hafez and Elton L. Daniel (eds.), *A Shi'ite Pilgrimage to Mecca, 1885–1886: The Safarnameh of Mirza Mohammad Hosayn Farahani*. Austin: University of Texas Press, 1990.

Field, Michael. *The Merchants: The Big Business Families of Arabia*. London: John Murray, 1984.

Findley, Carter. *Bureaucratic Reform in the Ottoman Empire: The Sublime Porte, 1789–1922*. Princeton University Press, 1980.

Fromkin, David. *A Peace to End All Peace: The Fall of the Ottoman Empire and the Creation of the Modern Middle East*. New York: Avon, 1990.

Gaudefroy-Demombynes, Maurice. *Le Pèlerinage à la Mecque*. Paris: Librarie Orientaliste, 1923.

Gellner, Ernest. *Muslim Society*. Cambridge University Press, 1981.

Ghawanimah, Hanadi Yusuf. *Al-Mamlakah al-Hashimiyyah al-Hijaziyyah*. Amman: Dar al-Fikr lil-Nashr wal-Tawzi', 1989.

Goldberg, Jacob. *The Foreign Policy of Saudi Arabia: The Formative Years, 1902–1918*. Harvard University Press, 1986.

Goldrup, Lawrence. 'Saudi Arabia, 1902–1932.' Unpublished PhD dissertation, University of California, Los Angeles, 1971.

Habib, John. *Ibn Sa'ud's Warriors of Islam: The Ikhwan of Najd and Their Role in the Creation of the Saudi Kingdom, 1910–1930.* Leiden: Brill, 1978.

Haim, Sylvia G. *Arab Nationalism: an Anthology.* Berkeley: University of California Press, 1962.

Hamzah, Fu'ad. *Qalb Jazirat al-'Arab.* Riyadh: al-Nasr al-Hadithah, 1968.

Hardach, Gerd. *The First World War, 1914–1918.* Harmondsworth: Penguin, 1987.

Helms, Christine. *The Cohesion of Saudi Arabia.* London: Croom Helm, 1981.

Hodgkin, E.C. (ed.). *Two Kings in Arabia: Sir Reader Bullard's Letters from Jeddah.* Reading, England: Ithaca Press, 1993.

Hurewitz, J.C. *The Middle East and North Africa in World Politics: A Documentary Record.* vol. 2, 1914–1945. New Haven: Yale University Press, 1979.

Issawi, Charles. *The Economic History of the Middle East, 1800–1914.* Chicago, University of Chicago Press, 1966.

———. *The Fertile Crescent, 1800–1914: A Documentary Economic History.* New York: Oxford University Press, 1988.

Jomier, Jacques. *Le Caravane Egyptienne des Pèlerins de la Mecque (XIIIᵉ–XXᵉ siècles).* Cairo: Imprimerie de l'Institut Français d'Archéologie Orientale, 1953.

Kayali, Hasan. *Arabs and Young Turks: Ottomanism, Arabism and Islamism in the Ottoman Empire, 1908–1918.* Berkeley: University of California Press, 1997.

———. 'Turco-Arab Relations and the Ottoman Rule in the Arab Provinces: The Case of the Hijaz, 1908–18.' Unpublished PhD dissertation, Harvard, 1988.

Kedourie, Elie. *Arabic Political Memoirs and Other Studies.* London: Cass, 1974.

———. *In the Anglo-Arab Labyrinth: The McMahon–Husayn Correspondence and its Interpretations, 1914–1939.* Cambridge University Press, 1976.

———. *The Chatham House Version and Other Middle Eastern Studies.* London: Wiedenfeld and Nicholson, 1970.

———. *England and the Middle East: The Destruction of the Ottoman Empire, 1914–1921.* Boulder, CO: Westview Press, 1987.

Kholaif, Ali Ibrahim. 'The Hijaz Vilayet 1969–1908: The Sharifate, the Hajj, and the Bedouins of the Hijaz.' Unpublished PhD dissertation, University of Wisconsin-Madison, 1986.

Ibn Khaldun, *The Muqaddimah,* trans. Franz Rosenthal. London: Routledge & Kegan Paul, 1987.

Khoury, Philip. *Urban Notables and Arab Nationalism in the Politics of Damascus, 1800–1920*. Cambridge University Press, 1983.

Kirkbride, Sir Alec. *An Awakening: The Arab Campaign 1917–1918*. University Press of America, 1971.

Kostiner, Joseph. 'The Making of Saudi Arabia, 1917–1936.' Unpublished PhD dissertation, London School of Economics, 1982.

———. *The Making of Saudi Arabia, 1916–1936: From Chieftaincy to Monarchical State*. New York: Oxford University Press, 1993.

Kramer, Martin. *Islam Assembled: The Advent of the Muslim Congresses*. New York: Columbia University Press, 1986.

Krause, Chester and Clifford Mishler. *1995 Standard Catalog of World Coins*. White Plains, NY: Krause Publications, 1994.

Landau, Jacob. *The Hijaz Railway and the Muslim Pilgrimage: A Case of Ottoman Propaganda*. Detroit: Wayne State University Press, 1971.

———. *The Politics of Pan-Islam: Ideology and Organization*. Oxford: Clarendon Press,1990.

Lapidus, Ira. *Muslim Cities in the Later Middle Ages*. Harvard University Press, 1967.

Lawrence, T.E. *Seven Pillars of Wisdom: A Triumph*.

Leatherdale, Clive. *Britain and Saudi Arabia, 1925–1939: The Imperial Oasis*. London: Cass, 1983.

Leslie, Shane. *Mark Sykes, His Life and Letters*. London: Cassell, 1923.

Lewis, Bernard. *The Emergence of Modern Turkey*. Oxford University Press,1968.

Long, David. *The Hajj Today: A Survey of the Contemporary Muslim Pilgrimage*. Albany: State University of New York Press, 1979.

Marmon, Shaun. *Eunuchs and Sacred Boundaries in Islamic Society*. New York: Oxford University Press, 1995.

McCusker, John J. *How Much is That in Real Money? A Historical Price Index for Use as a Deflator of Money Values in the Economy of the United States*. Worcester, MA: American Antiquarian Society, 1992.

McMunn, G., and Cyril Fall. *Military Operations in Egypt and Palestine from the Outbreak of the War with Germany to June 1917*. London: HMSO, 1928.

Maghribi, Muhammad 'Ali. *'Alam al-Hijaz fi al-Qarn al-Rabi' 'Ashrin lil-Hijrah*, 4 vols. Jeddah and Mecca, various publishers, 1981–1994.

Ibn Manzur, Muhammad ibn al-Mukarram. *Lisan al-'Arab*, vol.1, (first edition, Cairo, 1883–1890, edition used, Dar al-Ma'arif, n.p., n.d.).

Ibrahim Rif'at Basha. *Mir'at al-Haramayn*. 2 vols. Cairo: Matba'at Dar al-Misriyyah, 1925.

Midhat Bey, Ali Haydar. *The Life of Midhat Pasha*. London: John Murray, 1903.

Migdal, Joel. *Strong Societies and Weak States: State–Society Relations and State Capabilities in the Third World*. Princeton University Press, 1988.

Minault, Gail. *The Khilafat Movement: Religious Symbolism and Political Mobilization in India*. New York: Columbia University Press, 1982.

Mitchell, B.R. *Abstract of British Historical Statistics*. Cambridge University Press, 1964.

———. *British Historical Statistics*. Cambridge University Press, 1988.

Mousa [Musa], Suleiman [Sulayman]. *Al-Husayn bin 'Ali wal-Thawrah al-'Arabiyyah al-Kubra*. Amman: Dar al-Nashr wal-Tawzi', 1957.

———. *Al-Thawrah al-'Arabiyyah al-Kubra: Watha'iq wa-Asanid*. Amman: Da'irah al-Thaqafah wal-Funun, 1966.

———. *Al-Harakah al-'Arabiyyah: Sirat al-Marhalah al-Ula lil-Nahdah al-'Arabiyyah al-Hadithah*. Beirut: Al-Nahar, 1982.

———. *Al-Thawrah al-'Arabiyyah al-Kubra, al-Harb fil-Urdunn, 1917–1918: Mudhakkirat al-Amir Zayd*. Amman: n.p., 1976.

Muhammad, Muhammad 'Abd al-Jawwad. *Al-Tatawwur al-Tashri'i fi al-Mamlakah al-'Arabiyyah al–Sa'udiyyah*. Cairo University Press, 1977.

Mu'mini, Nidal Da'ud. *Al-Sharif Husayn bin 'Ali wal-Khilafah*. Amman: Lajnat Ta'rikh al-Urdunn, 1996.

Musil, Alois. *The Northern Hejaz: A Topographical Inquiry*. New York: American Geographical Society, 1928.

Nasif, Husayn Muhammad. *Madi al-Hijaz wa-Hadiruhu*. Cairo: n.p., 1930.

Nevakivi, Jukka. *Britain, France and the Arab Middle East, 1914–1920*. London: Athlone Press, 1969.

Niemeijer, A. *The Khilafat Movement in India, 1919–1924*. The Hague: Nijhoff, 1972.

Ochsenwald, William. *The Hijaz Railroad*. Charlottesville: University Press of Virginia, 1980.

———. *Religion, Society and the State in Arabia: The Hijaz under Ottoman Control, 1840–1908*. Columbus: Ohio State University Press, 1984.

Oppenheim, Max von. *Die Beduinen*. Leipzig: Harrasowitz, 1943.

Pakenham, Thomas. *The Scramble for Africa 1876–1912*. London: Abacus, 1992.

Peters, F.E. *The Hajj: The Muslim Pilgrimage to Mecca and the Holy Places*. Princeton University Press, 1994.

———. *Mecca: A Literary History of the Muslim Holy Land*. Princeton University Press, 1994.

Philby, H. St John. *Arabian Jubilee*. New York: John Day, 1953.

Prator, Sabine. *Der arabische Faktor in der jungturkischen Politik*. Berlin: Klaus Schwarz Verlag, 1993.

Qasimiyyah, Khayriyyah. *Al-'Alam al-Filastini*. Beirut: PLO, Markaz al-Abhath, 'Abhath Filastiniyyah' Series, No. 21.

Rabbow, Arnold. *Div-Lexicon Politischer Symbole*. Munich: Deutscher Taschenbuch Verlag, 1970.

Al-Rihani, Amin. *Ta'rikh Najd wa-Mulhaqatihi*. Beirut: Dar al-Rihani, 1954.

Al-Rasheed, Madawi Talal. *Politics in an Arabian Oasis: The Rashidi Tribal Dynasty*. London: I.B.Tauris,1991.

Al-Rawi, Ibrahim. *Min al-Thawrah al-'Arabiyyah al-Kubra ila al-'Iraq al-Hadith: Dhikriyyat*. Beirut: Maktabat Dar al-Kutub, 1969.

Rida, Rashid. *Al-Wahhabiyyun wal-Hijaz*. Cairo: Al-Manar, 1344.

Al-Rimawi, Suhaylah. *Al-Ittijahat al-Fikriyyah lil-Thawrah al-'Arabiyyah al-Kubra*. Amman: Lajnat Ta'rikh al-Urdunn, 1992.

Rosenthal, Franz. *The Herb: Hashish versus Medieval Muslim Society*. Leiden: E. J. Brill, 1971.

Rudd, Jeffery. 'Abdullah bin al-Husayn: The Making of an Arab Political Leader.' Unpublished PhD dissertation, SOAS, 1993.

Sa'id, Amin. *Al-Thawrah al-'Arabiyyah al-Kubra*. 3 vols. Cairo, 1934.

Samné, George. *Le Chérifat de La Mecque et l'Unité Syrienne*. Paris, 1919.

al-Sawwaf, Fa'iz Bakr. *Al-'Alaqat bayna al-Dawlah al-'Uthmaniyyah wa-Iqlim al-Hijaz, 1876–1916*. n.p.: Matabi' Sijill al-'Arab, 1978.

Sayigh, Anis. *Al-Hashimiyyun wal-Thawrah al-'Arabiyyah al-Kubra*. Beirut, 1966.

Schacht, Joseph. *An Introduction to Islamic Law*. Oxford: Clarendon Press, 1964.

Scoville, Sheila. 'British Logistical Support to the Hashemites of Hejaz: Ta'if to Ma'an, 1916–1918.' Unpublished PhD dissertation, University of California, Los Angeles, 1985.

———. *Gazetteer of Arabia: A Geographical and Tribal History of the Arabian Peninsula*. 2 vols. Graz: Akademische Druck u. Verlagsanstalt, 1979, 1995.

al-Sha'afi, Muhammad. *The Foreign Trade of Juddah*. n.p.: privately published, 1985.

Shaw, Stanford. *The Financial and Administrative Organization and Development of Ottoman Egypt, 1517–1798*. Princeton University Press, 1962.

———, and Ezel Shaw. *History of the Ottoman Empire and Modern Turkey, II, Reform, Revolution and Republic: The Rise of Modern Turkey, 1808–1975*. Cambridge University Press, 1977.

Shils, Edward. *Center and Periphery*. University of Chicago Press,1975.

Snouck Hurgronje, C. *Mekka in the Latter Part of the Nineteenth Century*. Leiden: E. J. Brill, 1931, rpt. 1970.

———. *Mekka: Die Stadt und ihre Herren*. The Hague: Nijhoff, 1888.

———. *The Revolt in Arabia*. New York: Putnam, 1917.

Stratkotter, Rita. *Von Kair nach Mekka. Sozial-und Wirtschaftsgeschichte der Pilgerfahrt nach den Berichten des Ibrahim Rif'at Basha: Mir'at al-Haramain*. Berlin: Klaus Schwarz Verlag, 1991.

Storrs, Sir Ronald. *Orientations*. London: Nicholson and Watson, 1937.

Stitt, George. *A Prince of Arabia: The Emir Shereef Ali Haider.* London: Geo. Allen and Unwin, 1948.

Tauber, Eliezer. *The Arab Movements in World War I.* London: Cass, 1993.

———. *The Emergence of the Arab Movements.* London: Cass, 1993.

Teitelbaum, Joshua. 'The Sa'udis and the *Hajj*, 1916–1933: A Religious Institution in Turbulent Times.' Unpublished MA thesis, Tel Aviv University, 1988.

Tibawi, A.L. *Anglo-Arab Relations and the Question of Palestine, 1914–1921.* London: Luzac, 1978.

Toledano, Ehud. *State and Society in Mid-Nineteenth Century Egypt.* Cambridge University Press, 1990.

Tresse, René. *Le Pélerinage Syrien aux Villes Saintes d'Islam.* Paris: Imprimerie Chaumette, 1937.

Troeller, Gary. *The Birth of Saudi Arabia: Britain and the Rise of the House of Saud.* London: Cass, 1976.

Twitchell, K.S. *Saudi Arabia: With an Account of the Development of its Natural Resources.* Princeton University Press, 1947.

Wahbah, Hafiz. *Jazirat al-'Arab fi al-Qarn al-'Ishrin.* n.p: n.p., n.d.

Wavell, A.J.B. *A Modern Pilgrim in Mecca and a Siege in Sanaa.* London: Constable, 1913.

Westrate, Bruce. *The Arab Bureau: British Policy in the Middle East, 1916–1920.* University Park, PA: Pennsylvania State University Press, 1992.

Wilson, Jeremy. *Lawrence of Arabia: The Authorized Biography of T. E. Lawrence.* New York: Atheneum, 1989.

Wilson, Mary. *King Abdullah, Britain, and the Making of Jordan.* Cambridge University Press, 1987.

Wilson, Peter. *A Question of Interest: The Paralysis of Saudi Banking.* Boulder, CO: Westview Press, 1991.

Winder, R. Bayly. *Saudi Arabia in the Nineteenth Century.* London: Macmillan, 1965.

Winstone, H.V.F. *The Diaries of Parker Pasha.* London: Quartet, 1983.

———. *The Illicit Adventure.* London: Cape, 1983.

Yapp, M. E. *The Near East Since the First World War.* Harlow: Longman, 1991.

al-Yassini, Ayman. *Religion and State in the Kingdom of Saudi Arabia.* Boulder, CO: Westview Press, 1985.

Zeine, Zeine. *The Emergence of Arab Nationalism.* Beirut: Khayat's, 1966.

———. *The Struggle for Arab Independence.* Beirut: Khayat's, 1960.

ARTICLES

Abdul Bari, Muhammad. 'The Early Wahhabis and the Sharifs of Mekka.' *Journal of the Pakistan Historical Society*, 1 (1955), pp. 91–104.

Abir, M. 'The "Arab Rebellion" of Amir Ghalib of Mecca (1788–1813).' *MES*, 7 (1971), pp. 185–200.

Abu-Manneh, Butrus. 'Sultan Abdul-Hamid II and the Sharifs of Mecca, 1880–1900.' *Asian and African Studies*, 9 (1973), pp. 1–21.

Arendonk, Van C. 'Sharif.' *EI²*.

Ayalon, Ami. 'The Hashemites, T.E. Lawrence, and the Postage Stamps of the Hijaz' in Asher Susser and Aryeh Shmuelevitz (eds). *The Hashemites in the Modern Arab World: Essays in Honour of the late Professor Uriel Dann*. London: Cass, 1995, pp. 15–30.

———. 'Malik in Middle Eastern Titulature.' *Die Welt des Islams*, 23–24 (1984), pp. 306–19.

———. 'Malik.' *EI²*.

Baldry, John. 'The Powers and Mineral Concessions in the Idrisi Imamate of 'Asir, 1910–1929.' *Arabian Studies*, 2 (1975), pp. 76–107.

———. 'The Turkish–Italian War in the Yemen, 1911–1912.' *Arabian Studies*, 3 (1976), pp. 51–89.

Bidwell, Robin. 'The Brémond Mission in the Hejaz, 1916–1917: A Study in Inter-Allied Cooperation' in R.L. Bidwell and G.R. Smith (eds), *Arabian and Islamic Studies: Articles Presented to R. B. Serjeant*. London: Longman, 1983, pp. 182–95.

Browder, Tim. 'Coinage of Hejaz Kingdom.' *Numismatic Scrapbook Magazine*, 26 (1960), pp. 3489–96.

Buzpinar, S. Tufan. 'The Hijaz, Abdulhamid and Amir Hussein's Dealings with the British.' *MES*, 31 (1995), pp. 99–123.

———. 'Opposition to the Ottoman Caliphate in the Early Years of Abudlhamid II: 1887–1882.' *Die Welt des Islams*, 36 (1996), pp. 59–89.

Casanova, M. 'Une Mine d'Or au Hidjaz.' Offprint of *Bulletin de la Section Géographique*. Paris: Imprimerie National, 1920.

Cohen, Ronald. 'Introduction' in Ronald Cohen and Elman Service (eds). *Origins of the State*. Philadelphia: Institute for the Study of Human Issues, 1978, pp. 1–17.

Cole, Juan and Moojan Momen. 'Mafia Mob and Shi'ism in Iraq: The Rebellion of Ottoman Karbala, 1824–1843.' *Past and Present*, 112 (1986), pp. 112–43.

Cleveland, William L. 'The Role of Islam as Political Ideology in the First World War' in Edward Ingram (ed.), *National and International Politics in the Middle East: Essays in Honour of Elie Kedourie*. London: Cass, 1986, pp. 84–101.

Davis Eric. 'Theorizing Statecraft and Social Change in Arab Oil-Producing Countries' in Eric Davis, Eric and Nicholas Gavrielides (eds), *Statecraft in the Middle East: Oil, Historical Memory and Popular Culture*. Miami: University of Florida Press, 1991, pp. 1–35.

De Jong, F. 'The Proclamations of al-Husayn b. 'Ali and 'Ali Haydar:' Some Observations and Notes Relative to MS Leiden Or. 12.482.' *Der Islam*, 57 (1980), pp. 281–7.

Deringil, Selim. 'Legitimacy Structures in the Ottoman State: The Reign of Abdulhamid II (1876–1909).' *IJMES*, 23 (1991), pp. 345–59.

Eldar, Dan. 'French Policy towards Husayn, Sharif of Mecca.' *MES*, 26 (1990), pp. 329–49.

Ende, Werner. 'The Nakhawila, a Shiite Community in Medina: Past and Present.' *Die Welt des Islams*, 37 (1997), pp. 263–348.

Gerber, Haim. 'Sharia, Kanun and Custom in the Ottoman Law: The Court Records of 17th Century Bursa.' *International Journal of Turkish Studies*, 2 (1981), pp. 131–47.

Gershoni, Yisrael. 'Ha-Le'om ha-'Aravi, Beit Hashim ve-Suriyah ha-Gedolah bi-Khtavav shel 'Abdallah.' *Ha-Mizrah he-Hadash*, 25 (1975), pp. 1–26.

Gibb, H.A.R. 'Amir al-Mu'minin.' *EI²*.

Haim, Sylvia. 'Blunt and al-Kawakibi.' *OM* 35 (1955), pp. 132–43.

Haim, Sylvia. 'The Abolition of the Caliphate and its Aftermath' in T.W. Arnold (ed.), *The Caliphate*. London: Routledge & Kegan Paul, 1965.

Hourani, Albert. 'Ottoman Reform and the Politics of Notables.' in William Polk and Richard Chambers (eds), *Beginnings of Modernization in the Middle East: The Nineteenth Century*. University of Chicago Press, 1968, pp. 41–68.

Hurvitz, Nimrod. 'Muhibb al-Din al-Khatib's Semitic Wave Theory and Pan-Arabism.' *MES*, 29 (1993), pp. 118–34.

Kedourie, Elie. 'The Surrender of Medina, January 1919.' *MES*, 13 (1977), pp. 123–43.

Khoury, Philip. 'Continuity and Change in Syrian Political Life: The Nineteenth and Twentieth Centuries.' *American Historical Review*, 96 (1991), pp. 1374–85.

Khoury, Philip and Joseph Kostiner. 'Introduction: Tribes and the Complexities of State Formation in the Middle East' in Philip Khoury and Joseph Kostiner (eds), *Tribes and State Formation in the Middle East*. Berkeley: University of California Press, 1990, pp. 1–22.

Kister, M.J. 'Mecca and Tamim.' Published chapter of PhD dissertation. *Tamim in the Period of the Jahiliyya: A Study in Tribal Tradition*. Hebrew University, 1964.

Kramer, Martin. 'Azoury: A Further Episode.' *MES*, 18 (1982), pp. 351–8.

———. 'Shaykh Maraghi's Mission to the Hijaz.' *AAS*, 16 (1982), pp. 121–36.

Kostiner, Joseph. 'The Hashemite 'Tribal Confederacy' of the Arab Revolt, 1916–1917' in Edward Ingram (ed.), *National and International Politics in the Middle East: Essays in Honour of Elie Kedourie*. London: Cass, 1986, pp. 126–43.

Lapidus, Ira. 'Muslim Cities as Plural Societies: The Politics of Intermediary Bodies.' *Proceedings of the International Conference on Urbanism in Islam*, Tokyo, 1989, vol. 1, pp. 134–63.

———. 'Traditional Muslim Cities: Structure and Change' in L. Carl Brown (ed.), *From Madina to Metropolis*. Princeton University Press, 1973, pp. 51–69.

———. 'Transforming Dualities: Tribe and State Formation in Saudi Arabia' in Philip Khoury and Joseph Kostiner (eds), *Tribes and State Formation in the Middle East*. Berkeley: University of California Press, 1990, pp. 226–51.

———. 'Tribes and State Formation in Islamic History' in Philip Khoury and Joseph Kostiner (eds), *Tribes and State Formation in the Middle East*. Berkeley: University of California Press, 1990, pp. 25–47.

McKale, Donald. 'German Policy toward the Sharif of Mecca.' *The Historian*, 55 (1993), pp. 303–14.

Mortel, Richard. 'The Husaynid Amirate of Madina during the Mamluk Period,' *Studia Islamica* 80 (1994), pp. 97–123.

———. 'The Origins and Early History of the Husaynid Amirate of Madina to the End of the Ayyubid Period.' *Studia Islamica*, 74 (1991), pp. 63–78.

———. 'Zaydi Shi'ism and the Hasanid Sherifs of Mecca.' *IJMES*, 19 (1987), pp. 455–72.

Mousa, Suleiman. 'The Role of Syrians and Iraqis In the Arab Revolt.' *Middle East Forum*, 43 (1967), pp. 5–17.

———. 'A Matter of Principle: King Husayn of the Hijaz and the Arabs of Palestine.' *IJMES*, 9 (1978), pp. 183–94.

———. 'Sharif Husayn and Developments Leading up to the Arab Revolt.' *New Arabian Studies*, 1 (1993), pp. 36–53.

Nettl, J.P. 'The State as a Conceptual Variable.' *World Politics*, 20 (1968), pp. 559–92.

Niblock, Tim. 'Social Structure and the Development of the Saudi Arabian Political System' in Tim Niblock (ed.), *State, Society and Economy in Saudi Arabia*. London: Croom Helm, 1982, pp. 75–105.

Ochsenwald, William. 'Arab Nationalism in the Hijaz' in Rashid Khalidi, Lisa Anderson, Muhammad Muslih, and Reeva Simon (eds.), *The Origins of Arab Nationalism*. New York: Columbia University Press, 1991, pp. 189–203.

———. 'The Commercial History of the Hijaz Vilayet, 1840–1908.' *Arabian Studies*, 6 (1982), pp. 57–76.

———. 'The Financial Basis of Ottoman Rule in the Hijaz, 1840–1877' in William Haddad and William Ochsenwald (eds), *Nationalism in a Non-National State: The Dissolution of the Ottoman Empire*. Columbus: Ohio State University Press, 1977, pp. 129–49.

———. 'A Modern Waqf: The Hijaz Railway, 1900–1948.' *Arabian Studies*, 3 (1976), pp. 1–12.

———. 'Opposition to Political Centralization in South Jordan and Hijaz, 1900–1914.' *Muslim World*, 63 (1973), pp. 297–306.

———. 'Ottoman Subsidies to the Hijaz,1877–1886.' *IJMES*, 6 (1975), pp. 300–7.

Philipp, Hans-Jurgen. 'Der beduinische Widerstand gegen die Hedschasbahn.' *Die Welt des Islams*, 25 (1985), pp. 31–83.

Porath, Yehoshua. 'The Palestinians and the Negotiations for the British–Hijazi Treaty, 1920–1925.' *AAS*, 8 (1972), pp. 20–48.

Rasheed, Madawi Talal. 'Durable and Non-Durable Dynasties: The Rashidis and Sa'udis in Central Arabia.' *British Journal of Middle Eastern Studies*, 19 (1992), pp. 144–58.

Reissner, Johannes. 'Die Idrisiden in 'Asir: Ein historische Uberblick.' *Die Welt des Islams*, 21 (1991), pp. 164–92.

Rosenfeld, Henry. 'The Social Composition of the Military in the Process of State Formation in the Arabian Desert.' *Journal of the Royal Anthropological Society*, 95 (1965), pp. 75–86; 174–94.

Serjeant, R. 'Haram and Hawtah, The Sacred Enclave in Arabia' in R. Serjeant (ed.), *Studies in Arabian History and Civilization*. London: Variorum Reprints, 1981, pp. 41–58.

Salame, Ghassan. '"Strong" and "Weak" States: A Qualified Return to the Muqaddimah' in Giacomo Luciani (ed.), *The Arab State*. Berkeley: University of California Press, 1971.

Shamir, Shimon. 'Midhat Pasha and the Anti-Ottoman Agitation in Syria.' *MES*, 10 (1974), pp. 115–41.

Shaw, Stanford J. 'The Nineteenth-Century Ottoman Tax Reforms and Revenue System.' *IJMES*, 6 (1975), pp. 421–59.

Silverfarb, Daniel. 'The British Government and the Khurmah Dispute, 1918–1919.' *Arabian Studies*, 5 (1979), pp. 37–60.

———. 'The Philby Mission to Ibn Sa'ud, 1917–1918.' *Journal of Contemporary History*, 14 (1979), pp. 269–86.

Snouck Hurgronje, C. 'Some of My Experiences with the Muftis of Mecca (1885).' *Asian Affairs*, 8 (1977), pp. 25–37.

Tauber, Eliezer. 'The Role of Lieutenant Muhammad Sharif al-Faruqi – New Light on Anglo-Arab Relations during the First World War.' *AAS*, 24 (1990), pp. 17–50.

———.Tauber, Eliezer.'Three Approaches, One Idea: Religion and State in the Thought of 'Abd al-Rahman al-Kawakibi, Najib 'Azuri and Rashid Rida.' *British Journal of Middle Eastern Studies*, 21 (1994), pp. 190–8.

Teitelbaum, Joshua. 'Pilgrimage Politics: The Hajj and Saudi–Hashemite Rivalry, 1916–1925' in Asher Susser and Aryeh Shmuelevitz (eds), *The Hashemites in the Modern Arab World: Essays in Honor of the late Professor Uriel Dann*. London: Cass, 1995, pp. 65–84.

———. 'Sharif Husayn ibn 'Ali and the Hashemite Vision of the Post-Ottoman Order: From Chieftaincy to Suzerainty.' *MES*, 34 (1998), pp. 103–22.

———. '"Taking Back" the Caliphate: Sharif Husayn ibn 'Ali, Mustafa Kemal, and the Ottoman Caliphate.' *Die Welt des Islams*, 40 (2000), pp. 412–24.

Thompson, Elizabeth. 'Ottoman Political Reform in the Provinces: The Damascus Advisory Council in 1844–45.' *IJMES*, 25 (1993), pp. 457–75.

Voll, John. 'Hadith Scholars and Tariqahs: An Ulama Group in the 18th Century Haramayn and Their Impact on the Islamic World.' *Journal of Asian and African Studies* 15 (1980), pp. 264–73.

Wasti, S. Tanvir. 'The Defense of Medina, 1916–1919.' *MES*, 27 (1994), pp. 642–53.

Wensinck, A.J. [C.E. Bosworth]. 'Makka.' *EI²*.

Wilson, Mary. 'The Hashemites, the Arab Revolt, and Arab Nationalism' in Rashid Khalidi, Lisa Anderson, Muhammad Muslih, and Reeva Simon (eds), *The Origins of Arab Nationalism*. New York: Columbia University Press, 1991, pp. 201–24.

INDEX